Distribution of Insurance-Based Investment Products

Pierpaolo Marano • Ioannis Rokas
Editors

Distribution of Insurance-Based Investment Products

The EU Regulation and the Liabilities

Springer

Editors
Pierpaolo Marano
Law Department
Catholic University of the Sacred Heart
Milan, Milano, Italy

Ioannis Rokas
Department of Business Administration
(em.) Athens University of Economics and Business
Athens, Attiki, Greece

ISBN 978-3-030-11667-5 ISBN 978-3-030-11668-2 (eBook)
https://doi.org/10.1007/978-3-030-11668-2

This Springer imprint is published by the registered company Springer Nature Switzerland AG.
The registered company address is: Gewerbestrasse 11, 6330 Cham, Switzerland

Preface

Insurance-based investment product (IBIP) is a new name for an old product. It is an **insurance product** falling under class III of life insurances. Class III of life insurances, according to new and old European insurance regulatory laws, includes life insurance against the "risk" of survival over a certain time, or the risk of death; combined (survival or death); life insurance with return of premiums; annuities insurance; as well as marriage insurance and birth insurance, when all these life insurances are **linked to "investment funds"**.

On a European level, this class was introduced by the first life insurance Directive 1979/267/EEC on the coordination of laws, regulations and administrative provisions relating to the taking up and pursuit of the business of direct life assurance. European legislation has not further defined the structure of the class III products, neither has it provided any rules or guidelines as regards the notion of investment funds to which that product is linked or any rules on the proportion between the insurance risk and the investment component of this product. These issues remain outside its harmonization scope. Some countries have not introduced any specific rules, and thus in their markets, products of class III are being sold from time to time without any risk component, while some other countries do require a minimum participation of 10% of the risk component. A specific minimum participation of the risk component is not provided under European law, although this is aligned with the nature of this product.

The actual sale of class III investment products by insurance undertakings gave an end to the regulatory ban of insurance products which included additional components alien to the transfer of risk; a taboo was broken. This evolution was in line with common sense: since insurance undertakings are the largest institutional investors in Europe, there was no reason for prohibiting the selling of insurance products combined with investment products.

The gradual increase of the volume of insurance products linked to investment funds that are distributed across Europe gave rise to concerns regarding the effective protection of a policyholder/consumer in its capacity as an investor, since originally at a European level neither insurance nor investment legislation included any special rules for such products. Certain national laws have introduced consumer protection rules focusing on additional information as regards the insurance linked to investment funds. In fact, the necessity of additional rules was acknowledged in the distribution and sales rather than in the manufacturing process of such products. Therefore, national rules focused on the provision of additional information to the applicants.

The question, which was answered in different ways by national legislators, was whether it was necessary to protect a policyholder in the same way as an investor: in other words, whether to vest insurance distributors/intermediaries with the same duties as those vested on the regulated distributors of investment products, or whether lighter duties would suffice. In this regard and until new rules were introduced, the legal framework of Europe was fragmented in this area, to the detriment of the functioning of the single market.

But 39 years after the launch of insurance products linked to investment funds as a special life insurance class, the time matured for the European legislator to move towards harmonizing customer protection rules. These rules are now included in Regulation (EU) No 1286/2014 "on key information documents for packaged retail and insurance-based investment products" (PRIIPs), Commission Delegated Regulation (EU) 2017/653 "supplementing Regulation (EU) No 1286/2014 by laying down regulatory technical standards with regard to the presentation, content, review and revision of key information documents and the conditions for fulfilling the requirement to provide such documents", Directive (EU) 2016/97 "on insurance distribution" (IDD), as well as Commission Delegated Regulation (EU) 2017/2359 "supplementing Directive 2016/97 with regard to information requirements and conduct of business rules applicable to the distribution of insurance-based investment products" (IBIPs Regulation). The European legislator, apart from providing special rules on the IBIP distributors, took a step further by imposing additional categorization between non-retail and retail insurance-based investment products. These retail products fall within the scope of the PRIIPs Regulation. It is worth noting that an IBIP is an insurance product offering a maturity or surrender value which is wholly or at least partially (in)directly exposed to market fluctuations. Thus, a consumer's loss in its capacity as an investor is covered by an investor's compensation or a guarantee scheme.

Insurance-based investment products are nowadays part of the regulated life insurance. As is the case with all insurance products, the new regulation distinguishes between customers who need additional protection and customers who do not. Customers of retail investment products are provided with additional information if the product is packaged with insurance, i.e. if the wrapper is an insurance contract.

The criterion as to who is the retail investor is set out in Directive 2014/65 (MiFID II). On the other hand, all customers of insurance-based investment products are protected by the IDD. Customers who are not (necessarily) protected by additional information rules are professional clients and insured covered for large risks within the meaning of the Solvency II Directive. Rules on financial products are now extended to cover IBIPs.

At this stage, answering the question of the nature of the contract of insurance-based investment products does not necessarily require an in-depth academic research on contract law.

Industry and customers need these products and the European regulator acknowledged these needs by introducing new rules, which focused on enhancing the information provided to the customer. These products include a combination of two types of financial services, which remain different and separate, but are at the same time, necessarily, wrapped in an insurance policy. They are not based on a "mixed" contract which alters the rules governing these two types of services. The insurance contract laws are not affected by the symbiosis with the contractual relations governing the investment component. Thus, the answer to the said question is that these products are both insurance and investment.

Almost all rules which contributed to the revision of the well-known insurance contract laws provided mainly over the last 40 years have aimed at the protection of the consumers and of the insured covered by non-large risks. The consumer protection wave has altered the traditional rules of the insurance contract laws. This is not repeated by the rise of the investment component in some insurance products. However, as insurance-based investment products are wrapped in an insurance contract, the rules on the requisite information apply to both financial products included in the policy. This influences to some extent the insurance contract doctrine and leads to the "mifidization" of the insurance-based investment products, as my colleague Pierpaolo Marano characterized the new tendency.

Milan, Italy — Pierpaolo Marano
Athens, Greece — Ioannis Rokas

Contents

Part I
The EU Discipline

The Notion of Insurance-Based Investment Products

A Cross-Sectoral Legal Approach in Europe

Ioannis Rokas and Athina Siafarika

Contents

Abbreviations

AIFMD	Alternative Investment Fund Managers Directive
AIFs	Alternative Investment Funds
CEIOPS	Committee of European Insurance and Occupational Pensions Supervisors (now EIOPA)

I. Rokas (✉)
Department of Business Administration, Athens University of Economics and Business, Athens, Greece

Rokas International Law Firm, Athens, Greece
e-mail: i.rokas@rokas.com

A. Siafarika
EY, Athens, Greece

P. Marano, I. Rokas (eds.), *Distribution of Insurance-Based Investment Products*, https://doi.org/10.1007/978-3-030-11668-2_1

CFD	Contract for Difference
COBS	Conduct of Business rules
DG	Directorate-General
EBA	European Banking Authority
EC	European Commission
ECB	European Central Bank
EIOPA	European Insurance and Occupational Pensions Authority
EMIR	European Market Infrastructure Regulation
EOS	Environmental and Social Objectives
ESAs	European Supervisory Authorities
ESFS	European System of Financial Supervision
ESMA	European Securities and Markets Authorities
FCA	Financial Conduct Authority
FTSE 100	Financial Times Stock Exchange 100 Index
IDD	Insurance Distribution Directive
IMD	Insurance Mediation Directive
KID	Key Information Document
KII	Key Investor Information
MiFID	Markets in Financial Instruments Directive
MiFIR	Markets in Financial Instruments Regulation
OTC	Over-the-Counter
PRIIPs	Packaged Retail and Insurance-Based Investment Products
PRIPs	Packaged Retail Investment Products
SPV	Special Purpose Vehicle
UCITS	Undertakings for the Collective Investment of Transferable Securities

1 Introduction

1.1 Overview of the Legal Framework

(a) Insurance-based investment products constitute an important example of the intersection of different financial sectors, each falling under the scope of its own sectoral regulation. They consist of broadly two components: the component of life insurance and the component of investment. A well-known form of an insurance product combined with an investment is represented by investment units (or indexes) to which the insurance product is linked ("**unit-linked policies**"[1] or index-linked policies, respectively).[2]

In practice the "link" between insurance and investment may vary significantly. For example, there are insurance policy structures where, even though both components (life insurance and investment) are present in the policy, they are nevertheless clearly distinct and separate, as long as the life-insurance part

---

[1] Galiatsos (2013), pp. 257 et seq.

[2] Fixed-index annuities and variable annuities are also provided.

consists of insurance premia while the investment part consists of separate funds channeled to investments.

(b) On the other hand, every "classic" life insurance policy, in which the insurer offers a maturity or surrender value (long-term life insurance policies), has a savings character. This is because part of the premium is not consumed by the risk, but it is collected and invested by the insurer in order to pay the fix sum provided in the insurance contract (in case of maturity or if the insured demands its repurchase of the policy), the payment of which is certain (the only uncertainty lying on the payment time). Thus, the policyholder of these insurance policies aims not only at risk coverage but also at a "safe" solution for his savings, enjoying at the same time fix interest, in line with the policy terms. Besides, it is the insurer who, in the case of the long-term life insurance policies (and generally in the case of "plain" insurance policies) holds the status of investor. It is worth to underline, at this point, that the European insurance industry is the largest institutional investor in Europe.[3]

Taking the above into consideration, it is of no surprise that contracts which are 'linked to investment funds', such as "unit-linked insurance policies" were developed in the context of insurance and in countries with liquid capital markets, such as in the UK and the US since the 1960s and 1970s.[4]

(c) The First Life Insurance Directive 1979/267,[5] subsequently codified by Directive 2002/83[6] and recently repealed by Directive 2009/138[7] (Solvency II), referred to "assurance….linked to investment funds" as a separate class of insurance (Annex I, class II of the Life Assurance Directive), thus enhancing cross-border provision of services for insurance undertakings. Besides, the European Court concluded[8] that Directive 1985/577 on contracts negotiated away from business premises,[9] which according its article 3(2)(d) does not apply to insurance contracts, does not apply equally to 'unit-linked' policies, since the latter are considered by the European legislator as insurance contracts as well.

However, at the time of the implementation of the first Life Assurance Directive, European law did not provide any special rules for the class III of life insurance categories on insurance contracts linked to investment funds, apart

[3] http://www.insuranceeurope.eu/protecting-long-term-investment.

[4] *Galiatsos* (2013), op.cit., p. 258.

[5] First Council Directive 1979/267 on the coordination of laws, regulations and administrative provisions relating to the taking up and pursuit of the business of direct life assurance.

[6] Directive 2002/83 concerning life assurance.

[7] Directive 2009/138 on the taking-up and pursuit of the business of Insurance and Reinsurance (Solvency II).

[8] Case C-166/11, Ángel Lorenzo González Alonso v Nationale Nederlanden Vida Cía de Seguros y Reaseguros SAE, Judgment of the Court (Fifth Chamber) of 1 March 2012, para 29. Reference for a preliminary ruling from the Audiencia Provincial de Oviedo [ECLI identifier: ECLI:EU:C:2012:119].

[9] Council Directive 1985/577 to protect the consumer in respect of contracts negotiated away from business premises.

from the provisions on technical reserves, thus, resulting in divergent national provisions in this regard. It is worth noting, though, that very often those national provisions "mirrored" the provisions of Directive 2004/39 on markets in financial instruments ("**MiFID**")[10]

(d) Directive 2014/65 ("**MiFID II**")[11] amended Directive 2002/92 on Insurance Mediation ("**IMD**") and introduced for the first time, explicit and special obligations for the insurer and the distributor of such products towards the policyholder.

(e) Directive 2016/97 on Insurance Distribution ("**IDD**"), replacing the IMD, complements the rules on the sale of investment products in MiFID II and in Regulation 1286/2014 on key information documents for packaged retail and insurance-based investment products ("**PRIIPS Regulation**").

1.2 MiFID and Insurance-Based Investment Products

(a) Insurance-based investment products can present an "unbundling" of the insurance part from the investment part, meaning that the insured person is able to identify which portion of his contract, and corresponding sum paid, constitutes insurance premium and which is invested.[12] Contrary to the common life insurance policies where the insurance sum is guaranteed[13] (fix sum), in insurance-based investments, the insurance part (like the investment part) of the policy may as well be expressed in investments, the risk for which is born by the insured. In this (admittedly, not very common) case where, for example, both the insurance and the investment part are expressed in units of investments, the insurance money to be paid is not a fixed sum of cash, but rather the value of a "fixed number of units". Thus, both, insurance part and investment part of insurance-based investment products can be exposed to the risks of the investment.

---

[10] CEIOPS, Report on National Measures regarding Disclosure Requirements and Professional Requirements for Unit-Linked Life Insurance Products, which are additional to the Minimum Requirements of the CLD and IMD (CEIOPS-DOC-20/09, 2 July 2009) available at: https://eiopa.europa.eu/CEIOPS-Archive/Documents/Reports/CEIOPS-Report-National-Measures-Unit-Linked-Life-insurance-products.pdf.

[11] In June 2014, the European Commission adopted new rules revising the MiFID framework. These consist of Directive MiFID II and Regulation 600/2014 (known as MiFIR). The application date of MiFID II and MiFIR, initially scheduled for 3 January 2017, has been extended to 3 January 2018. Hereinafter, where reference is made to MiFID, this shall mean Directive 2004/39/EC, while special reference is made to MiFID II and MiFIR.

[12] Münchener Rück Munich Re Group, Unit-linked Insurance- A general report, p. 5 available at: http://www.asf.com.pt/winlib/cgi/winlibimg.exe?key=&doc=18678&img=5977.

[13] Commission Staff Working Document, Impact Assessment accompanying the Communication from the Commission to the European Parliament and the Council on Packaged Retail Investment Products, SEC (2009) 556, p. 8.

(b) Investment products fall, as a rule, under the scope of MiFID which created a single market for investment services and activities aiming to ensure, inter alia, a harmonized and high level of protection for investors in financial instruments (as listed in Annex I of MiFID, including shares, bonds, money-market instruments, units in collective investment schemes etc.). Following the recent financial crisis, which revealed inefficiencies of the MiFID framework, the European Commission responded by initiating the MiFID II and MiFIR framework repealing MiFID. As with MiFID, insurance undertakings are expressly exempted from the new legislation.[14] As regards the scope of financial instruments to which MiFID II applies, this is broadly equivalent to MiFID, **thus not including insurance-based investments**.

However, MiFID II, apart from repealing MiFID, also amended the IMD, thus, often referred to as "IMD 1.5", which was subsequently repealed, as well, by the IDD. What is important to keep, though, is that the initial amendment of IMD by MiFID II (i.e. the IMD 1.5) intended to extend the MiFID-like level of protection to consumers enjoying products which would otherwise fall outside the scope of MiFID II, such as insurance-based investment products. Besides, the recent financial crisis resulted in an unprecedented decline in investors' and other consumers' of financial services trust in the financial sector. Thus, regulators focused on restoring that confidence, intervening in the full spectrum of financial services,[15] apart from MiFID II, **to achieve robust and uniform consumer protection across the financial sector**. Interestingly, national authorities, such as the UK FCA, amongst others, had already extended most of its conduct of business rules to insurance-based investment products in the UK, although the latter were not subject to MiFID, since such products were viewed as essentially falling in the same relevant market as MiFID- (and now MiFID II-) investment products, often regarded as substitutable to them.[16] Besides, Recital 87 of MiFID II confirms the need for consistent protection for retail clients, since insurance-based investments are often made available to them[17] as potential alternatives or substitutes to MiFID products.

[14] It should be noted, though, that the content of the exemption has been slightly amended in the case of MiFID II, so that it will now apply to "insurance undertakings or undertakings carrying out the reinsurance and retrocession activities referred to" in the Directive 2009/138 (Solvency II) **"when carrying out the activities referred to in that Directive"** (art.2 para 1(a) MiFID II).

[15] According to Recital (2) of the PRIIPs Regulation "Improving the transparency of PRIIPs offered to retail investors is an important investor protection measure and a precondition for rebuilding the confidence of retail investors in the financial market, in particular in the aftermath of the financial crisis".

[16] FCA, "Developing our approach to implementing MiFID II conduct of business and organizational requirements", March 2015, Discussion Paper DP15/3, p. 10 et seq.

[17] According to Recital (87) of MiFID II: "Investments that involve contracts of insurance are often made available to customers as potential alternatives or substitutes to financial instruments subject to this Directive. To deliver consistent protection for retail clients and ensure a level playing field between similar products, it is important that insurance-based investment products are subject to appropriate requirements".

However, at a European level, instead of extending the scope of application of MiFID (or MiFID II and MiFIR), the policy option finally chosen[18] was the enactment of special European rules applying MiFID-like level of protection to insurance-based investment products, given the "different market structures and product characteristics".[19] Those special provisions, though, resemble to the provisions of MiFID to such an extent (for the purposes of leveling the playing field across financial sectors and protecting consumers of financial services) that a trend towards a "*MiFIDization*"[20] of the insurance regulation reveals, at least when it comes to insurance-based investments. Of course, one could doubt[21] whether the choice of sectoral regulation achieves the goal of legal consistency among financial sectors and avoidance of regulatory arbitrage, since even minor differentiation between sectoral provisions will inevitably occur. That sectoral legislation principle has found its exception, however, with Regulation 1286/2014 on key information documents for packaged retail and insurance-based investment products ("**PRIIPs Regulation**"), being the first piece of "horizontal" or "cross-sectoral" legislation, covering banking, investment and insurance products, instead of limiting its scope of application to one of these sectors.[22]

[18] Both in the case of IMD 1.5 and subsequently through the provisions of IDD in relation to the provision of information conduct of business standards, conflicts of interest etc.

[19] Recital (87) of MiFID II further provides:"…Whereas the investor protection requirements in this Directive should therefore be applied equally to those investments packaged under insurance contracts, their different market structures and product characteristics make it more appropriate that detailed requirements are set out in the ongoing review of Directive 2002/92 rather than setting them in this Directive. Future Union law regulating the activities of insurance intermediaries and insurance undertakings should thus appropriately ensure a consistent regulatory approach concerning the distribution of different financial products which satisfy similar needs and therefore raise comparable investor protection challenges. The…EIOPA…and ESMA should work together to achieve as much consistency as possible in the conduct of business standards for those investment products. Those new requirements for insurance-based investment products should be laid down in Directive 2002/92".

[20] *P. Marano*, The "Mifidization": the sunset of life insurance in the EU Regulation on Insurance?, p. 2 et seq., available at: https://papers.ssrn.com/sol3/papers.cfm?abstract_id=2832952.

[21] *Gaetane/ Schaeken/ Willemaers*, Client protection on European financial markets –from inform your client to know your product and beyond: an assessment of the PRIIPs Regulation, MiFID II/MiFIR and IMD 2, p. 18, available at: https://papers.ssrn.com/sol3/papers.cfm?abstract_id=2494842&download=yes.

[22] *V. Colaert*, The Regulation of PRIIPs: Great Ambitions, Insurmountable Challenges?, p. 2, available at: https://papers.ssrn.com/sol3/Papers.cfm?abstract_id=2721644.

2 Retail Investment Markets and Products

2.1 Retail Investment Products

(a) The European market for retail financial services consists of loans payments, current and savings accounts, insurance, and other retail investments.[23] Especially the **retail investment markets** are characterized by **rapid financial innovation**, which has resulted in the structuring of a wide variety of retail investment products available to retail investors.

The term "**retail investor**" includes, in line with the direction followed by the EC during its consultation process, non-sophisticated, non-institutional investors, the primary focus being the individual or household, without though strictly excluding other categories.[24]

(b) Retail investment in the financial markets is largely channeled through "**packaged retail investment products**",[25] referred to as "**PRIPs**". PRIPs are a subset of retail financial products. In the case of PRIPs, financial product manufacturers intercede between retail investors and financial markets, "building" products normally designed to satisfy specific investment goals, with the intention of being sold to retail investors, either directly or through intermediaries.[26] Those financial services intermediaries—such as fund managing firms, insurance undertakings, credit institutions or investment firms[27]—are "manufacturing" those products in such a way so as to provide cost effective access to investment products for retail investors who otherwise would have neither the expertise nor the access to make such investments.[28] In the past, financial institutions used to distribute only products developed "in house", however, in recent times they have developed more open models of distribution, offering products by third parties as well.

(c) **Unit-linked policies and other insurance-based investment products of same nature fall under the scope of PRIPs**[29]

---

[23] European Commission Green Paper on retail financial services, COM (2015) 630 final, p. 3.

[24] Commission Staff Working Document, Impact Assessment accompanying the Communication from the Commission to the European Parliament and the Council on Packaged Retail Investment Products, SEC (2009)556, p. 8.

[25] Communication from the Commission to the European Parliament and the Council, "Packaged Retail Investment Products, SEC (2009)556, 557, p. 4 (http://ec.europa.eu/internal_market/finservices-retail/docs/investment_products/29042009_communication_en.pdf).

[26] Commission Staff Working Document, Impact Assessment accompanying the document Proposal for a Regulation of the European Parliament and of the Council on key information documents for investment products, SWD(2012)187 final, p. 5.

[27] Recital (12) and art.4 (4) of the PRIIPs Regulation.

[28] Commission Staff Working Document, op.cit. (note 16), Box 1: What are PRIPs, p. 21.

[29] Commission Staff Working Document, op.cit. (note 16) SWD (2012)/0191 final p. 26. In terms of terminology, it has to be noted, already, that upon the entry into force of the PRIIPs Regulation, packaged retail investment products generally referred to in this section as PRIPs, are considered

Other examples of PRIPs are investment funds such as UCITS and retail structured products.

(d) Packaged products are distinguished from non-packaged, such as investments in single equities or unstructured bonds, since the process of packaging investments adds an additional layer of complexity and cost that may make the key characteristics of the investment less transparent to the end investor, as we will further analyze below.[30]

(e) Before the launch of a European regulatory framework on packaged retail investment products, there was no widely-accepted legal definition in this regard, thus the scope of those products was initially based on common product characteristics, as well as on their shared core functionality providing retail investors with the prospect of capital accumulation over the medium to long term and compete for the same retail savings. Indeed, on 30 April 2009, the European Commission published a Communication on PRIPs[31] where it confirmed that they could ***"take a variety of legal forms which provide broadly comparable functions for retail investors"***[32]:

- They offer exposure to underlying financial assets, but in packaged forms, which modify that exposure compared with direct holdings,
- Their primary function is capital accumulation,
- They are generally designed with the mid-to long-term retail market in mind, and
- They are marketed directly to retail investors, although may also be sold to sophisticated investors.

(f) Based on the aforementioned criteria, the Commission prepared, and included in the same Communication, an initial non-exhaustive, nevertheless indicative, **list of the packaged retail investment products available at the time in the retail market**. The Commission highlighted in this regard that, due to the aforementioned financial innovation, new investment products are constantly emerging, however the list served "as a starting point for identifying packaged retail investment products". Thus, this initial basis-list titled **"Families of Packaged Retail Investment Products"** was the following[33]:

to be a subset of packaged retail and insurance-based investment products (**"PRIIPs"**), along with insurance-based investment products. In other words, in line with the PRIIPs regulation, PRIIPs consists of PRIPs and insurance-based investment products. Besides, the initial Proposal of the Regulation used the term "PRIPs", which, though, already included insurance-based investment products! We will refer to this change in terminology in the course of this article as well.

[30] Commission Staff Working Document, op.cit. SEC (2009) 556, p. 8, ref.4.

[31] Communication from the Commission to the European Parliament and the Council, "Packaged Retail Investment Products, SEC(2009) 556,557.

[32] Communication "Packaged Retail Investment Products, op.cit. p. 3.

[33] Communication from the Commission to the European Parliament and the Council, op. cit. (note 21), SEC(2009)556, 557.

- **Investment (or mutual) funds**. This is a type of collective investment, whereby pooled funds of a number of investors are invested. Subsequently, "units" of the fund are marketed to investors.
- **Investments packaged as life insurance policies**. Common examples in this regard are unit-linked life insurance policies, where a portion of the premium is invested in a fund, such as a UCITS. The returns in this case are linked to the performance of the fund,[34] since the policyholder usually bears the investment risk.[35]
- **Retail structured securities**. Structured securities are derived from or based on a single security, a basket of securities, an index, a commodity, a debt issue and/or a foreign currency.
- **Structured term deposits**. Structured term deposits offer a combination of a term deposit with an embedded option or an interest rate structure.[36]

(g) It has to be noted, though, that apart from similarities, retail investment products present differences as well. Those differences have also been described by the EC[37]:

- Different structure.
- Varying legal relationship between the investor and originator.
- Different risks associated with the products: for example counterparty risk, liquidity risk etc.
- Varying holding periods. For example, insurance-based products are typically held for longer than the average maturity of a structured security.
- Different tax treatment.
- Additional functionality. For example, in the case of unit-linked life insurance policy biometric risk coverage is included.

[34] In the case of the example given, the amount of the investment part varies on the market fluctuations, while the amount of the life insurance sum is a fix sum. It is not impossible that the insurance sum is also expressed in investments, such as units, where the insurer is obliged to pay the fix number of units in case the risk realizes or by the maturity of the policy or in case the insured demands its repurchase.

[35] It is common practice for the unit-linked policies to include condition whereby the investment decision lies to the policyholder.

[36] Also see MiFID II on structured deposits (art.4 para 1 (43) etc.).

[37] Impact Assessment accompanying the Communication from the Commission to the European Parliament and the Council on Packaged Retail Investment Products, Commission Staff Working Document, SEC (2009)556, p. 42.

2.2 Benefits and Risks for Retail Investors

It is unquestionable that packaged retail investment products are important investment tools for retail investors, who seek to achieve returns on their accumulated capital, as well as for the promotion of efficient capital markets and the economy.[38]

On the other hand, packaged retail investments entail risks. As highlighted by EIOPA, buying packaged retail investments is complex for consumers, especially in case of long term investments, since they might realize they were misguided after many years, compared to other consumer goods for which the assessment of quality and appropriateness can normally be made immediately.[39] Experience would not be useful either, since consumers are not frequently buying packaged retail investments.[40] Further risks for consumers derive from the "packaging" of those products, increasing complexity and reducing transparency, making their understanding rather difficult.[41] Besides, retail investors "suffer" from behavioral biases,[42] since they most commonly tend to focus on the "reward" or performance side of an investment rather than on costs, risks etc, while information asymmetry between retail investors and manufacturers/distributors of such packaged products increases the possibility for consumer detriment since retail investors are often confused about the true nature of their investment. For example, purchasers of structured products are often uncertain whether or not they are exposed to the risks of stocks and shares".[43]

The Impact Assessment accompanying the initial Commission proposal on "key information documents for investment products"[44] (later to become the so-called PRIIPs Regulation[45]) has defined the so-called "problem-drivers" linked to the "packaging" and distribution of packaged investment products available to retail investors[46]:

---

[38] Communication from the Commission to the European Parliament and the Council, op. cit (note 21), SEC(2009) 556,557, pp. 5&13.

[39] EIOPA Discussion Paper on Key Information Documents for Packaged Retail and Insurance-based Investment, JC/DP/2014/02, p. 17.

[40] EIOPA Discussion Paper on Key Information Documents for Packaged Retail and Insurance-based Investment, op.cit., p. 17.

[41] EIOPA Discussion Paper on Key Information Documents for Packaged Retail and Insurance-based Investment, op.cit., p. 17.

[42] EIOPA Discussion Paper on Key Information Documents for Packaged Retail and Insurance-based Investment, op.cit., p. 17.

[43] Consumer Decision-Making in Retail Investment Services: A behavioral Economics Perspective, 2010 (Executive Summary), p. 6.

[44] Commission Staff Working Document, Impact Assessment accompanying the document Proposal for a Regulation of the European Parliament and of the Council on key information documents for investment products, 2012. para. 2.1.

[45] The application of the PRIIPS Regulation (originally provided for 31.12.2016) was postponed to 1. 1.2018 according to the Commission proposal.

[46] Commission Staff Working Document, Impact Assessment accompanying the document Proposal for a Regulation of the European Parliament and of the Council on key information docu-

1. There is a wide variety of investment products available to consumers which take **different legal forms** and structures, though offering **comparable economic results**: Funds (whether UCITS or non-harmonised), investments packaged as life insurance policies (notably, unit-linked, index-linked and certain other "with-profits" products) and retail structured products (typically in the form of structured securities or structured term deposits).
2. Varying legal forms result in a fragmented regulatory environment with different levels of regulatory requirements applying, despite similarities in terms of economic outcomes. Such regulatory fragmentation incentivizes regulatory arbitrage, i.e. the structuring and marketing of products in such a way to take advantage of less onerous requirements across product groups.
3. There are powerful asymmetries of information between retail customers and industry, which remain unmitigated. This means that consumers of financial services suffer from severe informational problems, especially taking into account that most consumers find financial products complex and they make financial decisions infrequently. This makes the general case for policymakers to intervene to protect consumers.[47]

3 Insurance-Based Investment Products as a Subset of Retail Investment Products

Insurance-based investment products qualify as packaged retail investment products, since they offer exposure to underlying financial assets, but in packaged forms, and they are marketed directly to retail investors. Of course they may be marketed to non-retail investors as well. However, in such case, there is no clear case for regulatory intervention in favor of experienced and knowledgeable investors who qualify as professional clients.[48]

To put it simply, retail investments are packaged with life insurance policies, such as unit-linked or index-linked or fixed-index annuities and variable annuities policies, thus offering a maturity/surrender value which is exposed, partially or as a whole, to market fluctuations.[49] For example, the insured-investor purchases long-term life insurance[50] with the balance invested in a fund, such as a UCITS, and the

ments for investment products, op.cit.

[47] Commission Staff Working Document, Economic Review of the Financial Regulation Agenda "A reformed financial sector for Europe", COM (2014) 279 final, p. 146. See also Recitals (10) and (61) of IDD.

[48] See art.4(6)(b) of the PRIIPs Regulation.

[49] See already art.4(2) of the PRIIPs Regulation.

[50] However, life insurance contracts where the benefits under the contract are payable only on death or in respect of incapacity due to injury, sickness or infirmity, **are excluded from the scope** of insurance-based investment products as defined in both the IDD and the PRIIPs Regulation.

return[51] on the policy is linked to the performance of the funds in addition to the fixed sum of the insurance part of the policy. The UK FCA[52] refers to insurance-based investments as covering products packaged under insurance contracts, such as unit-linked and with profits policies, investment bonds, personal pensions provided by insurers, and annuities.[53] More broadly, the insurance industry refers to insurance-based investment products as comprising an insurance cover, consisting of protection against biometric risks (life insurance) faced by consumers, alongside an investment element.[54]

As regards the question whether the two components (investment and insurance) included in the policy have an impact on the application of investment and/or insurance legislation, we have to mention the following:

As already referred in the very beginning of this article the most important piece of legislation governing investment services and financial instruments is MiFID II[55] and MiFIR. The scope of financial instruments to which MiFID II Directive will apply is listed in its Annex I, including shares, money-market instruments, units in collective investment schemes, as well as types of financial derivatives. However, as with MiFID, **the new framework does not apply to insurance-based investments.**[56] Interestingly, though, despite the fact that insurance-based investment products do not fall under the scope of MiFID II, Recital 87 of that Directive confirms that **insurance-based investments are offered to consumers as "potential alternatives or substitutes" to financial instruments governed by MiFID II rules**. Given such substitutability between insurance-based investment products and MiFID II financial instruments, the European legislator has underlined in the preamble of MiFID II, a prominent piece of sectoral legislation, the need for an alignment of provisions governing those "substitutable" areas to prevent investor protection gaps.

On the same basis, IDD recognizes the potentially increased risk that insurance-based investment products represent to **consumers**. This is one of the reasons that IDD has included in its scope insurance-based investment products and has imposed additional requirements on distributors raising the level of policyholder's protection

---

[51] To be noted, here, that for example art.104 of Greek law 4099/2012 on UCITS provides that the insurance benefit (while not the insurance premium) in the case of life insurance may be paid through a transfer of units of UCITS to the insured, instead of cash. There is no similar explicit provision in Greek law as regards the payment of insurance premia through transfer of units, contrary to other jurisdictions such as in Luxembourg where this explicitly permitted. Germany on the other hand, prohibits the payment of premia otherwise than in cash.

[52] Financial Conduct Authority.

[53] FCA, op.cit., especially: Applying MiFID II rules to insurance-based investment products and pensions, p. 12.

[54] Insurance Europe, Insurance-based Investment Products' Benefits, p. 1 available at: http://www.insuranceeurope.eu/insurance-based-investment-products%E2%80%99-benefits.

[55] MiFID II and MiFIR replace MiFID and will apply as of 3.1.2018.

[56] To be noted that ESMA, the competent European supervisory authority, does not have any competency on the insurance sector and insurance products. ESMA guidelines are not addressed to insurance undertakings or distributors of insurance products.

to be aligned with MiFID.[57] Besides, according to the Recital of IDD (para.10) "*current and recent financial turbulence has underlined the importance of ensuring effective consumer protection* ***across all financial sectors***". In other words, a level playing field is to be achieved as regards products attaining the same or similar economic result, regardless of the originating institution.

4 What Forms Can Insurance-Based Investments Take?

In September 2010, a report titled *"Study on the Costs and Benefits of Potential Changes to Distribution Rules for Insurance Investments Products and other non-MiFID Packaged Retail Investment Products"*[58] (hereinafter the "Study") was published, commissioned by DG Internal Market and Services to investigate the costs and benefits to industry of potential changes to the distribution rules for insurance investment products and other packaged retail investment products that are not governed by MiFID-like rules.

The Study segmented insurance investment products, available in the market at the time (not provided by legal rules at a European level) and for the purposes of its cost-benefit analysis, into broadly four groups of life investment insurance products, as follows[59]:

1. A life insurance investment product which involves **the policyholder purchasing "units" in a fund**. It is commonly referred to as **unit-linked life insurance policy** (issued with or without a guarantee). Thereby, the value of the policy at maturity is dependent upon the growth of the fund in which the policy is invested and there is **generally no guarantee to the value of the policy when it matures**, i.e. investment risk is borne by the policyholder and market values directly determine outcomes for the policyholder.
2. A life insurance investment product where *the policy's cash value is tied to the performance of a financial index* (e.g. FTSE 100). This type is referred to as **index-linked insurance policy**.
3. A life insurance investment product where **benefits are partly guaranteed and partly dependent on the evolution of assets chosen by the policyholder**, usually UCITS. Then the amount paid by the insured-investor is partly invested in guaranteed assets (for the purpose to pay the fix life insurance sum, plus interest,

[57] European Commission MEMO, The Insurance Distribution Directive Frequently Asked Questions, Question 8: How are the rules different for insurance products with investment elements?, Brussels, 23 February 2016.

[58] Europe Economics, Study on the Costs and Benefits of Potential Changes to Distribution Rules for Insurance Investments Products and other non-MiFID Packaged Retail Investment Products, Europe Economics, 29.09.2010 available at http://ec.europa.eu/finance/consultations/2010/prips/docs/costs_benefits_study_en.pdf.

[59] Europe Economics, op. cit., p. 4.

provided in the policy) and partly in assets on the account and risk of the policyholder.[60]

4. A life insurance investment product where **the policyholder has some rights to participate in the profits of the insurance firm** (e.g. deriving from general expenses profit or from return on investments exceeding pre-defined minimum return) **in addition to some guaranteed minimum return**.

The Study (p. 34) verifies that the most common life insurance investment products in the EU (even though the list was not exhaustive) tend to be unit-linked products. The aforementioned types have evolved **through contractual agreements rather than provided by national legal provisions**, as long as of course the rights of the insured are not hindered.

The point of view presented above refers to the investment element when the investment risk is born by the policyholder, since **in terms of the insurance element and risk insured, those are aspects regulated by sectoral insurance regulation**. Thus, on the basis of **contractual freedom**, insurance-based investment products may be formed, where the sum for life insurance is either mirrored in investments (thus, instead of fix sum we have fix number of units most of the times) or constituted by cash plus fix interest and often participation in profits.

5 Towards a Legal Definition

5.1 General Remarks

By now, it should be common knowledge that, even though very often different investment products have the same economic effect, they are subject to different legal provisions, depending on their legal form, the originating institution and the distribution channels through which they reach retail investors. Those varying legal provisions refer to the disclosure of product information, conduct of business, management of conflicts of interest etc. For example, as already mentioned, MiFID (and from now on MiFID II) applied to investment products and not to insurance-based investments (sectoral legislation!), despite the fact that Member States such as the UK (so far) extended the scope of national legislation to insurance-based investments as well.

Such reality has become evident for the European Commission, already since 2007, when a call for evidence on the impact of the fragmented regulatory landscape for retail products on the protection of retail investors was launched.[61]

[60] We have already mentioned (note 35) that it is possible and very common for the part of the policy that represents the life insurance sum to be expressed in cash money while the investment part alone is linked to investment and that European law does not prohibit such a structure.

[61] Internal Market and Services Commissioner Charlie McCreevy said in Press release IP/07/1615, Brussels 26 October 2007: "A wide range of investment products are now available to help retail investors take responsibility for their long-term financial futures. Today, the EU legislative frame-

Following extensive consultations and studies, the Commission steadily refined a possible definition of retail investment products of the packaged form and more specifically of insurance-based investment products. Thus, by now, **the meaning of "insurance-based investment products" is defined in several European legal texts** as follows:

5.2 Insurance Distribution Directive

The Insurance Distribution Directive 2016/97 (**IDD**), defines the term **"insurance-based investment products"** as meaning an insurance product which **offers a maturity or surrender value** and where that maturity or surrender value is **wholly or partially exposed, directly or indirectly, to market fluctuation**, and does **not include** non-life policies, life insurance policies which cover only death, incapacity due to injury, sickness or disability, pension products, occupational pensions schemes and individual pension products.[62]

Interestingly, the European legislator has chosen to abstain from intervening in contractual freedom and consequently, from restricting entrepreneurial initiative and innovation as regards the types and legal forms a packaged product and, in our case, an insurance-based investment product can take. In other words, the European regulator does not specifically or separately regulate insurance-based investments from the perspective of contract law, but only from a consumer protection perspective, addressing information asymmetries afflicting retail investors/consumers. What is more, the European legislator does not prohibit the insurance sum to be expressed in investment units as well, thus reference is made to either fix number of units or fix sum of money calculated/paid in units of investments. Besides, as

---

work imposes different levels of product and fee disclosure, and different selling rules, depending on the legal form the product takes. I believe that there is a strong case for investigating whether these differences are harming investors and distorting markets".

[62] See Article 2 para 1(17) of IDD: 'insurance-based investment product' means an insurance product which offers a maturity or surrender value and where that maturity or surrender value is wholly or partially exposed, directly or indirectly, to market fluctuations, **and does not include**:

i. Non-life insurance products, as listed in Annex I to Solvency II Directive (Classes of non-life insurance),
ii. Life insurance contracts where the benefits under the contract are payable only on death or in respect of incapacity due to injury, sickness or disability,
iii. Pension products which, under national law, are recognized as having the primary purpose of providing the investor with an income in retirement, and which entitle the investor to certain benefits,
iv. Officially recognized occupational pensions schemes falling under the scope of Directive 2003/41or Solvency II Directive,
v. Individual pension products for which a financial contribution from the employer is required by national law and where the employer has no choice as to the pension product or provider.

already mentioned earlier, the European regulation remains neutral as regards insurance policies consisting of two separate parts, thus contractual freedom may form insurance-based products where the insurance sum or/and other benefits are expressed in investments.

IDD takes a step further, by making reference to **"non-complex" insurance-based investment products**, thus implying a distinction between complex and non-complex products. The reference is made in the context of article 30 IDD "Assessment of suitability and appropriateness and reporting to customers". More specifically, article 30 para 3 IDD allows Member States, under certain conditions, to derogate from the obligations set in paras 1 and 2 of article 30 IDD, i.e. from the assessment of suitability or appropriateness of an insurance-based investment product which, otherwise, are generally part of an advised or non-advised sale. The national discretion for a derogation refers to the case of a so-called **"execution-only" sale**, which is a type of sale where the insurance undertaking (or intermediary) executes the transaction requested by the customer, at the customer's (or potential customer's) initiative only, without prior vetting of the customer's knowledge, experience, financial situation and objectives.[63] Thus, if Member States choose to insert a national derogation, on the basis of article 30 para 3 IDD, in the case of "execution-only" sales, another condition specified in article 30 para 3 IDD has to be met, which relates to the complexity of the insurance-based investment product falling in the scope of such derogation. The assessment of such complexity is based on the nature of the financial instruments to which the insurance-based investment provides investment exposure, as well as the structure of the contract between the insurance undertaking (or intermediary) and the customer (art.30 para 3(a) IDD).[64] Article 30 para 3(a) describes two cases where insurance-based investment products qualify as "non-complex": (1) contracts linked to "non-complex" MiFID II financial instruments, as long as their structure allows the customer to understand the risks undertaken and (2) "other" non-complex insurance-based investment products. As underlined by EIOPA,[65] the list of specified non-complex financial instruments in MiFID II is limited to certain types of shares, bonds, money market instruments and structured deposits, and non structured UCITS, as set out in article 25 para 4(a) of MiFID II. However, apart from the "non-complex" financial instruments explicitly enumerated in MiFID II, article 25 para 4(a)(vi) makes reference to *"other non-complex financial instruments for the purpose of this paragraph"* which the Commission is empowered to specify through the adoption of delegated acts (art. 25 para 8 MiFID II). Thus, such MiFID II-based delegated acts and regulations need to be taken into account for the purpose of the application of article 30 para 3(a)(i) IDD, as well. On the other hand, even if products do not qualify as "non-

[63] Also see EIOPA, "Technical Advice on possible delegated acts concerning the Insurance Distribution Directive", EIOPA-17/048, 1 February 2017, p. 72 et seq.

[64] Also see EIOPA, "Technical Advice on possible delegated acts concerning the Insurance Distribution Directive", op.cit.

[65] EIOPA, "Technical Advice on possible delegated acts concerning the Insurance Distribution Directive", op. cit., p. 74.

complex" under MiFID II, they might still be deemed as "non-complex" under IDD. EIOPA has developed detailed technical advice for the assessment of complexity in this regard, on the basis that where an insurance-based investment product incorporates a structure which makes it difficult for the customer to understand the risks involved, it is in all cases not fit for distribution via execution-only sale,[66] while additional Guidelines will follow.

5.3 Regulation 1286/2014 on Key Information Documents for Packaged Retail and Insurance-Based Investment Products. From PRIPs to PRIIPs

As discussed in the beginning of this article, Regulation 1286/2014 (the **PRIIPs Regulation**) reflects an innovative policy option in the European regulation of financial services, since its scope of application is not sectoral, but rather cross-sectoral and functional, covering products with similar features "regardless of their form or construction" that are manufactured by the financial services industry to provide investment opportunities to retail investors[67]: the economic purpose of the product is preferred over the legal form.[68]

The original EC draft[69] Proposal for a Regulation, published in 2012, was referring to "**investment products**", while the final text of the Regulation refers to packaged retail and insurance—based investment products.[70] What might not be straightforward by the title of the draft Proposal, simply referring to "investment products", but is rather clarified in its preamble and definitions, is that—essentially—it intended to apply to **packaged investment products**.[71]

[66] EIOPA, "Technical Advice on possible delegated acts concerning the Insurance Distribution Directive", op. cit., p. 75.

[67] Recital (6) of the PRIIPs Regulation. Also, *V. Colaert*, op.cit. p. 4.

[68] *V. Colaert*, op.cit. p. 5.

[69] **Proposal for a Regulation of the European Parliament and of the Council on key information documents for investment products /* COM/2012/0352 final - 2012/0169 (COD) */**, available here: http://eur-lex.europa.eu/legal-content/EN/TXT/?uri=CELEX:52012PC0352.

[70] According to the initial draft Regulation (art.4), "investment product" means "an investment where regardless of the legal form of the investment, the amount repayable to the investor is exposed to fluctuations in reference values or in the performance of one or more assets which are not directly purchased by the investor". The draft Regulation also enumerated exceptions for certain cases.

[71] See art.4 of the draft Regulation along with Recitals (6) and (7) of its preamble:

> (6) "(…) This should include such investment products as investment funds, life insurance policies with an investment element, and retail structured products. For these products, investments are not of a direct kind achieved when buying or holding assets themselves. Instead these products intercede between the investor and the markets through a process of "packaging", wrapping or bundling together assets so as to create different exposures, provide different product features, or achieve different cost structures as compared with a

In 2014 a political agreement was finally reached between the European Parliament and the Council that led to the approval and publishing of PRIIPs Regulation. PRIIPs Regulation seeks to enable investors to better understand and compare the key features, risks, rewards and costs of different PRIIPs through a short and consumer-friendly **Key Information Document** (**KID**). Through KID retail investors will be provided with information about a broad range of investment opportunities including insurance-based investment products, structured investment products as well as collective investment schemes (investment funds). PRIIPs Regulation applies to both manufactures of PRIIPS and to those who are advising on or selling/ distributing a PRIIP to retail investors (art. 2).

5.4 The Current Scope of PRIIPs Regulation

(a) The definition of the products for which a KID must be produced occurs in articles 2 and 4 of the PRIIPs Regulation. Thereby, the Regulation distinguishes between insurance-based and non-insurance based PRIIPs (investment products), as well as instruments issued by SPVs. More specifically, according to article 4 para 3 of the PRIIPs Regulation, '**packaged retail and insurance-based investment product**' *means a product that is one or both of the following: (a) packaged retail investment product; (b) an insurance-based investment product.*

A **packaged retail investment product** is defined as an **investment**, including instruments issued by special purpose vehicles[72] or securitisation special purpose entities,[73] **where, regardless of the legal form of the investment, the amount repayable to the retail investor is subject to fluctuations because of exposure to reference values or to the performance of one or more assets which are not directly purchased by the retail investor** (art. 4 para 1, PRIIPs Regulation). On the other hand, an **insurance-based investment product, on the other hand**, means an insurance product which offers a maturity or surrender value and **where that maturity or surrender value is wholly or**

direct holding. Such "packaging" can allow retail investors to engage in investment strategies that would otherwise be inaccessible or impractical, but can also require additional information to be made available, in particular to enable comparisons between different ways of packaging investments".

(7) "(…) Assets that would be held directly, such as corporate shares or sovereign bonds, are not packaged investment products, and should therefore be excluded. (…) occupational pension schemes which fall under the scope of Directive 2003/41 (…) or Solvency II Directive (…) should not be subject to this Regulation. (…) Investment funds dedicated to institutional investors are not within the scope of this Regulation (…)".

[72] As defined in point (26) of Article 13 of Solvency II Directive.

[73] Entities as defined in point (an) of Article 4(1) of the Directive 2011/61.

partially exposed, directly or indirectly, to market fluctuations[74] (art.4 para 2 of PRIIPs).

However, comparing the initial draft Regulation with the final text of the Regulation, one can conclude that not much difference has been made in terms of terminology,[75] since insurance-based investment products are now included as a PRIIPs sub-category, while previously they were included in the one and single wider category of "investment products" (PRIPs). The amendment of the terminology used in the initial text of the draft by the final text of the Regulation has been characterized as "regrettable", undermining the overarching goal of the legislature to focus on the economic substance rather than on legal form, thus deviating in this regard from the traditional sectoral approach towards a more horizontal one.[76]

Further, as in the initial proposal, there are **exceptions** in the scope of PRIIPs. The exceptions[77] are a combination of **"true" exceptions** (those refer to products that would otherwise be in scope but are excluded solely by means of an explicit exception) and **clarifications** (it refers to products that might be viewed as out of scope of the Regulation under article 4, but which are identified for reasons of legal certainty).[78]

(b) The Recital of the Regulation provides again with useful guidelines in relation to the breadth of the scope of the Regulation[79]: investment products such as

[74] To be noted that Solvency II Directive makes reference, in art.132 para 3, to unit-linked and index-linked insurance policies: "...Where the benefits provided by a contract are directly linked to the value of units in a UCITS as defined in Directive 85/611, or to the value of assets contained in an internal fund held by the insurance undertakings, usually divided into units, the technical provisions in respect of those benefits must be represented as closely as possible by those units or, in case where units are not established by those assets. Where the benefits provided by a contract are directly linked to a share index or some other reference value other than those referred to in the second subparagraph, the technical provisions in respect of those benefits must be represented as closely as possible either by the units deemed to represent the reference value or, in the case where units are not established, by assets of appropriate security and marketability which correspond as closely as possible with those on which the particular reference value is based".

[75] Also see note 30 above.

[76] *V. Colaert*, op.cit. p. 5.

[77] Listed in art. 2 of the PRIIPs Regulation.

[78] Art.2 para 2 of the PRIIPs Regulation provides that the Regulation shall not apply to the following products: (a) non-life insurance products as listed in Annex I to Directive 2009/138; (b) life insurance contracts where the benefits under the contract are payable only on death or in respect of incapacity due to injury, sickness or infirmity; (c) deposits other than structured deposits as defined in point (43) of Article 4(1) of Directive 2014/65; (d) securities as referred to in points (b) to (g), (i) and (j) of Article 1(2) of Directive 2003/71; (e) pension products which, under national law, are recognised as having the primary purpose of providing the investor with an income in retirement and which entitle the investor to certain benefits; (f) officially recognised occupational pension schemes within the scope of Directive 2003/41 of the European Parliament and of the Council or Directive 2009/138; individual pension products for which a financial contribution from the employer is required by national law and where the employer or the employee has no choice as to the pension product or provider.

[79] See Recital (6) and (7) of the PRIIPs Regulation.

investment funds, life insurance policies with an investment element, structured products, structured deposits, as well as financial instruments issued by special purpose vehicles **fall within the scope** of the Regulation, regardless of the form/construction, **as long as** they constitute investments of an indirect kind and the amount repayable to the retail investor is subject to fluctuations. Directly held assets (corporate shares, sovereign bonds etc), deposits solely exposed to interest rates, insurance policies not offering investment opportunities and occupational pension products should not be considered as PRIIPs. Not surprisingly, investment funds dedicated to institutional investors are still excluded from the scope of this Regulation since they are not for sale to retail investors.[80]

The Regulation also clarifies that UCITS fall within its scope. Nevertheless, in view of the special regime already in place, namely Directive 2009/65 (UCITS), the PRIIPs Regulation will not apply, immediately upon entry into force, to UCITS and non-UCITS funds subject to UCITS-equivalent national regime, but instead following a transitional period of 5 years after the entry into force of this Regulation during which they would not be subject to this Regulation. After the expiry of that transitional period and in the absence of any extension thereto, UCITS should become subject to this Regulation.[81]

(c) To be noted that any distinction between packaged and non-packaged investments is subject to **changes due to innovation**. Most of the times, wherever the boundary is clearly drawn, the risk remains that financial engineering will develop products which, from an economic perspective, might be essentially similar to or the same as those captured by the defined legal scope but typically falling outside such scope or at least touching the limits of it.[82] Therefore, the delimitation of a clear-cut boundary may well encourage or facilitate regulatory arbitrage, contributing to further complexity in the market. This is again why in the PRIIPs Regulation the economic outcome was preferred over legal structures. Besides, contractual freedom can lead to such a great variety of products that is almost impossible to capture.

(d) In relation to those products currently out of scope, PRIIPs provides[83] on the one hand that Member States are allowed to regulate the provision of key information, while on the other hand the ESAs, in accordance with their mandate for consumer protection, should monitor the products which are currently excluded from the scope and, where appropriate, they should issue guidelines to address any problem identified.

(e) To be noted that the PRIIPs Regulation makes special reference to cases where retail investors pursue, along with the financial returns on their investment,

[80] See Recital (7) of the PRIIPs Regulation.

[81] See Recital (35) and art.32 para 1 of the PRIIPs Regulation.

[82] Commission Staff Working Document, Impact Assessment accompanying the document Proposal for a Regulation of the European Parliament and of the Council on key information documents for investment products, 2012.

[83] Recital (8) of the PRIIPs Regulation.

additional purposes **such as social or environmental goals** (Recital 19 thereof). Thus in case of PRIIPs targeting specific environmental or social objectives, article 8 para 4 of the PRIIPs Regulation empowers the Commission "to adopt delegated acts in accordance with article 30 specifying the details of the procedures used to establish whether a PRIIP targets specific environmental or social objectives".[84] In such case, where a KID states that a PRIIP targets environmental or social objectives (EOS PRIIP), the manufacturer must be able to demonstrate to stakeholders, and in particular to the potential retail investor, in supporting documentation to the KID, the relevance of these objectives for the whole value chain of the investment process.[85]

5.5 Types of Risks Inherent to PRIIPs

The ESAs[86] have examined[87] potential risks related to PRIIPs and their manufacturers. Such exercise resulted in a long list of types of risks, amongst which market risk, counterparty and credit risk, foreign-exchange, legal risk and operational risk were included. The list was further divided into three main types of risk: **market, credit and liquidity risk**.

i. **Market Risk.**[88] PRIIPs are by definition indirect investments and their value is dependent on the value of underlying asset(s) or reference values, such as equities, commodities, real estate, bonds, interest rates, foreign exchange rates, etc. The market risk of a PRIIP can therefore be defined as the risk of changes in the value of the PRIIP due to movements in the value of the underlying assets or reference values.
ii. **Credit Risk.**[89] Credit risk is generally perceived as the risk of loss on a given asset in relation to issuer's credit events (such as default).

[84] See already Joint Consultation Paper on "PRIIPs with environmental and social objectives", JC 2017 05, 10 February 2017, available at: https://esas-joint-committee.europa.eu/Publications/Consultations/JC_2017_05_CP_EOS_PRIIPs_final.pdf.

Further, the European Commission requested the ESAs to consider whether measures are required to ensure PRIIPs manufacturers have appropriate governance systems in place to ensure that disclosed EOS objectives are met.

[85] Joint Consultation Paper on "PRIIPs with environmental and social objectives", op.cit. p. 5.

[86] The three ESAs are the European Banking Authority (EBA), the European Securities and Markets Authorities (ESMA) and the European Insurance and Occupational Pensions Authority (EIOPA) and they are part of the European System of Financial Supervision (ESFS).

[87] EIOPA Discussion Paper on Key Information Documents for Packaged Retail and Insurance-based Investment, JC/DP/2014/02, p. 24.

[88] EIOPA Discussion Paper on Key Information Documents for Packaged Retail and Insurance-based Investment, JC/DP/2014/02, p. 25.

[89] See note 73.

iii. **Liquidity Risk.**[90] The PRIIPs liquidity risk relates to factors determining whether an investor can redeem his investment at the moment that the investor wishes to: for example, in case where the investor wishes to exit their investment before a scheduled maturity date in case of products with a fixed term, or products creating exposures to assets that may be or become illiquid (such as real estate, participations in long term projects). Especially in relation to **insurance-based products** those are not transferable in principle, thus **liquidity is only provided by the manufacturer**, the main question in this case being how costly would be for the retail consumer to exit the product.

6 Final Remarks

(a) Insurance-based investment products are a subset of (packaged) retail investment products or, according to the terminology used by the PRIIPs Regulation, a subset of packaged retail and insurance-based investment products. Both the IDD and PRIIPs define insurance-based investment products as insurance products offering to retail clients a maturity or surrender value which is wholly or partially exposed, directly or indirectly, to market fluctuations. Insurance products that do not offer investment opportunities are excluded from the scope. Unit-linked investment products are the most characteristic example of insurance-based investment products.
(b) On the one hand, contractual freedom can give rise to countless products, which may present a variety of legal forms although bearing similar or comparable economic results. Besides, innovation should not be hindered, but promoted. On the other hand, the delimitation of the term of insurance-based investment products and PRIIPs determine the scope of application of the applicable legal framework which aims to client-investor protection. To a certain extent, the breadth of the products covered by recent regulatory initiatives will define the successful attainment of the regulatory goals: mitigate information asymmetries, align divergent European and national regulatory responses across the financial sectors create a level playing field for financial services providers offering products with similar economic content but using different legal forms. This is why the European regulator opted for a regulatory approach based on economic results of products rather than their legal form or originating institution.
(c) Ultimately, the restoration of investor confidence, as well as of the efficiency of capital markets underpins the regulatory framework addressing insurance-based investment products and PRIIPs in general. It remains to be seen whether the application of the said framework and the prevailing policy choices underpinning it, will effectively reach the aforementioned goals.

[90] EIOPA Discussion Paper op. cit. p. 26.

References

Case C-166/11, Ángel Lorenzo González Alonso v Nationale Nederlanden Vida Cía de Seguros y Reaseguros SAE [ECLI identifier: ECLI:EU:C:2012:119]

CEIOPS (2009) Report on National Measures regarding Disclosure Requirements and Professional Requirements for Unit-Linked Life Insurance Products, which are additional to the Minimum Requirements of the CLD and IMD (CEIOPS-DOC-20/09) available at: https://eiopa.europa.eu/CEIOPS-Archive/Documents/Reports/CEIOPS-Report-National-Measures-Unit-Linked-Life-insurance-products.pdf

Colaert V., The Regulation of PRIIPs: Great Ambitions, Insurmountable Challenges?, available at: https://papers.ssrn.com/sol3/Papers.cfm?abstract_id=2721644

Commission Staff Working Document, Impact Assessment accompanying the Communication from the Commission to the European Parliament and the Council on Packaged Retail Investment Products, SEC (2009)

Commission Staff Working Document, Economic Review of the Financial Regulation Agenda "A reformed financial sector for Europe", COM (2014) 279 final

Commission Staff Working Document, Impact Assessment accompanying the document Proposal for a Regulation of the European Parliament and of the Council on key information documents for investment products, SWD(2012)187 final

Communication from the Commission to the European Parliament and the Council, "Packaged Retail Investment Products", SEC(2009)556

Consumer Decision-Making in Retail Investment Services: A behavioural Economics Perspective, 2010 (Executive Summary)

EIOPA, "Technical Advice on possible delegated acts concerning the Insurance Distribution Directive", EIOPA-17/048, 1 February 2017

EIOPA Discussion Paper on Key Information Documents for Packaged Retail and Insurance-based Investment, JC/DP/2014/02

ESAS Joint Consultation Paper on "PRIIPs with environmental and social objectives", JC 2017 05, 10 February 2017., available at: https://esas-joint-committee.europa.eu/Publications/Consultations/JC_2017_05_CP_EOS_PRIIPs_final.pdf

European Commission Green Paper on retail financial services, COM (2015) 630 final

FCA (2015) "Developing our approach to implementing MiFID II conduct of business and organizational requirements", Discussion Paper DP15/3

Gaetane/ Schaeken/ Willemaers, Client protection on European financial markets –from inform your client to know your product and beyond: an assessment of the PRIIPs Regulation, MiFID II/MiFIR and IMD 2, available at: https://papers.ssrn.com/sol3/papers.cfm?abstract_id=2494842&download=yes

Galiatsos (2013) Investments in private insurance, Hellenic Bank Association/Hellenic Banking Institute

Insurance Europe, Insurance-based Investment Products' Benefits, available at: https://www.insuranceeurope.eu/sites/default/files/attachments/Insurance%20based%20investment%20products%20benefits.pdf. http://www.insuranceeurope.eu/protecting-long-term-investment

Marano P., The "Mifidization": the sunset of life insurance in the EU Regulation on Insurance?, p. 2 et seq., available at: https://papers.ssrn.com/sol3/papers.cfm?abstract_id=2832952

Münchener Rück Munich Re Group, Unit-linked Insurance- A general report, available at: http://www.asf.com.pt/winlib/cgi/winlibimg.exe?key=&doc=18678&img=5977

The Legal Regime and the Relevant Standards

Kyriaki Noussia and Michele Siri

Contents

Both authors have elaborated the paper. Nevertheless, Sects. 1 and 2 can be attributed to Kyriaki Noussia and Sects. 3 to 7 to Michele Siri, while Sect. 8 was jointly drafted.

K. Noussia (✉)
School of Law, University of Exeter, Exeter, UK
e-mail: k.noussia@exeter.ac.uk

M. Siri
Jean Monnet Professor of European Union Financial and Insurance Markets Regulation, Law Department, University of Genoa, Genova, Italy
e-mail: michele.siri@unige.it

P. Marano, I. Rokas (eds.), *Distribution of Insurance-Based Investment Products*, https://doi.org/10.1007/978-3-030-11668-2_2

Abbreviations

AIFMD	Alternative Investment Fund Managers Directive
CEBS	Committee of European Banking Supervisors
CEIOPS	Committee of European Insurance and Occupational Pensions Supervisors (now EIOPA)
CESR	Committee of European Securities Regulators
COBS	Conduct of Business Rules
DG	Directorate-General
EBA	European Banking Authority
EC	European Commission
EIOPA	European Insurance and Occupational Pensions Authority
ESAs	European Supervisory Authorities
ESFS	European System of Financial Supervision
ESMA	European Securities and Markets Authority
ESRB	European Systemic Risk Board
FCA	Financial Conduct Authority
IBIP	Insurance-Based Investment Products
IDD	Insurance Distribution Directive
IMD	Insurance Mediation Directive
ISD	Investment Services Directive
ITS	Implementing Technical Standards
KID	Key Information Document
MiFID	Markets in Financial Instruments Directive
NCA	National Competent Authorities
PRIIPs	Packaged Retail and Insurance Based Investment Products
PRIPs	Packaged Retail Investment Products
RTS	Regulatory Technical Standards
TFEU	Treaty of the Functioning of the European Union
UCITS	Undertakings for the Collective Investment of Transferable Securities

1 Historical Analysis and Perspective of the Substantial Rules on the EU Regulation of Insurance Based Investment Products

Insurance-Based Investment Products (IBIPs) are an important feature of the insurance market, and as such they also pertain a highly value position in insurance law. They combine elements of life insurance and investment, and their historical route is one of great importance. As such, contracts relating to investment funds (e.g. unit-linked policies) have started being adopted (e.g. in the context of insurance) since the 1960s. This tendency and trend is also depicted in the way that the European Community, now European Union, has legislated starting from that time. In effect, in the last decades, the pattern for European legislation has been to legislate for banks in the first instance and then to apply the same rules with minor modifications to investment firms. Insurance regulation has followed a slightly different path in that there have been attempts to integrate insurance regulation with the regulation of banking and investment business at European level, and this was principally due to the fact of the different nature of underlying risks and business models involved.[1]

The slow opening of the market for financial services within the EU was partly due to the fear and danger of double regulation (i.e. different in home and host country). Further on, it was also due to the limited progress in the closely related area of the freedom of capital flows. Indeed, the Founding Treaties[2] themselves see them as connected, now in article 58(2) of the TFEU, however it is to be noted that the freedoms of capital flows was a rather slow process. By 1988, this freedom had been achieved in only three European countries, i.e. Germany, Netherlands and the UK, and this was done outside the EU framework; for, in relation to these countries this freedom of capital flows applied to any and to all countries worldwide. In fact, only the fundamental 1988 Directive freeing capital movements in the EU by the middle of 1990, did make the freeing of the regulation of financial services, a true and viable option which was possible to be achievable through the acceptance of home-country regulation of activities throughout the EU under some minimum harmonized standards, although it was still subjected to general and numerous exceptions, which were able to reactivate the host country rule in the event especially that this would be made in view of protecting smaller depositors and investors. However, the exceptions were increasingly limited by later Directives and case law.[3]

[1] For a selective literature review on the history of the evolution of the financial services sector, see representative bibliography as follows: Dalhuisen (2013), Welch and Parker (2014), Andoura and Timmerman (2008), De Grauwe and Gros (2009), Lannoo (2008), Backer (2008), Avgouleas (2009), Avgouleas (2012), Rix (2014), Alford (2006), p. 389; Chatzimanoli (2008), European Commission (2015) European Commission Green Paper on retail financial services, COM (2015) 630 final; European Commission (2016), Commission Delegated Regulation of 30 June 2016 supplementing Regulation (EU) No 1286/2014 of the European Parliament and of the Council on key information documents for packaged retail and insurance based investment products (PRIIPs) by laying down regulatory technical standards with regard to the presentation, content, review and revision of key information documents and the conditions for fulfilling the requirement to provide such documents (C(2016)3999 final); Lord Turner (2009), pp. 100–102; www.fsa.gov.uk/pubs/other/turner_review.pdf; Moloney (2013), pp. 955–965; Papaconstantinou (2016)p. 367; Snowdon/Lovegrove, MiFID Review, C.O.B. 2012, 94(Mar), 1–27, 20.

[2] Treaty establishing the European Coal and Steel Community (1951); Treaty establishing the European Atomic Energy Committee (1957); Treaty establishing the European Economic Community (1957); Treaty on European Union (1992); OJ C 191 29.7.1992.

[3] Dalhuisen (2013), p. 659.

1.1 Brief Citation of the Main Legislation

Given the analytical elaboration of the legislation in Chapter 1, we only provide a brief citation of the main legislative instruments. The First Life Insurance Directive 1979/267[4] was codified by Directive 2002/83[5] and then repealed by Directive 2009/138[6] (Solvency II). Directive 2004/39 on markets in financial instruments ("MiFID") was followed by Directive 2014/65 ("MiFID II"). The provision in the Insurance Mediation Directive (IMD) 1.5. as amended by MiFID II, was in a way a middle route solution and channel of amendment and in that sense has amended Directive 2002/92 on Insurance Mediation ("IMD") which was the first Directive to impose specific obligations for the insurer and the distributor of investment products. The IMD was replaced by Directive 2016/97 on Insurance Distribution ("IDD"), and further exemplified the rules on the sale of investment products contained in MiFID II and in Regulation 1286/2014 on packaged retail and insurance-based investment products ("PRIIPs Regulation").

The first example of a home state licensing system for financial services arose as early as 1985 with the first 'UCITS Directive'[7] which provided a passport for certain types of securities collective investment schemes, that could be marketed to the public in any member state, once they had been authorized by their home state. The UCITS Directive is also notable in that it introduced the division of responsibilities between the home State, responsible for licensing and prudential supervision of the UCITS and the host state, responsible for regulation of marketing of the product and other conduct of business rules. This was a distinction which was to be endorsed also in other Directives—such as MiFID—however, the precise dividing lines are unclear in practice and continue to generate controversy and debate between financial institutions and member states. The UCITS Directive as amended by two later Directives in 2001,[8] is unique as it serves the role of having been the only example of product regulation found in EU financial services law. As such, it has proved difficult to reconcile and develop in line with mainstream EU financial services regulation which focuses on regulation of the product or service provider.[9] However, its role and importance should not be undervalued. From a historical legal perspective, it is worth noting that the UCITS allowed for the products to be marketed EU wide. This concerned the operation of open-ended funds EU wide and proved of much greater importance as it introduced for the first time the notion of a European

[4] First Council Directive 1979/267 1979 on the coordination of laws, regulations and administrative provisions relating to the taking up and pursuit of the business of direct life assurance Official Journal L 063, 13/03/1979 P. 0001-0018.

[5] Directive 2002/83 on life insurance, OJ L 345, 19.12.2002, pp. 1–51.

[6] Directive 2009/138 (Solvency II), OJ L 335, 17.12.2009.

[7] Directive 85/611/EC on undertakings for collective investment in transferable securities [1987] OJ 1975/10.

[8] Directive 2001/107/EC on management companies and simplified prospectuses [2002]OJ L41/20, Directive 2001/108/EC on Investments of UCITS [2002]OJ L41/35.

[9] Welch and Parker (2014), pp. 115–119.

passport for financial services. A further 1993 proposal[10] sought to include money market funds and funds investing in units of other UCITS and allowed a UCITS to freely choose depositories in other member states if properly supervised in that state. It also proposed to allow the use of standard derivatives to better manage risk. UCITS is hence historically fundamental for firstly introducing the recognition of home regulation, subject to only a limited number of host regulator powers. This, in effect, became the model for all financial services in the EU. Hence, the aim of UCITS was to allow the marketing of collective investment schemes of open-ended type, or unit trusts, in all member states under certain minimum standards, regarding structure, activity or disclosure requirements.[11]

A further amending directive, known as UCITS IV, was adopted in July 2009, which, alongside with four Level 2 implementing measures, provided for a management company passport, with the management company being subject to prudential and conduct of business rules and resembling those rules contained in MiFID. UCITS IV also established a procedure for national and cross-border mergers of UCITS and introduced master-feeder structures to permit asset-pooling. The simplified prospectus was replaced by a key information document ('KID') setting out the required information in plain language and in investor-friendly terms. New notification procedures were introduced, allowing marketing of the fund in other member states immediately following notification by the home state regulator of the fund to the host state competent authority, whilst it also provided for measures to improve supervisory cooperation.

A further revision of UCITS was proposed by the Commission in July 2012[12] as one of three elements of its consumer policy response to the financial crisis with amendments aiming to clarify the duties and obligations of UCITS depositaries, to establish rules on the remuneration of UCITS managers and in addition to provide for a common approach by member states to sanctions for breach of UCITS requirements.

The PRIIPs is the result of the proposal of 2012 on PRIIPs[13] which encapsulated an effort to standardize the disclosure requirements across a range of retail investment products, including investments packaged as insurance policies. The proposal introduced the concept of KID. The PRIIPs KID is based on the UCITS KID and the product provider is responsible for producing the document. The task may be delegated, however the provider continues to retain the responsibility.[14] Further on, the KID features are analyzed.

---

[10] COM (93) 37 final [1993] OJ C59.

[11] Dalhuisen (2013), pp. 669–671. Can you also make reference to other authors who described the evolution of the regulation on financial services in the EU? There are dozens of works. Otherwise, it seems that you have just summarized what he wrote in his book.

[12] COM (2012)350.

[13] COM (2012)350.

[14] Welch and Parker (2014), pp. 115–119.

1.2 The European Passport Process

The liberalization of capital flows and payments of the 1988 EU Directive proved of major importance as it made the further liberalization of the financial services sector in the EU possible and it also accelerated the pace of this process occurring. The key element, for achieving this, was regulatory competition under a system of mutual recognition of home country standards of authorization capital and supervision for cross border activities EU wide, which resulted in the establishment of the European passport for financial service providers who were incorporated in the EU, and which were also subject to proper authorization and supervision in their home state. This approach was foreshadowed in the 1985 UCITS Directive and was firstly formulated as a more general policy in the June 1985 White Paper on the Completion of the Internal Market.[15] It happened in partial reliance in the case *Casis de Dijon*[16] on the basic idea of the principle of free movement of goods. Through the June 1985 White Paper on the Completion of the Internal Market,[17] this basic approach of mutual recognition of home-country rule was extended, by analogy, also to services. For the sector of the financial services also, the mutual recognition of home country regulation remained subject to the notion of general good, still being able to provide an exception to the home country rule in exceptional cases. The main consequence of this approach was regulatory competition between various home-country rules operating side by side, depending on the origin of the service provider involved. For the insurance business, such a liberalization process was depicted in the Third Generation or Liberalization Directives which incorporated the idea of mutual recognition of the home-country rule, subject to some harmonized rules for the authorization and supervision requirements. In effect, the Third Generation or Liberalization Directives reduced the impact general good in support of the host-country rule by making the notion subject to more specific rules. Notwithstanding the above efforts, the notion was not eliminated and, as per the case law evolution, proved capable to lead to some more fragmentation of regulation and supervision along national host country lines, which was mainly done to protect consumers and small investors in their territory, but at the same time was managed to be pushed back in the MiFID.[18] In its 2005 White Paper[19] the European Commission reviewed the progress and restated its objectives. It mentioned consolidation, better regulation, supervisory convergence, competition and global contribution. More open consultation and impact assessments were promised with a shift to a more risk- and principle-driven approach leading to simplification with only minimum legislative

---

[15] COM (85), 310 Final.

[16] Case 120/78 *Rewe-Zentral AG vs. Bundesmonopolverwaltung für Branntwein*, ECR 1979 p. 00649, http://eur-lex.europa.eu/smartapi/cgi/sga_doc?smartapi!celexplus!prod!CELEXnumdoc&lg=en&numdoc=61978J0120.

[17] COM (85), 310 Final.

[18] Dalhuisen (2013), pp. 669–674.

[19] White Paper on Financial Services Policy (2005–2010) COM (2005).

intervention. The idea was to make regulation market-, cost- and effect driven rather than seek mere intervention. The idea of harmonization of rules, at all levels and in all areas, was no longer the objective; rather, it served as a recognition of the fact that it was neither the regulation *per se*, nor its fine-tuning but ultimately only the market forces which could create the single market.[20]

2 The Route to Changes in the Financial Sector

The route to changes in EU legislation in financial services, and more specifically in insurance investment, envisages four levels of implementation. In Level 1 (framework level), primary Community legislation is envisaged based on framework principles. In Level 2 (implementation level), the Commission adopts Community legislation concerning the technical details of the framework principles. In this Level, technical advice could also be given by the Committee of European Securities Regulators (CESR) and the Committee of European Banking Supervisors (CEBS) which were also formed pursuant to the Lamfalussy proposals and represent the regulators of the Member States. The danger of both committees is that they may retain a purely domestic perspective. In Level 3, the implementation or transposition process in Member States is considered, in which connection the Committee of European Securities Regulators (CESR) and the Committee of European Banking Supervisors (CEBS) play a role in obtaining consistency and may issue guidelines or common, non-binding, standards. In Level 4, the Commission resumes its normal responsibility for enforcing EU legislation (under Art 17(1) TEU and Art 258 TFEU) and for compliance by Member States, where necessary, initiating compliance action before the European Court of Justice. At both Levels 2 and 3, three other standing committees function: one for commercial banking, one for investment business including UCITS, and one for insurance including pensions. A fourth committee operates at Level 2 for financial conglomerates. EcoFin set up a Financial Services Committee of its own (FSC). The whole set-up was reviewed in 2004. The Prospectus Directive 2003/71/EC[21] and the Market Abuse Directive 2014/57/EU[22] were among the first ones to emerge under the new regime, and are now consistent with and complementary to the Transparency Directive[23] and the revision of the ISD into MiFID. In its 2005 White Paper[24] the European Commission reviewed the progress and promised more open consultation and impact assessments with a view to better regulation, even at the costs of full harmonization.[25]

---

[20] Dalhuisen (2013), pp. 678–683.

[21] OJ L 345, 31.12.2003.

[22] OJ L 173, 12.6.2014, pp. 179–189.

[23] 2013/50/EU OJ L 294, 6.11.2013, pp. 13–27.

[24] White Paper on Financial Services Policy (2005–2010) COM (2005).

[25] Dalhuisen (2013), pp. 678–683.

The UCITS Directive of 1985 was updated in by two Directives of January 2002,[26] which broadened the types of assets in which UCITS can invest, regulated management companies, and allowed simplified prospectuses. These Directives had to be implemented by February 2004 and were consolidated in 2009 in UCITS IV.[27] Updates were proposed as of 2010 leading to UCITS V. It should be appreciated that UCITS only covers the cross-border activity in certain open-ended funds within the EU. It presupposes home-country approval and authorization, on the prerequisite basis of which a certificate is then issued. For general supervision of fund management, MiFID applies, although not to collective investment undertakings proper. The Directive on Alternative Investment Fund Managers (2011/61/EU)[28] deals with funds not under UCITS. As in so much financial regulation in Europe, the proposals were much inspired by suspicion of financial activities more generally, particularly in France and Germany, heightened after the 2008 banking crisis, but they met with a great deal of criticism from the beginning, it being clear that fund-management activities had not been at the heart of the crisis. Again, the danger simply is that these activities would leave the EU altogether,[29] and it remains to be seen, what will the situation be, post the shockwaves of BRexit and its effect on the financial markets.

However, it could be said to sum up that in the EU committee structure of financial supervisors, pursuant to the 1998 Action Plan following proposals in the Lamfalussy Report of 2000, a European Securities Committee (ESC) was formed, representing Member States (often at Ministry of Finance level) with powers to implement EU Level 1 framework legislation in the financial area, complemented by CEBS in London and CESR in Paris. As stated above, in the implementation or Level 3 stage in these Member States, the CEBS and CESR played a role in obtaining consistency and could issue guidelines or non-binding standards. At both Levels 2 and 3, there were three other standing committees: one for commercial banking, one for investment business including UCITS, and one for insurance, including pensions. A fourth committee operated at Level 2 for financial conglomerates. EcoFin set up its own FSC.

The whole set-up was reviewed in 2004 and then again in 2011. This Committee structure is now also referred to as the European System of Financial Supervisors (ESFS). Within it, the ESC remained in place but the CEBS was replaced by the European Banking Committee (EBC) in London and the CESR by the European Securities and Markets Committee (ESMA) in Paris. They were more independent from local regulators and meant to play a greater supervisory role at the EU level in the implementation of new directives and regulations, although they were still short of becoming EU regulatory bodies themselves, financial regulation remaining a Member State affair. Under Article 18 of the ESMA Regulation, the Council might

---

[26] EU Directives 200I/107/EC and 2001/108/EC, both of 21 January 2002, of the European Parliament and of the Council [2002] OJ L41/20 and 41/35.

[27] EU Directive 2009/65/EC of the European Parliament and of the Council 12009] OJ L302/32.

[28] OJ L 174, 1.7.2011, pp. 1–73.

[29] Dalhuisen (2013), pp. 685–704.

declare an emergency, however, empowering ESMA to demand action from national authorities or impose directly adequate measures in respect of market participants. For life insurance and occupational pensions, there is the European Insurance and Occupational Pensions Authority (EIOPA) in Frankfurt, replacing the earlier Committee of European Insurance and Occupational Pension Supervisors. At the initiative of the European Parliament, this framework is supplemented by the European Systemic Risk Board (ESRB), which operates under the ECB.[30] It monitors the risk build-up in the EU financial system in its entirety and may issue recommendations, especially whenever it detects risk concentrations and bubbles. The new set-up was the result of much political debate and wrangling and was a compromise. The new authorities have been given power to settle disputes among national supervisors if they cannot agree on cross-border issues, especially relevant in the resolution of banking collapses cross-border. They might also issue temporary bans on risky financial products and trading and might also set up uniform technical standards.[31]

2.1 The New European System of Financial Supervision

The three European Supervisory Authorities (ESAs), the European Banking Authority (EBA), the European Insurance and Occupational Pensions Authority (EIOPA) and the European Securities and Markets Authority (ESMA) form—in conjunction with the national supervisory authorities (National Competent Authorities, NCAs) and the European Systemic Risk Board (ESRB)—the new financial supervisory architecture in Europe: the European System of Financial Supervision (ESFS). The ESFS was developed based on recommendations of the High Level Group on Financial Supervision chaired by Jacques de Larosière to address previous shortcomings in the practice of financial supervision and to enhance cooperation and coordination between NCAs in Member States. The ESFS came into effect on 1 January 2011.[32]

From its onset in 2007, the global financial crisis revealed both gaps in the legislation which governs the financial system and shortcomings in the practice of financial supervision. In the European Union (EU), the crisis additionally highlighted deficiencies in the structures for cross-border crisis resolution; it shed light on the inconsistent application of the EU's legal framework for financial services and it tested supervisory cooperation and coordination between Member States, in some

[30] For the first 5 years, subsequently to be reviewed.

[31] Dalhuisen (2013), pp. 724–728.

[32] European Parliament, DG for Internal Policies: Review of the New European System of Financial Supervision (ESFS) Part 1: The work of the European Supervisory Authorities (EBA, EIOPA AND ESMA)—The ESFS's Micro Prudential Pillar, http://www.europarl.europa.eu/RegData/etudes/etudes/join/2013/507446/IPOL-ECON_ET(2013)507446_EN.pdf.

cases affecting the trust between national supervisors.[33] In order to address these issues and to achieve a more effective system of supervision, a new architecture for European financial supervision was developed based on the recommendations of the 2009 de Larosière Report.[34] This new arrangement, the European System of Financial Supervision (ESFS), was adopted in the form of regulations agreed by the European Parliament and the Council in late 2010[35] establishing, the European Systemic Risk Board (ESRB) responsible for the macro-prudential oversight of the financial system, focusing on systemic risk, three European Supervisory Authorities (ESAs) responsible for micro-prudential supervision of financial markets and activities: (a) the European Banking Authority (EBA), (b) the European Insurance and Occupational Pensions Authority (EIOPA), (c) the European Securities and Market Authority (ESMA), the Joint Committee to foster coordination amongst the three Authorities and with participation of national competent authorities (NCAs) in the three financial sectors.[36] The predecessors of the ESAs were Level 3 committees, i.e. CEBS, CEIOPS and CESR. The Level 3 Committees were based on comitology[37] and since the Lisbon Treaty entered into force, the legal basis for the new 'ex-comitology' framework has been Article 290 TFEU for delegated acts and Article 291(2) TFEU for implementing acts. The promotion from comitology committees to EU agencies was accelerated by the financial crisis and prepared by the de Larosière Report. The ESAs were established as decentralised agencies, i.e. independent legal entities under European public law, distinct from the EU institutions.[38] The ESAs assumed all tasks of the previous committees on 1 January 2011 supplemented by the additional new tasks set out in the ESA Regulations. The objective of the ESAs according to the Article 1(5) EBA and ESMA Regulations (Article 1(6) EIOPA Regulation) is to protect the public interest by contributing to the short, medium and long-term stability and effectiveness of the financial system,

[33] European Parliament, DG for Internal Policies: Review of the New European System of Financial Supervision (ESFS) Part 1: The work of the European Supervisory Authorities (EBA, EIOPA AND ESMA)—The ESFS's Micro Prudential Pillar, http://www.europarl.europa.eu/RegData/etudes/etudes/join/2013/507446/IPOL-ECON_ET(2013)507446_EN.pdf.

[34] The High-Level Group on Financial Supervision in the EU (chaired by J. de Larosière), Report, 25.2.2009; see Lannoo, K., The road ahead after de Larosière, CEPS Policy Brief No. 195, August 7, 2009.

[35] EBA Regulation (EU) No 1093/2010; EIOPA Regulation (EU) 1094/2010; ESMA Regulation (EU) 1095/2010, together referred to as the 'ESA Regulations', as well as ESRB Regulation (EU) 1092/2010 and Specific ECB Tasks Regulation Council Regulation (EU) 1096/2010.

[36] European Parliament, DG for Internal Policies: Review of the New European System of Financial Supervision (ESFS) Part 1: The work of the European Supervisory Authorities (EBA, EIOPA AND ESMA)—The ESFS's Micro Prudential Pillar, http://www.europarl.europa.eu/RegData/etudes/etudes/join/2013/507446/IPOL-ECON_ET(2013)507446_EN.pdf.

[37] For more information on comitology and comitology committees see http://europa.eu/legislation_summaries/glossary/comitology_en.htm.

[38] European Parliament, DG for Internal Policies: Review of the New European System of Financial Supervision (ESFS) Part 1: The work of the European Supervisory Authorities (EBA, EIOPA AND ESMA)—The ESFS's Micro Prudential Pillar, http://www.europarl.europa.eu/RegData/etudes/etudes/join/2013/507446/IPOL-ECON_ET(2013)507446_EN.pdf.

for the EU economy, its citizens and businesses.[39,40] The ESAs' establishment has occurred during a period of rapid and far-reaching change to legislative acts and regulatory standards for the financial sector in the EU and internationally. The ESAs were granted a range of powers to ensure supervisory consistency, avoid supervisory arbitrage and create a level playing field, but the intensity of use has varied markedly, with some powers not used at all. This has been a result of prioritising work on the Single Rulebook and the existence of legal obstacles for using certain powers. The development of the 'Single Rulebook', i.e. a harmonised set of rules based on first level directives and regulations supplemented by second level implementing and delegated acts has dominated the ESAs' workload, and consequently their regulatory role has been to the fore at the expense of other responsibilities.[41] At EU level it was felt that the ESAs have not used their supervisory consistency powers to the extent anticipated by stakeholders.

Unlike the ESMA and the EBA, the EIOPA inherited responsibility for two sectors, insurance and occupational pension funds, where national markets, products and legislation vary markedly from one Member State to another. The delay in the application of Solvency II, meant that any assessment of the EIOPA's performance could only have been preliminary.[42] The EIOPA had an important role to develop a common supervisory culture of EU insurance and occupational pensions markets which was timewise hindered by the delay in the implementation of the Solvency II and in effect that has meant that there has been inhibited convergence in the supervisory culture. The ESMA was born during the financial crisis and post-crisis environment characterised by a highly volatile market. This created a strong political will to restore confidence in the financial markets.

The ESMA is the only ESA entrusted with direct supervisory responsibilities. These powers cover entities or activities not regulated prior to the crisis and therefore these were not regulated by NCAs. For the other legislative initiatives already covering regulated financial activities, the focus of any new competence given to ESMA has been on developing the Single Rulebook, with some expansion of its

[39] European Parliament, DG for Internal Policies: Review of the New European System of Financial Supervision (ESFS) Part 1: The work of the European Supervisory Authorities (EBA, EIOPA AND ESMA)—The ESFS's Micro Prudential Pillar, http://www.europarl.europa.eu/RegData/etudes/etudes/join/2013/507446/IPOL-ECON_ET(2013)507446_EN.pdf.

[40] European Parliament, DG for Internal Policies: Review of the New European System of Financial Supervision (ESFS) Part 1: The work of the European Supervisory Authorities (EBA, EIOPA AND ESMA)—The ESFS's Micro Prudential Pillar, http://www.europarl.europa.eu/RegData/etudes/etudes/join/2013/507446/IPOL-ECON_ET(2013)507446_EN.pdf.

[41] European Parliament, DG for Internal Policies: Review of the New European System of Financial Supervision (ESFS) Part 1: The work of the European Supervisory Authorities (EBA, EIOPA AND ESMA)—The ESFS's Micro Prudential Pillar, http://www.europarl.europa.eu/RegData/etudes/etudes/join/2013/507446/IPOL-ECON_ET(2013)507446_EN.pdf.

[42] European Parliament, DG for Internal Policies: Review of the New European System of Financial Supervision (ESFS) Part 1: The work of the European Supervisory Authorities (EBA, EIOPA AND ESMA)—The ESFS's Micro Prudential Pillar, http://www.europarl.europa.eu/RegData/etudes/etudes/join/2013/507446/IPOL-ECON_ET(2013)507446_EN.pdf.

supervisory role but most often limited to the coordination of direct supervision by NCAs.[43]

2.2 *The Development of the EU Supervisory Structure*

Financial law as we know it today mirrors the traditional structure of the financial industry. It has thus been divided into banking, insurance and securities law in most legal systems, be they international, European or national.[44] Due to the blurring in practice of the above distinctions between the traditional sectors, the diverging regulatory and supervisory treatment of these sectors has been increasingly at odds with the economic reality. Therefore, several countries decided, in a first phase, to adapt their financial supervision structure. After several Member States started experimenting with a more cross-sectoral approach to parts of financial legislation, the European legislature also implemented cross-sectoral initiatives at EU level.

Insurance law crystallized quite separately from the other two sectors of financial law and came to develop into a set of rules distinct from general contract law. The first generation of European insurance law directives however made national legislatures introduce a generalized prudential and supervisory regime for the insurance sector. Later still, aspects of insurance intermediation were harmonized at the EU level.[45]

The 2014 introduction of a Banking Union brought a sea change to this long-standing characteristic of European financial supervision via the introduction of a supervisory system known as the "Single Supervisory Mechanism" (SSM). However, the Commission had, as early as 1999, already stressed the need for a "holistic", cross-sectoral approach to financial legislation in the EU. Yet, it was only in 2007 that the Council invited the Commission to review the consistency of EU legislation regarding the different types of retail investment products (such as unit-linked life insurance, investment funds, certain structured notes and certificates), to ensure a coherent approach to investor protection, to avoid any miss-selling possibilities and to stop the vulnerability and regulatory arbitrage in which the retail market for investment products had since years been succumbed to. Capitalizing on the impetus for improved retail investor protection in the wake of the crisis, the Commission decided that it would take steps to "bring the European legislative framework for mandatory disclosures and sales practices for PRIIPs into line with market reality".

---

[43] European Parliament, DG for Internal Policies: Review of the New European System of Financial Supervision (ESFS) Part 1: The work of the European Supervisory Authorities (EBA, EIOPA AND ESMA)—The ESFS's Micro Prudential Pillar, http://www.europarl.europa.eu/RegData/etudes/etudes/join/2013/507446/IPOL-ECON_ET(2013)507446_EN.pdf.

[44] Colaert (2015), pp. 1579–1584.

[45] As part of the European System of Financial Supervision, three European Supervisory Authorities (ESAs) have been established, i.e. the EBA, EIOPA and ESMA; Colaert (2015), pp. 1579–1599.

The initiative to regulate PRIIPs intended to tackle the divergence in financial regulation in relation to highly similar, but legally distinct, investment products available to retail investors. However, the more horizontal EU approach to financial regulation has not been achieved by means of a single legislative document as one might have expected. Next to a "horizontal" PRIIPs Regulation with respect to product information, an attempt to level the playing field with respect to sales rules was made in two pre-existing sector-specific EU directives, i.e. the MiFID and the IMD.[46]

2.3 *PRIIPs: Evolution and Role*

The PRIIPs Regulation represents an innovative approach within the scope of the regulation of EU financial services, and applies cross-filed, for it covers multiple common featured products which may have different forms or routes but all have been created so as to provide investment opportunities to retail investors.[47] The aim of the PRIIPs Regulation is to encourage efficient EU markets by helping investors to better understand and compare the key features, risk, rewards and costs of different PRIIPs, through access to a short and consumer-friendly Key Information Document (KID).[48]

The PRIIPs Regulation applies to persons who manufacture PRIIPs, or advise on or sell PRIIPs. Hence, a PRIIP manufacturer (or any other person who changes an existing PRIIP, such as a distributor) is required to prepare a KID for each PRIIP that they produce and to publish each KID on their website. A person who advises a retail investor on a PRIIP or sells a PRIIP to a retail investor must provide the retail investor with a KID in good time before any transaction is concluded. In addition to advisers, this will impact intermediaries such as distributors. Where the retail investor initiates the transaction by means of distance communications, the KID may be provided after the conclusion of the transaction so long as it is not possible to provide the KID in advance and the retail investor consents. The retail investor must be told that it is not possible to provide the KID in advance, and that they can delay the transaction, to receive and read the KID before concluding the transaction.[49]

The KID includes all the information relevant for the investment decision of the individual retail investor in a concise way. The KID is an addition to the existing retail investor information obligations. The products covered by the new regulation include investment funds, structured products and structured deposits (packaged retail investment products), as well as life insurances with investment elements

[46] Colaert (2015), pp. 1579–1599.

[47] Recital (6) of the PRIIPs Regulation.

[48] FCA, PRIIPs disclosure: Key Information Documents, 12/5/2017, https://www.fca.org.uk/firms/priips-disclosure-key-information-documents.

[49] FCA, PRIIPs disclosure: Key Information Documents, 12/5/2017, https://www.fca.org.uk/firms/priips-disclosure-key-information-documents.

(insurance-based investment products), such as life insurances based on funds or index-linked life insurances. Taken together, these categories are referred to as PRIIPs, which the regulation is named after. However, certain types of life insurance, such as life insurance products where the benefits are only payable upon death or incapacity for work, are not within the scope of the regulation. This is also applicable for other insurance products, such as life insurances for which the redemption value is not exposed to market fluctuations.

The regulator aims to establish a "level playing field" between providers of financial products and insurance products respectively, with regards to retail investor information standards. Generally, the KID must be provided to the investor before the PRIIP is purchased, or, before the investor has undertaken any obligation. An exception applies only when the investor initiates the transaction, concludes the transaction using a mean of long distance communication, the provision of a KID is not possible. In such a case, the investor has to be informed that the provision of a KID is not possible and that he has the option to delay the transaction in order to receive the KID before concluding the transaction and that the investor actively consents receiving the KID after the transaction. The harmonizing aim of the Regulation is apparent from the power granted to EIOPA to temporarily intervene in the promotion or sale of insurance-based investment products in the EU. This is consistent with the powers granted to other ESAs under MiFID II in respect of specific non-insurance investments.[50]

2.4 A Cross-Sectoral Product Disclosures

The PRIIP Regulation reach only partially a consistent regulatory approach towards the distribution by firms to consumers of investment products which satisfy similar investor needs and raise comparable investor protection challenges.[51] The divergence existing in the regulatory regime in the EU in relation to PRIIPs at sector level, meant that the legal requirements had been different depending on the method of distribution and the legal form of the product. There are concern that retail investors are not afforded equal protection across the sectors and furthermore that there was lack of a consistent approach to providing retail investors with key information on final costs, product risks and rewards Hence, the Commission proposed a two-pronged European-level approach with rules on the form and content of key investor disclosures and associated marketing materials on the one hand and rules on sales which would include the management and disclosure of conflicts of interest, on the other hand[52] and published proposals on the regulation of PRIIPs to close gaps and inconsistencies in current rules across Europe, by introducing a horizontal approach

[50] Pinsent Masons, "Are the KIDs alright?", 2016 https://www.pinsentmasons.com/en/media/legal-updates/are-the-kids-alright/.

[51] Snowdon-Lovegrove, MiFID Review, C.O.B. 2012, 94(Mar), 1–27, 20.

[52] Moloney (2013), pp. 955–965.

to the regulation of mandatory pre-contractual product disclosures and sales practices for PRIIPs.

Previously, pre-contractual product disclosures were regulated—pursuant to different European Directives, including the Prospectus Directive (PD), the Undertakings for Collective Investment in Transferable Securities (UCITS) Directive, the Solvency II Directive, the Insurance Mediation Directive (IMD) and the Markets in Financial Instruments Directive (MiFID). The PRIPs disclosure regime would adopt the same principles as the UCITS Directive's Key Investor Information Document (KIID) with an aim to assist retail investors' decision making, by providing them with key, information in a streamlined form on a timely basis.

In essence, KIIDs as uniform disclosure documents are providing standardised information about PRIIPs in a way that is designed to give retail investors sufficiently clear, comparable information on the range of products available. Regulation (EU) No 1286/2014 (PRIIPs Regulation)[53] required manufacturers of PRIIPs to draw KIDs for these products before they are made available to retail investors, and those selling or advising on these products to provide the KIDs to retail investors in good time before they buy those products.

The PRIIPs Regulation empowers the European Banking Authority established by Regulation (EU) No 1093/2010, the European Insurance and Occupational Pensions Authority established by Regulation (EU) No 1094/2010 and the European Securities and Markets Authority established by Regulation (EU) No 1095/2010 to jointly develop regulatory technical standards (RTS) specifying the elements of the KID, namely the presentation and the content of the KID, including methodologies for the calculation and presentation of risks, rewards and costs within the document (Article 8(5) of the PRIIPs Regulation). Article 10(2) of the PRIIPs Regulation also empowers the European Supervisory Authorities (ESAs) to develop RTS on the review, revision and publication of the KID and Article 13(5) on the conditions for fulfilling the requirement to provide the KID in good time to the retail investor. On 6 April 2016, the ESAs jointly submitted the draft RTS to the Commission. On 30 June 2016, the Commission adopted a Delegated Regulation supplementing the PRIIPs Regulation (Delegated Regulation)[54] which specifies the presentation and the content of the KID and its standardised format, the methodology underpinning the presentation of risk and reward and the calculation of costs, the conditions and the minimum frequency for reviewing the information contained in the KID and the conditions for fulfilling the requirement to provide the KID to retail investors. On

[53] Regulation (EU) No 1286/2014 of the European Parliament and of the Council of 26 November 2014 on key information documents for packaged retail and insurance-based investment products (PRIIPs) (OJ L 352, 9.12.2014, p. 1).

[54] Commission Delegated Regulation of 30 June 2016 supplementing Regulation (EU) No 1286/2014 of the European Parliament and of the Council on key information documents for packaged retail and insurance-based investment products (PRIIPs) by laying down regulatory technical standards with regard to the presentation, content, review and revision of key information documents and the conditions for fulfilling the requirement to provide such documents (C(2016)3999) http://ec.europa.eu/finance/docs/level-2-measures/priips-delegated-regulation-2017-1473_en.pdf.

14 September 2016, the European Parliament objected to the Delegated Regulation.[55] To address the concerns expressed by the European Parliament, the Commission, in a letter of 10 November 2016, proposed to the ESAs amendments to the Delegated Regulation, as regards multi-option PRIIPs, performance scenarios, comprehension alert and presentation of administrative costs in relation to biometric components of insurance-based investment products. Under the sixth subparagraph of Article 10(1) of Regulation (EU) No 1093/2010, of Regulation (EU) No 1094/2010 and of Regulation (EU) No 1095/2010, the ESAs may amend the draft RTS within six weeks, following the Commission's proposed amendments and resubmit the amendments in a formal Opinion to the Commission. On the expiry of that period, the ESAs did not adopt the final Opinion. Consequently, under the seventh subparagraph of Article 10(1) of Regulation (EU) No 1093/2010, of Regulation (EU) No 1094/2010 and of Regulation (EU) No 1095/2010, the Commission may adopt RTS with the amendments it considers relevant. The Commission's amendments to the Delegated Regulation concern multi-option PRIIPs, performance scenarios, comprehension alert and presentation of administrative costs in relation to biometric components of insurance-based investment products. In April 2016, the ESAs submitted draft RTS to the Commission, combining RTS developed under Articles 8(5), 10(2) and 13(5) of the PRIIPs Regulation. The Commission endorsed the bundling given the interconnectedness of the three RTS in an effort to ensure that the requirements introduced by them are fully consistent. A single legal act also ensures that stakeholders would be able to locate easier PRIIPs provisions.

3 IDD and the Client Protection

The IDD plays a significant role in the promotion of consumer protection within the distribution of insurance products across the EU, especially if considered that MiFID II does not cover the distribution of insurance-based products. In particular, the IDD ensures greater transparency of insurance distributors in relation to the price and costs of their products but also provides higher standards concerning product information and conduct of business (COB) rules. In performing this function, the IDD provides many rules following the similar MiFID II rules. However, many differences (e.g. those concerning the regulation of inducements) exist and pose a risk for segmentation and regulatory arbitrage.[56] Moreover, while MiFID II aspires to a maximum harmonisation, the IDD expressly aims at a minimum harmonisation, which means that any Member States can impose stricter rules to

[55] Position of the European Parliament of 1 December 2016 and Decision of the Council of 8 December 2016; http://ec.europa.eu/finance/docs/level-2-measures/priips-delegated-regulation-2017-1473_en.pdf.

[56] Colaert (2017), pp. 229–244; and Kern, A. (2018), Marketing, Sale and Distribution. Mis-selling of Financial Product. A study requested by the ECON Committee, 31.

protect customers.[57] The Insurance Distribution Directive (EU) 2016/97 have been supplemented by two delegated regulations—based on the European Insurance and Occupational Pensions Authority (EIOPA) Technical Advice to the Commission[58]—concerning product oversight and governance requirements for insurance undertakings and insurance distributors, information requirements and conduct of business rules.[59]

Insurance-based investment products are defined as those products "which offer(s) a maturity or surrender value and where that maturity or surrender value is wholly or partially exposed, directly or indirectly, to market fluctuations".[60] They do not include: (a) non-life insurance products, (b) life insurance contracts where the benefits under the contract are payable only on death or in respect of incapacity due to injury, sickness or disability, (c) pension products which are recognized as having the primary purpose of providing the investor with an income in retirement, and which entitle the investor to specific benefits, (d) officially recognized occupational pension schemes, and (e) individual pension products for which a financial contribution from the employer is required by national law and where the employer or the employee has no choice as to the pension product or provider.[61]

The IDD aims explicitly to harmonise national provisions concerning insurance[62] And reinsurance[63] distribution across the Union,[64] and targets not only—as in the past—insurance brokers or intermediaries, but several types of persons or institutions which distribute insurance-based investment products ('IBIPs') to third parties, such as agents, 'bancassurance' operators, insurance undertakings, travel agents and car rental companies.[65] However, customers—regardless of the distribution

---

[57] Recital 3 of the IDD.

[58] EIOPA 17/048, Technical Advice on Insurance Distribution Directive (1 February 2017).

[59] Respectively, Commission Delegated Regulation (EU) 2017/2359 of 21 September 2017 supplementing Directive (EU) 2016/97 of the European Parliament and of the Council with regard to information requirements and conduct of business rules applicable to the distribution of insurance-based investment products; and Commission Delegated Regulation (EU) 2017/2358 of 21 September 2017 supplementing Directive (EU) 2016/97 of the European Parliament and of the Council with regard to product oversight and governance requirements for insurance undertakings and insurance distributors.

[60] Art 1(17) IDD.

[61] Id.

[62] 'Insurance distribution' is defined as the "activities of advising on, proposing, or carrying out other work preparatory to the conclusion of contracts of insurance, of concluding such contracts, or of assisting in the administration and performance of such contracts". See Article 1(1) IDD.

[63] 'Reinsurance distribution' is defined as the activities of advising on, proposing, or carrying out other work preparatory to the conclusion of contracts of reinsurance, of concluding such contracts, or of assisting in the administration and performance of such contracts, in particular in the event of a claim, including when carried out by a reinsurance undertaking without the intervention of a reinsurance intermediary. See Article 1(2) IDD.

[64] Recital 2 IDD.

[65] Recital 5 IDD. For a deeper analysis of the scope of the IDD, see also Maesschalck (2017), pp. 63–65.

channel—should benefit from the same level of protection and equal treatment.[66] In particular, in line with the MiFID II regime for financial instruments and structured deposits, within the IDD regime customer protection is ensured by specific provisions concerning the conduct of business rules and product governance requirements. In this regard, since the IDD empowers the Commission to adopt specific Delegated Acts concerning such requirements, on February 2016 the European Commission requested the European Insurance and Occupational Pensions Authority (EIOPA) for its technical advice for the development of IDD Delegated Acts. Two Commission Delegated Regulations were published in autumn 2017 and specifically targeted conduct on business rules and product and oversight governance.[67]

The IMD already provided conduct of business ['COB'] rules,[68] but these necessary provisions did not provide an adequate level of protection covering the full life-cycle of the distribution process and did not ensure an exhaustive disclosure of information to the client. Modelled after MiFID II, the IDD now requires insurance distributors to 'act honestly, fairly and professionally following the best interests of (their) clients'.[69] The IDD then provides specific requirements—recently further specified under corresponding Delegated Regulations (EU) 2017/2358 and (EU) 2017/2359—concerning the: (a) disclosure of information duties; (b) cross-selling practices; (c) conflict of interest; (d) inducements, and (e) assessment of suitability and appropriateness.

According to the IDD, all information addressed by the insurance distributor to customers or potential customers should be 'fair, clear and not misleading'.[70] Articles from 18 to 24, and 29 address the content, as well as the form and procedures that insurance distributors should perform in the disclosure of information to the client.

First of all, before the conclusion of an insurance contract the insurance intermediary and undertaking should disclose: (i) its identity and address and that it is an insurance intermediary/undertaking; (ii) whether it provides advice about the insurance products sold; (iii) the procedures enabling customers and other interested parties to register complaints about insurance intermediaries and the out-of-court complaint and redress procedures.[71] Moreover, the insurance intermediary should communicate the register in which it has been included and the means for verifying that it has been registered and whether it is representing the customer or is acting for and on behalf of the insurance undertaking.[72]

The insurance intermediary should also provide information concerning potential conflict of interests, such as whether it has a holding, direct or indirect,

---

[66] Recital 6 IDD.

[67] See Commission Delegated Regulations (EU) 2017/2358 and (EU) 2017/2359.

[68] Article 12–13 IMD.

[69] Article 17(1) IDD and Article 24(1) MiFID II.

[70] Article 17(2) IDD and Article 24(3) MiFID II.

[71] Article 18 IDD.

[72] Article 18 (a) IDD.

representing 10% or more of the voting rights or of the capital in a given insurance undertaking, or whether a given insurance undertaking or parent undertaking of a given insurance undertaking has a holding, direct or indirect, representing 10% or more of the voting rights or of the capital in the insurance intermediary.[73] Similarly, in relation to the contracts proposed or advised upon, it should inform whether: (i) it gives advice on the basis of a fair and personal analysis; (ii) it is under a contractual obligation to conduct insurance distribution business exclusively with one or more insurance undertakings; or (iii) it is not under a contractual obligation to conduct insurance distribution business exclusively with one or more insurance undertakings and does not give advice on the basis of a fair and personal analysis.[74] Information concerning all costs and related charges should be promptly disclosed to the clients, to allow them to understand the overall cost as well as the cumulative effect on the return on the investment.[75]

Before the conclusion of the contract, the insurance distributor should specify the demands and needs of the customer, provide the customer with objective information about the insurance product in an understandable form, but also ensure that the contract proposed is consistent with the client's demands and needs.[76] In the event that the insurance intermediaries give their advice on the basis of fair and personal analysis, they should advise on the basis of an analysis of a sufficiently large number of insurance contracts available on the market.[77]

4 Non-complex Insurance-Based Investment Products

In February 2016, EIOPA was asked with a formal "Request for Advice" by the European Commission to provide technical advice on possible delegated acts to further specify certain aspects of the IDD. In relation to non-complex insurance-based investment products, the Commission sought EIOPA's response as to the criteria to assess such products. Drawing from the relevant provisions in the IDD (articles 30(3) (a), 30(6)) and in MiFID II (article 57) although an assessment of the suitability or appropriateness of an IBIP for the customer by the insurance distributor is generally required as part of an advised or non-advised sale (IDD article 30 (1),(2)), Member States are allowed (IDD article 30(3)) to derogate from these obligations and to not require either a suitability or appropriateness test to be conducted, where various conditions are satisfied. Such sales ("execution only") although carried out only at the initiative of the customer still require the insurance distributor to specify the demands and needs of the customer prior to the conclusion of the contract (IDD article 20(1)). One of the conditions specified in Article 30(3) to

[73] Article 19 (1) (a–b) IDD.

[74] Article 19(1)(c) IDD.

[75] Article 29(1) IDD.

[76] Art 20 (1) IDD.

[77] Article 20(3) IDD.

determine whether an IBIP can be distributed as an execution-only sale relates to the complexity of the IBIP. IBIPs can be considered non-complex when they only provide investment exposure to the financial instruments deemed non-complex under MiFID II and do not incorporate a structure which makes it difficult for the customer to understand the risks involved (IDD article 30(3)(a)(i)).

In accordance with Article 25(8) of MiFID II, the Commission is empowered to adopt delegated acts on the criteria to identify "other non-complex financial instruments" referred to in Article 25(4)(a)(vi) of the same Directive. Also, Article 30(3)(a)(ii) of IDD acknowledges the possibility that IBIP may not fall within the scope of Article 30(3)(a)(i), but may still be deemed a non-complex product. EIOPA considered that where an IBIP incorporates a structure which makes it difficult for the customer to understand the risks involved, it is in all cases not fit for distribution via an execution-only sale. EIOPA's evidence gathering has shown that there are only a limited number of IBIP types currently sold execution-only. Whilst the numerous Member States allow for the sale of certain products on a non-advised basis, only a limited number allow for products to be sold by means of execution-only transactions. In relation to the criteria for the assessment of other non-complex financial instruments, as per the draft Commission Delegated Regulation under MiFID II, EIOPA has included the provisions in its technical advice where these criteria address product features, which are considered to be equally applicable to IBIPs.[78] Regarding the nature of any guarantee provided by the insurance undertaking, where the latter provides a guarantee regarding the surrender and maturity value of an IBIP, the customer is not fully exposed to the performance of the financial instruments in which the insurance undertaking has invested or to which the customer's benefits are linked. In view of this, depending on the nature of the guarantee, IBIPs could be regarded as non-complex, even though the contract may provide investment exposure that is not limited to financial instruments deemed non-complex under MiFID II. In this case, EIOPA considered that as a minimum the customer should be guaranteed to receive, at both surrender and maturity, at least the amount of the premiums that they have paid, minus legitimate costs levied.

In accordance EIOPA issued the following technical advice: "An IBIP shall be considered as non-complex for the purposes of Article 30(3)(a)(ii) of Directive (EU) 2016/97 if it satisfies all of the following criteria: (a) the contractually guaranteed minimum surrender and maturity value is at least the amount of premiums paid by the customer minus legitimate costs levied. (b) it does not incorporate a clause, condition or trigger that allows the insurance undertaking to materially alter the nature, risk or pay-out profile of the IBIP; (c) there are options to surrender or otherwise realise the IBIP at a value that is available to the customer; (d) it does not include any explicit or implicit charges which have the effect that, even though there

[78] However, in these cases it was still necessary to modify some of the MiFID II requirements to appropriately reflect the insurance sector. In particular, regarding the provision in point (d) of the technical advice, given that exit penalties have been a feature of long term insurance based investment products that are considered to have led to consumer detriment, this is intended to exclude products with unreasonable exit charges, including fiscal penalties.

are technically options to surrender the IBIP, doing so may cause unreasonable detriment to the customer, because the charges are disproportionate to the cost to the insurance undertaking of the surrender; (e) it does not in any other way incorporate a structure which makes it difficult for the customer to understand the risks involved."

Contracts for IBIPs can be complicated and difficult to understand for consumers. Distributors, either insurance undertakings or insurance intermediaries, therefore play an important role in processing information for the consumer and guiding consumers in choosing suitable insurance policies. Prior to the advent of the IDD, consumer protection standards for the sales of insurance-based investment products were not considered sufficient at EU level to reduce the risk of mis-selling of those products, as the IMD did not contain specific rules for the sale of life insurance products with an investment element. This was so in spite of the fact that these products are generally more complicated and represent higher risks for retail consumers than other insurance products. Hence, IDD stipulated additional conduct of business rules for the sale of IBIPs, and it provided for the case that differentiation should exist between complex and non-complex IBIPs.

Where an IBIP is considered non-complex, Member States may allow insurance distributors to not undertake some of the assessments (suitability and appropriateness) during the sales process that is normally necessary for the distribution of IBIPs. The EIOPA technical advice on the criteria to be used to assess "other non-complex IBIPs" aimed to facilitate the identification of "other non-complex IBIPs", such that only those products for which the risks are readily understood by customers, can be sold by execution-only. It also aimed to promote the consistent application of the IDD with respect to the identification of "other non-complex insurance-based investments" to be consistent with the line taken in the delegated acts expected to be adopted under Article 25(8) of MiFID II. Those aims are aligned with those under the IDD, i.e. the aim of improving insurance regulation in a manner that will facilitate market integration, the aim of establishing the conditions necessary for fair competition between distributors of insurance products and the aim of strengthening consumer protection, in particular with regards to IBIPs. It follows that an overly strict approach would not only be disadvantageous for insurance undertakings and insurance intermediaries, but also for customers and potentially for NCAs.

Hence, the adoption of criteria based on MiFID II seemed like the best solution in many respects, i.e. firstly because it was considered as striking the appropriate balance between the interests of insurance distributors and those of their customers and because it was considered as enabling the necessary flexibility at NCA level via the provision of criteria for other "non-complex insurance-based investments" at EU level. Not least, at customer level, it seemed reasonable to prevent insurance undertakings and insurance intermediaries from making insurance products available for sale via execution-only which do not meet the criteria while enabling customers to execute an order for products if the criteria are met.[79]

[79] EIOPA (2017a) Technical Advice on possible delegated acts concerning the Insurance Distribution Directive, 1/2/2017, EIOPA-17/048, https://eiopa.europa.eu/Publications/Consultations/EIOPA%20Technical%20Advice%20on%20the%20IDD.pdf.

5 Conflicts of Interest Regulation

The IDD and its delegated regulation[80] follow MiFID II provisions and those of its delegated regulation.[81] Article 23 of MiFID II, Article 28 of the IDD does not define or prohibit conflicts of interest. However, in the relevant delegated regulation we find provisions specifying certain situations which should be taken into account in the assessment of conflict of interest,[82] and the requirement for insurance intermediaries and insurance undertakings to establish, implement and maintain specific conflicts of interest policy to be followed for the identification, prevention and management of such conflicts of interest.[83] In particular, insurance intermediaries and insurance undertakings shall assess whether they, a relevant person or any person directly or indirectly linked to them by control, have an interest in the outcome of the insurance distribution activities, in the event such an interest: (a) is distinct from the customer's or potential customer's interest in the outcome of the insurance distribution activities; and (b) has the potential to influence the outcome of the distribution activities to the detriment of the customer.[84]

This assessment should be performed, by way of example, in the following situations:

(a) the insurance intermediary or insurance undertaking, a relevant person or any person directly or indirectly linked to them by control is likely to make a financial gain, or avoid a financial loss, to the potential detriment of the customer;
(b) the insurance intermediary or insurance undertaking, a relevant person or any person directly or indirectly linked to them by control has a financial or other incentive to favour the interest of another customer or group of customers over the interest of the customer;
(c) the insurance intermediary or insurance undertaking, a relevant person or any person directly or indirectly linked by control to an insurance intermediary or an insurance undertaking is substantially involved in the management or development of insurance-based investment products, in particular where such a person has an influence on the pricing of those products or their distribution costs.'[85]

As for the conflict of interest policy, this should include the circumstances—related to the specific insurance distribution activity—which constitute or may give a rise to a conflict of interest which could damage customers' interest, as well as the

[80] Articles 3–7 of the Commission Delegated Regulation (EU) 2017/2359.

[81] Commission Delegated Regulation (EU) 2017/565. See also the Explanatory Memorandum, Commission Delegated Regulation (EU) 2017/2359, p. 3.

[82] Article 3 of the Commission Delegated Regulation (EU) 2017/2359.

[83] Article 4 of the Commission Delegated Regulation (EU) 2017/2359.

[84] Article 3(2) of the Commission Delegated Regulation (EU) 2017/2359.

[85] Article 3(2) of the Commission Delegated Regulation (EU) 2017/2359.

procedures to be followed and the measure to be adopted for the management of such conflicts.[86] The policy should be assessed and periodically review, on an at least annual basis, and amended in case of any deficiency.[87] As regard to the insurance intermediaries, who are under a contractual obligation to conduct insurance distribution business exclusively with one or more insurance undertakings, EIOPA has clarified that the conflict of interest policy remains a requirement under the responsibility of that intermediary.[88]

EIOPA considers it essential that intermediaries who distribute exclusively on behalf of one or more insurance undertakings are required to establish, implement and maintain an efficient conflicts of interest policy, set out in writing and suited to their size and organisation and the nature, scale and complexity of their business in accordance with Article 4(1) of Delegated Regulation 2017/2359. This requirement "does not prohibit intermediaries who distribute exclusively on behalf of one or more insurance undertakings, from receiving assistance and guidance from an insurance undertaking to which they are tied, in developing a conflict of interest policy". However, EIOPA holds the regulatory responsibility of establishing, implementing and operating the policy remains with the insurance intermediary.

As in MiFID II, the disclosure of a conflict of interest should be avoided, except for the situations in which the organisational and administrative arrangements are insufficient for the prevention of risks of damage to the interests of the customer.[89] In such a case, the disclosure should be made on a durable medium and include sufficient detail,[90] Which means that it should provide a specific description of the conflict of interest in question, explain its general nature, sources, and associated risks for consumers, and state that the organizational and administrative arrangements established within the conflict of interest policy are not sufficient to ensure, with reasonable confidence, the prevention of such risks.[91] Finally, the senior management of the insurance distributors should receive, at least annually, written reports on the situations in which a conflict of interest arose, and of these the insurance intermediary of undertaking should keep a record.[92]

In EIOPA's view,[93] an insurance intermediary or insurance undertaking is not exempted from further managing conflicts of interests if it discloses the conflicts of interest to the consumer. The legal basis for such conclusion is the Recital 5 of Delegated Regulation 2017/2359 clarifies that the disclosure of conflicts of interest by an insurance intermediary or an insurance undertaking cannot exempt it from the

[86] Article 4(2) of the Commission Delegated Regulation (EU) 2017/2359.

[87] Article 7(1) and Recital 5 of the Commission Delegated Regulation (EU) 2017/2359.

[88] EIOPA Q and A on Regulation (2018), No. 1622.

[89] Article 6(1) and Recital 5 of the Commission Delegated Regulation (EU) 2017/2359.

[90] Article 28(3) IDD.

[91] Article 6(2) and Recital 5 of the Commission Delegated Regulation (EU) 2017/2359.

[92] Article 7(2) and Recital 5 of the Commission Delegated Regulation (EU) 2017/2359.

[93] EIOPA Q and A on Regulation (2018), No. 1625. See also No. 1627 as regard to the application of proportionality in relation to the measures set out in the IDD for managing conflicts of interest.

obligation to maintain and operate the organisational and administrative arrangements that are the most effective means of preventing damage to customers. EIOPA considers that "disclosure is a measure of last resort". Thus, the insurance intermediary or insurance undertaking has to take "all reasonable steps to prevent the conflicts of interest from adversely affecting the interests of its customers and only when the conflicts of interests cannot be prevented, disclosure of the conflicts of interest to the customer is expected". As part of the disclosure, EIOPA considers it important that "the customer is advised that organisational and administrative measures established to prevent or manage conflicts of interest are not sufficient to ensure, with reasonable confidence, that risks of damage" to the interests of the customer will be prevented. Such a report is not addressed to the insurance undertaking, given the reference in Art. 7 only to report on conflicts of interest to their senior management of the intermediary.

6 Inducements Regime

According to the IDD, the insurance intermediary should inform the client whether, in relation to the insurance contract, any inducement,[94] i.e. any fee, commission or non-monetary benefit paid or provided by any party except the customer, is paid. The payment of inducements is only allowed if it '(a) does not have a detrimental impact on the quality of the relevant service to the customer, and (b) does not impair compliance with the insurance intermediary's or insurance undertaking's duty to act honestly, fairly and professionally in accordance with the best interests of its customers'.[95] This seems a less stringent discipline compared to that provided in MiFID II, which imposes specific bans and strict limitations to fees and commission paid in connection to financial advice.[96]

However, all the rebates are relevant, irrespective of their origin. Thus, even the rebates different rates from fund managers, are captured by the assessment under Article 29(2), IDD to ensure that it does not have a detrimental impact on the quality of the relevant service to the customer and that it does not impair compliance with the insurance intermediary's or insurance undertaking's duty to act honestly, fairly and professionally in accordance with the best interests of its customers.[97]

EIOPA consider the insurance undertaking who receives the rebate, is obliged to consider "all relevant factors which may increase or decrease the risk of detrimental impact on the quality of the relevant service to the customer, and which have potential to impair compliance with the insurance undertakings duty to act honestly, fairly and professionally in accordance with the best interests of its customers, including the fact that different rates are received from fund managers". Insurance undertakings

[94] Article 19(1)(e) IDD.

[95] Article 29(2) IDD.

[96] Art 24(7) and (9) of MiFID II.

[97] EIOPA Q and A on Regulation (2018), No. 1630.

may also consider EIOPA's Opinion on monetary incentives and remuneration[98] between providers of asset management services and insurance undertakings in which the risk of customer detriment related to the practice of receiving rebates from asset managers they are addressing, including the application of the Product Oversight and Governance requirements.[99]

As requested by the IDD,[100] the Commission further specified in a delegated act the criteria for assessing whether inducements paid or received increase the risk of a detrimental impact on the quality of the relevant service.[101] In particular, an inducement has to be considered to have a detrimental impact on the quality of the relevant service to the customer when "it is of such a nature and scale that it provides an incentive to carry out insurance distribution activities in a way that is not in compliance with the obligation to act honestly, fairly and professionally in accordance with the best interests of the customer".[102] Furthermore, insurance distributors should conduct an overall analysis taking into account 'all relevant factors which may increase or decrease the risk of detrimental impact on the quality of the relevant service to the customer', as well as 'any organizational measures taken by the insurance intermediary or insurance undertaking carrying out distribution activities to prevent the risk of detrimental impact'.[103]

EIOPA considers it important that insurance intermediaries and insurance undertakings demonstrate compliance with Article 8 of Delegated Regulation 2017/2359, which requires that an overall analysis is performed, taking into account any relevant factors that may increase or decrease the risk of detriment to customers an assessment of relevant inducement schemes.[104] Regarding the frequency of such assessments, EIOPA recommend that "insurance intermediaries and insurance undertakings consider all relevant factors which may increase or decrease the risk of detrimental impact on the quality of the relevant service to the customer or risk of impairing compliance with the intermediary's or insurance undertaking's obligation to act fairly, honestly and professionally in accordance with the best interests of the customer, and assess for themselves at what frequency the assessment is required in order to maintain continual compliance with the criteria set out in Article 29(2), IDD". For example, if there are no changes or modifications to the inducement scheme, the frequency can be appropriately extended, where no other indicators (such as customer complaints or others) give reason to do so. Anyway, The details of the assessment should be recorded in order to demonstrate and enable competent authorities to monitor that the inducement complies with the criteria set out in Article 29(2), IDD.

[98] EIOPA (2017b).

[99] See P. Marano, "The Product Oversight and Governance: Standards and Liabilities", in this volume.

[100] Article 29(4) IDD.

[101] Article 8 Commission Delegated Regulation (EU) 2017/2359.

[102] Article 8(1) Commission Delegated Regulation (EU) 2017/2359.

[103] Article 8(2) Commission Delegated Regulation (EU) 2017/2359.

[104] EIOPA Q and A on Regulation (2018), No. 1623.

The insurance intermediary or insurance undertaking is required to consider the amount of inducement being paid in comparison to the value of the product or service being provided. EIOPA holds that insurance intermediaries and insurance undertakings need to consider whether "the customer is receiving value for the payment in relation to the services they have received".[105] In any case, the amount of the inducement being paid should not be disproportionate and not excessive to the services being provided. In this respect, in case of a rebate from a fund manager, insurance undertakings should also consider EIOPA's Opinion on monetary incentives and remuneration[106] between providers of asset management services and insurance undertakings in which the risk of customer detriment related to the practice of receiving rebates from asset managers are addressed. Regardless of whether a personal recommendation is provided, a rebate should be assessed in accordance with Article 29(2), IDD.[107]

7 Assessment of Suitability and Appropriateness

IDD provides specific conduct of business rule, not derived from MiFID II regime, known as the demands and needs test. The scope of this test is not prescribed in the Directive or the Delegated Regulation and is subject to national implementation. However, EIOPA provided some guidance regarding minimum expectations for this test and how it may relate to the assessment of suitability.[108] Recital 7 of Delegated Regulation 2017/2359 clarifies that the assessments of suitability and appropriateness are without prejudice to the obligation, for insurance intermediaries and insurance undertakings, to consider and specify, prior to the conclusion of any insurance contract, on the basis of information obtained from the customer, the demands and needs of that customer.

The demands and needs test provides a protection for customers to avoid cases of mis-selling (Recital 44, IDD) and it applies to all insurance contracts, not just IBIPs. Article 30, IDD applies "without prejudice" to the demands and needs test as covered by Article 20(1), IDD. The demands and needs test has to be performed in any event prior to the conclusion of the contract and is distinct from the suitability assessment in advised cases, and the suitability assessment can also be provided at any time during the customer relationship. The assessment of demands and needs is required whether or not advice is being provided and the specifying of the demands and needs would not amount to a suitability assessment. Depending on the national implementation, where advice is being provided, the demands and needs test and assessment of suitability could be seen as a continuum, rather than as a break.

---

[105] EIOPA Q and A on Regulation (2018), No. 1631.

[106] EIOPA (2017b).

[107] EIOPA Q and A on Regulation (2018), No. 1635.

[108] EIOPA Q and A on Regulation (2018), No. 1638.

The main information concerning the customer's needs, typically includes, for example, personal information (age, profession, place of residence etc.) or the information particularly linked to the type of product requested. This information should enable the insurance intermediary or insurance undertaking to assess whether certain products can be offered or not according to their capacity of meeting the demands and needs of the customer. This could lead to a selection of a range of comparable products for consideration during the suitability assessment where advice is being given or during the appropriateness assessment where no advice is given.

Where the customer is provided with advice the information, which will be obtained by the insurance intermediary or the insurance undertaking, will need to include other more specific and detailed elements, like the customer's financial situation, including their ability to bear losses, their investment objectives, including their risk tolerance, and other correlated information. In the EIOPA view, the final outcome should be a personalised recommendation where it is specifically explained why that particular product best meets the customer demands and needs.

Under the IDD[109] And the Delegated Regulation,[110] the provisions concerning the assessment of suitability and appropriateness are almost identical to the corresponding provisions under MiFID II and its specific Delegated Regulation.[111] In particular, the suitability assessment requires that the insurance intermediary or undertaking, in the case of sales with advice, gathers information about their client's knowledge, experience, investment objective and risk tolerance—in order to recommend to the client the IBIPs that are best aligned with the client's profile,[112] which means that it meets the client's investment objectives, risk tolerance, financial situation and that its nature and characteristics are adequate in respect to the client's knowledge and experience.[113]

If the insurance product is not suitable for the individual customer or the suitability cannot be determined but the customer still wishes to conclude the contract it is up to Member State implementation law to establish if the contract can still be concluded. In the EIOPA view Paragraphs 5 and 6 of Article 9 of Delegated Regulation 2017/2359 cover the cases where a recommendation cannot be made due to the insurance intermediary or the insurance undertaking not obtaining the necessary information or there being no products that are suitable for the customer or potential customer.[114] In these circumstances the customer may agree to proceed with concluding the contract as a sale without advice (in conformity with the applicable rules of national law), and subject to an assessment of appropriateness unless it is possible to sell the contract on an execution only basis, (see recital 12 of Delegated Regulation 2017/2359). Where the distributor cannot obtain the necessary

[109] Article 30 of IDD.

[110] Articles 9–19 of the Commission Delegated Regulation (EU) 2017/2359.

[111] Commission Delegated Regulation (EU) 2017/565.

[112] Article 30(1) of IDD and Article 9 of the Commission Delegated Regulation (EU) 2017/2359.

[113] Article 9(2) of the Commission Delegated Regulation (EU) 2017/2359.

[114] EIOPA Q and A on Regulation (2018), No. 1639.

information to assess the appropriateness of the contract, the distributor shall warn the customer that the contract might not be appropriate. Only when the customer asked to proceed with concluding the contract despite this warning, the distributor may perform the sale. In all cases, Article 20(1), IDD provides that any contract proposed must always be consistent with the demands and needs of the customer.

The insurance intermediary or undertaking should adopt measures to ensure that the information collected about the clients is reliable, and communicate them that the suitability assessment is performed in their best interest.[115] It should then provide the customer with the so-called 'suitability statement', which includes an outline of the advice given, as well as information about how the recommendation meets the customer's investment objectives, risk tolerance, financial situation, knowledge and experience.[116]

The appropriateness requirement provides that, in the event of sales requiring no advice, the insurance intermediary or insurance undertaking gathers information on the client to assess if the product or services offered or demanded were appropriate for the customer.[117] In the event the product is deemed not appropriate for the customer, the insurance intermediary or insurance undertaking should warn the customer or potential customer.

EIOPA believes that the level of detail will be case-specific and depend upon the individual circumstances of the sale including the nature of the product or service offered or demanded, the risks involved and the knowledge and experience of the customer.[118] It is worth noting that Article 17(1) of Delegated Regulation 2017/2359 requires that the information obtained shall include information to the extent appropriate to the nature and type of product or service offered or demanded. Therefore, it should relate to the product overall, including where relevant, such as in the case of a unit-linked insurance contract, the underlying investment assets. Article 19(3) of Delegated Regulation 2017/2359 contains requirements for records to be kept in relation to the appropriateness assessment, in particular regarding the result of the assessment, warnings given to the customer and storage in an accessible manner for future reference.

As under MiFID II, this assessment is not required concerning non-complex products as defined by MiFID II.[119] However, due to the specific structures of insurance products, the Commission Delegated Regulation under IDD provides, among the criteria for non-complex IBIPs, an additional condition concerning products including a specific guarantee.[120]

Moreover, the insurance intermediary or insurance undertaking should establish a record of documents agreed with the customer containing rights and obligations of the parties, as well as other terms related to the provision of services to the

[115] Article 10 and 11 of the Commission Delegated Regulation (EU) 2017/2359.

[116] Article 14(1) of the Commission Delegated Regulation (EU) 2017/2359.

[117] Article 30(2) of IDD and Article 14 of the Commission Delegated Regulation (EU) 2017/2359.

[118] EIOPA Q and A on Regulation (2018), No. 1636.

[119] Article 30(3) IDD and 25(4)(a) MiFID II.

[120] Article 16(a) of the Commission Delegated Regulation (EU) 2017/2359.

customer. The customer should also be provided with periodic reports on the service, which include a number of communications proportionate to the type and complexity of the IBIP involved.[121] In the context of periodic reporting to customers, the insurance intermediary also expected to develop and provide 'adequate reports on the service provided'. There could be some overlapping between the insurance intermediary primarily responsible for reporting to customers on costs and charges and providing periodic reports to customers, and the insurance undertaking which is always responsible for delivering information on the product, as required under the Solvency II Directive. According to EIOPA concerning the obligations to provide appropriate reporting under Articles 29(1) and 30(5), IDD and Article 18 of Delegated Regulation 2017/2359, it will depend upon who is providing the service.[122] This may generally be expected to be an insurance intermediary, except where the insurance undertaking is providing services when distributing directly. Thus, the insurance undertaking remains responsible always for delivering the information required by Article 185 of Directive 2009/138/EC (Solvency II).

8 Conclusions

Following the wave of other regulatory changes, such as MiFID II and PRIIPS Regulation, the IDD intends to strengthen consumer protection, improve the competitive landscape of the European insurance industry, and reduce cross-sectoral inconsistencies. However, the Directive is aimed at minimum harmonization and therefore does not preclude Member States from maintaining or introducing more stringent provisions, provided that these are consistent with the Directive. IDD also introduces product oversight and governance requirements similar to MiFID II. In relation to assessing the suitability and appropriateness of this is conducted by insurance companies that provide advice to customers on IBIPs so as to enable them to recommend to the customer or potential customer the IBIPs that are suitable for that person. Insurance based investment products are an essential feature of insurance industry. However, it has not always been easy to make them widely known to the wider public due to the slow opening of the market for financial services within the EU. IDD will hopefully provide a more harmonised and more efficient legal framework, fostering the convergence of investor protection within the financial sectors as a whole.

[121] Articles 30(4) and (5) IDD.

[122] EIOPA Q and A on Regulation (2018), No. 1645.

References

Alford D (2006) The Lamfalussy process and EU Bank regulation: another step on the road to Pan-European regulation? Annu Rev Bank Financ Law 25:389

Andoura S, Timmerman P (2008) Governance of the EU: the reform debate on European agencies reignited. In: EPIN Working Paper No. 19, European Policy Institutes Network, Brussels, October 2008

Avgouleas E (2009) The global financial crisis and the disclosure paradigm in European financial regulation: the case for reform. Eur Company Financ Law Rev 6(4)

Avgouleas E (2012) Governance of global financial markets: the law, the economics, the politics. International corporate law and financial market regulation. Cambridge University Press, Cambridge

Backer LC (2008) Monitor and manage: MiFID and power in the regulation of EU financial markets. Yearb Eur Law 27

Case 120/78 *Rewe-Zentral AG vs. Bundesmonopolverwaltung für Branntwein*, ECR 1979 p. 00649. http://eur-lex.europa.eu/smartapi/cgi/sga_doc?smartapi!celexplus!prod!CELEXnumdoc&lg=en&numdoc=61978J0120

Chatzimanoli D (2008) Law and governance in the institutional organisation of EU financial services - The Lamfalussy procedure and the single supervisor revisited. Thesis, European University Institute, Florence

Colaert V (2015) European Banking, securities and insurance law: cutting through sectoral lines? Common Mark Law Rev 52:1579–1616

Colaert V (2017) Building blocks of investor protection: all-embracing regulation tightens its grip. J Eur Consum Mark Law (6):229–244

Dalhuisen J (2013) Dalhuisen on transnational comparative, commercial, financial and trade law: vol 3: financial products, financial services and financial regulation. Hart, Oxford

De Grauwe P, Gros D (2009) A new two-pillar strategy for the ECB, CEPS Policy Brief No. 191. CEPS, Brussels

EIOPA (2017a) Technical Advice on possible delegated acts concerning the Insurance Distribution Directive, 1/2/2017, EIOPA-17/048. https://eiopa.europa.eu/Publications/Consultations/EIOPA%20Technical%20Advice%20on%20the%20IDD.pdf

EIOPA (2017b) Opinion on monetary incentives and remuneration between providers of asset management services and insurance undertakings, 11 December 2017, EIOPA-BoS-17/295. https://eiopa.europa.eu/Publications/Opinions/Opinion%20on%20monetary%20incentives%20and%20remuneration%20between%20providers%20of%20asset%20management%20services%20and%20insurance%20undertakings.pdf

EIOPA (2018) Q and A on Regulation - Answers - Commission Implementing Regulations laying down Implementing Technical Standards, (EU) 2017-2359 Info requirements and conduct of business rules applicable, published on: July 16 2018. https://eiopa.europa.eu/Pages/Guidelines/Q-and-A-on-Regulation-Answers-Commission-Implementing-Regulations.aspx

European Commission (2015) European Commission Green Paper on retail financial services, COM (2015) 630 final

European Commission (2016) Commission Delegated Regulation of 30 June 2016 supplementing Regulation (EU) No 1286/2014 of the European Parliament and of the Council on key information documents for packaged retail and insurance based investment products (PRIIPs) by laying down regulatory technical standards with regard to the presentation, content, review and revision of key information documents and the conditions for fulfilling the requirement to provide such documents (C(2016)3999 final)

European Parliament (2013) DG for Internal Policies: Review of the New European System of Financial Supervision (ESFS) Part 1: The work of the European Supervisory Authorities (EBA, EIOPA AND ESMA) – The ESFS's Micro Prudential Pillar. http://www.europarl.europa.eu/RegData/etudes/etudes/join/2013/507446/IPOL-ECON_ET(2013)507446_EN.pdf

European Parliament (2017) Position of the European Parliament of 1 December 2016 and Decision of the Council of 8 December 2016. http://ec.europa.eu/finance/docs/level-2-measures/priips-delegated-regulation-2017-1473_en.pdf
FCA (2017) "PRIIPs disclosure: Key Information Documents". https://www.fca.org.uk/firms/priips-disclosure-key-information-documents
Lannoo K (2008) Concrete Steps towards More Integrated Financial Oversight, CEPS Task Force Report, CEPS, Brussels, December 2008
Lord Turner (2009) A regulatory response to global financial crisis. Lord Turner Review, London, UK, pp 100–102. www.fsa.gov.uk/pubs/other/turner_review.pdf
Maesschalck ND (2017) The insurance distribution directive: what does it change for intermediaries and for others? In: Marano P, Siri M (eds) Insurance regulation in the European Union. Palgrave Macmillan, pp 63–65
Moloney J (2013) Resetting the location of regulatory and supervisory control over EU financial markets: lessons from five years on. Int Comp Law Q 62(4):955–965
Papaconstantinou G (2016) Investment bankers in conflict: the regime of inducements in MiFID II and the member states' struggle for fairness. Eur Rev Contract Law 12(4):356–390, 367
Pinsent Masons (2016) Are the KIDs alright?, 2016. https://www.pinsentmasons.com/en/media/legal-updates/are-the-kids-alright/
Rix C (2014) A practitioner's guide to the regulation of insurance, 5th edn. Sweet & Maxwell, London
Snowdon P, Lovegrove S (2012) MiFID review, C.O.B. 94(Mar), 1–27, 20
Welch J, Parker P (2014) European financial services, 83. In: Walker G, Purves R (eds) Financial services law. Oxford University Press, Oxford

Further Readinngs

EIOPA (2014a) Discussion Paper on Key Information Documents for Packaged Retail and Insurance-based Investment, JC/DP/2014/02
EIOPA (2014b) EIOPA, EBA, ESMA, ESAs' response to the intention of the European Commission to amend the draft Regulatory Technical Standards (RTS) jointly submitted by EBA, ESMA and EIOPA under Articles 8(5), 10(2) and 13(5) of Regulation (EU) No 1286/2014. https://esas-joint-committee.europa.eu/publications/letters/esas-2016-81%20joint%20letter%20on%20rts%20on%20priips.pdf
EIOPA (2016) EIOPA, EBA, ESMA, ESAs' response to the intention of the European Commission to amend the draft Regulatory Technical Standards (RTS) jointly submitted by EBA, ESMA and EIOPA under Articles 8(5), 10(2) and 13(5) of Regulation (EU) No 1286/2014. https://esas-joint-committee.europa.eu/publications/letters/esas-2016-81%20joint%20letter%20on%20rts%20on%20priips.pdf
ESMA (2016) Final draft regulatory technical standards, JC 2016, 21 https://www.esma.europa.eu/sites/default/files/library/jc_2016_21_final_draft_rts_priips_kid_report.pdf
European Commission (2001) Committee of Wise Men on the Regulation of European Securities Markets, Final Report, Brussels, 15.2.2001; more information on the Lamfalussy process at http://ec.europa.eu/internal_market/securities/lamfalussy/
European Commission (2009) "Staff Working Document, Impact Assessment accompanying the Communication from the Commission to the European Parliament and the Council on Packaged Retail Investment Products", SEC 2009, 356
European Commission (2010) The European Union's Roadmap for Financial Reform under the political authority of Commissioner Michel Barnier, 2010. http://ec.europa.eu/internal_market/finances/docs/roadmap/finanial_reform_en.pdf
European Commission (2016) Intention of the Commission to amend the draft Regulatory Technical Standards jointly submitted by EBA, ESMA and EIOPA under Articles 8(5), 10(2) and 13(5) of Regulation (EU) No 1286/2014, Ares(2016)6353871 - 10/11/2016. https://esas-

joint-committee.europa.eu/Publications/Letters/Ares%206353871_Letter%20to%20EBA%20 ESMA%20and%20EIOPA%20-%20PRIIPs%20draft%20RTS.pdf
FCA (2015) "Developing our approach to implementing MiFID II conduct of business and organizational requirements", Discussion Paper DP15/3
Hopt K (2007) European company and financial law, 4th edn. Oxford University Press
Huertas M (2017) A little less conversation, a little more action? EU unveils the CMU action plan for retail financial services. J Int Bank Law Regul 32(8):323–330
Kounadis J (2017) Cross-selling practices under MiFID II: a comprehensive analysis of the new regime. J Int Bank Law Regul 32(8):331–340
Lehmann M, Kumpan C (2017) Financial services law. Beck, Munchen
Mollers T (2015) European legislative practice 2.0: dynamic harmonisation of capital markets law - MiFID II and PRIIP. Bank Finance Law Rev 31(1):141–176
Moloney N (2014) EU securities and financial markets regulation. Oxford University Press
Schaeken – Willemaers - Gaetane (2014) 'Client Protection on European Financial Markets – From Inform Your Client to Know Your Product and Beyond: An Assessment of the PRIIPs Regulation, MiFID II/MiFIR and IMD 2' (July 1, 2014). Revue Trimestrielle de Droit Financier (Autumn 2014). Available at SSRN: https://ssrn.com/abstract=2494842
Veerle C (2017) MiFID II in relation to other investor protection regulation: picking up the crumbs of a piecemeal approach. In: Busch D, Ferrarini G (eds) Regulation of the EU financial markets: MiFID II and MiFIR. Oxford University Press
Walker G, Purves R, Blair M (eds) (2014) Financial services law, 3rd edn. Oxford University Press, Oxford

The Product Oversight and Governance: Standards and Liabilities

Pierpaolo Marano

Contents

Abbreviations

EOS-PRIIPS	Targets specific environmental or social objectives
ESAS	Notwithstanding this, the European supervision authorities
FCA	Financial conduct authority
FSA	Financial services authority
IDD	Insurance distribution directive
IMD1	Insurance mediation directive

P. Marano (✉)
Department of Law, Catholic University of the Sacred Heart, Milano, Italy
e-mail: pierpaolo.marano@unicatt.it

P. Marano, I. Rokas (eds.), *Distribution of Insurance-Based Investment Products*, https://doi.org/10.1007/978-3-030-11668-2_3

KID	Key information document
POG	Product oversight and governance
PRIIP	Packaged retail and insurance-based investment product

1 Where do the Product Oversight and Governance (POG) Come From?

The concept of POG was mainly developed in the United Kingdom (UK),[1] as one of the regulatory responses to the financial crisis of 2007. POG was introduced in the UK with reference to financial products before being adopted by the EU in the Market in Financial Instruments Directive (MiFID II) and, then, extended to all insurance products through the Insurance Distribution Directive (IDD), with the exception of the insurance products covering the large risks. Since the UK has gone ahead of the European Union, the UK legal framework and supervisory practices can be considered as the benchmark for the EU regardless of the event of Brexit. This makes it useful in order to analyse how the UK has elaborated the POG especially with regard to insurance-based investment products, which satisfy investor's needs similarly to those satisfied by financial products and therefore raise comparable investor protection challenges.[2]

With the acknowledgment of real and significant failings in the UK regulatory framework, the UK HM Treasury issued a consultation paper in July 2010 aiming to lay the foundation for a new legal framework of the financial sector due to the failure of the UK regulators in recognising and responding to the problems that were emerging in the financial system.[3]

Following up this consultation, the Financial Services Authority (FSA) issued a Discussion Paper on Product intervention in January 2011. This paper presented the new regulatory approach adopted by the business conduct authority in 2010, which involves earlier regulatory intervention, engaging with firms to ensure that new products truly do serve the needs of the customers to whom they are marketed.[4] FSA announced, in fact, they are more willing than previously to target products when

[1] Some inspiration can be found in the Resolution n. 9019104 of 2 March 2009 on illiquid investment products, which was issued by the Italian authority responsible for regulating the Italian financial market (CONSOB). The principle of "acting honestly, fairly and professionally in accordance with the best interest of customers" (see Article 19.1 MiFID) was interpreted in the sense of requiring issuers of illiquid investment products to design their commercial policy evaluating the compatibility of each product with the characteristics and needs of the customers to whom they are offered. Thus CONSOB requires the definition of business processes to allow, even in abstracts terms, the assessment of the financial needs of the selected target market compared to those satisfied by the products which should be offered to them, in the concrete selection phase of the products to be distributed and, more importantly, in the possible engineering phase. In addition, the activities above shall be approved by the administrative body and verified by the compliance function.

[2] See Recital no. 87 of MiFID II.

[3] HM Treasury, *A new approach to financial regulation: judgement, focus and stability.*

[4] See Perry et al. (2011), pp. 1–33.

specific problems emerge, rather than focusing so much on selling practices as they have in the past. Thus, FSA aims to take rapid action to stop problems from growing and affecting large numbers of consumers, and to deter the creation of products likely to lead to consumer detriment.[5] The new approach complements and does not replace the previous one that was based on the assumption that effective consumer protection would be achieved provided sales processes were fair and product feature disclosure was transparent. After receiving 84 responses to Discussion Paper above, the FSA believed that a product intervention approach, whose rationale is explained in detail in the Discussion paper,[6] is an essential means of achieving an appropriate level of consumer protection.[7]

The key features of this approach anticipate those adopted by the EU and this was also one of the purposes of the Discussion Paper.[8] The tools developed for the new intensive and intrusive supervisory approach include:

- Product oversight[9];
- Product strategy[10];
- Target market[11];

---

[5] FSA, Discussion Paper on Product Intervention, January 2011, p. 16.

[6] See FSA, Discussion Paper, cit., p. 23 ff.

[7] FSA, Feedback on Discussion Paper on Product Intervention, June 2011.

[8] See Annex II, point 15: "Given the EC's willingness to consider similar issues in the MiFID review, responses to this DP may be used to influence our position in EU negotiations rather than to set new standards at UK level. It may be that an appropriate action for us is to work with our colleagues at EU level, rather than pursuing a national approach".

[9] Authority assesses whether firms ensure that the fair treatment of customers is built into their oversight arrangements. What they look for includes:

- A board engaged in ensuring products deliver the right outcomes for consumers;
- Clearly allocated responsibilities for oversight of product governance; and
- The effective inclusion of control functions such as Compliance in oversight arrangements.

[10] Product strategy covers such areas as the firm's plans to develop and distribute its existing and new products over the next few years, how the firm sees the market for its products developing and where it considers strategic opportunities will arise. Supervisory approach considers how firms set their product strategy and whether they include adequate challenge of it, including:

- Controls in place to ensure that customers' needs are reflected in setting and implementing the product strategy; and
- Evidence that these controls have led to improvements from a customer perspective.

[11] Supervisory approach considers how the firm has defined its target market; how it tests that this is the right approach and the surrounding governance procedures. What authority looks for includes:

- Policies and procedures that support the design of products appropriate to a specified target market;
- A design process that leads to an appropriate matching of products to the needs of the target market;
- Clear consideration of what customer usage or needs the product would not fulfil;
- A target market that is plausible in terms of size or shape; and
- Products designed to meet customer needs, not simply to copy a competitor's product, for example.

- Distribution strategy[12];
- Incentives[13];
- Risks and stress testing[14];
- Price and value[15];
- Execution and review.[16]

---

[12] Authority asks firms to provide evidence that the fair treatment of customers is built into the development and oversight of the distribution strategy. Therefore, supervisory approach includes:

- Controls in place that ensure the distribution channels and strategy are compatible with the needs of the target market;
- Details of the target market, product features and risks being accurately conveyed to distributors;
- Interactions and communications with distributors that are likely to lead to fair customer outcomes; and
- The firm taking action to address any mismatches between the actual distribution/sales and the intended target market.

[13] Firms need to include measures to avoid conflicts of interest in their remuneration policies. Therefore, the review of remuneration and other incentive practices for in-house staff includes:

- How sales staff are incentivised;
- Whether the incentives increase the risk of mis-selling; and
- Whether those risks are adequately controlled.

[14] By 'stress testing' authority is referring to scenario modelling or other forms of analysis used to identify how the product might function under a range of market conditions and how the customer could be affected. In the consumer protection context, supervisory approach is considering the stress testing of a product from the consumer's point-of-view, rather than stress and scenario testing for prudential purposes, to manage risks to the firm. Therefore, it considers the depth and breadth of risk assessment and stress testing undertaken, looking for, among other things:

- Clear identification and management of the risks to the customer;
- Robust stress and scenario testing to ensure the delivery of fair customer outcomes; and
- Evidence that subsequent changes to product features actually mitigate the risks to the customer.

[15] Supervisory approach looks for warning signals that indicate a product may not offer reasonable value for money for customers, including whether:

- Product design is driven by features that benefit the customer and not by a business model that is dependent on poor customer outcomes;
- Product costs are compatible with the objectives of the product; and
- Conflicts of interest have been avoided or managed effectively.

[16] Authority also expects firms to ensure that their products continue to work well for their customers. Supervisory approach considers the quality of their regular reviews, the use they make of customer feedback and the ongoing active management of the product. Therefore, it includes:

- No outstanding risks to customers resulting from flawed implementation;
- Appropriate mechanisms in place to ensure that lessons learned (e.g. from complaints) are fed back into the product development process;
- Evidence that post-sale analysis is used to make changes that have improved customer outcomes in existing or new products; and
- Appropriate action is taking place if the product is no longer behaving as expected (for instance because of changes to wider market conditions or legislative changes). It may be, for example, that the firm should stop selling the product to new customers on the same basis, contact existing customers to explain the problem and suggest ways in which they could deal with it.

In addition, this intensive supervisory strategy requests an appropriate background to evaluate the outcomes. Thus, authority has specifically recruited staff with experience and expertise in product design in order to ensure authority has the necessary skills to supervise firms effectively.[17]

The new supervisory approach has been completed turning some of FSA previously published material on treating customers fairly and the responsibilities of product providers and distributors into rules. FSA Handbook related to "The Responsibilities of Providers and Distributors for the Fair Treatment of Customers" provides guidance for POG, which are inferred from some Principles of Businesses, making a clear distinction between (i) provider responsibilities and (ii) distributor responsibilities.

With reference to provider[18] responsibilities, the following Principles are particularly relevant when undertaking product or service design[19]:

- Principle 2 (*'A firm must conduct its business with due skill, care and diligence'*);
- Principle 3 (*'A firm must take reasonable care to organise and control its affairs responsibly and effectively, with adequate risk management systems'*);
- Principle 6 (*'A firm must pay due regard to the interests of its customers and treat them fairly'*).

Principle 2 is also relevant when providing information to distributors,[20] and Principles 2, 6 and 7 (*'A firm must pay due regard to the information needs of its clients, and communicate information to them in a way which is clear, fair and not*

[17] See FSA, *Discussion Paper on Product intervention*, point 4.15.

[18] In particular, the term "provider" include persons who offer services such as portfolio management (through distributors or otherwise) as well as those who develop, manage or package products such as life insurance, general insurance or investment products or who develop or enter into home finance transactions (i.e. mortgages, home reversion plans and home purchase plans).

[19] In particular, a firm:

(1) Should identify the target market, namely which types of customer the product or service is likely to be suitable (or not suitable) for;
(2) Should stress-test the product or service to identify how it might perform in a range of market environments and how the customer could be affected;
(3) Should have in place systems and controls to manage adequately the risks posed by product or service design.

[20] In particular, a firm:

(1) Should make clear if that information is not intended for customer use;
(2) Should ensure the information is sufficient, appropriate and comprehensible in substance and form, including considering whether it will enable distributors to understand it enough to give suitable advice (where advice is given) and to extract any relevant information and communicate it to the end customer. As part of meeting this standard, the provider may wish to consider, with regard to each distribution channel or type of distributor, what information distributors of that type already have, their likely level of knowledge and understanding, their information needs and what form or medium would best meet those needs (which could include discussions, written material or training as appropriate).

misleading') are relevant when selecting a distribution channel.[21] In the area of information to customers, Principles 3, 6, and 7 are relevant,[22] whereas Principles 2, 6 and 7 are particularly important in the area of post-sale responsibility.[23]

Regarding distributor responsibilities, Principles 3, 6 and 7 are particularly relevant in the area of financial promotions,[24] and Principles 2, 6 and 7 when providing

---

[21] In particular, a firm:

(1) Should decide whether this is a product where customers would be wise to seek advice;
(2) Should review how what is occurring in practice corresponds to (or deviates from) what was originally planned or envisaged for the distribution of its products or services given the target market. This involves collecting and analysing appropriate Management Information such that the firm can detect patterns in distribution as compared with the planned target market, and can assess the performance of the distribution channels through which its products or services are being distributed;
(3) Should act when it has concerns, for example by ceasing to use a particular distribution channel.

[22] In particular, a firm:

(1) Should pay regard to its target market, including its likely level of financial capability;
(2) Should take account of what information the customer needs to understand the product or service, its purpose and the risks, and communicate information in a way that is clear, fair and not misleading;
(3) Should have in place systems and controls to manage effectively the risks posed by providing information to customers.

[23] In particularly a firm:

(1) In supplying information direct to the customer, must ensure that the information is communicated in a way which is clear, fair and not misleading;
(2) Should periodically review products whose performance may vary materially to check whether the product is continuing to meet the general needs of the target audience that it was designed for, or whether the product's performance will be significantly different from what the provider originally expected and communicated to the distributor or customer at the time of the sale. If this occurs, the provider should consider what action to take, such as whether and how to inform the customer of this (to the extent the customer could not reasonably have been aware) and of their option to seek advice, and whether to cease selling the product;
(3) Should communicate to the customer contractual 'breakpoints' such as the end of a long tie-in period that may have a material impact on a customer that the customer cannot reasonably be expected to recall or know about already;
(4) Should act fairly and promptly when handling claims or when paying out on a product that has been surrendered or reached maturity. In doing this, the provider should meet any reasonable customer expectations that it may have created with regard to the outcomes or how the process would be handled;
(5) Must establish, implement and maintain effective and transparent customer complaint-handling systems.

[24] In particular, a firm:

(1) Should have in place systems and controls to manage effectively the risks posed by financial promotions;
(2) In passing on a promotion created by a provider, must act with due skill, care and diligence. A firm will not contravene the financial promotions rules where it communicates a promotion produced by another person provided the firm takes reasonable care to establish that another firm has confirmed compliance with the relevant detailed rules, amongst other matters.

information to a customer before or at the point of sale.[25] Principles 2 and 6 are particularly relevant when advising on selection of a provider,[26] and Principles 3 and 6 in the area of post-sale responsibility.[27]

FSA's product intervention approach is coherent with the one drafted in the 2011 Treasury's consultation on the structure and powers of the new Financial Conduct Authority (FCA)[28] announcing that "FCA will have a fundamentally different approach to the one of the FSA in the way it intervenes to mitigate risk financial services.[29] The FCA will have a lower risk appetite for issues affecting a whole

---

[25] In particular, a firm:

(1) Should consider, when passing provider materials to customers, whether it understands the information provided;
(2) Should ask the provider to supply additional information or training where that seems necessary to understand the product or service adequately;
(3) Should not distribute the product or service if it does not understand it sufficiently, especially if it intends to provide advice;
(4) When providing information to another distributor in a distribution chain, should consider how the further distributor will use the information, such as whether it will be given to customers. Firms should consider what information the further distributor requires and the likely level of knowledge and understanding of the further distributor and what medium may suit it best for the transmission of information.

[26] In particular, a firm:

(1) Should consider the nature of the products or services offered by the provider and how they fit with the customer's needs and risk appetite;
(2) Should consider what impact the selection of a given provider could have on the customer in terms of charges or the financial strength of the provider, or possibly, where information is available to the distributor, how efficiently and reliably the provider will deal with the distributor or customer at the point of sale (or subsequently, such as when queries/complaints arise, claims are made, or a product reaches maturity).

[27] In particular, a firm:

(1) Should comply with any contractual obligation it has to the customer, for example to provide ongoing advice or periodic reviews. In connection with this, it should also consider its responsibility to maintain adequate systems and controls to deliver on such reviews;
(2) Should consider any implied or express representation it made (during meetings, correspondence or promotional material, for example). Where a customer has reasonable expectations based on the prior statements of a distributor, for example that performance will be monitored, the distributor should meet these expectations;
(3) Where involved in handling claims or paying out on a product that has been surrendered or reached maturity, should meet any reasonable expectations that the distributor has created in the customer's mind with regard to how the process would be handled;
(4) Must establish, implement and maintain effective and transparent customer complaint-handling systems;
(5) Should pass any communications received from customers (intended for or suited to providers to act upon) to providers in a timely and accurate way.

[28] HM Treasury, A new approach to financial regulation: building a stronger system, February 2011.

[29] The joint FSA and Office of Fair Trade document on Payment Protection Products, issued in November 2011, is in the same path, while FSA's guidance on Retail Product Development and

sector, sub-sector or type of product – it will be less prepared to see detriment actually occurring, instead seeking to act in a more preventative manner". As a result of this new approach, the FCA "will entail, for example, proactively intervening earlier in a product's life cycle, with greater scrutiny of firms' product design and product governance complementing the traditional focus on sales and marketing, and the disclosure of information".[30]

In conclusion, the UK experience shows that POG has been developed with reference to financial products, namely products maintaining the investment risk on the investor, requiring manufacturers to demonstrate the value for customer of the products they are designing. POG was already embedded in principles on business conduct, but regulatory intervention was deemed necessary to detail POG. Thus, business conduct switched from a principle-based regulation to a detailed-based regulation.[31]

POG aims at anticipating customer protection at the design stage for product marketing because it enables supervisory authorities to have a clearer picture of the businesses processes that are behind the products marketed to customers. A more structured design and marketing process, involving the board of directors and where company functions are constantly attentive to meeting customer needs and interests, should prevent the customer bias without intervention of supervisory authorities.

On the other hand, the early knowledge of the design process should facilitate the authorities to exercise their intervention powers in order to prevent or reduce detriments arising from products that are not developed in the best interest of the customers.[32] To this purpose, authorities need to be properly equipped with skilled staff in order to quickly understand the design of the products,[33] if the intervention powers to be exercised promptly.[34]

Finally, the concept of POG outlines that business conduct becomes a matter of firm's organization because the POG embeds the customer's protection in the organizational rules applying to manufacturer and distributors. Thus, firms are called to comply with internal procedures aiming at creating products that have a real value for the customers to which they will be offered, and not just a value for the shareholders, directors and senior management of the undertaking.

Governance—Structured Product Review, issued in March 2012, focus on the key issues of governance which arise in the development and marketing of structured products by applying FSA Handbook on "The Responsibilities of Providers and Distributors for the Fair Treatment of Customers" to these products.

[30] HM Treasury, A new approach to financial regulation: building a stronger system, February 2011, p. 69.

[31] In a broader perspective, see Marcacci (2017), pp. 305 ff.

[32] Ferran (2012), pp. 264 ff. See also: Tomic (2018), pp. 229–255; Busch (2017), pp. 409–420.

[33] P. Brandt, Product distribution round-up, in Compliance Officer Bulletin, April 2011, p. 8 noted "This is not to say that current supervisory staff are inadequate; however, it appears that what the FSA is proposing is a radical and challenging benchmark which requires a significant investment in resourcing levels, training and overall staff quality".

[34] About the genesis of product intervention, see Moloney (2012), pp. 186 ff.

2 The Transposition of the POG Into the IDD

POG rules were not included in the initial draft proposal of the IDD, which was issued by the European Commission in July 2012, and the introduction of POG for the insurance industry was not preceded by a specific activity of the European Commission, even in terms of cost/benefit analysis.

Notwithstanding this, the European Supervision Authorities (ESAs) adopted a Joint position on manufacturers' products oversight and governance processes in 2013, where the legal basis of EIOPA's involvement was founded (i) in the possibility that product governance provisions may be included in the Insurance Mediation Directive (IMD1) or any future legislative act replacing IMD1 and (ii) as part of the principle set forth by Recital 16 of Solvency II under which the main objective of insurance and reinsurance regulation and supervision is the "adequate protection of policyholders and beneficiaries". This, because such a principle is supplemented by additional requirements in Articles 41(1) and 41(6) of Solvency II, which include having effective systems of internal control and governance to provide for sound and prudent management of the business.[35]

Accordingly, the first public consultation on Guidelines for POG, which was launched by EIOPA in 2014, was only addressed to "manufacturers", i.e. an insurance undertaking that designs and brings to the market, products to be offered to consumers, as the legal basis of this regulatory intervention was founded in Solvency II.[36] "Distributors" fell within the scope of the Guidelines in the second public consultation in 2016, as the IDD was adopted in the meantime. It should be mentioned that, within the scope of the second public consultation in 2016, fall both insurance undertakings (which do not manufacture the insurance product) and insurance intermediaries, as according to the IDD provisions, the latter are also considered to be distributors of insurance products.

However, the issued Guidelines on POG were qualified by EIOPA as "preparatory", providing early guidance and supporting national authorities and market participants with the implementation of POG requirements in preparation for formal requirements provided for in IDD.[37] Article 25 of IDD sets POG rules forth and the European Commission is empowered to adopt delegated acts to further specify the principles set out in this Article, taking into account in a proportionate way the activities performed, the nature of the insurance products which were sold and the nature of the distributor. Thus, POG rules of the IDD are supplemented by

[35] See Joint Position of the European Supervisory Authorities on Manufacturers' Product Oversight & Governance Processes, at point 22. The Joint position is available at https://www.eba.europa.eu/documents/10180/15736/JC-2013-77+%28POG+-+Joint+Position%29.pdf.

[36] Consultation Paper a available at https://eiopa.europa.eu/Publications/Consultations/2014-10-27_EIOPA-BoS-14-150_POG_guidelines_rev.pdf.

[37] These Guidelines are available at https://eiopa.europa.eu/Pages/News/EIOPA-publishes-Preparatory-Guidelines-on-Product-Oversight-and-Governance.aspx.

Commission Delegated Regulation (EU) 2017/2358 of 21 September 2017, which is based on the Technical advice provided by the EIOPA in February 2017.[38]

The Commission Delegated Regulation specifies the criteria and practical details for the application of POG rules, affirming that these rules are mainly addressed at manufacturers of insurance products and oblige them to maintain, operate and review a POG policy in order to ensure on a continuous basis that all insurance products marketed are appropriate for their specific target market. Insurance distributors have to support this by operating product distribution arrangements to ensure that they have all the information needed to sell the product in line with the POG policy set by the manufacturer. Should be mentioned, whether an insurance distributor is qualified as the manufacturer of an insurance product, the insurance distributor has the corresponding obligations. Thus, POG rules are built around two players—manufacturer and distributor—as POG imposes separate duties for both of them. Nevertheless, general provisions are also set forth for both, whilst the same entity can play the role of manufacturer and distributor.

The Commission Delegated Regulation was adopted to complement the IDD. Article 25 of IDD is mainly a "copy and paste" of Article 16 of MiFID II.[39] The affinity between financial products and insurance-based investment products is evident,[40] while affinities with other insurance products do not seem obvious. Notwithstanding this, the same rules apply to all insurance products and are clearly borrowed from those applicable to financial products.[41] POG is therefore an example of the "Mifidization" of insurance regulation, which is the transposition—

[38] The Final report is available at https://eiopa.europa.eu/Publications/Reports/EIOPA%20Final_Report_on_IDD_Technical%20Advice.pdf.

[39] Recital No. 55 of IDD asserts: "In order to ensure that insurance products meet the needs of the target market, insurance undertakings and, in the Member States where insurance intermediaries manufacture insurance products for sale to customers, insurance intermediaries should maintain, operate and review a process for the approval of each insurance product. Where an insurance distributor advises on, or proposes, insurance products, which it does not manufacture, it should in any case be able to understand the characteristics and identified target market of those products. This Directive should not limit the variety and flexibility of the approaches which undertakings use to develop new products".

[40] Recital No 87 of MiFID II states "Investments that involve contracts of insurance are often made available to customers as potential alternatives or substitutes to financial instruments subject to this Directive. To deliver consistent protection for retail clients and ensure a level playing field between similar products, it is important that insurance-based investment products are subject to appropriate requirements".

[41] Recital No. 87 of MiFID II states "Whereas the investor protection requirements in this Directive should therefore be applied equally to those investments packaged under insurance contracts, their different market structures and product characteristics make it more appropriate that detailed requirements are set out in the ongoing review of Directive 2002/92/EC rather than setting them in this Directive. Future Union law regulating the activities of insurance intermediaries and insurance undertakings should thus appropriately ensure a consistent regulatory approach concerning the distribution of different financial products which satisfy similar investor needs and therefore raise comparable investor protection challenges".

sometimes uncritical—of the regulatory solutions adopted for financial products to the insurance ones.[42]

The conclusion is that MiFID II rules on POG as well as other rules also applicable to insurance-based investment products, e.g. the ones of the Regulation (EU) No 1286/2014 on Packaged Retail and Insurance-based Investment Product (PRIIP), will also be taken into account in the analysis carried out in the following paragraphs on POG rules applicable to insurance-based investment products.

3 Who Is the Manufacturer?

Manufacturers are the main recipients of POG rules. Both insurance undertakings and insurance intermediaries can qualify as manufacturers depending on the role they play in designing insurance products.[43]

IDD makes reference to design activity only, while EIOPA[44] does provide a description of such an activity.[45] The Joint Position of the ESAs' on Manufacturers' Product Oversight & Governance Processes, however, provides a definition of manufacturer "for the purpose of this Joint Position only", which makes reference to the development and issuance of a product or the modifications or the combinations of the products.[46] Furthermore, MiFID II includes "the creation, development, issuance and/or design" of financial instruments within the scope of POG. Thus, IDD should be interpreted as inclusive of all decision-making processes (designing and developing)[47] related to products that will be marketed or distributed to customers.

In the case of insurance undertaking playing a "passive" role or a non-exclusive role in the decision-making process, a distinction should be made whether the insurance undertaking has (i) outsourced the design activities or (ii) contributed to the design of the product with another entity.

Manufacturers designating a third party to design products on their behalf shall remain fully responsible for compliance with the product approval process (Article

[42] Cousy (2009), pp. 245–254; Marano (2017b), pp. 219–234; Marano (2017a), and Cousy (2017), pp. 10 ff. and 45 ff.

[43] See Article 25(1) of IDD.

[44] See Technical Advice on possible delegated Acts concerning the Insurance Distribution Directive, EIOPA-17-048 (https://eiopa.europa.eu/Publications/Consultations/EIOPA%20Technical%20Advice%20on%20the%20IDD.pdf).

[45] In particular, an insurance intermediary shall be considered as a manufacturer: "if the insurance intermediary has a decision-making role in designing and developing an insurance product for the market". Furthermore, the manufacturing activity is defined by reference to activities/practices (e.g. handling customer—claims, tailor made contracts which are designed at the request of a customer to meet the individual demands and needs of that customer), that cannot qualify as manufacturing and that suffice for a distributor to be characterised as a manufacturer.

[46] See Joint Position of the ESAs' on Manufacturers' Product Oversight & Governance Processes, 2013, cit., at p. 2, point 6.

[47] See article 3(1) of the Commission Delegated regulation.

4(5) of Commission Delegated Regulation). The outsourcing to an entity other than an insurance intermediary falls outside the scope of the co-manufacturer's rule because Article 25(1) of IDD prevents this entity to be likely to be regarded as manufacturer. Thus, insurance undertaking will be solely responsible for the outsourced activity,[48] and for compliance with the product approval process. This clarification is relevant in the case of insurance-based investment products because Regulation (EU) No 1286/2014 on Packaged Retail and Insurance-based Investment Product (PRIIP) provides a definition of PRIIPs manufacturer,[49] which shall draw up for that product a key information document (KID) according to the requirements of that Regulation and shall publish the document on its website. Thus, if an insurance undertaking designates a third party (a PRIIP manufacturer) to design insurance products, the latter can be an entity falling outside the scope of POG, when such an entity is not an insurance intermediary. In this case, the insurance undertaking shall be the one entity to have to comply with POG rules because of the outsourcing of the manufacturer of an insurance-based investment product to an entity that cannot be considered as co-manufacturer.

On the other hand, if an insurance intermediary and an insurance undertaking are both manufacturers within the meaning of Article 2 of Commission Delegated Regulation,[50] they are qualified as co-manufacturers. If an insurance intermediary is involved in the designing process of insurance products, a decision-making role shall be assumed where insurance intermediaries autonomously determine the essential features and main elements of an insurance product, including its coverage, price, costs, risk, target market and compensation and guarantee rights, which are not substantially modified by the insurance undertaking providing coverage for the insurance product.[51] The above list of essential features and main elements of an insurance product should be considered as exhaustive of the conditions which must be satisfied in the evaluation of the role played in the decision-making process. They express, on the whole, a position of supremacy on insurance undertaking; therefore insurance intermediary should meet these conditions all together to be considered as co-manufacturer. If so, co-manufacturers shall sign a written agreement which specifies their collaboration to comply with the requirements for manufacturers referred to in Article 25(1) of IDD, the procedures through which they shall agree on the

---

[48] See Article 49(1) of Solvency II.

[49] Article 4(4) sets forth that PRIIPs manufacturer is: (i) any entity that manufactures PRIIPs, or (ii) any entity that makes changes to an existing PRIIP including, but not limited to, altering its risk and regard profile or the costs associated with an investment in PRIIPs.

[50] Article 2 sets forth "This Regulation shall apply to insurance undertakings and to insurance intermediaries that manufacture insurance products that are offered for sale to customers ('manufacturers') (…)". Furthermore, Article 3(4) sets forth "An insurance intermediary and an insurance undertaking that are both manufacturers within the meaning of Article 2 of this Delegated Regulation, shall sign a written agreement which specifies their collaboration to comply with the requirements for manufacturers referred to in Article 25(1) of Directive (EU) 2016/97, the procedures through which they shall agree on the identification of the target market and their respective roles in the product approval process."

[51] See Article 3(2) of Commission Delegated Regulation.

identification of the target market and their respective roles in the product approval process.[52] In addition, if the insurance intermediary involved in the decision-making process also falls within the scope of MiFID II, only one target market needs to be identified,[53] and this identification shall comply with the IDD (see par. 9 below).

IDD does not rule out that the co-manufacturing is done by two insurance undertakings without involving an insurance intermediary.

This is the case of a life insurance product combining two different classes, e.g. unit-linked and assurance on survival to a stipulated age or on earlier death, each of them managed by one of the two insurance undertakings, whilst the product is distributed through the distribution channel selected by one of the undertakings. The foregoing case is likely when the two undertakings are based in different countries and the product is distributed in one of them. It may happen that the parent company designs a product and merely asks the subsidiary established in another Member State to distribute it in the latter State. This case should also be within the scope of the co-manufacturing rules because applying these rules a double need would be met. The insurance undertaking based in the country where product is distributed (host country) should be able to better perform both the target market/scenario analyses and the monitoring on the distribution channel. Moreover, the supervisory authority of the host country is a position to exercise the early intervention power on the insurance undertaking based in the host country and, therefore, before product is brought to the market or distributed to customers in that country.

POG rules of IDD do not mention insurance undertakings and insurance intermediaries based in a third country and carrying out their businesses in the EU Member States, whilst the Articles 9 and 10 of Commission Delegated Directive (EU) 2017/593 of 7 April 2016 supplementing MiFID II could be a useful reference for the Member States as regulation on financial products deals with this issue. The IDD shall not affect a Member State's law in respect of insurance and reinsurance distribution activities pursued by insurance and reinsurance undertakings or intermediaries established in a third country and operating on its territory, provided that equal treatment is guaranteed to all persons carrying out insurance and reinsurance distribution activities on that market.[54] The principle of equal treatment therefore requires national legislation to apply POG rules to products marketed in the country without taking into account the nationality of the manufacturer. Thus, the same principle can be recalled *a fortiori* in the case of activities carried out by insurance entities based in third countries.

[52] See Article 3(4) of Commission Delegated Regulation.

[53] See Article 9(9) of Commission Delegated Directive (EU) 2017/593 of 7 April 2016 supplementing MiFID II.

[54] See Article 1(6) of IDD.

4 The Product Approval Process

POG rules call manufacturers for a 'product approval process' covering the maintenance, operation and review of product oversight and governance arrangements for insurance products and for significant adaptations to existing insurance products before those products are brought to the market or distributed to customers, as well as rules for product distribution arrangements for those insurance products. The product approval process shall contain measures and procedures for designing, monitoring, reviewing and distributing insurance products, as well as for corrective action for insurance products that are detrimental to customers (Article 4). The product approval process shall be set out in a written document ("product oversight and governance policy"), which shall be made available to the relevant staff, and manufacturers shall regularly review their product approval process to ensure that the process is still valid and up to date, and they shall amend the product approval process where necessary (Article 4). The relevant actions, which are taken by manufacturers in relation to their product approval process, shall be duly documented, kept for audit purposes and made available to the competent authorities upon request (Article 9).

Some aspects of the product approval process need to be thoroughly investigated.

(i) The product approval process also applies to existing insurance products, in case of significant adaptations.

   Two conditions must be fulfilled in this regard and they refer to time and significance of adaptations. The starting date of application of the Commission Delegated Regulation should be aligned with the entry into application of the national measures transposing the IDD (Recital No.13 and Article 13 of the Commission Delegated Regulation). Thus, the products within the scope of POG rules are those still marketed at that time, even though they were designed before. With reference to the other condition, i.e. the significance of adaptations, the evaluation has to be done irrespective to the type of product and of the requirements applicable at the point of sale (see Recital No.1). POG rules do not identify the conditions for determining when adaptation has to be considered relevant and, therefore, the issue is referred back to the national level. We can expect the adaptation to be considered as relevant, at least, whenever it constitutes a novation of the contract for the national laws.

(ii) The product approval process shall contain measures and procedures for corrective actions.

   POG rules expressly apply only to new products as well as existing products in the case of significant adaptations concerning products marketed *after* such adaptations.[55] Thus, corrective actions should only cover these products

[55] EIOPA was requested to introduce such a limit in the Technical advice to the European Commission. However EIOPA decided to be silent on this issue asserting that it was not in EIOPA's remit to address this question as this is a legal question falling in the competence of the European

excluding those marketed *before* the entry into force of POG, which have not been subject to significant adaptations.[56] However, if national insurance law allows for unilateral amendments to ongoing contracts and in favour of policyholders, corrective actions should also cover products marketed before the POG in order to avoid lawsuits for breach of equal treatment or to support the existence of discrimination between policyholders.

(iii) The corrective actions refer to insurance products that are detrimental to customers.

The regulatory framework only refers to customer detriment. The detriment can arise from any event embedded in the insurance-based investment product, including its features. Manufacturers are requested to review the insurance products taking into account "any event that could materially affect the potential risk to the identified target market" (Article 25 (1)(4) of IDD). Thus, the product approval process shall ensure that the design of insurance products: (i) takes into account the objectives, interests and characteristics of customers; (ii) does not adversely affect customers; (iii) prevents or mitigates customer detriment.[57]

The IDD makes no reference to market integrity or to the orderly functioning or to the stability of financial markets, unlike the financial instruments.[58] Nevertheless, the IDD calls Member States to ensure that competent authorities monitor the market and EIOPA may facilitate and coordinate such monitoring (see Article 1 (5)). In addition, market monitoring and product intervention powers have been introduced by the Regulation (EU) No 1286/2014 on key information documents for packaged retail and insurance-based investment products (PRIIPs).

EIOPA or competent national authority may prohibit or restrict, in the Union or in/from the Member State, the marketing, distribution or sale of insurance-based investment products if a list of conditions is fulfilled including where "the proposed action addresses a significant investor protection concern or a threat to the orderly functioning and integrity of financial markets or to the stability of the whole or part of the financial system" in the Union or within at least one Member State.[59] POG rules were introduced to anticipate the customer's protection by increasing the scrutiny of the authorities over the products. The timely pursuit of these tasks requires that the authorities can ascertain

---

Commission and, ultimately, in the competence of the EU Court of Justice (see Technical advice, at p. 8).

[56] EIOPA does generally not expect insurance undertakings to change existing contracts, in particular, in cases where this would contradict rules of national law. Depending on market developments, EIOPA may issue further guidance on this issue to explain best practices that have been developed by market participants (see Technical advice, p. 14).

[57] See Article 4(3) of Commission Delegated Regulation.

[58] See Article 9(2)(4) of Commission Delegated Directive (EU) 2017/593 of 7 April 2016 supplementing MiFID II.

[59] See Articles 16(2) (a) and 17(2) (a).

whether the above conditions are met also by evaluating the analysis carried out on such profiles by manufacturers. Thus, it is likely that authorities refer to these somewhat vague conditions when they fulfil the above-mentioned duties.

In conclusion, manufacturers should ensure that the design of the insurance-based investment products does not lead to problems with market integrity as well as they have to consider whether the product may represent a threat to the orderly functioning or to the stability of financial markets.

(iv) The measures and procedures for designing, monitoring, reviewing and distributing insurance products should be chosen and applied in a proportionate and appropriate manner.

The reference to proportionality means that those measures should be relatively simple for straightforward and non-complex products that are compatible with the needs and characteristics of the mass retail market. In the case of more complex products with a higher risk of consumer detriment, more exact measures should be required (Recital No.2) while reference to complex product includes insurance-based investment products not covered by Article 30(3) of IDD. In the technical advice, EIOPA suggested to do not differentiate between or to exempt specific products, specific services (e.g. non-advised sales) or services for specific customers (professional customers). The European Commission allows differentiating between products based on the level of their complexity, while proportionality does not refer to the "quality" of the target market and the service provided at the point of sale because they should be embedded into the product—lower or higher—complexity.

(v) The product approval process shall be set out in a written document ("product oversight and governance policy"), which shall be made available to the relevant staff.

This policy will enable competent authorities to supervise and assess whether the regulated entities comply with the regulatory requirements on POG, thus promoting customer's protection in the end.[60] This is to say that such a policy is part of the system of governance of insurance undertakings that provides for sound and prudent management of their business. Thus, the written policy shall be the subject to prior approval by the administrative, management or supervisory body of the manufacturer or equivalent structure (in the case of two tier systems)[61] as well as any material changes.[62] Moreover, the administrative, management or supervisory body of the manufacturer or equivalent structure: (i) is ultimately responsible for the establishment, subsequent reviews and continued compliance of the POG arrangements, and (ii) ensures that the POG arrangements are appropriately designed and implemented into the governing structures of the manufacturer.[63]

[60] See EIOPA, Final Report on Consultation Paper n. 16/006 on Technical Advice on possible delegated acts concerning the Insurance Distribution Directive, February 2017, p. 34.

[61] See Article 41(3)(2) of Solvency II.

[62] See EIOPA, Final Report on Consultation Paper n. 16/006, cit., p. 35.

[63] See EIOPA, Final Report, cit., p. 35.

The Commission Delegated Regulation, however, merely states "The manufacturers' body *or* structure responsible for the manufacturing of insurance products shall: (a) endorse and be ultimately responsible for establishing, implementing and reviewing the product approval process; (b) continuously verify internal compliance with that process" (see Article 4(4)). This standard is not consistent with the considerations before exposed. It seems to allow the POG to be entirely governed by structures that are subjected to the administrative, management or supervisory body of the manufacturer, as an alternative to manufactures' body. POG rules on insurance products would therefore be less stringent than those introduced for financial products in identifying the body responsible for setting up and monitoring the POG.

Commission Delegated Directive (EU) 2017/593 of 7 April 2016 supplementing MiFID II requires investment firms to ensure that (i) the management body has effective control over the firm's product governance process[64] and (ii) the compliance reports to the management body systematically include information about the financial instruments manufactured by the firm, including information on the distribution strategy (see Article 9(6)).[65] An interpretation consistent with the provision for financial products is, therefore, to state that the manufacturer's board of directors is empowered of the policy approval and it is regularly updated on its execution by the system of internal control,[66] while a corporate structure or unit will be responsible for overseeing and managing the entire product design and marketing including any changes and remedial actions. In any case, the system of internal control shall have access to this policy in order to carry out assessments including compliance, which are mandatory according to Solvency II.

The product oversight and governance policy is made available to the relevant staff, but POG rules neither provides a definition of relevant staff nor identifies the structure responsible for performing that task. Relevant staff includes the manufacturer's body or structure responsible for the manufacturing of insurance products.[67] Furthermore, it should include the staff involved in designing and manufacturing insurance products, in line with the requirement for manufacturers to appoint people

[64] In addition, EBA Guidelines on product oversight and governance arrangements for retail banking products, issued in March 2016, require the manufacturer's management body to endorse the establishment of the arrangements and subsequent reviews in order to ensure that product oversight and governance arrangements are an integral part of its governance, risk management and internal control framework (see Guideline No. 2).

[65] Article 9(7) sets forth "Member States shall require investment firms to ensure that the compliance function monitors the development and periodic review of product governance arrangements in order to detect any risk of failure by the firm to comply with the obligations set out in this Article".

[66] See EBA Guidelines, cit, which identify senior management, with support from representatives of the manufacturer's compliance and risk management functions, as responsible for continued internal compliance with the product oversight and governance arrangements. Thus, "They should periodically check that the product oversight and governance arrangements are still appropriate and continue to meet the objectives as set out in Guideline 1.1 above, and should propose to the management body that the arrangements be amended if this is no longer the case" (see Guideline No. 2).

[67] See Article 4(4) of Commission Delegated Regulation.

who have the necessary skills, knowledge and expertise to properly understand the insurance products sold and the interests, objectives and characteristics of the customers belonging to the target market.[68] Manufacturers' management who are responsible, and accountable to the management body, for the day-to-day management of the institution shall be charged of the task to make available the policy to the relevant staff.[69]

5 Product Designing

5.1 Target Market

Articles 5 and 6 of Commission Delegated Regulation deal with the target market and product testing.

With reference to the target market, manufacturers shall only design and market insurance products that are compatible with the needs, characteristics and objectives of the customers belonging to the target market. The product approval process shall, for each insurance product, identify the target market at a sufficiently granular level, taking into account the characteristics, risk profile, complexity and nature of the insurance product.

Reference to the target market raises at least the three following issues.

(i) The difference between the target market for manufacturers and the assessment at the point of sale.

The identification of the target market has to be distinguished from the individual assessment, which is made by the insurance distributor at the point of sale, whether an insurance product is consistent with the demands and needs, and in case of insurance-based investment products, whether the insurance product is suitable and appropriate for the individual customer (see Article 30 of IDD). Thus, a proper identification of the target market concerns the duties and responsibilities of the manufacturer, while the distributor is solely or mainly—depending on national law—responsible for the assessment of customers at the point of sale.

(ii) The elements to be considered for the target market.

When assessing whether an insurance product is compatible with a target market, manufacturers shall take into account the level of information available to the customers belonging to that target market and their financial literacy.

The generic reference to the level of information should be integrated with more detailed criteria. EIOPA advised to take into account criteria such as the demands and needs, and, where relevant with regard to the complexity and

---

[68] See Article 5(4) of Commission Delegated Regulation.

[69] See Guideline No 2.4 issued by EBA, cit., p. 10.

nature of the product, the knowledge and experience in the investment field, financial situation, the investment objectives and the financial literacy of the typical customer of the target market.[70] Moreover, EIOPA listed a number of criteria for all insurance products,[71] while other criteria are additional for the insurance-based investment products.[72]

The criteria advised for insurance-based investment products are quite in line with the list of five categories provided in the Guidelines on POG issued by ESMA.[73] This authority also acknowledges that "manufacturers usually don't have direct client contact and, therefore, their target market identification may be based *inter alia* on their theoretical knowledge and experience of the product"[74]; while EIOPA states "The level of knowledge and understanding of the product could also include experience of targeted consumers with similar products".[75]

(iii) The skills of the staff involved in designing and manufacturing insurance products.

Together with elements related to the customers, the Commission Delegated Regulation calls manufacturers to ensure that staff involved in designing and manufacturing insurance products have the necessary skills, knowledge and expertise to properly understand the insurance products sold and the interests, objectives and characteristics of the customers belonging to the target market.

---

[70] See EIOPA, Final Report on Consultation Paper n. 16/006, cit., p. 38.

[71] EIOPA, Final Report, cit., p. 38 makes reference to (i) the level of the target market's knowledge and understanding of the complexity of the product and (ii) the objectives, demands and needs of the customers belonging to the target market.

[72] EIOPA, Final Report, cit., p. 38 f. quotes: (i) the age of the customers belonging to target market; (ii) the occupational situation of the customers belonging the target market; (iii) the level of risk tolerance of the customers belonging the target market; (iv) the financial situation of the customers belonging the target market; (v) the financial and non-financial objectives and investment horizon of the customers belonging the target market.

In addition, these criteria are detailed by EIOPA in the Q&A on Regulation, (EU) 2017-2358, published on the 16th July 2018. Thus, the description of the target market could include the age (category) of the customers belonging to target market, the personal household and dependents situation of the customers belonging to the target market, the occupational situation and the relevant occupational pension and insurance scheme of the customers belonging the target market, the level of risk tolerance of the customers belonging the target market, the financial situation of the customers belonging the target market, the financial and non-financial objectives and investment horizon of the customers belonging to the target market. Further criteria to define the target market may also include the pay-out characteristics of the IBIP (e.g. life long payments, lump sum or insurance coverage for surviving spouse in case of death), the tax deductibility for premiums, the need for capital guarantees, natural premiums depending on age, and a possible cut-off coverage at a certain age.

[73] ESMA, Final Report, Guidelines on MiFID II product governance requirements, June 2017, p. 34.

[74] ESMA, Final Report, cit., p. 34.

[75] EIOPA, Final Report, cit., p. 39.

These rules comply with the general principle of good governance stated in Article 258(1)(e) of Commission Delegated Regulation (EU) No 2015/35 under Solvency II requesting insurance undertaking to employ personnel with the skills, knowledge and expertise necessary to carry out the responsibilities allocated to them properly, and EIOPA called, as necessary, the staff involved in designing products to receive, for instance, appropriate professional training to understand the characteristics and risks of the relevant products and the interests, objectives and characteristics of the target market.[76]

5.2 *Product Testing*

An essential element of the product design process is product testing. Article 6 of Commission Delegated Regulation sets forth that manufacturers shall test their insurance products appropriately, including scenario analyses where relevant, before bringing that product to the market or significantly adapting it, or in case the target market has significantly changed. That product testing shall assess whether the insurance product over its lifetime meets the identified needs, objectives and characteristics of the target market. Manufacturers shall test their insurance products in a qualitative manner and, depending on the type and nature of the insurance product and the related risk of detriment to customers, quantitative manner.

POG rules do not prescribe specific testing methods to be applied, but give a broad discretion to market participants to choose the appropriate form and method of product testing.[77] Nevertheless, the scenario analysis is always requested for insurance-based investment products,[78] even though in a range proportionated to the complexity of the product, its risks and relevance of external factors with respect the product performance.[79]

Keeping in mind the objectives of the defined target market, EIOPA advised that the assessment could imply considering a list of questions specifically for insurance-based investment products, which are of an explanatory and exemplary nature only.[80] Thus, such list does not prevent to make also reference to the provisions set

---

[76] EIOPA, Final Report on Consultation Paper n. 16/006, cit., p. 39. See also EIOPA, Q&A on Regulation, (EU) 2017-2358.

[77] EIOPA, Final Report, cit., p. 39.

[78] EIOPA, Q&A on Regulation, (EU) 2017-2358 states "EIOPA considers it important that product testing of insurance-based investment products should always include scenario analysis. Events like declining stock prices should be identified and the effect on the outcomes of the product should be analyzed. In addition, the costs structure should be analyzed in light of such events and the connection with the needs and objectives of the target market. In general, costs always should be reasonable and transparent".

[79] EIOPA, Final Report, cit., p. 39 f.

[80] Here is the list of questions:

– What would happen to the risk and reward profile of the product following changes to the value and liquidity of underlying assets?

forth by the Article 9 of Commission Delegated Directive (EU) 2017/593 of 7 April 2016 supplementing MiFID II, including the consideration of the charging structure proposed for the insurance-based investment products.[81]

The scenario analysis does not necessarily coincide with what the manufacturer of an insurance-based investment product is required to produce in the Key Information Document (KID), which also contains information on the risk and reward profile of the product. We have already pointed out that manufacturer of PRIIPs can be an entity other than insurance undertaking or insurance intermediaries. Thus, the rules governing this manufacturer are different from those applicable under POG. EIOPA outlined that "Performance scenarios expected to be presented in the KID and the range of scenarios used for testing the product may present similarities; however, may not necessarily be identical".[82]

Manufacturers need to define the level of complexity of the product in order to determine whether they should be used, in addition to qualitative criteria, quantitative criteria. Some of the quantitative criteria are used in the product's design, such as scenario analyses for insurance-based investment products. Thus, it is reasonable they are also used for testing. In line with the purpose of the testing phase, tests should focus on customer satisfaction by demonstrating that the product is able to meet interests and needs of the target market.

In addition, manufacturers will have to define the process to be followed for conducting the tests. In particular, they have to identify the criteria for passing the test as well as the staff who has to perform the testing. The criteria should be predetermined, so as to avoid manipulations of the results. For this reason, manufactures should appoint staff for testing other than product developers thus avoiding a self-referential process. The principle of proportionality also applies in this case; therefore, for manufacturers who cannot distinguish the development and test structures, the basic requirement is that the test methodology and the related activities are formalized and that at least the system of internal control receives evidence before approval of the product.

- How is the risk/reward profile of the product balanced, taking into account the cost structure of the product?
- When a product benefits from a certain tax environment or other condition; what happens if these conditions change?
- What are the terms and conditions, and how do they affect the outcome of the product?
- What will happen when the manufacturer faces financial difficulties?
- What will happen if the customer terminates the contract early?

[81] See Article 9(12) which requests to consider: (a) financial instrument's costs and charges are compatible with the needs, objectives and characteristics of the target market; (b) charges do not undermine the financial instruments return expectations, such as where the costs or charges equal, exceed or remove almost all the expected tax advantages linked to a financial instruments and (c) the charging structure of the financial instrument is appropriately transparent for the target market, such as that it does not disguise charges or is too complex to understand.

[82] EIOPA, Final Report on Consultation Paper n. 16/006, cit., p. 41, states: "Performance scenarios are disclosed to customers whereas scenarios for testing the products cover a large range of factors that determine the performance of the product".

Product testing is relevant for the responsibilities. Article 6(2) of Commission Delegated Regulation sets forth that manufacturers shall not bring insurance products to the market if the results of the product testing show that the products do not meet the identified needs, objectives and characteristics of the target market. The liability arises not only whether the results of the product testing show that the products do not meet the purposes above and the product is still marketed, but also if the product testing is manipulated to show a fictitious result and, therefore, only apparently favourable to the customer.

6 Product Monitoring and Review, Remedial Actions

Article 7 of Commission Delegated Regulation details the product monitoring and review that was introduced by Article 25(4) of IDD. Manufacturers shall continuously monitor and regularly review insurance products they have brought to the market, to identify events that could materially affect the main features, the risk coverage or the guarantees of those products. They shall assess whether the insurance products remain consistent with the needs, characteristics and objectives of the identified target market and whether those products are distributed to the target market or they are reaching customers outside the target market.

EIOPA outlined that product monitoring is of a permanent nature and it requires manufacturers to remain alert to crucial events that would substantially affect the main features, the risk coverage and the guarantees of the products, e.g. the potential risk or return expectations.[83] However, monitoring must also be guided by the principle of proportionality with respect to the size, scope, contractual duration and complexity of the products, both regarding the monitoring frequency and the Key Performance Indicator (KPI) to be monitored.

Product review takes place instead periodically as determined by manufactures, thereby taking into account the size, scale, contractual duration and complexity of the insurance products, their respective distribution channels, and any relevant external factors such as changes to the applicable legal rules, technological developments, or changes to the market situation (see Article 7 of the Commission Delegated Regulation).

In conclusion, from an organizational point of view, the manufacturers must set up an alert system defining a process under which the business units monitoring certain information will report to the monitoring managers the occurrence of alert situations.

EIOPA stated the importance that the manufacturer and the distributor coordinate their reviews and should aim to have similar frequencies of reviews. Manufacturers should consider: (i) what information they need to review a product and (ii) what information they already have. If they need additional information from distributors, they can choose how to gather that information and from which

[83] EIOPA, Final Report on Consultation Paper n. 16/006, cit., p. 41.

distributors.[84] Also this request to manufacturers should be evaluated in line with the principle of proportionality taking into account the distribution channels. In fact, the coordination of the frequencies is reasonable with tied distributors, whilst can be disproportionate with multi-tied and independent distributors because the latter have distribution agreements with several manufacturers.

Depending on the findings of the product monitoring and product review, the manufacturer may be obliged to take appropriate action to mitigate the situation and prevent further occurrences of the detrimental event.

POG rules do not specify the remedial actions the manufacturers are supposed to take. Article 7 merely imposes manufacturers to promptly inform concerned insurance distributors and customers about the remedial action taken. Although the manufacturers will adopt remedial actions in accordance to national laws, EIOPA might issue further guidance on this issue to explain the best practices that have been developed by market participants. In the meantime, EIOPA stated as a general principle, and, in accordance with national legal framework, the manufacturer can only make changes to the product that are consistent with the interests, objectives and characteristics of the already existing target market and these changes do not have an adverse impact on the customer to which the product has been sold already.[85]

In addition, EIOPA considers manufacturers and distributors should take appropriate action when they become aware of an event that could materially affect the potential expectations regarding product guarantees and, when such an event occurs, they should take appropriate action on a case-by-case basis.[86] To this purpose, EIOPA identified a not exhaustive list of actions.[87] Thus, such list can be supplemented with the changing the insurance-based investment product to avoid unfair contract terms, as mentioned in Article 9(15)(d) of Commission Delegated Directive (EU) 2017/593 of 7 April 2016 supplementing MiFID II.

Finally, manufacturers have to make product monitoring and review, as well as to take remedial actions, during the product lifetime. EIOPA outlined that the product lifetime is understood as capturing the entire life cycle of a product, which begins at the moment when the product is being designed and only finishes once there is no product left on the market. It covers situations when the product is no longer being sold, but there are still customers who own the product. The end of the life cycle of the product is reached only when the last product has been withdrawn from the market.[88]

---

[84] EIOPA, Final Report on Consultation Paper n. 16/006, cit., p. 41.

[85] EIOPA, Final Report, cit., p. 43.

[86] EIOPA, Final Report, cit., p. 42.

[87] EIOPA, Final Report, cit., p. 42 lists: (i) the provision of any relevant information on the event and its consequences on the product to the customer, or the distributors of the product if the manufacturer does not offer directly the product to the customer; (ii) changing the product approval process; (iii) changing the product; (iv) proposing a new product to the customer; (v) changing the target market; (vi) stopping further issuance of the product; (vii) contacting the distributor to discuss a modification of the distribution process; (viii) terminating the relationship with the distributor; (ix) informing the relevant competent authority; (x) or informing the customer.

[88] EIOPA, Final Report, cit., p. 42.

7 The Products with Environmental or Social Objectives

The ESAs provided technical advice in July 2017,[89] in order to assist the Commission on the possible content of the delegated acts on the procedures used to establish whether a PRIIP targets specific environmental or social objectives ("EOS-PRIIPs" socially responsible investment funds), under Regulation (EU) No 1286/2014.[90]

The European Commission asked Joint Committee to give advice in relation to the details of the internal product governance procedures PRIIPs manufacturers put in place. This should include consideration of what processes, systems and controls would be appropriate to ensure such internal product governance procedures are followed and validated. To this purpose, the European Commission has identified three process steps for determining whether PRIIPs manufacturers have appropriate governance systems in place to ensure the disclosed environmental or social objectives are met, and invited the Joint Committee to consider these steps. One of these steps refers to the development and operation of processes, systems and controls to ensure that the investment strategy is properly implemented and adhered to over time. This could include regular reviews to ensure assets remain in line with the investment strategy, periodic reviews and reporting lines to responsible senior management.

The advice provided by the Joint Committee has not identified new obligation on this step relying on existing sectorial product governance and oversight measures.

This conclusion is based on the analysis *inter alia* of the Article 25 of IDD, and of Articles 41, 44 and 132(2) of Solvency II, which led the Joint Committee to state that the targeting of environmental or social objectives as part of the investment objectives and strategy of a PRIIP, and relative disclosure will have the consequence that these objectives would need to be integrated into the normal oversight, governance and monitoring activities of the PRIIP manufacturer in view of the PRIIPs they offer.

Criticisms from the associations of consumers to the conclusion above are based on the following arguments.

---

[89] See Joint Technical Advice, July, 2017, which is available at https://esas-joint-committee.europa.eu/Publications/Technical%20Advice/Joint%20Technical%20Advice%20on%20the%20PRIIPs%20with%20environmental%20or%20social%20objectives.pdf.

[90] Article 8(3)(c) of Regulation (EU) No 1286/2014 requires a section of the Key Information Document (KID) entitled 'What is this product?' to outline the nature and main features of the PRIIP. Under point (ii) this shall include:

> Its objectives and the means for achieving them, in particular whether the objectives are achieved by means of direct or indirect exposure to the underlying investment assets, including a description of the underlying instruments or reference values, including a specification of the markets the PRIIP invests in, *including, where applicable, specific environmental or social objectives targeted by the product*, as well as how the return is determined.

Investors will not have any information on whether the provider has met its investment objectives or not and by how much: the provider only has to disclose these objectives "and how these will be achieved". Moreover, the ESAs seem therefore to assume that these objectives will be achieved, and that providers just have to review internally "the progress made in achieving the specified and disclosed objectives".[91] However, a recent research would demonstrate on the contrary that some "EOS PRIIPS" not only massively failed to achieve their investment objectives over the long term, but also failed to disclose this important warning to investors.[92] Such a warning is required by the MiFID Directives (see Article 27(2) of the MiFID I implementation directive and article 44(2) of MiFID II delegated regulation (EU) 2017/565 of 25 April 2016), but seems omitted in the most relevant information document: the KID.[93]

The criticisms are not fully shared.

The labelling of these products as EOS-PRIIPs is an issue other than information to customers. A more stringent regulation on the classification of a product as EOS-PRIIP as well as the management and disclosure of the related risks, it is agreeable to protect customer who wish to invest in these products.

Failure to achieve the objectives of the EOS-PRIIPs is an event, however, that is likely to affect the potential expectations regarding the product and it should be assessed as detrimental to customer. Thus, the manufacturer is under the obligation to monitor and review the product and to adopt remedial actions in order to avoid the detriment for both current customers and *a fortiori* potential customers, whilst the "open list" of remedial actions should be able to neutralize the risks reported by consumer associations.

This conclusion is in line with the European Parliament Resolution of 29 May 2018 on sustainable finance (2018/2007(INI)), which calls for common guidelines in order to harmonise the definition of ESG factors and their introduction in all new and revised legislation (see point 10); calls on the Commission to deliver a delegated act to specify the details of the procedures used to establish whether a packaged retail- and insurance-based investment product targets specific environmental or social objectives (see point 11); suggests that the Commission establishes a binding and proportionate labelling system for institutions offering retail bank accounts, investment funds, insurance and financial products, indicating the extent to which underlying assets are in conformity with the Paris Agreement and ESG goals (see point 20); emphasises that the identification, management and disclosure of ESG

---

[91] See Better Finance, Press release, ESAs advise on PRIIPS with Environmental or Social Objectives, which is available at http://betterfinance.eu/fileadmin/user_upload/documents/Position_Papers/Financial_Markets_Infrastructure/en/ESAs_advise_on_PRIIPS_with_environmental_or_social_objectives_01.pdf.

[92] See Better Finance helps investors identify potential falsely active funds ("closet indexers"), and asks regulators to investigate further, which is available at http://betterfinance.eu/fileadmin/user_upload/documents/Press_Releases/en/Other_investors/EN_-_Press_Release_and_Annexes_2_3_-Better_Finance_replication_of_ESMA_study_on_Closet_Indexing.pdf.

[93] Better Finance, Press release, cit.

risks are integral parts of consumer protection and financial stability and should thus fall under the mandate and supervisory duties of the ESAs (see point 38).

The Commission published amended IDD Delegated Act integrating Environmental, Social and Governance (ESG) considerations and preferences into investment advice for insurance-based investment products on 4 January 2019. The proposed amendments are in line with the European Parliament Resolution. They provide a definition of the ESG and require insurance intermediaries and insurance undertakings providing advice on insurance-based investment products (*i*) to collect the ESG preferences expressed by the customer and (*ii*) to explain in the suitability statement provided to the customer how the recommendation takes into account the ESG preferences expressed by the customer.

8 The Distribution Channels

Manufacturers have duties of properly selecting, informing and monitoring distribution channels, while distributors have to cooperate with manufacturers in monitoring the distribution of the insurance products to the identified target market, and they can set up or apply a specific distribution strategy. The co-operation between manufacturers and distributors has to be formalized in the product distribution arrangements.

Article 8 of Commission Delegated Regulation deals with distribution channels and sets forth that manufacturers shall carefully select distribution channels that are appropriate for the target market, thereby taking into account the particular characteristics of the relevant insurance products. EIOPA outlined the manufacturers need to select insurance distributors that have the necessary knowledge, expertise and competence to understand the product features and the characteristics of the identified target market, correctly place the product in the market and give the appropriate information to customers.[94]

The reference to an appropriate selection of the distribution channel should also allow selection within the distribution channel depending on the characteristics of the product to be marketed as well as the target market. Some business units or branches of a bank may have customers and sales people who are more suited to that product than other branches of the same bank; some brokers or agents may have a specific background that allow them to distribute a complex insurance-based investment product, while other brokers or agents are more appropriate with non-complex insurance-based investment product. Thus, in the selection of the distribution channel, a generic evaluation of the type of distributor (e.g. bank, agent, broker) it is not sufficient. The manufacturer must ascertain that the people who actually distribute the product are not only aware of its characteristics and of the target market, but also have the skills to distribute it correctly, or must commit to training such people properly.

[94] EIOPA, Final Report on Consultation Paper n. 16/006, cit., p. 43.

The selected distribution channel has to get all appropriate information on the insurance products and the product approval process, including the identified target market of the insurance product, in order to understand both of them (see Article 25(1)(5) and (6) of IDD).

In addition, the distributors are expected to know from manufacturers the "suggested distribution strategy" (see Article 8(2) of Commission Delegated Regulation). This strategy shall address the question on how insurance products are distributed to the customers, in particular whether the product should be sold only where advice is given. This statement is coherent with the provision of Article 11 of Commission Delegated Regulation requesting insurance distributors, when they become aware that an insurance product is not in line with the interests, objectives and characteristics of its identified target market or become aware of other product-related circumstances that may adversely affect the customer to promptly inform the manufacturer "and, where appropriate, amend their distribution strategy for that insurance product".[95]

Article 25(1)(3) of IDD requires manufacturers to take reasonable steps to ensure that the insurance product is distributed to the identified target market. Thus, Article 8(4) of Commission Delegated Regulation requires manufacturers to monitor that insurance distributors act in accordance with the objectives of the manufacturers' product approval process. The monitoring activities shall be reasonable, taking into consideration the characteristics and the legal framework of the respective distribution channels. That monitoring obligation shall not extend to the general regulatory requirements, in particular the conduct of business rules as laid down in IDD, with which insurance distributors have to comply when carrying out insurance distribution activities for individual customers.

The monitoring activity calls for cooperation from distributor too.

To support product reviews carried out by manufacturers, insurance distributors shall upon request provide manufacturers with relevant sales information, including, where appropriate, information on the regular reviews of the product distribution arrangements.[96] In turn, insurance distributors shall regularly review their product distribution arrangements to ensure that those arrangements are still valid and up to date. They shall amend product distribution arrangements where appropriate.[97]

In addition, insurance distributors shall set out the product distribution arrangements in a written document and make it available to their relevant staff.[98] The product distribution arrangements shall: (a) aim to prevent and mitigate customer detriment; (b) support a proper management of conflicts of interest; (c) ensure that the objectives, interests and characteristics of customers are duly taken into account.[99] The insurance distributors' body or structure responsible for insurance

[95] See also EIOPA, Final Report on Consultation Paper n. 16/006, cit., p. 45 f.

[96] See Article 10(6)(3) of Commission Delegated Regulation.

[97] See Article 10(6)(1) of Commission Delegated Regulation.

[98] See Article 10(1)(2) of Commission Delegated Regulation.

[99] See Article 10(2) of Commission Delegated Regulation.

distribution shall endorse and be ultimately responsible for establishing, implementing and reviewing the product distribution arrangements and continuously verify internal compliance with those arrangements.[100]

The described structure of the product distribution arrangements requires manufacturers and distributors to renegotiate existing agreements, which are mainly focused on strictly commercial profiles. The most delicate part of this negotiation is probably related to the flow of information that could become a source of responsibility for the manufacturer and/or the distributor.

Manufacturer is responsible for accepting what is reported by distributor without any possibility to verify the accuracy of the data communicated by distributor, if the distribution is detrimental to customers. This is, because manufacturer (i) fails to comply with monitoring rules that exclude an uncritical acceptance of the information received and (ii) delays to take the remedial actions that a timely and correct knowledge would have made necessary.

On the other hand, a distributor is responsible for transmitting information that is not eligible to support product review carried out by manufacturer because information is false or intentionally omissive. Distributor breaches the duty to provide information to manufacturer as well as the duty to have in place an effective POG system failing to implement or review the product distribution arrangement properly.

9 The "Negative" Target Market and the Sales Outside the Positive Target Market ("Grey Area")

The policy proposals on target market, which have been made to the European Commission by EIOPA, was the target market to be identified at a sufficient granular level depending on the characteristics, risk profile, complexity and nature of the product, avoiding groups of customers for whose demands and needs, and, where relevant, knowledge and experience in the investment field as well as financial situation and investment objectives, the product is *generally* not compatible. Moreover, where relevant from a consumer protection perspective, in particular, for insurance-based investment products, the manufacturer shall also identify groups of customers for whom the product is *generally* not compatible.[101]

The use of the term "generally" suggests that exceptions are allowed, but the rules of Commission Delegated Regulation are apparently more restrictive because no reference is made to the distribution on exceptional basis to a target other than the positively identified one.

Manufacturers shall provide insurance distributors with all appropriate information on the insurance products, the identified target market and the suggested distribution strategy (Article 8(2)). Thus, the possibility for distributors to sell the product out of the target would not be coherent with the standard above.

[100] See Article 10(5) of Commission Delegated Regulation.

[101] See EIOPA, cit., p. 39.

In addition, manufacturers shall not bring insurance products to the market if the results of the product testing show that the products do not meet the identified needs, objectives and characteristics of the target market (see Article 6(2)). If distributors were allowed to sell the product out of the target, distributors would modify *de facto* the results of product testing.

Finally, insurance distributors, when reviewing their product distribution arrangements, shall verify that the insurance products are distributed to the identified target market (see Article 10(6)). This target is the one provided by the manufacturer because any specific distribution strategy set up or applied by insurance distributors shall be in accordance with the distribution strategy set up and the target market identified by the manufacturer (see Article 10(4)).

However, Recital No. 9 of Commission Delegated Regulation states compliance with target market should not prevent insurance distributors from distributing insurance products to customers who do not belong to that target market, provided that the individual assessment at the point of sale justifies the conclusion that those products correspond to the demands and needs of those customers and, where applicable, that insurance-based investment products are suitable or appropriate for the customer.

The rules of Commission Delegated Regulation must be understood, therefore, as a general discipline that can be waived in the case mentioned in Recital No. 9. The insurance distributor may distribute, on an exceptional basis, insurance products to a customer, who does not belong to the identified target market, provided that the insurance distributor can prove that the respective insurance product meets the demands and needs of the individual customer, and, in the case of insurance-based investment products, is appropriate or suitable for the customer.

The selling to a negative target market is also allowed under MiFID II and the level playing field with financial products leads to analyse how the negative target market is regulated.

ESMA issued Guidelines on MiFID II requirements for POG in June 2017.[102] ESMA allows deviations from the target market making reference to "negative target market" and "grey area" as situations that do not prevent the distribution to the customers under certain circumstances.

In particular, "When providing investment advice adopting a portfolio approach and portfolio management to the client, the distributor can use products for diversification and hedging purpose. In this context, products can be sold outside of the product target market, if the portfolio as a whole or the combination of a financial instrument with its hedge is suitable for the client".[103] Thus, distributors can deviate from the target market "if the recommendation or sale fulfils the suitability requirements conduced with a portfolio view as well as other applicable legal requirements".[104]

---

[102] ESMA Final Report with Guidelines is available at https://www.esma.europa.eu/press-news/esma-news/esma-publishes-final-report-product-governance-guidelines-safeguard-investors.

[103] ESMA Final Report, p. 42.

[104] ESMA Final Report, p. 42.

The consequences of these sales are different, however, for the distributor.

In the case of negative target market, the distributor should always report the sale to the manufacturer and disclose to the client, "even if those sales are for diversification or hedging purposes", and the sales into the negative target "should be a rare occurrence".[105]

On the other hand, the distributor is not required to report sales outside of the positive target market but not in the negative target market—the "grey area"—to the manufacturer if these sales: (i) are for diversification and hedging purposes, and (ii) are still suitable given the client's total portfolio or the risk being hedged.[106]

In addition, deviations from the target market (outside the positive or within the negative) "which may be relevant for the POG process of the manufacturer (especially those that are recurrent) should be reported to the manufacturer".[107] However, this duty concerns the sales falling into the grey area (outside the positive target market),[108] when diversification and hedging purposes do not recur.[109]

It may be questionable if insurance-based investment products can be offered for diversification or hedging purposes, within a portfolio management strategy specifically involving other life insurance products, even though Article 9(7) of Commission Delegated Regulation (EU) 2017/2359 of 21 September 2017[110] deals with advice that involves switching between underlying investment assets.

IDD is still aiming at minimum harmonization and should therefore not prevent Member States from maintaining or introducing more stringent provisions in order to protect customers provided that such provisions are consistent with Union law, including the IDD (see Recital No. 3 of IDD). Thus, despite Recital No. 9 is permissive, Member States can prevent distribution of insurance products, in particular insurance-based investment products, outside the positive target market.

In addition, in the absence of national provisions that prohibit the off-target sale, Recital No. 9 requires POG rules on insurance products to be interpreted as allowing the off-target sale on an exceptional basis "provided that the insurance distributor can prove that the respective insurance product meets the demands and needs of the individual customer, and, in the case of insurance-based investment products, is appropriate or suitable for the customer".[111]

---

[105] ESMA Final Report, p. 42.

[106] ESMA Final Report, p. 42.

[107] ESMA Final Report, p. 46 f.

[108] ESMA, Final Report, p. 46 make the example of "the sales outside the positive target market as a result of non advised sales i.e. where clients approach a firm to purchase a certain products without any active marketing by the firm or having been influenced in any way by that firm), where the firm does not have all the necessary information to conduct a thorough assessment of whether the client falls within the target market, which might be the case, for instance, for execution platforms that only operate under the appropriateness regime".

[109] ESMA Final Report, p. 47.

[110] Concerning information requirements and conduct of business rules applicable to the distribution of insurance-based investment products.

[111] See also EIOPA, Q&A on Regulation, (EU) 2017-2358.

In the case of off-target sale of insurance-based investment products, therefore, member States (and EIOPA) should look at MiFID II to regulate the reporting to manufacturers of the sales outside the positive target market by distributors.

10 Potential Compliance Gaps: FCA Thematic Review of Product Development and Governance

Predictability of POG compliance is difficult because POG has just been detailed by the EU legislator and has not yet been fully implemented by recipient entities in the member States. Nevertheless, the UK's experience can provide useful guidelines on potential gaps at least with reference to insurance-based investment products, due to their strong similarities with financial products.

Since publishing finalised guidance on structured products in 2012, the FCA has continued to review how this market serves retail clients. Evidences are held in a paper issued in March 2015 and they are based on supervisory work with retail and wholesale firms as well as consumer research. The foregoing considerations, which have highlighted how the UK entered his name on POG's rules on financial products adopted by the EU, lead us to believe that this survey anticipates possible gaps national supervisory authorities might find in relation to firms' compliance with POG rules of insurance-based investment products.

The FCA observed that some firms failed to (i) define a clear target market of end customers at the product design stage and identify relevant need(s) which their product would serve, (ii) conduct sufficiently robust analysis and stress-testing, (iii) properly assess whether products are likely to represent value for money for end customers, and/or (iv) monitor how the product was distributed to check that distributors had sufficient information about the product and its target market to fulfil their own obligations towards the end customer.

More details on the results just summarized are useful in understanding the gaps that other supervisors are likely to find in the implementation of POG in their national markets.

With reference to target market, the FCA's expectations were that firms should identify a target market not only for generating ideas for products, but to ensure that products address specific investor needs and are designed in a way that the end customer can understand. Consideration of target market factors should permeate all aspects of product development and distribution, as noted above, as well as ensuring the selection of appropriate distribution channels and the promotion of the product accompanied by sufficient and correct information.[112]

Review showed that firms had identified the distribution channels for their structured products. However, most firms were unable to evidence that they had taken sufficient steps to identify the needs of a specific target market for their products and

---

[112] FCA, *Structured Products: Thematic Review of Product Development and Governance,* March 2015, p. 14.

then use this information to inform decisions on product development, the selection of distribution channels and their marketing/promotion strategy.

Gaps are recorded from both retail firms and wholesale firms.

Although some retail firms made their own market research and/or consumer testing, this tended to be focused on identifying the factors that made potential products attractive to customers (and could be used to market them more successfully), rather than understanding and seeking to serve the needs and objectives of end customers. Firms were also influenced by feedback from intermediaries regarding which types of product were likely to sell.[113]

Wholesale firms typically used a matrix describing the notional target market for different types of product. Some firms adopted the principle that only 'simple products' should be sold to retail investors, however, the definition of a 'simple product' was not always consistent and some did not have a clear view on what a 'simple product' was (and whether these 'simple' products were understood by their customers).

Regarding firms' approaches to product stress testing and modelling, FCA highlighted the need to minimise statistical bias that could adversely influence an end customer. Although the use of historical back-testing to evaluate product performance helps product design, the FCA was concerned that firms had not always made adjustments to compensate for the following issues with back-testing: (i) economic conditions vary over time so the period over which the back-testing takes place has a significant impact on the outcomes; (ii) when back-testing is based upon multiple time periods that overlap, the results may not always be an accurate reflection of a product's potential performance, (iii) firms compared the potential performance of the product produced by their back-testing to the current yields available and did not take account of the yields available historically. This has an obvious benefit in an environment when rates are lower (as they are currently), as the performance of certain products tends to correlate with the interest rate available at time of issuance.[114]

The FCA's survey identified the following common weaknesses in the evaluation of potential product performances: (i) the selection and calibration of modelling approaches did not reflect the statistical properties of prices observed in the real world[115]; (ii) some firms used unrealistic and/or optimistic growth rates.[116] The net effect of these issues is the production of modelling simulations that may not accu-

[113] FCA, *cit.*, p. 14.

[114] FCA, *cit.*, p. 17.

[115] FCA, *cit.*, p. 17. For example, the distribution of equity returns resulting from a local volatility model may not necessarily match the equity returns observed in the real world. Further, if the growth rate is adjusted to include an equity premium in a local volatility model, the distortion may increase.

[116] FCA, *cit.*, p. 18. For example, the relevant growth rate may differ if the underlying is an equity (investor receives dividends) or an equity index (investor pays the dividend). This distinction was not addressed by most firms, despite the majority of products offered being dependent on equity index performance.

rately reflect potential market scenarios and cold lead to more optimistic estimate of potential product performances.[117]

In addition, the value for money test performed by the firms considers whether modelled product returns would exceed a chosen threshold. Some firms' threshold tests placed undue reliance on the maximum possible returns suggested by their modelling, rather than the most likely returns.[118] Firms did not always take into account any difference in credit risk between the issuer/guarantor of the structured product and the provider of the alternative product, and factor this into their value for money assessment.[119]

Finally, the FCA pointed out that a number of firms employed external specialists for the quantitative modelling and/or assessment of a product's expected return.[120] Some firms appeared to be using these results as a validation for their decision to approve a product post-launch rather than as a tool by which to test the proposition prior to launch. They were not always able to demonstrate they had conducted appropriate due diligence on these third parties and on the robustness of the methodology being used, despite they are responsible for the modelling even in case of outsourcing.[121]

With reference to the selection of distribution channels, the FCA's survey reveals that some firms' ongoing monitoring of distributors was insufficient. Many firms appeared to take assurances from distributors at face value without having sufficient information to satisfy themselves that distributor' policies and procedures were appropriate for their product and target market.[122]

In addition, the firms provided very little assistance where sales were conducted through private banks, on the assumption that banking staff in sales functions had the necessary product knowledge.[123] This finding is extremely important in the model of bancassurance, which is the predominant distribution channel in life insurance of most of the EU Member States, and it is a serious warning for the entities involved in this model because firms need to ensure that their chosen distribution channels have enough information to form an adequate understanding of their products.

Regarding the information to distributors, the FCA was concerned that the level of ongoing due diligence performed by manufacturers on distributors could inhibit their ability to check that products are reaching the target market.[124]

The FCA also expects firms to have transparent and auditable product approval frameworks for new structured products ensuring that the product approval process is not compromised as a result of commercial, time or funding pressures, allows for

[117] FCA, *cit.*, p. 18.

[118] FCA, *cit.*, p. 18.

[119] FCA, *cit.*, p. 18.

[120] FCA, *cit.*, p. 18.

[121] FCA, *cit.*, p. 18.

[122] FCA, *cit.*, p. 16.

[123] FCA, *cit.*, p. 16.

[124] FCA, *cit.*, p. 20.

review and challenge by the compliance, risk and legal functions, and is not undermined by senior management over-ride.[125]

The review on wholesale firms has found that in some firms there was a lack of recent reviews/tests undertaken by compliance and/or internal audit on structured products. Given the retail focus of many of these products, firms should review their current/planned arrangements to ensure compliance and/or internal audit coverage of this area is adequate.[126]

On the other hand, the retail review suggested that the governance around the launch of new products in some firms was overly focused on the profitability of the product rather than meeting identified investment needs for customers in the target market. The FCA had particular concerns about how firms assessed whether new products represented value for money for end customers.[127]

IDD does not make reference to price and value of insurance products. EIOPA aimed at introducing a reference to fair value of these products, which was proposed in the draft Technical Advice submitted to the public consultation ended in October 2016. However, the Final Report does not mention the fair value and EIOPA stated that it was not his intention to introduce a price control via the policy proposals on product oversight and governance.

Although a reference to "fair value" or "value for money" is not expressly mentioned, the experience of the UK supervision should teach that these elements are, in the last instance, the benchmark for manufacturers in the products' design, if products aim at being in line with the best interests of the customers.

11 Are There New Liabilities from POG?

POG consists of procedures aiming to better protect costumers. The failure to comply with POG requirements exposes to liability both supervised entities and supervisors. National law primarily governs their liabilities, but the EU regulation provides interesting ideas for setting up national liabilities.

POG policy on insurance-based investment products shall be coherent with the general rules for insurance products and those additional to these products of Article 28 to 30 of IDD as detailed by Commission Delegated Regulation (EU) 2017/2359 on conflicts of interest,[128] inducements and inducements schemes,[129] the procedures for the assessment of suitability,[130] or appropriateness,[131] of the customer or potential customer and providing of advice.[132]

---

[125] FCA, *cit.*, p. 21.

[126] FCA, *cit.*, p. 21.

[127] FCA, *cit.*, p. 21.

[128] See Article 4 of Commission Delegated Regulation (EU) 2017/2359.

[129] See Article 8 of Commission Delegated Regulation (EU) 2017/2359.

[130] See Articles 9 to 11 and 17 of Commission Delegated Regulation (EU) 2017/2359.

[131] See Articles 15 and 17 of Commission Delegated Regulation (EU) 2017/2359.

[132] See Articles 12 and 14 of Commission Delegated Regulation (EU) 2017/2359.

Thus, a misalignment or a contradiction between the POG rules and those of the other policies and procedures that are relevant for the purposes of POG, it is likely to be detected by the supervisory authority. This mismatch could be the indicator of a malfunctioning of the internal control system and/or a substantial non-compliance with the POG rules.

POG rules could also be relevant in relations with individual policyholders. The product approval process requires the manufacturer to demonstrate that the product has been designed with customer interest and needs in mind. Moreover, the effectiveness of remedial actions depends on the timeliness and granularity of the information on the lasting validity of the product and on its correct distribution. The assessment of how the different steps of the designing, monitoring and review activities have been carried out by manufacturer/distributor could affect the decision of any dispute between the manufacturer/distributor and the policyholder, at least in the event of national laws and judges that may also allow to acquire such documentation even in a judgment between the manufacturer and/or/distributor and the policyholder.

On the other hand, the EIOPA and national supervisory authorities are empowered to monitor new and existing financial activities and to adopt guidelines and recommendations with a view to promoting the safety and soundness of markets and convergence of regulatory practice.[133] In light of this task, Article 15 of Regulation (EU) No 1286/2014 of 26 November 2014 specifies that: "EIOPA shall monitor the market for insurance-based investment products which are marketed, distributed or sold in the Union. Competent authorities shall monitor the market for insurance-based investment products which are marketed, distributed or sold in or from their Member State".

The monitoring of the market can be done with a retrospective approach and/or a forward-looking approach. POG has been introduced as part of the intervention powers of the supervisory authorities and, therefore, it should be also appreciated in view of the interplay with these powers, which are expressly addressed to PRIIPs. These powers may be exercised in coherence with a forward-looking approach because PRIIPs Regulation allows EIOPA or the national competent authority "to impose the prohibition or restriction [...] on a precautionary basis before an insurance-based investment product has been marketed or sold to investors" (see Articles 16 (2) and 17 (2)).

The intervention of the authority, however, may not be limited to the imposition of prohibitions or restrictions on the manufacturer. If the authority exercises the above powers before the marketing of a product, the authority necessarily assesses compliance with POG rules of that product. Thus, national laws could punish the manufacturer for failure to comply with the requirements of POG. National laws shall regulate how this liability has to be punished, whilst such liability does not replace civil liability for damages suffered by individual customers. They will be able to claim for damages individually or through collective or class actions whether provided in national law.

[133] See Article 9(2) of Regulation (EU) No 1094/2010.

The ability to exercise the above powers before the marketing or selling of insurance-based investment products, however, it is likely to give rise to a liability also by supervisory authorities.

Recital No. 25 of Regulation (EU) No 1286/2014 states that "those powers should be used exclusively in the public interest and should not give rise to civil liability on the part of the competent authorities". Each Member State therefore must determine whether to grant this exemption of liability to national authorities. This exemption, however, refers to the consequences of exercising these powers. The rationale of the exemption is because a potential liability could discourage authorities from using their powers. Thus, the exemption could not cover the civil liability for *failure* to exercise the powers of intervention. Authorities should be liable of the damage suffered by the insured that bought a product not complying with POG *and* which was not to be sold if the authority had exercised its powers of intervention.

What to say in case of *delay* in exercising the powers?

The rationale of the exemption from liability is to provide an incentive to authorities to use the intervention powers in accordance with the conditions set out in the Regulation (EU) No 1286/2014. Nevertheless, authorities are empowered of monitoring products and prohibiting the marketing since their design. Failure to supervise at that stage prevents authority to exercise their powers in a timely manner.

If the damage to customer is already materializing with product sales, there is a connection between the inertia of authority and the damage suffered by the customer. Thus, the exemption from civil liability would not be supported by an adequate justification. Exemption protects authorities that exercise their monitoring and intervention powers, while delay in their exercise, in principle, it is equivalent to a failure to exercise such powers. In both cases, the damage would not have occurred if the authorities had supervised.

On the other hand, a delay does not occur when the damage is materialising *after* the marketing of the product *and* depends on causes that are unknown at the time of product's design or difficult to detect at that time. Although the damage was already embedded in the product, there is no link between the authority's conduct and the damage suffered by customer because authority used its intervention powers when detriment to customer has become predictable.

12 Is the Failure to Comply with POG an Unfair Commercial Practice?

Compliance with POG rules is part of the professional diligence expected from manufacturers and distributors, which are requested to act honestly, fairly and professionally in accordance with the best interests of their customers (see Art. 17 (1) of IDD). POG rules aim at increasing customers' protection and, therefore, they embedded such protection in the organizational rules of manufacturers and distributors. Thus, POG supplements the current EU legislation on customers' protection.

The EU legislation on customers' protection includes Directive 2005/29/EC concerning unfair business-to-consumer commercial practices. This Directive is of maximum harmonization allowing Member States to impose requirements more restrictive or prescriptive than those introduce by this Directive, in relation to 'financial services' as defined in Directive 2002/65/EC including insurance products.

Business-to-consumer commercial practices are defined as "any act, omission, course of conduct or representation, commercial communication including advertising and marketing, by a trader, *directly connected* with the promotion, sale or supply of a product to consumers", while trader means "any natural or legal person who, in commercial practices covered by this Directive, is acting for purposes relating to his trade, business, craft or profession and *anyone acting in the name of or on behalf of a trader"*.

The definition of commercial practice is very broad.[134] The distribution of insurance products is mainly based on an indirect distribution scheme, where an insurance intermediary/distributor acts on behalf of the manufacturer. This is the case, e.g., of the bancassurance that has been successful for life insurance and insurance-based investment products in most of the EU Member States.

The importance of indirect distribution is the reason why IDD requires (i) manufacturers to make available to distributors all appropriate information on the insurance product and the product approval process, including the identified target market of the insurance product and (ii) insurance distributors to have in place adequate arrangements to obtain the information on the insurance product and the product approval process from the manufacturer, and to understand the characteristics and identified target market of each insurance product (see Article 25 (5) (6) of IDD).

POG rules govern the design of products for their marketing to customers' targets. The unfair design of the product is likely to affect the target and be detrimental to the average customers of this target, regardless of the distribution activity. Misleading information provided to distributor from the manufacturer is likely to be evaluated as unfair commercial practice because (i) this is a business-to-business practice that is directly connected to the sale of a product to consumers and (ii) acts or omissions (or, it may be, negligence) occurred in the supply chain of distributor.[135]

National laws could be clearer on that when implementing the IDD. It should be noted that they could also impose requirements, which are more restrictive or prescriptive than those of Directive 2005/29/EC. Member States may leave the issue to the interpretation of national courts, but this is likely to create uncertainty both in customer protection and in fair competition.

---

[134] Stuyck (2015), p. 732 ff., provides an overview of the ECJ's rulings aiming to limit the concept of commercial practice as well as of trader.

[135] Office of Fair Trading (OFT), *Guidance on the Consumer Protection from Unfair Trading Regulations 2008*, considers within the scope of Consumer Protection from Unfair Trading Regulations 2008 "Any aspect of a business-to-business practice that is directly connected to the sale of a product to consumers" (see page 15), specifying that "For example where a trader sells a product to a consumer, acts or omissions which occur further up the supply chain may also constitute commercial practices" (see point 4.3).

References

Busch D (2017) Product governance und produktintervention unter miFid ii/miFir. J Econ Bank Law 9:409–420
Cousy H (2009) Le secteur des assurances sera-t-il mifidisé? Bulletin des Assurances 89(3):245–254
Cousy H (2017) Changing insurance contract law: an age-old, slow and unfinished story. In: Marano P, Siri M (eds) Insurance regulation in the European Union. Solvency II and beyond. Palgrave Macmillan
FCA, Structured Products: Thematic Review of Product Development and Governance, March 2015
Ferran E (2012) Regulatory lessons from the payment protection insurance mis-selling scandal in the UK. Eur Bus Organ Law Rev 13:264ff
FSA, Discussion Paper on Product Intervention, January 2011
FSA, Feedback on Discussion Paper on Product Intervention, June 2011
HM Treasury, A new approach to financial regulation: judgement, focus and stability
Marano P (2017a) Sources and tools of the insurance regulation in the European Union. In: Marano P, Siri M (eds) Insurance regulation in the European Union. Solvency II and beyond. Palgrave Macmillan
Marano P (2017b) The mifidisation: the sunset of life insurance in the EU regulation on insurance? In: Liber Amicorum in Honour of Ioannis K. Rokas, Athens, pp 219–234
Marcacci A (2017) European regulatory private law going global? The case of product governance. Eur Bus Organ Law Rev 18:305–332
Moloney N (2012) The legacy effects of the financial crisis on regulatory design in the EU. In: Ferran E, Moloney N, Hill JC, Coffee JC Jr (eds) The regulatory aftermath of the global financial crisis. Cambridge University Press, Cambridge
Perry J, Moulton R, Barwick G, Small M, Green J, Kay N (2011) The new UK regulatory landscape. Compliance Off Bull 84(Mar):1–33
Stuyck J (2015) The court of justice and the unfair commercial practices directive. Common Mark Law Rev 52:721–752
Tomic K (2018) Product intervention of supervisory authorities in financial services. In: Grima S, Marano P (eds) Governance and regulations' contemporary issues. Emerald Publishing

ADR and Insurance-Based Investment Products

Jacquetta Castle and Jonathan Hyde

Contents

Abbreviations

ADR	Alternative Dispute Resolution
CEFAREA	Centre Francaise d'Arbitrage de Reassurance et d'Assurance
EC	European Commission
EEA	European Economic Area
EIOPA	European Insurance and Occupational Pensions Authority
EU	European Union

J. Castle (✉)
ArgoGlobal, London, UK

British Insurance Law Association, London, UK
e-mail: jacquetta.castle@argo-global.com

J. Hyde
DWF LLP, London, UK
e-mail: jonathan.hyde@dwf.law

P. Marano, I. Rokas (eds.), *Distribution of Insurance-Based Investment Products*, https://doi.org/10.1007/978-3-030-11668-2_4

FFSA	Federation Francaise des Societes d'Assurance
FOS	Financial Ombudsman Service
GDV	Gesamtverband der Deutschen Versicherungswirtschaft
IBIPs	Insurance-Based Investment Products
IDD	Insurance Distribution Directive
IMD	Insurance Mediation Directive
IPF	Direccion General de Seguros y Fondos de Pensiones
IRSG	Insurance and Reinsurance Stakeholder Group
ODR	Online Dispute Resolution
PPI	Payment Protection Insurance
RIAD	International Association of Legal Protection Insurance

1 Introduction

ADR[1] is not a new process,[2] but its prevalence globally has increased exponentially since the 1970s,[3] not least as a result of dissatisfaction with the costs, delays, uncertainty of outcome, complexity and other difficulties of court processes in resolving disputes. ADR has its roots in informal processes designed to resolve all manner of disputes, including those concerning IBIPs, without reference to the courts. Increasingly some of the most sophisticated ADR schemes have been adopted in the areas of insurance, which only looks set to increase following recent EU legislation in this area. As the European internal market has enlarged over the past five decades, ADR has gained increased importance in Europe. In particular, the central pillar of the EU of free trade across Member State borders creates greater numbers of cross-border transactions, including in the distribution of investment-based insurance products, which invariably leads to greater numbers of complaints about insurance intermediaries and/or IBIPs that need to be resolved satisfactorily. ADR has become an increasingly important means of dealing with such disputes about IBIPs effectively, and has therefore received active support within the EU from the EC and (to varying degrees) Member States.[4]

This chapter explores the development of ADR in the EU with particular reference to its application to insurance intermediaries and IBIPs. By its nature this cannot be comprehensive, but we aim to summarise the key background, framework

[1] ADR refers to any and all processes of concluding disputes other than by obtaining judgement from a formal Court system (c.f. Fitzpatrick (1993), who argues that "'Alternative' justice, including popular justice, is set in a dynamic of opposition to the formalized and centralized power of the state", p. 454). It therefore encompasses, *inter alia*, conciliation, mediation, arbitration and ombudsmen.

[2] "This idea is not new of course: conciliation, arbitration, mediation have always been important elements of the means of dispute settlement. However, there is a *new element* in that modern societies have developed *new reasons* to prefer such alternatives." Cappelletti (1993), p. 287 (emphasis original).

[3] Social anthropology after World War II has especially highlighted ways in which many cultures resolve their disputes without "going to court" (c.f. Roberts and Palmer (2005), p. 5 and pp. 21–38).

[4] Hodges et al. (2012), p. 1.

and issues involved. We start by summarising briefly the growing importance of ADR as a matter of EU policy generally, before considering the various steps that have been taken to promote it over the past 20 years, in particular specific ADR schemes established in the UK, France, Germany and Spain to deal with insurance disputes. We then consider the creation and development of the EU cross-border out-of-court complaints network for financial services ("FIN-NET") that is important for the resolution of cross-border disputes, including those concerning IBIPs, evaluating its work to date and its future direction. We conclude by considering some of the opportunities and challenges that face ADR in the context of disputes over IBIPs in the future. At the time of writing this chapter it is not known the precise form that Brexit will take and to what extent, if at all, the UK will participate in these EU ADR structures in the future. Given that ADR is well-developed in the UK, that the UK Ombudsman has played an enthusiastic role as a leading member of FIN-NET, and the benefits of ongoing participation, it may be assumed that the UK would want to retain as much of the existing system as possible.

2 The Development of ADR for Insurance-Based Investment Products in the EU

2.1 Overview

Many Member States have promoted ADR over the past three decades,[5] and from the late 1990s it has gained greater prominence at EU level too,[6] including in resolving disputes about insurance products as discussed in more detail below. Before analysing the issues involved, it is a useful exercise to chart the chronological development of ADR in the EU, and EU initiatives to promote ADR.

In 1998, the EC released a communication on "out-of-court settlement of consumer disputes", aimed at those involved in resolving disputes within the court system.[7] In the same year, the EC adopted a Recommendation to promote ADR by requiring certain minimum guarantees in its use.[8]

In 1999, EU leaders emphasised the importance of ADR in cross-border disputes at the European Council on Justice at Tampere.[9] The following year, EU leaders asked the EC and the EU Council of Ministers to consider how to use ADR in dis-

[5] Hodges et al. (2012) note the development of ADR in other Member States over this time (*Consumer ADR*, chapters 2 to 10).

[6] C.f. Hodges (2015), p. 263.

[7] Hodges et al. (2012), p. 425.

[8] Recommendation 98/257/EC on the principles applicable to the bodies responsible for the out-of-court settlement of consumer disputes [1998] OJ L 115/31. See Hodges et al. (2012), p. 7, pp. 425–426.

[9] Hodges et al. (2012), p. 4.

putes about e-commerce to enhance consumer confidence.[10] In 2001, the EC adopted a further Recommendation,[11] this time specifically targeted at ADR schemes seeking a consensual resolution of disputes outside the court system (but not customer complaints services or ADR provided by a business).[12]

In 2002, the IMD[13] encouraged Member States to establish an ADR scheme in the insurance sector.[14] The same year, the EC launched a Green Paper on ADR in civil and commercial law, which led to the non-binding European Code of Conduct for Mediators in 2004,[15] and the first Mediation Directive[16] in 2008.[17] These steps were intended to promote mediation as a quick and cost-effective means of resolving cross-border disputes, including those concerning IBIPs, and encourage Member States to adopt it accordingly, but did not require them to do so.

In 2008, the EC issued a consultation throughout the EU on ADR in respect of financial services in particular.[18] It extolled the virtues of ADR for consumers to resolve their disputes with financial services providers, including disputes concerning IBIPs, and noted that the EC was examining ways in which it could further improve such mechanisms.[19] The EC sought views in particular on improving the coverage of such ADR and how it might create comprehensive coverage for consumers,[20] and make them aware of it.[21] In 2009, the EC published the responses to its consultation.[22] Overall, the EC found support among stakeholders for improving ADR schemes in financial services, but views differed as to how this could best be achieved.[23] Other studies were carried out into the use of ADR in the EU at the same time.[24]

---

[10] *Ibid.*

[11] Recommendation 2001/310/EC on the principles for out-of-court bodies involved in the consensual resolution of consumer disputes [2001] OJ L 109/56. It set out four minimum guarantees: impartiality; transparency; effectiveness; and fairness.

[12] Hodges et al. (2012), p. 8 and pp. 425–426.

[13] Directive 2002/92/EC on insurance mediation [2003] OJ L 9/3.

[14] Hodges et al. (2012), p. 10.

[15] See http://ec.europa.eu/civiljustice/adr/adr_ec_code_conduct_en.pdf.

[16] Directive 2008/52/EC on certain aspects of mediation in civil and commercial matters [2008] OJ L 136/3.

[17] Hodges et al. (2012), p. 4, pp. 8–10.

[18] Commission (EC) "Alternative Dispute Resolution in the Area of Financial Services – Consultation Document", 11 December 2008.

[19] *Ibid.*, p. 1.

[20] *Ibid.*, pp. 7–8.

[21] *Ibid.*, pp. 8–9.

[22] Commission (EC) "Summary of the responses to the public consultation on alternative dispute resolution in the area of financial services", 14 September 2009.

[23] *Ibid.*, p. 3.

[24] Hodges et al. (2012), p. 20. The ADR Directive also claims to be based on improving the single market as discussed by the European Parliament and the EC between 2010 and 2011 (e.g. Recitals 8 to 10).

Also in 2009, the Solvency II Directive[25] imposed a specific duty on non-life insurance undertakings to inform the policyholder of the undertaking's complaint-handling arrangements, and the existence of any appropriate complaints body.[26] In her paper, Dr Alkistis Christofilou noted that "a respective duty is provided in the case of life assurance as well", and that EIOPA[27] has "issued implementing Guidelines to insurance undertakings", albeit there is no specific reference to ODR.[28] Nevertheless, in Solvency II the EU clearly signalled to insurance undertakings its expectation that they should endeavour to resolve consumer complaints by means other than formal court processes. Indeed, Christofilou explained how Article 203 of Solvency II went a step further and required that Member States "provide for the availability of arbitration mechanisms".[29] She noted how "the industry has not reacted negatively to the initiative", and cited the example of RIAD taking a "positive stance with regard to legal protection insurers covering mediation costs".[30] It therefore seems that insurance undertakings are not adverse to the EU's pressure on them to embrace ADR in disputes with consumers. Reflecting the growing importance of ADR in the context of insurance, Christofilou noted that the Principles of European Insurance Contract Law specifically do not preclude access by a policyholder, insured or beneficiary to any out-of-court complaint and redress mechanisms that are available to them.[31]

Two further measures concerning ADR were proposed in 2011, and enacted in 2013: the ADR Directive,[32] and the ODR Regulation.[33] The language of these enactments was more forceful than previous legislation and showed a clear determination by the EU to require Member States to improve their ADR offerings, both in terms of gaps in coverage and quality, as well as raising consumer awareness as to available mediation options. Interestingly, the two enactments applied to domestic as well as cross-border matters. Both measures were designed, at least in part, to address the issues and concerns identified in the previous studies and research into the use of ADR in the EU noted above, including as concerns IBIPs.

The role and future of FIN-NET was considered further in the EC's Green Paper on retail financial services, in particular identifying the need for improving the effectiveness of ADR; for increasing consumer awareness of ADR redress options;

---

[25] Directive 2009/138/EC of the European Parliament and of the Council of 25 November 2009 on the taking-up and pursuit of the business of Insurance and Reinsurance (Solvency II) [2009] OJ L 335/1.

[26] *Ibid.*, Article 183(1), as discussed by Christofilou (2016), p. 288.

[27] See https://eiopa.europa.eu/.

[28] *Online Dispute Resolution*, pp. 288–289.

[29] *Ibid.*, p. 289.

[30] *Ibid.*

[31] *Ibid.*

[32] Directive 2013/11/EU on alternative dispute resolution for consumer disputes and amending Regulation (EC) No 2006/2004 and Directive 2009/22/EC [2013] OJ L 165/63.

[33] Regulation (EU) No 524/2013 on online dispute resolution for consumer disputes and amending Regulation (EC) No 2006/2004 and Directive 2009/22/EC [2013] OJ L 165/1.

and generally improving access by consumers to compensation where retail financial products and/or insurance had been mis-sold.[34] In response to the Paper, consumer organisations emphasised the need for consumer trust in financial services providers, including providers of insurance, especially in cross-border situations.[35] As a result, 2016 and 2017 saw increased efforts to promote FIN-NET, which are summarised below.[36] Further changes to the ADR landscape as it concerns insurance intermediaries and the distribution of insurance products may follow as a result of the Green Paper,[37] and Brexit.

In the meantime, on 22 February 2016[38] the EU implemented the successor to the IMD, the IDD,[39] in express recognition of issues with the IMD.[40] The IDD is intended to provide consumers with a level playing field with distributors, including regarding IBIPs[41]; improve the internal market for insurance products and services[42]; and facilitate appropriate and effective out-of-court complaint and redress procedures to settle disputes between distributors and consumers.[43] In the latter regard, the IDD requires Member States to establish appropriate ADR procedures (or use existing ones) and ensure participation in them, which is more forceful that the

[34] Commission (EU) "Green Paper on retail financial services", 10 December 2015, pp. 19–20.

[35] Commission (EU) "Summary of contributions to the Green Paper on retail financial services" (COM (2015), 630 final), 3–4.

[36] In September 2017, the Parliament adopted a resolution on the implementation of the First Mediation Directive that encouraged Member States to promote the use of mediation in civil and commercial disputes, and sought the EC's input on extending the use of mediation across Member State boarders whilst controlling mediation service quality: http://www.europarl.europa.eu/sides/getDoc.do?pubRef=-//EP//TEXT+TA+P8-TA-2017-0321+0+DOC+XML+V0//EN&language=EN.

[37] E.g. the EC's Consumer Financial Services Action Plan, published on 23 March 2017 (https://ec.europa.eu/info/publications/consumer-financial-services-action-plan_en) and the Study on the Distribution of Retail Investment Products, published on 24 April 2018 (https://ec.europa.eu/info/publications/180425-retail-investment-products-distribution-systems_en).

[38] Member States are now required to transpose the IDD by 1 July 2018, and to apply it to relevant firms by no later than 1 October 2018, when the IDD will repeal the IMD; nevertheless, the IDD will have retrospective effect from 23 February 2018 in the interests of certainty, as that was its intended application date (Directive 2018/411/EU). Subsequently, EIOPA is required to report to the EC, and the EC to report to the Parliament and Council, on various aspects of its application and the insurance market (Directive (EU) 2016/97 on insurance distribution (recast) [2016] OJ L 26/19, Articles 11(5) and 41).

[39] Directive (EU) 2016/97 on insurance distribution (recast) [2016] OJ L 26/19. Regulation (EU) 2017/2359 supplementing Directive (EU) 2016/97 of the European Parliament and of the Council with regard to information requirements and conduct of business rules applicable to the distribution of insurance-based investment products [2017] OJ L 341/8 provides further requirements to insurance intermediaries and insurance undertakings to ensure that IBIPs are suitable for particular consumers, and to deal with conflicts of interest.

[40] *Ibid.*, Recitals 1 and 7. C.f. Consultation document on the Review of the IMD, Commission Staff Working Paper, discussing the various problems in the EU insurance market following the IMD.

[41] *Ibid.*, Recitals 6 and 10.

[42] *Ibid.*, Recitals 9, 19, 34 and 36.

[43] *Ibid.*, Recital 38 and Article 15.

IMD's encouragement to that end.[44] The IDD specifically focuses on IBIPs given their increasing complexity and innovation, so that consumers can be properly informed and advised about investing in them,[45] although it is perhaps arguable whether the majority of IBIPs that are currently sold are in fact complex and difficult for consumers to understand, especially where the insurance undertaking provides a guarantee at maturity.[46]

Empowered by the IDD, in October 2017 EIOPA published guidance focused on the assessment of whether an IBIP is complex or non-complex in the context of "execution-only" sales to consumers (i.e. where an IBIP is transacted without any advice or assessment of the customer's personal situation).[47] The guidance emphasised the need to identify where a consumer may find it difficult to understand the risks of the IBIP in which they are interested,[48] and that consumers should only be exposed on an "execution-only" basis to non-complex IBIPs with sufficiently transparent risks for the consumer to understand without difficulty.[49]

This is potentially important as regards ADR for IBIPs. It limits the extent to which IBIPs can be transacted on an "execution-only" basis, which transactions may not be subject to a national ADR scheme because they do not involve advice being given to the consumer. It appears that complex IBIPs will only be transacted where advice is given to the consumer, giving them the opportunity to seek redress from the relevant national ADR scheme governing that advice process if they are subsequently dissatisfied with the IBIP. Non-complex IBIPs may also remain subject to ADR where they cannot be transacted on an execution-only basis because of the difficulty of the consumer understanding the risks involved, although in practice consumers may be sufficiently familiar with a number of non-complex IBIPs. As a result of this guidance the class of consumers who may not have recourse to an ADR scheme for their IBIP may therefore be relatively small, limited to those who could properly understand the risks of the IBIP themselves.

[44] *Ibid.*, Article 15(1).

[45] *Ibid.*, Recitals 33, 42, 56, 57, 61 and 67, and Articles 26 to 30; these requirements are therefore relaxed for professional clients (Recital 51). These additional requirements are aligned with the MiFID II Directive (2014/65/EU).

[46] See the response of EIOPA's IRSG to EIOPA's consultation: https://eiopa.europa.eu/Publications/Comments/EIOPA%20Insurance%20and%20Reinsurance%20Stakeholder%20Group%20%28IRSG%29_23-05-2017.pdf.

[47] EIOPA-17/651, 4 October 2017 (https://eiopa.europa.eu/Publications/Guidelines/EIOPA-17-651-IDD_guidelines_execution_only_EN.pdf); c.f. Article 30(3) of the IDD.

[48] *Ibid.*, p. 3.

[49] *Ibid.*, p. 4. The German response to EIOPA's consultation behind this guidance disagreed that IBIPs are complicated and difficult for consumers to understand, arguing that German consumers were well aware of them (https://eiopa.europa.eu/Publications/Comments/German%20Insurance%20Association%20%28GDV%29_23-05-2017.pdf). The Association of British Insurers was similarly concerned that IBIPs could be wrongly classified as complex (https://eiopa.europa.eu/Publications/Comments/Association%20of%20British%20Insurers%20%28ABI%29_23-05-2017.pdf). As noted above, IRSG made a similar comment to EIOPA (https://eiopa.europa.eu/Publications/Comments/EIOPA%20Insurance%20and%20Reinsurance%20Stakeholder%20Group%20%28IRSG%29_23-05-2017.pdf).

This will hopefully encourage the suitable recommendation of IBIPs to consumers, and confidence in the cross-border European market for them, although tighter restrictions could also stifle innovation in IBIPs especially if they add to confusion as to the complexity of various IBIPs. In their paper, Poufinas and Zygiotis have criticised the EU's lack of coherence and consistency in its laws concerning IBIPs and the product information provided to consumers, compromising both transparency and consumer trust.[50] They argue that transparency is essential for consumer satisfaction and trust, leading to increased consumer retention and market performance.[51] Consequently, they recommend that insurers should embrace the EU's proposed regulation to increase consumer protection and trust.[52] However, the most recent requirements for IBIPs in the EU have yet to be fully tested so it remains to be seen whether they will have the result that the EU desires, and which will benefit insurance undertakings; as noted above, the IMD did not succeed in these regards as had been hoped.

2.2 Competence of the EU

There is some debate over the competence of the EU to prescribe its latest measures on ADR. Professor Hodges and his co-authors in their book, *Consumer ADR*, explain how the EU initially had to employ "soft law instruments" in respect of ADR as it did not have express power in this area.[53] They argued that the Lisbon Treaty in 2009 gave the EU wide powers to provide civil justice measures, in particular under Article 81 and the new Article 81(2). They concluded that "the EU can adopt ADR measures on the basis of this Article", albeit only in cross-border matters.[54] Hodges and his co-authors argued in the alternative that the EU can rely on sector-specific provisions regarding consumer protection, such as Article 169 of the Lisbon Treaty.[55] They noted nevertheless that "most EU measures regarding consumer law have been adopted on the basis of Article 114 [of the Lisbon Treaty]",[56] which relates to the internal market, although they considered that Article 169(2)(b) might be more appropriate as being expressly concerned with the interests of consumers and their protection,[57] which ADR in the EU is intended to serve.

The competence of the EU to rely on Articles 114 and 169 may not be so clear-cut, however, where the EU is seeking to influence domestic affairs rather than cross-border matters. Dr Rühl noted that the ADR Directive and the ODR Regulation

[50] Pufinas and Zygiotis (2017), p. 406.

[51] *Ibid.*, p. 416.

[52] *Ibid.*

[53] *Consumer ADR*, p. 5.

[54] *Ibid.*, p. 6.

[55] *Ibid.*, p. 7.

[56] *Ibid.*

[57] *Ibid.*

both took their justification from Articles 114 and 169(1)(a) of the Lisbon Treaty, i.e. they were adopted in furtherance of the functioning of the internal market.[58] However, she argued that it is "unclear" whether in fact these measures have objectively contributed to the functioning of the internal market.[59] She contended that the EU has assumed, or simply referred to, the problems with the internal market that both measures are said to help correct, without empirically demonstrating that the internal market is indeed affected so as to engage Articles 114 and/or 169.[60] The authors/draftsmen of both the ADR Directive and the ODR Regulation appear conscious of this issue as they expressly rely on the internal market and consumer protection as their rationale (e.g. Recitals (1) and (6) of each measure), which would perhaps not be necessary if the question were beyond doubt.

While the position is far from clear, the absence of quantifiable evidence that EU legislation intended to address alleged deficiencies in ADR within Member States engages one or both Articles remains a potential issue in terms of the justification of these measures as regards domestic matters. These uncertainties should not, however, affect the EU's competence to deal with issues across Member State borders.

2.3 ADR in the UK for Insurance-Based Investment Products

In order to examine the role of ADR for IBIPs in different EU jurisdictions we shall highlight a few specific example countries, starting with the UK which has the most active scheme in Europe. The use of an Ombudsman to resolve disputes between consumers and private-sector insurance undertakings was first introduced in the UK in 1981 with the Insurance Ombudsman. It was established to resolve complaints on a "fair and reasonable" basis, rather than by strict application of the law. Its decisions bound insurance undertakings, whilst leaving consumers free to litigate in court if they wished. This freedom for consumers was particularly important in overcoming their reluctance to take disputes about insurance contracts to court, given their legal complexities, cost and asymmetry of experience with the insurance products in question as compared to the insurance undertakings themselves. Dr Julian Farrand, the second Insurance Ombudsman (between 1989 and 1994), helped in particular to develop the importance of ADR in resolving disputes about insurance products in the UK.[61]

[58] Rühl (2015), pp. 433–434. She agrees that Article 81(1) only applies to cross-border matters.

[59] *Ibid.*, p. 435.

[60] *Ibid.*, pp. 438–439. C.f. Hodges et al. (2012), p. 20.

[61] Rickett and Telfer (2003), p. 185. During his 5 years in office, Dr Farrand oversaw an increase in complaints handled by his department from 2000 a year to 8133 a year, alienating many insurance companies in the process (*Pensions poach new Ombudsman from insurance: Julian Farrand succeeds Michael Platt*, The Independent, 1 August 1994).

With effect from 1 December 2001 the FOS took over,[62] among other things, the role of the Insurance Ombudsman to resolve disputes between insurance undertakings and consumers, obtaining jurisdiction over insurance policies and investment products. From 14 January 2005, the FOS also acquired jurisdiction over insurance intermediaries. Like the Insurance Ombudsman, the FOS resolves complaints based on what is, in the Ombudsman's opinion, fair and reasonable in all the circumstances of the case.[63] The Ombudsman will take into account relevant law, regulations, practice, guidance and standards, but is not required to follow them prescriptively.[64] The Ombudsman may award up to £150,000 plus interest and costs based on what it considers to be fair compensation, whether or not a court would do so.[65] Also like the Insurance Ombudsman, an Ombudsman decision by the FOS is binding on the insurance undertaking[66] but not the consumer, who may still pursue their complaint in court.[67] There is no right of appeal against an Ombudsman's decision, but in certain limited circumstances it can be subject to judicial review by the court.[68]

Before complaining to the FOS, consumers first need to give the business in question chance to resolve their complaint. If this is unsuccessful or there is no final response from the business within 8 weeks then the consumer can refer their complaint to the FOS. If the business has provided a final response letter rejecting the complaint, the consumer must refer the complaint to the FOS within 6 months of the date of that letter.[69]

Consumers can complain to the FOS orally, or in writing, or digitally. An Adjudicator is assigned to each case, who will try to resolve the complaint in the first instance. The Adjudicator will normally attempt conciliation between the parties, but if that is unsuccessful they may issue a decision. Either party may appeal then that decision to an Ombudsman for a fresh consideration of the complaint.[70]

The FOS is by far the most active scheme in the EU in the context of financial services, and unsurprisingly also has a much larger budget than other member ADR schemes.[71] Its total operating costs in 2014/15 were around £240m, which were paid

---

[62] See http://www.financial-ombudsman.org.uk/.

[63] Dispute Resolution: Complaints in the Financial Conduct Authority Handbook ("DISP") 3.6.1R. Since 2013, FOS publishes reports of Ombudsman's determinations, save where the Ombudsman informs the FOS that it would be inappropriate to do so (DISP 3.6.8G).

[64] DISP 3.6.4R.

[65] DISP 3.7.2R, 3.7.4R and 3.7.5G.

[66] DISP 3.7.12(1)R; c.f. DISP 3.7.13G.

[67] So long as they have not accepted the Ombudsman's decision (*Clark and Clark v In Focus Asset Management and Tax Solutions Limited* [2014] EWCA Civ 118).

[68] For a recent (unusually successful) example, see *R (Aviva Life and Pensions (UK) Limited v Financial Ombudsman Service* [2017] EWHC 352 (Admin).

[69] Hodges et al. (2012), p. 276. The FOS also applies jurisdictional rules as to whether a complaint was referred to it in time and/or the complainant was eligible (DISP 2.7 and 2.8).

[70] *Ibid.*

[71] Hodges et al. (2012), pp. 382–384.

by financial services firms in the first instance but ultimately passed on to consumers in those firms' fees and charges.[72] This was a vast increase from the FOS' initial budget of £21.4m in 2000/01, although its costs have more than doubled in the last 5 years alone.[73] Rapid increases in complaints about PPI led to a significant increase in the FOS' size: it went from entering 2010/11 with around 120,000 new mis-selling cases, to entering 2012/13 and 2013/14 with around 400,000 new mis-selling complaints in each year.[74] The FOS received a total of 1.49m PPI complaints between 2001 and 2016, of which 90% have been received since 2010.[75] However, the number of PPI complaints may now finally be starting to reduce.[76] In order to deal with mass cases such as those involving PPI, the FOS has developed a procedure to appoint a lead case where it identifies a common principle within a group of cases so as to deal efficiently with an issue that will determine a number of other cases.[77]

Whilst 74% of complainants have been satisfied by how the FOS has handled their complaints, only around 52% felt that it took a reasonable length of time.[78] Even so, in 2014/15 only 24% of survey respondents could name the FOS without prompting, despite it spending £330,000 in that period raising awareness.[79] Furthermore, the vast majority of PPI complaints were not brought by consumers direct but by claims management companies, who received between £3.8bn and £5bn of the £22.2bn total compensation paid out to consumers of PPI.[80] Around half of consumers do not use the FOS despite it being free for them, most commonly because of doubts about its effectiveness or concerns about stress.[81]

The FOS takes great pains to inform businesses how to improve their complaint-handling processes based on the data that it accumulates in dealing with complaints against them.[82] It also liaises with the Financial Conduct Authority and the Office of Fair Trading to identify emerging issues that could lead to widespread consumer detriment.[83]

---

[72] Report by the Comptroller and Auditor General, *Financial Services Mis-Selling: Regulation and Redress* (National Audit Office, 24 February 2016), p. 7.

[73] *Ibid.*, p. 26.

[74] *Ibid.*, p. 10. It also almost tripled the number of case handlers and adjudicators, as well as adopting new strategies to deal with volume of similar complaints, and developing new case management software to assist with decision-making (p. 41).

[75] *Ibid.* In 2014/15, after PPI the largest number of complaints dealt with by the FOS concerned "other types of general insurance" (p. 16).

[76] *Financial Ombudsman Service Annual Review 2016/17: Fairness in a Changing World*, p. 49.

[77] Hodges et al. (2012), pp. 278–279.

[78] *Financial Services Mis-Selling*, p. 10.

[79] *Ibid.*, pp. 43–44. Around 80% of respondents nevertheless had "some awareness" of the FOS.

[80] *Ibid.*, p. 10. They may charge between 25% and 33% of the redress paid to consumers (p. 44).

[81] *Ibid.*, p. 44. Such doubts and concerns are not limited to problems with financial services: Pleasence (2006), chapter 3.

[82] Hodges et al. (2012), pp. 277–278.

[83] *Ibid.*, p. 279.

The FOS was a founder member of FIN-NET, which is discussed further below.

2.4 ADR in France for Insurance-Based Investment Products

In summarising the EU's attempts to promote ADR above, we do not wish to suggest that all Member States have been slow to recognise its benefits for resolving insurance disputes. Three Member States in particular were quick to adopt ADR in this way, in addition to the UK.

In 1993, France established a private and voluntary mediation scheme through the *mediateur* of the FFSA. The FFSA represents around 90% of the insurance market and is able to rule on disputes involving members who have signed its Mediation Charter. Under the Charter, insurers and insureds can seek advice from an in-house *mediateur*, and six companies have appointed in-house *mediateurs*. Alternatively, the matter can be referred to the FFSA-appointed *mediateur*, who is appointed unanimously by the Chairman of the National Consumer Institute of Consumption (*Institut National de la Consommation*), the Chairman of the Advisory Committee of the National Insurance Council (*Commission Consultative du Conseil National des Assurances*) and the Chairman of the FFSA, for a renewable term of office of 2 years, and who is a member of FIN-NET.[84]

The *mediateur* has a fairly broad jurisdiction, and there are few limits on the cases they can hear. There is no charge for the mediation service, no limits on the amount at stake and no time limits apply. Article 8 of the Charter specifically provides that the *mediateur* should achieve an amicable solution that cannot replicate the approach of the court, although they should take into account elements of law and equity. However, the *mediateur* can only accept a referral after all of the other means of redress made available by the insurance undertaking in question have been exhausted. In addition, if the mediation does not result in an agreed resolution the *mediateur* can only issue a non-binding written opinion, and the parties are free to litigate the dispute at court.[85]

Hodges *et al* reported that 5316 requests for mediation were made to the *mediateur* in 2010, although that number is a significant increase on the volume of requests between 1995 and 2000 (around 500 per year) and between 2001 and 2005 (around 1300 per year); the greatest increase in volume of requests appears to have been since 2006.[86] However, as many as 45.9% of requests were rejected by the *mediateur* in 2010, and many that proceeded were for small sums (around €100). Of the cases handled by the mediateur, only around 391 formal recommendations were issued in 2010. The majority favoured companies (54.7%), but were acted on by the parties in whole or part in all but 2.5% of cases.[87]

---

[84] *Ibid.*, pp. 51–52. See www.acam-france.fr/mediateurs.

[85] *Ibid.*, p. 53.

[86] *Ibid.*, p. 55.

[87] *Ibid.*, p. 56.

While mediation is useful for disputes between insurance undertakings and consumers, arbitration remains the favoured ADR process for resolving disputes between insurers and reinsurers or between reinsurers. In 1995, France established an insurance and reinsurance arbitration centre accordingly, the CEFAREA, with rules of conduct and procedure, a list of arbitrators and model arbitration clauses.[88]

2.5 *ADR in Germany for Insurance-Based Investment Products*

The most established Ombudsman scheme in Germany is the Insurance Ombudsman,[89] which was created on 1 October 2001 on the initiative of the GDV. Given the particularly large volume of insurance contracts in Germany (more than 400 million, of which more than 90 million involve capital savings), it was considered a service of general interest to the population. The GDV was keen to level the playing field between insurance undertakings and consumers, who could find their insurance contracts complex and difficult to understand, and not have the resources to fight insurance undertakings through court. Hirsch noted the inherent complexity and "juridification" of insurance products, combined with their fundamental importance to society, as reasons compelling to use of ADR between insurers and consumers.[90] The GDV thereby hoped to increase confidence in the insurance industry, and required all insurance undertakings to inform their customers about the Ombudsman.[91]

Accordingly, Germany is perhaps not in the same position as some other Member States concerning IBIPs. The GDV has asserted that German consumers may not find IBIPs especially complicated or difficult to understand and that significant provisions are already in place to protect consumers' interests with IBIPs, for example ensuring that consumers receive accurate calculations of the surrender value of their IBIPs and setting down detailed rules for allocating surpluses to consumers.[92] In these circumstances it may not be inappropriate to limit the consumer's recourse to an ADR process if they are unhappy with their IBIP but nevertheless fully understood what they were buying in advance. Confidence in the market should not be unduly affected by this, and there is less asymmetry between the consumer and insurance undertaking. In order to protect consumers, appropriate ADR should nevertheless remain available for complex IBIPs or IBIPs that are difficult for consumers to understand. In addition, the position in Germany underlines the importance of

---

[88] Hodges et al. (2012), p. 52.

[89] See www.versicherungsombudsmann.de.

[90] Hirsch (2011), p. 562.

[91] Hodges et al. (2012), p. 90.

[92] See the GDV's submissions to EIOPA in respect of its proposed guidance under the IDD for IBIPs: https://eiopa.europa.eu/Publications/Comments/German%20Insurance%20Association%20%28GDV%29_23-05-2017.pdf.

consumer education about financial services and IBIPs, as a potential means of avoiding disputes arising altogether between consumers and insurance undertakings.[93]

The Ombudsman is independent of the trade association (in funding and function) is private, and is part of FIN-NET. It is supported by an Advisory Council, comprising a range of consumer, insurance and parliamentary members, which plays an important role in the Ombudsman's decisions, procedures and appointments, thereby guaranteeing its independence.[94] Around 95% of private insurance undertakings are members of the Insurance Ombudsman Association (*Versicherungsombudsman e.V.*), and fund the Ombudsman by an annual contribution and case fees (€100 per claim, adjusted at the end). This means that the Ombudsman is free of charge for consumers. Consumers also retain the right to reject any decision by the Ombudsman and take their dispute to court, whereas its decisions bind insurance undertakings.[95] An exception is complaints raising important, but unsettled, issues of legal principle, which the Ombudsman leaves to be addressed by the courts.[96]

The Ombudsman procedure is intentionally far more informal that a court process. The consumer must have complained to the insurance undertaking in question and given it at least 6 weeks to reply before they can refer their complaint to the Ombudsman. However, that complaint can be made orally or in writing to the Ombudsman, to which the respondent has around a month to reply. The Ombudsman can accept complaints by consumers against insurance undertakings that are members of the Ombudsman Association, so it cannot accept all insurance-based complaints. The Ombudsman process is entirely written, and the Ombudsman can itself can reject complaints if they would use too much of its resources. Otherwise, as noted above the Ombudsman will only generally agree to withdraw a complaint that concerns a test case of fundamental importance, and the insurer agree to pay the consumer's costs of litigating at court regardless of whether they win or lose.[97]

As the Ombudsman process is intended to be informal, it assists consumers in making complaints. Lawyers are not needed, and are generally not used by the parties. Instead, the Ombudsman initially tries to use conciliation to bring the parties to a mutually acceptable resolution. This is often successful, and the Ombudsman will encourage an insurance undertaking in this regard by indicating if they are likely to rule against the insurance undertaking in any decision about the complaint. Where the Ombudsman makes a decision, they apply the law although there is a degree of flexibility in interpretation where the facts are not clear. The Ombudsman can make

[93] C.f. Godwin and Ramsey (2015), pp. 212–238.

[94] Hirsch (2011), p. 564.

[95] Hodges et al. (2012), pp. 90–91. Since May 2007, the Ombudsman has also dealt with complaints against insurance intermediaries and advisers, in addition to insurers (Hirsch 2011, p. 565).

[96] Hirsch (2011), p. 565.

[97] Hodges et al. (2012), pp. 91–92. C.f. Hirsch (2011), p. 567.

a legally binding decision up to €10,000, and give non-binding recommendations up to €100,000.[98]

Like the French *mediateur*, the volume of complaints dealt with by the Ombudsman has increased during their lifetime, and ranges between around 18,000 and 19,000 a year.[99] The vast majority of these complaints involved less than €5000 or €10,000, and were decided in favour of the insurance undertaking. However, unlike the *mediateur* the Ombudsman accepts the overwhelming majority of the complaints brought to them. In 2010, the Ombudsman cost around €3.2m and had an income of around €3.6m. The Ombudsman has generally been considered a success, and its model was copied in other areas (e.g. transport).[100]

Hirsch has noted how the successful Ombudsman model benefits insurers as well as consumers.[101] Insurers thereby communicate clearly to consumers that they take consumer interests seriously, which improves both insurers' image and the confidence of customers in the industry. In fact, good complaint management is essential to insurers for good relationships with consumers, which ADR can achieve in a particularly effective way by facilitating understanding between the parties.

2.6 ADR in Spain for Insurance-Based Investment Products

In 2002, Spain established the IPF as a measure to reform the financial system.[102] The IPF consults on and assesses complaints free of charge that concern insurance contracts and pension plans issued by insurance entities, and insurance mediators. Individuals and organisations can make use of the IPF, including insurance takers and beneficiaries. Complaints can concern the behaviour of the entity in question, or where its acts or omissions have damaged another's interests or rights.[103]

A claimant must give the financial services company chance to resolve the complaint before referring it to the IPF, meaning that the company must have dismissed the complaint or failed to respond to it for 2 months. In reality, most complaints may be resolved between the consumer and the financial services company direct as Spanish insurance law may be said to favour consumers and so increase pressure on companies to respond constructively to complaints. The claimant can then submit their complaint to the IPF on paper or digitally, and the IPF will liaise between the parties to obtain their comments. The IPF will then apply the law (not equity) to resolve the complaint, and in its recommendation say whether the financial services company breached insurance or pensions regulations, or good practice and financial

[98] *Ibid.*, p. 92.

[99] Hirsch (2011), p. 567.

[100] Hodges et al. (2012), pp. 93–94.

[101] Hirsch (2011), pp. 567–568.

[102] See http://www.dgsfp.mineco.es/reclamaciones/index.asp.

[103] *Ibid.*, p. 222.

customs; however, the IPF will not assess any economic damage that may have been caused. Any decision by the IPF is not binding and so cannot be appealed.[104]

In 2010, the IPF considered around 9574 cases, which was an increase on the previous year. Just over half of these cases were accepted by the IPF, of which half were decided in favour of the financial services company, and about a quarter in favour of the consumer (the balance were terminated in other ways).[105] As noted above, many consumers may not need to rely on ADR and involve the IPF to resolve their complaints against financial services companies because Spanish insurance law firmly encourages those companies to deal with complaints constructively. In this context the higher rate of decisions by the IPF in favour of financial services companies, compared to its decisions in favour of consumers, may reflect a lack of merit in the complaints that the IPF considers; it is possible that companies deal with many meritorious complaints themselves, so a disproportionate number of complaints to the IPF are by consumers who are unwilling to accept a fair resolution to their complaint.

3 FIN-NET

3.1 Introduction

FIN-NET was launched in February 2001 as the network for financial disputes, including those about IBIPs, in the EU, Iceland, Liechtenstein and Norway[106]; its membership is comprised of ADR institutions in these countries. FIN-NET is premised on the tenet that, as discussed above, ADR offers a preferable means of resolving disputes to the formal court process.[107] In comparison to the court, ADR is seen to be a quicker, cheaper and easier process,[108] and therefore beneficial to consumers. This may be especially important in the context of insurance products, whose complexity can regularly produce a "structural asymmetry" between the insurer and the consumer.[109] The advantages of ADR may be increased further in the context of cross-border insurance disputes, where the court in each country operates

[104] *Ibid.*, pp. 222–223.

[105] *Ibid.*, p. 223.

[106] Commission (EC) "FIN-NET activity report 2001-2006", 21 June 2007, p. 2. The ADR Directive specifically notes FIN-NET as an example of networks of ADR entities that "should be strengthened" within the EU (Recital (53)).

[107] Commission (EC) "FIN-NET – Settling cross-border financial disputes out of court: Consumer guide"; and Recitals (4) and (5) of the ADR Directive.

[108] There may, however, be no logical reason to assume that settlements necessarily produce superior outcomes, despite their potential to do so (Galanter and Cahill 1994, pp. 1376–1377). Others have argued more forcefully against the merits of settlement when compared to formal court adjudication (e.g. Fiss 1984, pp. 1073–1090; Nader 1993, pp. 1–25), but there may be no need to see the issue in such polarised terms (Moffitt 2009, pp. 1203–1246).

[109] Hirsch (2011), p. 562.

in a different language and under different procedural rules. FIN-NET thus recognises the freedom with which consumers in the EEA can choose insurance products across borders, and the need to provide easy access to justice for them when disputes arise. In this way, FIN-NET may foster confidence in the internal market and encourage consumers to shop for insurance products across borders.[110]

Recognising that many European countries already operated ADR schemes in the financial services sector that dealt with complaints about financial services in that country,[111] FIN-NET sought to connect those various schemes in order to facilitate consumers from one county using an ADR scheme in a different country where they had purchased financial services,[112] including insurance. Having provided the necessary information, the consumer could then rely on his or her national ADR scheme to lodge the complaint, e.g. about an insurance product, with the relevant scheme in the financial services provider's home country. That ADR scheme would then handle the consumer's complaint in exactly the same way as if it had been made by someone in that country. If it would be more efficient, the consumer's own domestic ADR scheme may ask that the consumer contact the ADR scheme in the other country directly. FIN-NET is thus essentially a network of certain financial services ADR schemes in the EEA.

3.2 *Membership of FIN-NET*

2001 was considered to be a pilot year for FIN-NET. After its launch, Member States began notifying ADR schemes to the EC for membership of FIN-NET. By September 2002, it had 38 members.[113] Its membership had increased to 59 by the end of 2016 covering 26 EEA countries, including Slovakia for the first time.[114] As at May 2018, FIN-NET had 60 members in 27 countries, following the addition of the Mediation Centre of Slovenian Insurance Association,[115] but still lacked members in Bulgaria, Cyprus, Latvia and Romania. As noted above, the national ADR schemes for insurance in the UK, France and Germany are all members of FIN-NET.

In order to join FIN-NET before 12 May 2016, a Member State regulator had to certify to the EC that its ADR scheme complied with all seven principles of

[110] C.f. the discussion above of the competence of the EU to legislate in this area under Articles 114 and/or 169 of the Lisbon Treaty.

[111] And the fact that the jurisdictions of most ADR schemes are limited to financial services providers and/or transactions that take place in the country in which they are established.

[112] (EC) FIN-NET: "Settling cross-border financial disputes out of court: Consumer guide".

[113] FIN-NET activity report 2001-2006, p. 3.

[114] FIN-NET activity report 2016, p. 2.

[115] https://ec.europa.eu/info/business-economy-euro/banking-and-finance/consumer-finance-and-payments/consumer-financial-services/financial-dispute-resolution-network-fin-net/fin-net-network/members-fin-net-country_en.

Recommendation 98/257/EC. These are independence, transparency, adversarial principle, effectiveness, legality, liberty and representation. With effect from 12 May 2016, the procedure has changed as a result of FIN-NET amending its operating rules in light of the ADR Directive and the ODR Regulation.[116] Consequently, since that time FIN-NET's work has been guided by the ADR Directive.[117] As a result, new applicants need to be notified by their competent national authorities as complying with the principles above.[118] It is arguable whether an opt-out approach to membership of FIN-NET might better protect consumers,[119] particularly given the asymmetry that can exist between them and insurance undertakings in the context of cross-border insurance intermediation.

Membership of FIN-NET is subject to its Memorandum of Understanding, which expressly deals with cross-border co-operation between its members within the framework of the ADR Directive and the ODR Regulation.[120] The Memorandum sets out the procedures and co-operation that apply to FIN-NET members in handling cross-border disputes, including those concerning IBIPs, but it is essentially voluntary and so does not give rise to any legal rights or obligations.[121]

The ADR Directive permits variations between Member States as to how the access to ADR required by the Directive is achieved. The schemes under FIN-NET's umbrella vary considerably, including schemes specifically tailored to insurance,[122] as well as those that handle financial services[123] or consumer complaints in general.[124] Thresholds for complaints are also very different, in terms of the schemes' financial thresholds, time limits for bringing complaints and limits on redress awards that can be made.[125] Their coverage also varies, and 22 Member States provide coverage across all relevant financial sectors.[126] The processes used and the status of the decisions of individual services also vary, from conciliation to adjudication, and from recommendations with no binding force to binding determinations. However, many members employ a three-fold model of sequencing or escalating ADR processes, starting with direct contact between consumers and businesses, moving on to mediation and concluding with a form of adjudication (although each

[116] Although very few complaints were received by FIN-NET members via the EU on-line platform in 2016, but FIN-NET expects this to increase in 2017 (FIN-NET activity report 2016, p. 3).

[117] FIN-NET activity report 2016, p. 2.

[118] Commission (EC) "FIN-NET activity report 2015", October 2016, p. 3. A transitional period of 2 years applies to existing FIN-NET members who have not yet been notified as ADR-compliant.

[119] Petrauskas and Gasiunaite (2012), pp. 184–185.

[120] See https://ec.europa.eu/info/sites/info/files/memorandum-of-understanding_en.pdf.

[121] Hodges et al. (2012), p. 16.

[122] E.g. in Belgium, Croatia, Denmark, Finland, France, Germany, Iceland, Italy, Luxembourg and Spain.

[123] Which may also include insurance, e.g. in the Netherlands, Ireland and the UK.

[124] E.g. in Sweden, which can deal with insurance disputes.

[125] Hodges et al. (2012), pp. 379–380.

[126] FIN-NET activity report 2015, p. 3.

of these stages may be divided into one or more further steps).[127] As noted above in the context of Germany, the key purpose for any insurance ADR process must be effectiveness so as to foster consumer confidence in the industry; it is therefore appropriate that members of FIN-NET are not bound by too prescriptive a process.

Because of its membership requirements,[128] FIN-NET does not represent an exhaustive network of all ADR schemes that deal with financial services, or insurance, disputes in the EEA. Some ADR schemes were not certified to the EC by their Member States as complying with Recommendation 98/257/EC, whereas others are treated as affiliates until such time as they meet FIN-NET's membership requirements.[129]

3.3 *Operation of FIN-NET*

Since its inception in 2001, members of FIN-NET have handled exponentially more cases. In 2001, its members handled 335 cases,[130] whereas in 2016 they handled 2571 cases, of which 592 concerned insurance.[131] Measured by increase in caseload, ADR in Europe is therefore a demonstrable success. However, it is difficult to assess what this data shows for each member of FIN-NET. Historically such cases have not been evenly distributed between FIN-NET's members. Instead, a small number have dealt with the majority of cases.[132]

FIN-NET's activity reports contain examples of its work in particular areas of financial services, including insurance. Recent examples in the past few years cover a wide variety of situations: travel insurance, health insurance, life insurance, car insurance, pension insurance and insurance to guarantee a loan contract. Although it does not yet provide any case studies on IBIPs, it is helpful to consider how these examples show FIN-NET affecting the resolution of cross-border insurance disputes by ADR in the EEA and where consumers may otherwise be disadvantaged.

Perhaps unsurprisingly, a number of the cases reported by FIN-NET concerned travel insurance. In 2013, the French *mediateur* persuaded their German colleague to cover both an insured elderly lady who missed her flight after injuring herself, and her friend who travelled with her.[133] That same year, two Hungarian citizens were refused cover by their Irish travel insurer when their flight was cancelled due

---

[127] Hodges et al. (2012), pp. 405–408.

[128] See Sect. 3.2 above.

[129] E.g. the Swiss Banking Ombudsman has been an observer (now affiliate) for many years. The *Arbitro Bancario Finianziario* of Italy was a candidate scheme for FIN-NET in 2010, before joining as a member in 2011.

[130] FIN-NET activity report 2001-2006, p. 7.

[131] FIN-NET activity report 2016, p. 5. This was a lower number of insurance disputes than the peak of 1263 in 2013, and less than the 699 insurance disputes in 2015.

[132] Hodges et al. (2012), p. 16; c.f. pp. 378–379.

[133] FIN-NET activity report 2013-2014, pp. 8–9.

to strikes. The Hungarian Financial Arbitration Board liaised with the Irish insurer, who then made an offer to the Hungarians that settled the case.[134] In 2015, a dispute arose over cover for flights that were cancelled due to the insured's sickness. After intervention from the National Board for Consumer Disputes (SE), the case was settled without the need for a formal recommendation by the Board.[135] In 2016, a UK citizen received assistance from the Irish Financial Services Ombudsman when an Irish travel insurer refused to pay for his hospital care abroad.[136]

A number of cases reported by FIN-NET have also dealt with health insurance. In 2013, an EU citizen bought health insurance with a Maltese provider, which subsequently imposed large increases on his premiums. After the business failed to resolve his complaint, he referred it to the Malta Financial Services Authority, whose Consumer Complaints Unit persuaded the business to terminate the policy and refund all premiums.[137] In 2014, a resident of Amsterdam complained when his UK-based insurer refused to cover two email consultations with a doctor. The FOS upheld the complaint and determined that the consultations should be covered.[138]

As noted above, FIN-NET has also dealt recently with complaints about other areas of insurance. In 2014, a French consumer purchased insurance from a Maltese company to guarantee a loan contract. The insurer declined cover, so the French *mediateur* liaised with his colleague in Malta. They decided that the insurer was entitled to refuse cover as the consumer had failed to declare two diseases for which they had been taking medical treatment.[139] Also in 2014, a Lithuanian citizen was involved in a car accident in Poland and claimed various sums from their insurance company. The Polish insurer tried to lower the indemnity provided to the consumer, but this was rejected by the Insurance Ombudsman.[140] In 2015, a French consumer involved the *mediateur* in contacting his colleague in Luxembourg after the consumer tried and failed to cancel a pension insurance product from an insurance undertaking there. As a result, the insurer agreed to reimburse the amounts paid and cancel the contract.[141] Also in 2015, a consumer complained to the FOS after her Spanish life insurer refused to pay out on her policy. The FOS was unable to consider the complaint as the insurer was based in Spain, but it used FIN-NET to provide the correct Spanish authority with details of the complaint, and informed the consumer how to pursue it.[142]

[134] *Ibid.*, p. 10.

[135] FIN-NET activity report 2015, p. 7.

[136] FIN-NET activity report 2016, pp. 5–6.

[137] FIN-NET activity report 2013-2014, p. 9.

[138] *Ibid.*, pp. 10–11.

[139] FIN-NET activity report 2013-2014, p. 10.

[140] *Ibid.* The Lithuanian Insurance Supervisory Commission was established in 2003 to handle disputes about insurance, but its functions were passed to the Bank of Lithuania in 2012 (Hodges et al. 2012, pp. 122–123).

[141] FIN-NET activity report, 2015, p. 7.

[142] *Ibid.*, pp. 7–8.

In 2016, FIN-NET members also assisted consumers to deal with banking issues between Member States. The FOS helped a German consumer who was unhappy with her British bank, and the FOS also put a Greek citizen in contact with her Hellenic bank over issues withdrawing cash in England.[143]

3.4 Evaluation of FIN-NET

3.4.1 Evaluation by the CSES

In 2009, DG Internal Market and Services commissioned an evaluation of FIN-NET by the Centre for Strategy and Evaluation Services.[144]

As regards relevance, the resulting report's conclusions were positive. It found that whilst the volume of cross-border financial services activity was relatively limited, almost all stakeholders saw a need to support consumers in dealing effectively with cross-border disputes.[145] It also found overwhelming support for FIN-NET's approach,[146] which was not duplicated by the other networks established by the EC to assist consumers in cross-border disputes.[147]

The report also reached positive conclusions about FIN-NET's quantitative performance, albeit in the context of a limited cross-border trade in financial services.[148] The report estimated that the number of complaints with which FIN-NET members dealt was in proportion to the level of underlying cross-border trade.[149] It also found that very few cases were not handled via the network of FIN-NET members to an ultimate conclusion.[150]

However, important problems with FIN-NET's effectiveness were also uncovered, in particular a lack of consumer awareness of it,[151] the inconsistency between aspects of the different member ADR schemes[152] (although the ADR Directive expressly permits variety in this regard), and gaps in the coverage of those schemes in certain financial services sectors and Member States.[153] Even so, members of FIN-NET were clear that it had encouraged co-operation between them, along with information- and experience-sharing.[154] FIN-NET is nevertheless considering

---

143 FIN-NET Activity Report 2016, p. 6.

144 DG Internal Market and Services, Evaluation of FIN-NET (2009).

145 *Ibid.*, p. 38.

146 *Ibid.*, pp. 39–40.

147 *Ibid.*, pp. 40–41.

148 *Ibid.*, pp. 11–13 and p. 29.

149 *Ibid.*, pp. 41–42.

150 *Ibid.*, p. 42.

151 *Ibid.*, p. 44.

152 *Ibid.* The report also criticised the limited activity and involvement of some members (p. 46).

153 *Ibid.*, pp. 43–44.

154 *Ibid.*, p. 45.

whether national ADR schemes should remain empowered to define their own redress systems in light of the extent of integration in the retail financial services market.[155] Greater homogeneity may be possible following the exit of the UK from the EU.

Finally, the report considered that FIN-NET was run with reasonable efficiency, although it was difficult to gauge that accurately in the circumstances.[156] It also identified FIN-NET's website as needing further attention and development.[157]

Accordingly, the report recommended that FIN-NET should maintain what it did well whilst continuing its efforts to increase its membership and reduce coverage gaps, and adopt measures to raise its profile and improve its website.[158] We turn to discuss a number of the points below.

3.4.2 Lack of Awareness

Consumer and business awareness of FIN-NET remains a challenge of which it is acutely aware. To address this, it has suggested a formal "awareness campaign".[159] FIN-NET is not alone in cross-boarder entities facing this problem.[160] Nevertheless, we consider that this is a fair criticism and the priority for Member States should be to focus in on ensuring that potential stakeholders have a full understanding of the systems. This approach may usefully inform FIN-NET's ongoing efforts to increase its own profile in the awareness of businesses and consumers. These efforts were assisted in September 2016, when two German State Secretaries from the Ministry of Finance and the Ministry of Justice offered the German government's support to FIN-NET.[161] Further, in March 2017 the EC announced a future FIN-NET awareness-raising campaign as part of its action plan on consumer financial services, including modernisation of its website, a promotion video and a social media campaign.[162]

Increased awareness can be greatly facilitated where a country's dispute resolution architecture is fundamentally geared towards ADR.[163] For those countries that do not have deeply well-established ADR systems, it is likely to require a significant period of concerted effort by the national governments and ADR schemes to reach this point. Nevertheless, there is no substitute for a reliable and efficient means of providing relevant information, as well as ensuring that the information itself is clear and accessible; this should reduce the instances of disputes being directed to

155 FIN-NET activity report 2015, p. 3.

156 DG Internal Market and Services, Evaluation of FIN-NET, p. 50.

157 *Ibid.*, p. 54.

158 *Ibid.*, pp. 63–67. C.f. Inchausti (2014), pp. 197–208.

159 FIN-NET activity report 2015, p. 3.

160 Rühl (2015), p. 449. C.f. Hodges et al. (2012), pp. 408–409 and pp. 430–433. As noted above with the FOS, even established national schemes can face similar problems.

161 FIN-NET Activity Report, p. 3.

162 *Ibib.*

163 Hodges et al. (2012), p. 408.

an inappropriate ADR scheme.[164] Timing may also be important, ensuring that consumers are provided with the information at each key stage, such as when a dispute arises and again when direct discussions between the consumer and the business fail.[165] Awareness of ADR processes for resolving insurance disputes is good within some members, such as the UK, France and Germany considered above, so it should be possible to include sufficient information within documents passing between consumers and insurance businesses that consumers from other countries are also aware of their ADR options.

3.4.3 Gaps in Coverage

FIN-NET is not alone in failing to achieve its potential in cross-border ADR.[166] Gaps in coverage remain a serious challenge to its effectiveness in the EEA. The ODR Regulation may help to reduce gaps in coverage by providing consumers with a single online portal for complaints, at least where they are concluded online.[167] However, they may then still be reliant on the existence and competence of an appropriate ADR scheme to resolve their disputes.[168]

FIN-NET will still therefore have an important role to play in facilitating discussion about this issue, even after enactment of the ADR Directive, particularly as the Directive does not require ADR schemes in any one country to accept complaints about businesses established in another country.[169] It therefore remains vital that FIN-NET members can continue to assist consumers by referring appropriate complaints to each other across borders, although the network's usefulness in this regard is necessarily limited by the effectiveness of its members. It is therefore somewhat surprising that FIN-NET has recently made attaining membership more difficult. This places the onus back on Member States to establish ADR schemes that comply with FIN-NET's Memorandum of Understanding in order to increase its membership. Nevertheless, FIN-NET remains conscious of the need to improve its level of coverage, particularly in Member States where it is not yet present.[170]

In doing so, there may be issues with the links of Member State ADR schemes to the insurance industry, and thus their impartiality. Under the ADR Directive Member States are specifically required to ensure that all disputes covered by the Directive are subject to an appropriate ADR entity (Article 5(1)). As noted above, some successful ADR schemes arise from industry initiatives, such as the GDV in Germany and the French *mediateur*. However, not all Member State ADR schemes follow the

[164] *Ibid.*, p. 409.

[165] Rühl (2015), p. 450.

[166] *Ibid.*, pp. 444–445.

[167] *Ibid.*, p. 448. In its first year, the EU reported that the ODR platform was used by 24,000 consumers: http://europa.eu/rapid/press-release_IP-17-727_en.htm.

[168] *Ibid.*, pp. 448–449.

[169] *Ibid.*, p. 448.

[170] FIN-NET Activity Report 2016, p. 4.

same pattern, such as the Netherlands and the UK.[171] There is no single solution for all Member States, so the success or otherwise of any particular ADR scheme may depend in no small part on the suitability of that entity for the culture of the country in question.[172] As noted above, the key requirement for any successful insurance ADR process must be its effectiveness, and the confidence that it therefore produces in the industry for IBIPs.

Success may also depend on the ADR process that is used. To the extent that a scheme endeavours to conciliate or mediate a dispute, it may be inappropriate to require parties to submit to it. The precise content and structure of such processes vary tremendously as a result of their varying degrees of informality.[173] Nevertheless, choice and control for those using the processes are essential. Professor Fuller considered that the "central quality" of mediation is "its capacity to reorient the parties towards each other, not by imposing rules on them, but by helping them to achieve a new and shared perception of their relationship".[174] The centrality of this relationship may be especially pronounced in disputes concerning insurance products, which may be long-term investments. Coercion to conciliation or mediation can reduce the reactive devaluation that might otherwise attach to one party suggesting those processes to another,[175] but it can also severely undermine their effectiveness. Research in England has noted how pressure to mediation in particular may "propel" cases into the procedure, but that "this is not necessarily particularly effective in terms of settlement rates" and can instead increase costs and delays.[176]

There is also a subtle, but potentially equally damaging, risk that if the EU requires parties to use conciliation or mediation then it could contaminate these informal processes by "integrating [them] in the overall structure of state political and legal domination".[177] Once integrated, conciliation and/or mediation "loses autonomy and is put to service in a diffuse peripheral area of political domination… as a kind of state-produced non-state power".[178] Thus, even whilst the state seems to retract as disputes are handed over to conciliation and/or mediation, it is in reality expanding as its control extends into those processes.[179] It has been said that the state thereby defuses public anger at perceived injustice at little cost to itself by co-

[171] *Ibid.*, p. 154, pp. 247–276.

[172] It may therefore be less suitable in countries whose culture already prizes co-operation and informal compliance, such as the Netherlands and Sweden (Hodges et al. 2012, pp. 164–165 and pp. 251–252).

[173] There is no universal professional qualification for conciliation or mediation, or requirement to be qualified in any formal sense. However, as noted above the EC launched its voluntary Code of Conduct for Mediators in 2004.

[174] Fuller (1971), p. 325.

[175] Barendrecht and de Vries (2005), p. 97.

[176] Genn et al. (2007), p. 205.

[177] De Sousa Santos (1980), p. 387.

[178] *Ibid.*

[179] *Ibid.*, p. 391.

opting conciliation and/or mediation to its assistance.[180] This is not a role, of course, that those processes are intended to play and to utilise them in this way poses a risk of ultimately compromising their effectiveness.

3.4.4 Language

Finally, it hardly needs to be said that the multiplicity of languages across the EEA represents an enormous practical difficulty in the effectiveness of ADR schemes in cross-border disputes, including those concerning insurance intermediaries and products.[181] It has been noted above how FIN-NET can assist in this area, facilitating communication between national ADR schemes across borders to assist consumers who may not otherwise be able to complain effectively. This difficulty may be less pronounced for the larger insurance undertakings and/or intermediaries, which are themselves international organisations capable of dealing with consumers and ADR schemes in multiple languages. Even then, each country's ADR scheme operates in a particular language, and smaller insurance organisations may struggle to work in any other language. It is possible that the ODR Regulation will assist with this issue by establishing an online portal that consumers can use in any of the EU's official languages.[182]

This is another area in which practice among ADR schemes varies considerably. Most schemes will accept a complaint in their own language and in English, but few accept complaints in many more languages, or in any language whatsoever.[183] In addition, only a small number of schemes issue their decisions in different languages or translate their decisions.[184] There may be no reason in principle why individual ADR schemes cannot operate in more languages, but in practice issues of cost and proportionality may play a significant role.

Petrescu has noted how language issues might be especially important in terms of best practice for entities operating in insurance.[185] In particular, it affects key aspects of insurance business such as communications with consumers, management of websites, knowing consumers and managing and settling disputes between businesses and consumers. It will therefore be important to resolve language issues if ADR is to be truly effective for disputes over IBIPs.

---

[180] Abel (1982), p. 281.

[181] FIN-NET's use of only three languages has been criticised: see DG Internal Market and Services, Evaluation of FIN-NET (2009), 66, which recommended making all "key information" available in all 25 languages of the EEA.

[182] Rühl (2015), p. 451.

[183] DG Internal Market and Services, Evaluation of FIN-NET (2009), p. 19.

[184] *Ibid.* The Financial Ombudsman Service in the UK resolves disputes in 49 languages (Hodges et al. 2012, p. 281).

[185] Petrescu (2016), pp. 232–236.

4 Conclusion

This chapter has discussed the increasing importance placed by the EU on resolving disputes, including disputes about IBIPs, by ADR. Some of the most advanced national services have focused on financial services and insurance products for many years now, and in the past 20 years there has also been considerable focus by the EU on these areas. The approach of the EU in this regard has gradually hardened, from initial encouragement towards ADR, to more recent direct legislation requiring greater use of ADR schemes to resolve such disputes as summarised at the beginning of this chapter.[186] EIOPA's recent guidance on IBIPs suggests that strict limits will be imposed on transactions involving them that are potentially not subject to ADR because they were transacted on an "execution-only" basis. It remains to be seen what effect the requirements for ADR in the IDD, with its focus on IBIPs, will have once the IDD has come fully into force.

Whilst this change may be broadly welcomed in improving access to justice, in particular across borders, it raises particular issues for the effectiveness ADR processes that are by nature voluntary and non-binding. Any challenge to the effectiveness of an ADR process is especially concerning in the context of IBIPs, as that can reduce consumer confidence in those investments. In an industry where there may often by substantial asymmetry between insurance business and consumer, particularly given the potential complexity of IBIPs, it is vital that consumer confidence remains high.

FIN-NET plays an important role in ADR in the EEA, uniting a number of the relevant ADR schemes in a single network that demonstrably assists consumers to resolve cross-border disputes effectively, especially concerning IBIPs, albeit with some gaps in coverage. FIN-NET nevertheless faces a particular challenge in making insurance businesses and consumers aware of its work, ensuring that they are not only informed about it but also understand it, which FIN-NET is looking to address. Progress in this area should be possible as consumer awareness is good of some capable national ADR schemes for insurance within FIN-ET members, such as the UK, France and Germany. Language also plays an important part, as few members of FIN-NET (or other relevant ADR schemes) operate in more than a few languages. It is important that these issues are addressed so as not to undermine the effectiveness of insurance ADR processes, and consumer confidence in IBIPs.

It remains to be seen whether recent advances in ODR will help to address some of these issues.[187] By comparison with other jurisdictions, EU initiatives to resolve

[186] Indeed, the European Court of Justice has recently ruled that the ADR Directive does not prevent national legislation imposing compulsory mediation on consumers as a pre-condition to litigation, so long as the parties are not denied their rights to access the judicial system (*Menini and another v Banco Popolare Societa Cooperativa*, Case C-75/16, 14 June 2017).

[187] In December 2017, the EU published the findings of its on-line study researching compliance of on-line traders with the ODR Regulation, which showed that only 28% of EU on-line traders presented a link to the ODR platform on their websites (*Online Dispute Resolution: Web-Scraping of EU Traders' Websites: Final Report*, JUST/2016/CONS/FW/CO03/0104, 1 December 2017, p. 28).

insurance disputes by ODR may appear underdeveloped.[188] Christofilou noted developments in ODR in America since the 1990s, which have produced technology to assist adjusters and lawyers to accelerate the settlement of insurance claims.[189] Even this technology is not a perfect solution by itself, however, as actors in the insurance industry must be willing to engage with it, on both sides of the fence (i.e. both insurance undertakings and consumers).[190] As well as showing greater interest in this regard, those involved with insurance disputes in the EU will also need to consider the extent to which automated ODR systems can meet market needs to resolve disputes; they may be better suited to quantum analysis rather than determining liability, and should be fitted to the experience and sophistication of the parties using them.[191] The ODR Regulation is helpful, but for the reasons given above it is too soon to draw any conclusions about its effectiveness in operation. It remains to be seen whether regulation alone can achieve these aims, and whether key stakeholders in insurance disputes will take the initiative to explore the potential of ODR to resolve their disputes. To the extent that ODR can assist to resolve standard aspects of insurance claims, the cost benefit for both insurance undertakings and consumers may merit further investment in this area.

Such challenges as we have discussed may reflect the underlying fact that cross-border trade in insurance, as in other financial services, remains relatively low. This limits the amount of international interest in the resulting disputes, and the justification in straightened economic times for investing the resources necessary to address them. Nevertheless, whilst challenges to the EU's goal of an ever-closer union remain, particularly in light of Brexit, ADR looks set to play an increasingly important role in dealing effectively with the disputes that will unavoidably arise about insurance intermediaries and insurance products.

References

Abel RL (1982) The contradictions of informal justice. In: Abel RL (ed) The politics of informal justice. Academic Press, London/New York

Barendrecht M, de Vries BR (2005) Fitting the forum to the fuss with sticky defaults: failure in the market for dispute resolution services. Cardozo J Confl Resolut 7:83–118

Cappelletti M (1993) Alternative dispute resolution processes within the framework of the worldwide access to justice movement. Modern Law Rev 56:282–296

Christofilou A (2016) Online dispute resolution and insurance. In: Marano P et al (eds) The "Dematerialized" insurance. Springer, Cham

Clark and Clark v In Focus Asset Management and Tax Solutions Limited [2014] EWCA Civ 118

---

[188] C.f. Christofilou (2016), pp. 278–279, and pp. 292–294 (discussing Benoam, the online arbitration system established in Israel in 2002 to resolve subrogation claims between insurance undertakings in car accidents where there is no personal injury).

[189] *Ibid.*, pp. 273–274.

[190] *Ibid.*, p. 274.

[191] *Ibid.*, p. 275.

Commission (EC) "Alternative Dispute Resolution in the Area of Financial Services – Consultation Document", 11 December 2008
Commission (EC) "FIN-NET – Settling cross-border financial disputes out of court: Consumer guide"
Commission (EC) "FIN-NET activity report 2001-2006", 21 June 2007
Commission (EC) "FIN-NET activity report 2015", October 2016
Commission (EC) "FIN-NET activity report 2016"
Commission (EC) "Summary of the responses to the public consultation on alternative dispute resolution in the area of financial services", 14 September 2009
Commission (EU) "Green Paper on retail financial services", 10 December 2015
Commission (EU) "Summary of contributions to the Green Paper on retail financial services" (COM (2015), 630 final)
Consultation document on the Review of the IMD, Commission Staff Working Paper
De Sousa Santos B (1980) Law and community: the changing nature of state power in late capitalism. Int J Sociol Law 8:379–397
DG Internal Market and Services, Evaluation of FIN-NET (2009)
Financial Ombudsman Service Annual Review 2016/17: Fairness in a Changing World
Fiss OM (1984) Against settlement. Yale Law J 93:1073–1090
Fitzpatrick P (1993) The impossibility of popular justice. In: Merry SE, Milner N (eds) The possibility of popular justice. University of Michigan Press, Ann Arbor
Fuller LL (1971) Mediation – its forms and functions. South Calif Law Rev 44:305–339
Galanter M, Cahill M (1994) Most cases settle: judicial promotion and regulation of settlements. Stanford Law Rev 46:1339–1391
Genn H, Fenn P, Masson M, Lane A, Bechai N, Gray L, Vencappa D (2007) Twisting arms: court referred and court linked mediation under judicial pressure, Ministry of Justice Research Series, 1/07
Godwin A, Ramsey I (2015) Financial products and short-form disclosure documents: a comparative analysis of six jurisdictions. Cap Mark Law J 10(2):212–238
Hirsch G (2011) The german insurance ombudsman. Zeitschrift für die gesamte Versicherungswissenschaft 100(4):561–569
Hodges C (2015) Verbraucher-Ombudsstellen: Besserere Regulierung und Beilegung von Streitigkeiten. Zeitschrift für das Privatrecht der Europäischen Union
Hodges C, Benöhr I, Creutzfeldt-Banda N (2012) Consumer ADR in Europe. Hart, Oxford
Inchausti FG (2014) Specific problems of cross-border consumer ADR: what solutions? Zeitschrift fur das Privatrect der Europaischen Union 11(4):197–208
Menini and another v Banco Popolare Societa Cooperativa, Case C-75/16, 14 June 2017
Moffitt M (2009) Three things to be against (Settlement Not Included). Fordham Law Rev 78(3):1203–1246
Nader L (1993) Controlling processes in the practice of law: hierarchy and pacification in the movement to re-form dispute ideology. Ohio State J Disput Resolut 10:1–25
Online Dispute Resolution: Web-Scraping of EU Traders' Websites: Final Report, JUST/2016/CONS/FW/CO03/0104, 1 December 2017
Petrauskas F, Gasiunaite A (2012) Alternative dispute resolution in the field of consumer financial services. Jurisprudence 19(1):179–194
Petrescu RM (2016) Identifying best practices in insurance, Challenges of the knowledge society, 232–236
Pleasence P (2006) Causes of action: civil law and social justice, 2nd edn. TSO, London
Pufinas T, Zygiotis Z (2017) How transparency affects investment-linked insurance products. Int Adv Econ Res 23:405–418
R (Aviva Life and Pensions (UK) Limited v Financial Ombudsman Service [2017] EWHC 352 (Admin)
Report by the Comptroller and Auditor General, *Financial Services Mis-Selling: Regulation and Redress* (National Audit Office, 24 February 2016)

Rickett CEF, Telfer TGW (eds) (2003) International perspectives on consumers' access to justice. Cambridge University Press, Cambridge

Roberts S, Palmer M (2005) Dispute processes: ADR and the primary forms of decision making, 2nd edn. Cambridge University Press, Cambridge

Rühl G (2015) Alternative and online dispute resolution for cross-border consumer contracts: a critical evaluation of the European Legislature's recent efforts to boost competitiveness and growth in the internal market. J Consum Policy 38:431–456

Part II
Liability in the Context of Distribution

France

Yannis Samothrakis

Contents

Abbreviations

ACPR	Autorité de contrôle prudentiel et de résolution
EEA	European Economic Area
IDD	Directive (EU) 2016/97 on insurance distribution
KID	Key Information Document
ORIAS	Organisme pour le Registre des Intermédiaires en Assurance

Y. Samothrakis (✉)
Clyde & Co LLP, Paris, France
e-mail: Yannis.Samothrakis@clydeco.com

P. Marano, I. Rokas (eds.), *Distribution of Insurance-Based Investment Products*, https://doi.org/10.1007/978-3-030-11668-2_5

PRIIPS Regulation	Regulation 1286/2014 on key information documents for packaged retail and insurance-based investment products
Solvency II Directive	Directive 2009/138/EC of the European Parliament and of the Council of 25 November 2009 on the taking-up and pursuit of the business of Insurance and Reinsurance

1 Introduction: Sources of Insurance Law in France

Insurance-based investments products in France consist in insurance contracts falling under branch 22 of Article R. 321-1 of the Insurance Code, i.e. "Insurance linked to investment funds" otherwise referred to as unit-linked insurance contracts.

As analysed in more details under [Chapter I], this generic term can cover a great variety of insurance-based investment products. Few other areas of insurance law have been subject to such fluctuations, as case law and statutory changes generated a great level of uncertainty for years. While the legal dust seems to have somehow settled, innovation in the actual structure of contracts remains arguably in the hands of the legislator, while insurance companies have limited powers of initiative in a narrowly defined regulatory framework.

The law applicable to insurance contracts in general comes from a number of sources and its nature is rather composite.

As a starting point, French positive law does not provide any definition of insurance, insurance operation or insurance contracts, arguably because of the complexity of agreeing on such a definition.[1]

In spite of its numerous specificities, insurance constitutes a contractual operation which is subject to the fundamental concepts of civil law found, *inter alia*, in the Civil Code as recently amended.[2] As such, it is "*formed by the meeting of an acceptance and of an offer by which the parties indicate their willingness to commit*".[3]

The offer is often referred to as *pollicitation*, i.e. a firm offer which must be precise enough to be accepted as such by the other party, which entails that it contains the essential elements of the contract, namely the object and the price.[4]

The reminder of this principle is essential in light of the developments that follow, mainly because aside from the many formalistic constrains affecting the conclusion of insurance based insurance products, their formation remains subject to the fundamental principle of offer and acceptance.

---

[1] Bigot et al. (2014).

[2] French contract law was subject to a major reform contained in ordinance n°2016-131 of 10 February 2016 amending the Civil Code and which entered into force on 1st October 2016.

[3] Article 113 of the Civil Code (our translation).

[4] Malaurie and Aynès (2016).

1.1 The Main Sources of French Statutory Insurance Law

1.1.1 EU Law as a Primary Source of French Insurance Law

The precedence of EU law has long been recognised by both Supreme Courts, i.e. the Civil Supreme Court[5] (*Cour de cassation*) and the Adminsitrative Supreme Court[6] (*Conseil d'Etat*).

In that context, as for every EU Member State, French insurance law consists to a large extent in the transposition of the EU insurance directives now consolidated under the Solvency II Directive.

Other relevant instruments of EU law have been analysed in detail under Chapter I; while it is not within the scope of this chapter to provide an exhaustive list of the sources of EU law, let us nevertheless stress the importance of other instruments which do not specifically target insurance or financial services but are fundamental in the functioning of the single market.

Such instruments include the Rome I Regulation on contractual obligations[7] which, in spite of its perceived shortcomings,[8] is a significant tool in structuring insurance covers spanning several jurisdictions, as well as the Rome II Regulation on non-contractual obligations.[9]

1.1.2 The Insurance Code, the Mutual Code and the Social Security Code

Unit-linked insurance contracts may be offered by French-authorised undertakings falling under the following categories:

- Limited companies (which includes the *sociétés anonymes* and the Societas Europeae);
- Mutuals;
- Provident institutions (*institutions de prévoyance*), a specific type of undertakings co-managed by employers and employees.

Each is subject to specific provisions of either the Insurance Code (limited companies and some mutuals); the Mutual Code (certain types of mutuals); and the Social Security Code (provident institutions).

---

[5] Cass. Ch. mixte, 24 mai 1975, Société Cafés Jacques Vabre.

[6] CE Ass. 20 octobre 1989, Nicolo.

[7] Regulation (EC) No 593/2008 of the European Parliament and of the Council of 17 June 2008 on the law applicable to contractual obligations (Rome I).

[8] See *inter alia* the report of the European Commission set up an Expert Group on European Insurance Contract law of 24 January 2014 available at: http://ec.europa.eu/justice/contract/files/expert_groups/insurance/final_report_en.pdf.

[9] Regulation (EC) No 864/2007 of the European Parliament and of the Council of 11 July 2007 on the law applicable to non-contractual obligations (Rome II).

While some differences in drafting do exist between the Codes,[10] they are of no relevance for the purpose of this Chapter and as such, we will focus on the provisions contained in the Insurance Code.

Contracts offered in France by insurance undertakings operating either under freedom of services or freedom of establishment will be subject to the relevant provisions of the Insurance Code.

1.2 Case Law

In addition to what has been mentioned above, insurance operations are also subject to a variety of other sources of law which can be found in any type of statutory or regulatory instrument including other codes, acts of Parliament and more generally for business-to-consumer schemes, in the ever-evolving corpus of consumer-protection legislation.

In addition, changes to insurance law are often treated as measures ancillary to more politically strategic issues and as such are arguably not drafted with the attention to clarity and consistency that the complexity of insurance requires.[11]

In that context, the role of the Courts in interpreting insurance law has been significant, alas not always fostering consistency and clarity. This is particularly the case for the law applicable to insurance-based investment contracts where statutory provisions and case law have generated a great level of uncertainty.

1.3 The Role of the Supervisor

The French insurance supervisor ACPR (*Autorité de contrôle prudentiel et de resolution*) is given a wide range of powers which are listed in the Financial and Monetary Code.

In particular, Article L. 612-29-1 of the Financial and Monetary Code authorises the ACPR to approve certain codes of conducts issued by professional associations, thus making them enforceable against the members of such associations:

> Where a professional association representing the interests of one or more categories of persons subject to the competence of the ACPR or subject to its control issues a code of conduct in relation to distribution and customer protection designed to specify the rules

[10] Essentially between the Insurance Code and the Mutual Code as Article L 923-23 of the Social Security Code generally refers back to the Insurance Code.

[11] As an example, the Constitutional Court recently stroke out a provision allowing for the termination of mortgage insurance at any time because "…*these additions were not, at this stage of the procedure, directly related to a provision still under discussion. Nor were they intended to ensure compliance with the Constitution, to coordinate with texts under consideration or to correct a material error*"—in other words, the inclusion of the specific provision had no relation with the rest of the Act. Decision n° 2016-741 of 8 December 2016.

> applicable to its members, the authority shall verify its compatibility with the laws and regulations applicable to them. The association may request the authority to approve all or parts of the codes of good practice in relation to distribution and customer protection policies. The publication of the approval by the Authority of these codes makes them enforceable against all the members of this association under the conditions fixed by the codes or the decision of approval.

The ACPR's powers go further, as the same article grants it the power to "*determine the existence of good professional practices*" and to "*formulate recommendations defining rules of good professional practice with regard to distribution and customer protection*".

Finally, the ACPR also has the ability to issue other *soft law* instruments, in particular positions and recommendations, always pursuant to article L. 612-29-1 of the Financial and Monetary Code. In theory, these recommendations should not be adding to the law but merely providing the ACPR's own interpretation or clarification of how it intends to enforce them. In practice however, several examples illustrate that recommendations can go much further than that. For instance, its recommendation of 8 January 2013 on unit-linked life insurance[12] provides (under paragraph 4.1.5) that:

> the information gathered previously be updated as necessary to ensure that the advice provided is adapted to the client's profile:
>
> - at the time of taking the life insurance contract;
> - in the event of a new payment, partial surrender or switch between investments, where such transactions are likely to result in a material change in the life insurance contract.

While article L. 132-27-1 of the Insurance Code does provide for the obligation to collect such information at the time of taking the contract, the ongoing duty imposed on insurers to check such information during the life of the contract is a pure creation by the ACPR.

2 The Distribution of Investment-Based Insurance Products

In order to analyse the liability of different actors in the distribution of insurance-based investment products, it is essential briefly to summarise the types of contracts we refer to as well as the different actors involved in their distribution.

[12] *Recommandation sur le recueil des informations relatives à la connaissance du client dans le cadre du devoir de conseil en assurance-vie*, available at http://acpr.banque-france.fr/fileadmin/user_upload/acp/publications/registre-officiel/Recommandation-2013-R-01-de-l-ACP.pdf.

2.1 Typology of Investment-Based Insurance Products in France

Unsurprisingly, the Insurance Code does not provide a definition of insurance-based investment contracts. In fact, the term itself is alien to the different legal concepts underpinning French insurance law as it refers to the purpose (the *investment* element) rather than to the nature of the contract.

The Insurance Code[13] defines the insurance operations that are under the State's control as, among other types of insurance "*companies which, in the form of direct insurance, contract obligations whose performance depends on human life, undertake to pay capital in the event of marriage or the birth of children or invite investment by the public with a view to capitalisation and contract specific obligations for said purpose.*" (official translation).

The criterion is therefore the nature of the risk covered, i.e. human life.[14]

French law does not explicitly distinguish categories of insurance-based investment contracts. Different typologies therefore result from market practice with the most common offers being referred to as *multisupports* contract, i.e. contracts offering the policyholder the ability to link the value of their investments by reference to a variety of funds or assets.

Benefits have traditionally been either expressed in euros (reference is then made either to contracts in Euros or to Euro funds or *fonds en Euros*) or by reference to units whose value is determined by the value of one or more assets: currencies, shares of securities or real estate vehicles (SICAV,[15] shares, FCP[16] units, SCI[17] shares etc.).

When benefits are "in Euros", the insurer will be able to provide a guarantee which may be either equal to the premiums paid, or may also contain a guaranteed rate of return pursuant to Article A. 132-1-1 of the Insurance Code which provides for the method of calculation.

The Insurance Code also requires insurers to share their technical and financial results with the policyholders in compliance with a methodology provided under Articles L. 132-20 *et seq.* As such, when benefits are "in Euros", the insurer will allocate profit sharing in compliance with the requirements of these provisions.

When benefits are calculated by reference to units, the units to which the value of the benefits are linked must offer sufficient protection.[18]

---

[13] Article L 310-1 of the Insurance Code.

[14] Article L. 310-1-1 of the Insurance Code.

[15] *Société d'investissement à capital variable*, i.e. investment company with variable capital.

[16] Fonds communs de placement, i.e. investment funds.

[17] *Société civile immobilière* is a specific type of civil (as opposed to commercial) company whose sole purpose is to detain and manage real property.

[18] Article L. 131-1 of the Insurance Code.

The Insurance Code[19] provides a limitative list of eligible assets that may compose the units, which includes *inter alia*:

- Bonds or other securities issued or guaranteed by a state which is a member of the OECD;
- Company-issued bonds;
- Bonds or shares in securitisation vehicles;
- Investment funds;
- Shares exchanged on a recognised stock exchange;
- Shares in insurance and reinsurance companies;
- Etc.

Finally, we should mention a recent legislative innovation introduced by law 2013-1279 of 29 December 2013 commonly referred to as *euro croissance* contracts.

In essence, the legislator's purpose was to find a way to direct the significant amounts of savings currently held in euro funds or contracts towards the real economy. The mechanism of the *euro croissance* gives the ability to the policyholder to invest in more volatile assets while benefitting from a guarantee of the premiums paid provided the benefits of the contract remains invested for a contractually-set time.

2.2 *The Persons Involved in the Distribution Process*

While the nature of the persons involved in the distribution of insurance-based investment products do not raise any particular difficulty in most cases, it is useful to have a closer look at some specific scenarios which may have an impact on the issue at stake.

2.2.1 The Insurer

Direct insurance may only be conducted in France by[20] (in essence):

(i) Insurance companies whose head office is in France and authorised by the French regulator ACPR (Autorité de Contrôle Prudentiel et de Résolution);
(ii) Insurance companies whose head office is in a state which is party to the European Economic Area (EEA), as long as they are duly licensed in their own country and conducting insurance business in France via the so-called European passport:

[19] Article R. 131-1 of the Insurance Code.

[20] Article R. 131-1 of the Insurance Code.

- either directly (freedom of services—*libre prestation de services—LPS*[21]);
- or through a branch (freedom of establishment—*liberté d'établissement*[22]);

(iii) Branches of insurers established outside of the EEA may only conduct direct insurance business in France if they have obtained both a license and a "special authorisation" (which is discretionary, of a political nature and refusal is final) from the ACPR pursuant to article L. 329-1 of the Insurance Code.

In addition, it is forbidden to insure a risk located in France with an insurance company not authorised to cover such risk (with the exception of marine and aviation insurance).[23]

2.2.2 The Insurance Intermediary

Only companies authorised as an insurer or an insurance intermediary are entitled to distribute insurance policies in France.

France has adopted an ordinance[24] as well as a decree[25] transposing the Insurance Distribution Directive (IDD). The present chapter takes into account such transposition which will enter into force on 1st October 2018 except for specific training obligation which will apply from 23 February 2019. As such, unless otherwise indicated, we refer to the provisions of the Insurance Code as amended.

The definition of insurance distribution, of insurance intermediaries and distributors is a faithful transposition of the relevant provisions of Article 2 IDD.[26]

The different categories of insurance intermediaries have not changed following the transposition of the IDD and are as follows:

(a) Insurance intermediaries authorised in France:

   (i) brokers (*courtiers*);
   (ii) general insurance agents (*agents généraux d'assurance*): they act exclusively for an insurer and propose only insurance policies of this insurer;
   (iii) insurance commissioners (*mandataires d'assurance*) and agents of insurance commissioners (*mandataires d'intermédiaires d'assurances*): they are offering cover on behalf of an insurance company (*mandataires d'assurance*) or of another intermediary (*mandataires d'intermédiaires d'assurances*).

(b) Insurance intermediaries authorised to conduct insurance distribution business in a state which is a party to the EEA and which have notified to such state's regulator their intention to conduct insurance mediation business in France.

[21] Article L. 362-2 of the Insurance Code.

[22] Article L. 362-1 of the Insurance Code.

[23] Article L. 310-10 of the Insurance Code.

[24] Ordinance n°2018-36 dated 16 May 2018.

[25] Decree dated 1st June 2018.

[26] Article L. 511-1 of the Insurance Code.

Insurance intermediaries falling under (a) have to be registered with the ORIAS (*Organisme pour le Registre des Intermédiaires en Assurance*), which is a registry listing all insurance intermediaries in France.

Amongst others conditions, insurance intermediaries shall obtain a professional civil liability insurance (*assurance responsabilité civile professionnelle*) and a financial guaranty (*garantie financière*), in accordance with articles L. 512-6 and L. 512-7 of the Insurance Code (save for some specific situations for the *mandataires d'assurance* and *mandataires d'intermédiaires d'assurance*).

A list of insurance intermediaries authorised in France is available on the website of ORIAS at https://www.orias.fr/search.

It is customary to consider that general insurance agents and insurance commissioners will be acting on behalf of the insurer, while brokers act on behalf of their clients, i.e. the policyholders.

Nevertheless, in practice and especially in the context of the distribution of insurance-based investment products, insurers will delegate tasks to brokers especially at the crucial pre-contractual stage.

This of course has an impact on the issue of liability. As will be analysed further below, determining whether the broker is executing its own obligation or acting on behalf of the insurer will have obvious implications in case of breach.

In addition, it is possible for a broker established in France only to work with a limited number of insurance undertakings.

2.2.3 The Special Case of Group Insurance Contracts

Several EU Member States know the concept of group or collective insurance contracts. The Insurance Code provides under Article L. 141-1:

> A group insurance contract is a contract contracted by a legal entity or a head of business in view of membership by a group of persons meeting the conditions stipulated in the contract in order to cover risks happening during a lifespan, risks affecting a person's physical integrity or maternity risks, risks of incapacity for work or risks of disability or risk of unemployment.
>
> The members must have a common link with the policyholder. (official translation)

Group insurance contracts are a very popular way of customising insurance-based investment contracts to a specific group of persons which have a common interest.

For instance, major insurers have long "sponsored" associations which offer dedicated products to their members.

Once becoming members, the persons "adhere" to the group insurance contract and are each referred to as *adherent*. We will use the term *insured* in the next developments for ease of read.

More generally, policyholders are typically employers, professional or trade bodies, associations, or even brokers.

The contractual setup includes at least the following:

- The framework agreement between the policyholder and the insurer, which provides the conditions under which the policyholder may propose the *adhesion* to the insurance contract provided by the insurer. Such contract does not qualify as an insurance contract[27] not least because at the time it is entered to, no risk has yet been insured.
- The *adhesion* by the individuals, which is the equivalent of a person taking an individual contract with an insurer. According to case law, the process actually creates a contractual relationship between the insured and the insurer, so that in practice, the insurer's obligations towards such member are the same as towards the policyholder of an individual policy.

Nevertheless, as we will see below, the presence of the policyholder may add a layer of complexity when determining the liability in the context of distribution of insurance-based investment contracts.

3 The Duty to Provide Information: Pre-contractual Information

The nature of pre-contractual information for unit-linked insurance contracts has been a significant source of litigation due to unclear legal provisions as well as fluctuating (and arguably *contra legem*) case law.

As expected, the pre-contractual stage and the information provided is the most crucial step in the underwriting process.

Indeed, whether pre-contractual information has been delivered at the appropriate time and in the precise format required by the law will generate liability.

3.1 Form and Content of the Pre-contractual Information

Pre-contractual information is subject to two set of provisions: those applicable to all insurance contracts, and those specific to unit-linked insurance contracts. While it is impossible to provide an exhaustive list of all the information that must be provided to the prospective policyholder, this section will list the key ones.

[27] Kullmann et al. (2017).

3.1.1 Provisions Applicable to All Insurance Contracts

The Insurance Code[28] provides that the insurer must communicate to the prospective policyholder, before the conclusion of the contract, an information sheet on the price and covers as well as either (1) a copy of the draft contract or (2) an information notice on the contract. Such notice must, *inter alia*, the cover, the exclusions and the obligations of the policyholder. It must also indicate the law applicable (if other than French law) as well as how complaints can be made.

3.1.2 Provisions Specific to Life Insurance Contracts

Two options are given to the insurer[29]:

Provide on the one hand what the Insurance Code refers to as an insurance proposal or draft contract (in practice, the terms and conditions) and on the other hand a separate information notice containing the key features of the contract; or

Provide only what the Insurance Code refers to as an insurance proposal or draft contract (in practice, the terms and conditions), as long as a table summarising the key features of the contract is included on the first page.

Content of the terms and conditions

The insurance contract must contain specific provisions[30]:

- the surnames and addresses of the contracting parties,
- the insured person,
- the nature of the risks covered,
- the moment from which the risk is covered and the term of said cover,
- the amount of said cover,
- the insurance premium or contribution,
- the law governing the contract when it is not governed by French law,
- the address of the registered office of the insurer and, where appropriate, of the branch granting the cover,
- the name and address of the authorities in charge of supervising the insurance company providing the cover.

Option (i): Information Notice

When the first option is chosen, then the information notice's content must comply precisely and exactly with the provisions of art. A. 132-4 *et seq.* of the Insurance Code, in summary:

---

[28] Article L. 112-2 of the Insurance Code.

[29] Article L. 132-5-2 of the Insurance Code.

[30] Article L.112-4 of the Insurance Code.

- Name, legal form and address of the insurer;
- Commercial denomination of the contract;
- Term of the contract;
- Modes of premium settlement;
- Duration and method of exercise of cancellation rights;
- Claims procedure;
- Specific requirements for insurance-based insurance contracts:
  - Charges in case of surrender
  - List and characteristics of all units as well as any charges levied on the units or on the mathematical provision
- Group contracts: name and address of the policyholder, termination and transfer procedure;
- Tax treatment of the contract;
- Calculation and attribution method of profit-sharing;
- Conflict-resolution procedure.

Option (ii): Information Table

When the second option is chosen, then the table's content must comply precisely and exactly with the provisions of art. A. 132-8 of the Insurance Code.

The courts are extremely strict in that respect. For instance, not providing the information in the right order will constitute a breach of such provision.

In summary, the following must be provided:

- **The nature of the contract**: this must appear in very apparent fonts.[31] It must indicate whether the contract is an individual or a group life insurance contract or an endowment contract. In the case of group contracts, this indication shall be supplemented by the following words: "the rights and obligations of the participant may be modified by means of amendments to the contract concluded between (name of the insurance undertaking) and (the name of the policyholder). The participant is informed beforehand of these modifications".
- **The cover offered**: including the supplementary and non-optional guarantees, with reference to the clauses defining them. It must also be specified whether the contract provides the payment of a capital or an annuity.
- **Profit-sharing**: the information box must specify the existence or not of a contractual profit-sharing, where applicable, the percentage of the latter. It must also indicate the reference to the clause specifying the conditions for the allocation of

[31] There is surprisingly significant case law in relation to what constitutes "very apparent print". Generally, the fonts used must stand out and therefore not be used for any other section of the document (Cass. Civ. 1st, 1st December. 1998, n° 96-18.993) so that the attention of the policyholder is specifically drawn to it (Cass. Civ. 1st, 11 Dec. 1990, n° 89-15.248). A typical option will be bold and/or capitalised fonts.

technical and financial profits, which must be included in the contract in application of Article L. 132-5 of the Insurance Code.

- **Surrender option or transferability**.
- **Consolidation of costs**: Costs and indemnities of any kind levied by the insurer mentioned in Article R. 132-3 and, where applicable, the ones incurred by the unit, are indicated in the same heading. Reference is made to a contractual clause or to the simplified prospectus for the details of these costs and the information box must contain this information. With regard to the charges levied by the insurer, the heading must distinguish:
  - "entry and payment costs": maximum amount or percentage of the fees charged at the time of the purchase and the payment of premiums;
  - "contractual expense": maximum amount or percentage, on an annual basis, of charges levied and not linked to the payment of guarantees or premiums;
  - "exit costs": maximum amount or percentage of expenses on arrears receipts, indemnities mentioned in article R. 132-5-3 of the Insurance Code (redemption indemnities);
  - "other costs": maximum amount or percentage of other costs and allowances.
- **Recommended duration of the contract**.
- **The Beneficiary's designation procedures**: these procedures shall be indicated as set out in Article A. 132-9 of the Insurance Code.

3.1.3 Information Specific to Unit-Linked Life Insurance

It is not within the scope of this chapter to provide an exhaustive description of the requirements in relation to the information that must be provided to policyholders in relation to the specific features of unit-linked insurance contracts, not least because of the sheer volume of rules applicable in that respect.

In that respect, the policyholder is provided with an amount of information impossible to process. Articles A. 134 *et seq.* of the Insurance Code provide a detailed list of such information. In particular, the insurance contract should contain a summary of its characteristics including the investments policy and objectives, the risk and return profile of the underlying assets etc.

Some key elements of the information provided include:

- A personalised table containing the surrender value of the contract for the first 8 years. If not possible, then such table must contain a simulation based on a generic number of units and be completed by a literal explanation of the calculation. If some charges or levies cannot be known in advance (thus making the simulation impossible), then three examples must be provided with an increase, stability or decrease of the unit value.[32]

[32] Article A. 132-4-1 of the Insurance Code.

- A warning that the insurer only guarantees the number of units and not their value, as well as the indication that the value of units reflects the value of the underlying assets, is not guaranteed and may go up or down depending in particular on the evolution of financial markets.[33]
- Charges levied by the insurer on each unit, the total charges on the units, where applicable whether the value of the unit is linked to a specific index.[34]
- Whenever the policyholder switches their investments to a new unit, then the information on this unit must be provided as if the investment had occurred at inception.[35]

3.2 PRIIPS and the Key Information Document

Regulation 1286/2014 on key information documents for packaged retail and insurance-based investment products ("**PRIIPS Regulation**") has not been the subject of any specific transposition or instruction by the French legislator and the ACPR in relation to insurance based investment contracts. The ACPR has not indicated that it intends to provide further advice to insurance companies in relation to PRIIPS.

As such, we refer to Chapter I for a detailed analysis of the PRIIPS Regulation provisions as well as on the content of the Key Information Document ("**KID**").

Unfortunately, the adoption of the PRIIPS Regulation did not trigger any initiative to review the already complex and sizeable amount of documents provided to the policyholder. The KID will therefore simply an addition to the pack of information the policyholder is to receive.

3.3 Delivery of the Pre-contractual Information

The obligation to provide the pre-contractual information lies with the insurer.[36] While the insurer may—and often does—delegate this obligation to the intermediary, this will not impact the policyholder's ability to cancel the policy.

In the specific case of group insurance contracts, the policyholder must deliver to the member a notice drawn up by the insurer which explains the covers and the conditions for its entry into force, as well as the formalities to be fulfilled in the event of damage. The burden of proof of the delivery of the note to the member and the information relating to the contractual modifications falls on the policyholder.[37]

[33] Article A. 132-5 of the Insurance Code.

[34] Article A. 132-7 of the Insurance Code.

[35] Article A. 132-4-3 of the insurance Code.

[36] Article L.132-5-2 of the Insurance Code.

[37] Article L. 141-4 of the Insurance Code.

Where the link between the member and the policyholder does not make it compulsory to adhere to the contract, the notice provided by the policyholder includes, in addition to the information above, those contained in the information notice.[38]

The information box mentioned in the first paragraph of Article L. 132-5-2 is inserted at the beginning of the notice. At the time of joining, the policyholder must give the participant the example of cancellation letter.[39]

4 The Duty to Provide Advice

4.1 Nature of the Duty to Provide Advice

French law imposes a general duty on insurance distributors to provide advice and to warn policyholders if the cover they are contemplating is not adequate. So-called "execution-only" distribution is not permissible in France: there are no exemptions to the duty to provide advice and France has not implemented the option offered by 30 para 3 IDD.[40]

In fact, the Civil Code itself now imposes a general duty to inform on any party to a contract, introduced by the order of 10 February 2016 mentioned under 1 above.

According to article 1112-1 of the Civil Code, the party who knows information the importance of which is decisive for the consent of the other party must inform the other party if the latter ignores such information or relies on the former's knowledge.

The Consumer Code also provides that a professional has a general duty to inform the consumer pursuant to Article L. 111-1.

The advice is generally understood to be the provision of information in relation to the insurance contract and its features, while the warning obligation targets specifically the adequacy—or lack thereof—of the cover to the specific situation of the policyholder. The latter warning obligations has arisen as a necessity to address the situation where the conditions imposed by the insurer to cover a claim rendered the policy useless for the policyholder, in particular in the field of mortgage insurance which has given rise to significant litigation.[41]

In addition, the mere provision of the pre-contractual documentation is not sufficient and regardless of whether the contract is clear, the insurer may have breached its obligation to provide advice if its erroneous advice has led the policyholder to accept its stipulations.[42]

---

[38] Article L. 132-5-3 of the Insurance Code.

[39] Referred to in the third paragraph of Article L. 132-5-2.

[40] See Chapter I para 5.2 on the optional exemption provided under article 30 para 3 IDD.

[41] Kullmann et al. (2017), *op. cit.* n°51.

[42] Cass. 1st Civ., 9 May 2001.

Such advice is not limited to the inception of the contract: the duty to provide advice and to warn policyholders does not stop at the moment when the contract is concluded but extends to its whole duration[43] according to case law.

This is also the ACPR's position in its Recommendation on the collection of information relating to the knowledge of the customer in the context of information duties in life insurance.[44] In this document, the ACPR indicates that insurers should update the information previously collected in order that the advice provided be adapted to the client's profile upon taking the policy, but also upon successive top ups, partial surrenders and switch of investments when such operations may trigger a significant change of the insurance contract.[45] When looking at the detail of the ACPR's recommended inquiries under this recommendation,[46] it is difficult to imagine how insurers may meet this requirement fully in practice.

Even more so when considering the extent of the information and warning obligation as interpreted by the Courts. An interesting case provides an insight into how far such obligation must go[47]: a policyholder had taken a home content insurance policy with an insurance company and later decided to switch to another contract from the same insurer. While the former insurance contract contained a cover for theft of jewellery, the new one did not. Following a loss, the insurer thus refused to cover the value of the stolen jewellery. The Cour de Cassation ruled that the insurance agent should have drawn the attention of the policyholder on the fact that cover for theft of jewellery was not included in the new insurance contract.

As to the actual content of the advice, it will depend to some extent on the level of expertise of the policyholder as long established by case law[48]: a policyholder who knows his or her risk and has contracted in full knowledge will require a lower level of protection.

4.2 *The Distributor's Duties*

The transposition of the IDD has aligned the obligations which of the insurer and of the intermediary, which were previously treated differently under the relevant provisions of the Insurance Code.

---

[43] Cass. 2nd Civ., 5 July 2006: in this case, the insurance agent should have warned the policyholder that her change in circumstances rendered the policy inadequate.

[44] Recommendation on the collection of information relating to the knowledge of the customer in the context of information duties in life insurance, 2013-R-01 of 8 January 2013.

[45] Paragraph 4.1.5.

[46] Paragraph 4.2.

[47] Analysed in Astegiano-La Rizza, A., *Le contenu de l'information de l'assuré*, Revue Générale de Droit des Assurances 2007 p. 464.

[48] Cass. Civ. 1st., 12 May 1987 mentioned in Kullmann et al. (2017), *op. cit.* n°53.

4.2.1 General Principle (Article L. 521-1 of the Insurance Code)

Article L. 521-1 of the Insurance Code provides as a general principle that insurance distributors must always act honestly, fairly and professionally in accordance with the best interest of the policyholder or the insured.

Regarding information, including marketing communications, addressed by the insurance distributor to the potential policyholder or the potential insured article L. 521-1 provides that the information must be clear, accurate and not misleading. Furthermore, marketing communications shall always be clearly identifiable as such.

Finally, article L. 521-1 provides that the insurance distributor must not be remunerated or must not remunerate or assess the performance of its employees in a way that conflicts whit their duty to act in accordance with the best interests of the policyholder or the insured. In particular, an insurance distributor must not make any arrangement by way of remuneration, sales targets or otherwise that could provide an incentive to itself or its employees to recommend a particular insurance product to a potential policyholder or potential insured when the insurance distributor could offer a different insurance product which would better meet the needs of the potential policyholder or potential insured.

Article R. 521-1, I of the Insurance Code states that the insurance distributor must provide the policyholder or the insured with the address and contact of its complaint service (if this service exists) and the address of the ACPR. The insurance distributor shall also provide the policyholder or the insured with procedures for the mediation process.

4.2.2 Conduct of Business Rules (Articles L. 521-4 and L. 521-6 of the Insurance Code)

Prior to the conclusion of each insurance contract, article L. 521-4 of the Insurance Code provides that the insurance distributor must specify in writing, on the basis of information obtained from the potential policyholder or the potential insured, the demands and the needs of the latter. The insurance distributor shall also provide the potential policyholder or the potential insured with objective information about the proposed insurance product in a comprehensive, fair and not misleading form in order to allow the latter to make an informed decision.

The insurance distributor has to propose a contract which is consistent with the insurance demands and needs of the potential policyholder and the potential insured. The insurance distributor also has to specify reasons that lead to this advice.

Prior to the conclusion of any specific contract, when the insurance distributor offers a personalised recommendation service, this service consist in explaining why, among several insurance product or several choices in the product, a particular product or choice would best meet the demands and needs of the potential policyholder or the potential insured (article L. 521-4, II, of the Insurance Code).

Article L. 521-4, III, of the Insurance Code also provides that details previously mentioned which rest in particular on information communicated by the potential policyholder or the potential insured shall be modulated according to the complexity of the insurance product. Those details have to be communicated to the potential policyholder or the potential insured in a comprehensive, fair and not misleading form in order to allow the latter to understand the consistence of the proposed product with its demands and need and to make an informed decision.

Article R. 521-4 of the Insurance Code also specifies that the insurance distributor, who is acting in this capacity, has to indicate in any mail or publicity its name or legal name, professional address and where appropriate its registration number of intermediary.

Article L. 521-6 of the Insurance Code provides information conditions. Therefore, all information referred to in article L. 521-4 shall be communicated to the policyholder or the insured on paper.

The information communicated can also be provided on a durable medium other than paper under the condition that the potential policyholder or the potential insured has chosen the medium support after having given the choice between information on paper or durable medium support.

Finally, the information may be provided by means of a website if it is addressed personally to the policyholder or the insured or if the following conditions are met:

1. The use of this means is appropriate in the context of the business conducted between the insurance distributor and the policyholder or the insured;
2. The policyholder or the insured gave their consent to the use of this means;
3. The insurance distributor has notified electronically to the policyholder or the insured the address of the website, and the place on the website where that information can be accessed;
4. It is ensured that that information remains accessible on the website for such period of time as the policyholder or the insured may reasonably need to consult it.

The insurance distributor should check that providing information on a durable medium other than paper or by means of a website is appropriate in the context of business conducted with the policyholder or the insured. The provision by the latter of an e-mail address and if the validity if that e-mail address is checked by the insurance distributor, shall be regarded as such evidence.

Where the information is communicated using a durable medium other than paper or by means of a website, a paper copy shall be provided to the customer upon request and free of charge. Article R. 521-2 of the Insurance Code further specifies that any information provides by the insurance distributor shall be communicated in clear, fair and not misleading way.

5 Remedies

5.1 Specific Regime Applicable to Pre-contractual Information in Investment-Linked Life Assurance

The sanction in case of breach of the above provisions is that the cancellation period of 30 days, provided under Article L. 132-5-1 of the Insurance Code, will only start on the day on which the insurer provides a fully compliant set of documents for up to 8 years after the inception date of the contract.

As a consequence, the sanction for the insurer is that it will bear the investment risk of the policy, as the policyholder may exercise his/her cancellation right at any time, thus obtaining the full repayment of the premiums—even though the surrender value may have (and usually has) dropped below the value of premiums.

This is of particular concern not only to French insurers, which have found themselves generally on the losing end in case of litigation, but also for insurers established in the EEA and distributing their products under the freedom of establishment or freedom to provide services. Indeed, their products may not fit easily in the very strict requirements imposed by Article A. 132-4 and A. 132-8 of the Insurance Code, e.g. in relation to profit sharing, charges structure, benefits definitions or nature of the unit.

It is nevertheless comforting that after years of severe criticisms, the *Cour de Cassation* has finally accepted that a policyholder could not exercise his or her right of cancellation in bad faith.[49]

5.2 Liability in Case of Breach of Duty

5.2.1 Legal Basis for the Claim Against the Insurer or the Intermediary

Finally, an important point is that when the policyholder exercises his or her right of withdrawal under Article L. 132-5-2, he or she may also bring a claim against the insurer under the liability provisions under Articles 1240 (formerly 1382) and 1231-1 (formerly 1147) of the Civil Code. However, such claim will be subject to the legal framework applicable to civil liability which entails that the policyholder will need to prove that he or she has suffered a prejudiced and establish a causal link between such loss and the failure of the insurer to deliver the pre-contractual information.[50]

Such action may be directed towards the insurer or the intermediary when improper advice is alleged.

---

[49] Cass. Civ. 2nd, 19 mai 2016.

[50] Cass. Civ. 2nd, 15 December 2011.

One of the issues was to determine the legal basis for an action against the insurer or the intermediary in case of wrong pre-contractual advice: would it be on the basis of tort (*responsabilité délictuelle*) or of contractual liability? The *Cour de Cassation* has ruled that contractual liability was the appropriate legal basis.[51]

It is also worth reminding that French law distinguishes between a best endeavours obligation (*obligation de moyens*) and an obligation of result (*obligation de résultat*) the latter being of course the stricter form of obligation. The obligations of the insurer and of the intermediary to provide advice are best endeavours obligations. As such, they cannot be held automatically liable in case of deterioration of the policy's surrender value. However, the provision of false information will trigger the insurer's liability if the policyholder suffers a loss as a result. The *Cour de Cassation* has ruled that this was the case when the insurance agent had provided false information on the guaranteed capital and was thus subsequently held liable to pay the amount falsely communicated to the policyholders.[52]

5.2.2 Loss of Opportunity: The Consequence of the Breach of Duty

In addition to the penalty seen under Sect. 5.1 above, i.e. the ability for the policyholder to claim back premiums paid, since 2009 the *Cour de Cassation* has accepted the aggregation of this penalty, which is specific to insurance law, and the payment of damages arising from contractual liability mentioned under 5.2.1.

When the policyholder has been wrongly advised about the financial risks that the investment-bases insurance contract entails, he/she may:

- waive the contract and obtain reimbursement of all premiums paid,
- and/or claim damages for damages caused by the breach of duty to provide advice.

If the policyholder decides to make a claim against the insurer or the intermediary for a possible breach of the duty to provide advice, his or her argument must be based on the principles of ordinary law (*droit commun*); the liability of the insurer or the intermediary must be subject to the existence of damage causally linked to the breach of duty. The causal link only exists if the damage alleged by the policyholder is indeed the direct consequence of the insurer's failure to provide information.

In that case, the loss-of-opportunity's theory is a possible solution.

5.2.3 Loss-of-Opportunity's Compensation in Case of Breach of Duty

Indeed, the policyholder can claim compensation for loss-of-opportunity; the opportunity for the policyholder to have been able to take out insurance adapted to his/her needs, thanks to the advice given by the insurer or intermediary. For

[51] Cass. Civ. 1st, 9 July 1996.

[52] Cass. Civ. 2nd, 8 September 2005.

example, it's the case when the insurer fails to advice a 71 years old man, who "could only wish to give his partner the most important tax advantages possible for the transmission of his capital by contracting a life-insurance contract", about the impossibility of benefiting from such advantages; in that case, the policyholder lost the opportunity to act differently in order to manage his savings and to find a more favorable solution to ensure the transmission of his capital to his wife after his death.[53]

Even if it is incumbent upon the insurer or the intermediary to prove that the duty to provide advice has been properly performed,[54] it is the policyholder who avails himself or herself of the damage of loss-of-opportunity to prove it and convince the judge that he or she would have sought and found insurance, but also to prove that he or she had the means to pay the corresponding premium.[55] The cost of insurance is taken into consideration by the judge.

Therefore, the policyholder must prove:

- the non-adequacy of the investment-based insurance contracts: in the case of life insurance, the damage caused by the breach of duty to provide advice amounts to a loss-of-opportunity of obtaining better returns when making the investments, but not merely the opportunity to opt for a less risky asset-management option,[56]
- and that the non-adequacy could have been avoided if the insurer or the intermediary had not failed in their duty to provide advice.

The issue of course is that the fact giving rise to liability is the disappearance of a favorable event which is uncertain: doubt remains as to the damage claimed by the policyholder; finding another contract more appropriate for the policyholder being a theoretical proposition.

In a 1997 report, the *Cour de Cassation* explained that there was "a hazard of knowing whether duly informed, the victim would have taken out a non-compulsory personal insurance, and if so, what type of insurance and what amount of guarantee".

Indeed, it can be said that if the policyholder had been properly informed, or cautioned against the maladjustment of the insurance contract to his or her situation and duly advised on his or her interest in seeking insurance, he or she could have taken an insurance contract with another insurer, or would have behaved in a different way.

The judge must therefore decide between two solutions:

- the policyholder could have obtained a more appropriate product, and the damage is equivalent to what this guarantee would have provided,
- the policyholder could not have obtained it, and no prejudice could be withheld.

---

[53] Cass. Civ. 2, 3 October 2013, 12-24957.

[54] Cass. Civ. 2, 2 June 2005.

[55] Cass. Com. 31 May 2011, 10-20.043.

[56] Cass. com. 9 December 2014, 13-23.673.

The judge often distinguishes according to age or situation of fortune; an elderly contractor who has ceased his professional activity would probably not have taken out a unit-linked contract if he had known that he was preparing to retire.

On the other hand, "a person who is very knowledgeable about financial matters - as evidenced by the judicious allocation of his capital could not misunderstand the scope of the contractual information he received on his investment-based insurance contract",[57] nor when the policyholders have taken out an insurance contract on the advice of a wealth management firm and were thus able to ask for any necessary clarification on the terms of the contract.[58]

Indeed, in terms of loss-of-opportunity, judges consider that breach of duty to provide advice cannot benefit those who already have the information, or who, considering their level of education, should have it.[59]

The judge is required to seek the chances of success of the policyholder's pursuit for insurance. The judge must assess, in accordance with the case-law on loss-of-opportunity, its "real and serious" nature (*caractère réel et sérieux*). A loss of opportunity with only a tiny probability of being realized is assimilated to a hypothetical prejudice, and cannot be compensated.[60]

5.2.4 Quantification of the Loss of Opportunity

French judges are used to quantify the probability of the opportunity to happen; in other words the probability that the expected event will occur.[61]

As far as the French judge is concerned, compensation of a loss-of-opportunity must be measured with regards to the lost opportunity and cannot be equal to the benefit that would have been provided if it had been achieved.[62]

This is why a lower Court cannot award damages equivalent to the entire value of the investment-based insurance contract as if it had been wholly lost when the policyholders only lost the opportunity of seeing the amount of the contract increased.[63]

Moreover, the *Cour de Cassation* emphasised that the determination of the amount of the loss-of-opportunity to have made a better investment due to the lack of advice from the intermediary falls within judges' discretion and can be done by fixing a lump sum.[64]

On the other hand, if the policyholder cannot prove that he could have found a more appropriate contract with another insurer and could have paid for it, the judge

---

[57] Luc Mayaux, Traité de Droit des assurances, Tome 4.

[58] Cass. com. 9 December 2014, 13-23.673.

[59] Cass. Civ 1. 18 February 2003.

[60] Cass. Com. 1 December 2015, 14-22.134.

[61] Sabard (2013), p. 23.

[62] Cass. com. 15 February 2011, 09-16779.

[63] Cass. Civ 2, 13 September 2012, 11-19408.

[64] Cass. com., 12 juill. 2011, 10-17579.

declares the loss-of-opportunity null and void,[65] because the loss cannot be declared certain and the policyholder is not entitled to any compensation. For example, that is the case when the policyholder claims a disability coverage which the insurer could not have granted in any event, the policyholder being already in a state of invalidity.[66]

6 Conclusion

French law provides a complex set of detailed rules in relation to the documents and advice to be provided by distributors of insurance based investment products, now complemented by the KID pursuant to the PRIIPS Regulation.

On the one hand, these rules as interpreted by the courts have proven to be a significant source of liability for insurance companies with severe consequences in case of non-compliance. They also constitute a notable barrier to entry for insurance companies located in other EEA States.

On the other hand, we have serious doubts as to whether the mass of information provided to policyholders, especially at pre-contractual stage, achieves the objective of optimal information on the nature and risks of the insurance based investment products being offered.

On the contrary, the various documents often contain similar information presented differently, which is particularly blatant in the case of the information notice and the PRIIPS Regulation KID.

A rationalisation of the pre-contractual information in order to reduce the amount of document and foster their consistency would reduce liability risks for insurance companies as well as distributors, encourage innovation and reinforce policyholder protection to the greater benefit of the economy.

References

Bigot J et al (2014) Traité de droit des assurances, Le contrat d'assurance Tome I, 2nd edn. LGDJ, Paris

Kullmann J et al (2017) Lamy Assurances. Wolters Kluwer, Alphen aan den Rijn

Malaurie P, Aynès L (2016) Droit des obligations, 8th edn. LGDJ, Paris

Sabard O (2013) L'évaluation de la perte de chance par le juge judiciaire. Les Petite Affiches 218:23

[65] Cass. Com., 22 September 2009, 08-18141.

[66] Cass. Civ 1, 4 February 1997, 95-12.572.

Germany

Katica Tomic

Contents

Abbreviations

2. FiMaNoG	Second Financial Markets Reform Act
AltZertG	Act on Certification of Old-Age Provision and "Basic Pension" Contracts
BGB	German civil code
BVerfG	The Federal Constitutional Court
DIHK	German Chamber of Trade and Commerce
ECJ	European Court of Justice
GewO	German Trade, Commerce and Industry Regulation Act
GG	Basic Law for the Federal Republic of Germany
HGB	German Commercial Code

K. Tomic (✉)
Rechtsanwälte BVM, Vienna, Austria

P. Marano, I. Rokas (eds.), *Distribution of Insurance-Based Investment Products*, https://doi.org/10.1007/978-3-030-11668-2_6

IDD	Directive (EU) 2016/97 on insurance distribution
MiFID	Markets in Financial Instruments Directive
PRIIPs	Packaged Retail and Insurance-based Investment Products
UCITS	Undertakings for the Collective Investment of Transferable Securities
VAG	German Insurance Supervision act
VersVermV	Regulation on Insurance Mediation and Advice
VVG	Insurance contract act
VVG-Info-Verordnung	Regulation on information obligation for insurance contracts

1 Introduction

1.1 Basic Information on Insurance-Based Investment Products in Germany

The German life insurance market offers a wide range of innovative life insurance products such as unit-linked life insurance, hybrid life insurance, and variable annuities that satisfy basic customer needs. Those products are used as investment and savings vehicles as well as for financial protection, providing payments in case of death, disability, longevity and illness. According to the statistics,[1] the sales of hybrid policies (unit-linked with a guaranteed element) are increasing and sales of pure unit-linked policies, where the investment risk is entirely for the policyholder, are limited in German insurance market. The two-main unit-linked product types are endowment and annuity products and they cover biometrical risks, i.e., endowment products cover mortality risk and annuities.

1.2 The Historic Development of Insurance-Based Investment Products in Germany

In this chapter, we will focus on historical development of insurance-based investment products in German insurance market. The German life insurance market has been deregulated since 1994 as a result of the creation of the European Single Market. For that reason, innovative products such as unit-linked insurance products still have rather small market shares. For better understanding this topic, we will

[1] Gesamtverband der Deutschen Versicherungswirtschaft e.V, Statistisches Taschenbuch der Versicherungswirtschaft 2017, copy of the document available at URL: https://www.gdv.de/resource/blob/12208/b2a04a76a1597e051d5a3a6d210b8a11/download-statistisches-taschenbuch-2017-data.pdf.

focus on history and evolution of insurance-based investment products, regulatory framework in the German insurance market. In Germany, the market of insurance-based investment products is less mature than in other EU countries even though considerable number of German life insurance companies are selling these products. This chapter will help us to understand reasons for that.

The introduction of unit-linked products has been one of the most significant innovations in the field of life insurance over the past several decades. We can divide its development in the German insurance market in different phases. Unit-linked insurance policies were developed in the context of insurance in countries with well-developed investment markets (e.g. USA and UK) which is consistent with the view that financial development and overall economic development move in tandem. The German insurance market was relatively passive in the decades after the Second World War[2] and economic growth has started in the 1950s.[3] Unit-linked insurance policies were introduced for the first time in Germany in 1970[4] and they were caused by external factors, such as legislative and economic forces which we will explain below.

In Germany, the first holding companies were officially founded in 1965.[5] The background of formation of these companies was to improve the supply of equity based capital to mid-sized companies which had no access to the organised capital market. Therefore, due to the lack of competition, insurance companies were inadequately developed.[6] In Germany, the equity ratio of the companies is traditionally much lower than in other industrial countries.[7] This situation was caused by quick economic growth in the post-war period with low profits, high taxation as well as growing labour costs.[8] This growth was primarily financed by third parties.[9] In the 1970s, the percentage of investors from the business sector and banks was approx. 70%.[10] The remaining 30% were provided from funds from the European Recovery Program (ERP).[11] German insurance companies had no aspiration to offer innovative life insurance products such as unit-linked life insurance because of the high profit margins for conventional insurance products (and low margins for unit-linked

---

[2] Pyka and Hanusch (2006), p. 126.

[3] Eichengreen and Ritschl (2008).

[4] Bernhardt (2010), p. 29.

[5] Gaida (2002), p. 217.

[6] Döring (2010), p. 50.

[7] Historical data for the Germany DAX (*Deutscher Aktienindex*) Stock Market Index of the 30 major German companies from 1970 to 2017 are available at: https://tradingeconomics.com/germany/stock-market.

[8] Pyka and Hanusch (2006), p. 126.

[9] Günter and Frommann (1998), p. 11.

[10] In the German equity market, the silent partnership in the company's (*Stille Gesellschaft*) became established as the dominant legal form because of the huge level of its acceptance in the partner companies. The disadvantages of this company form are the inability to influence company management and the uncertainty about the availability of liquid funds in case of partnership dissolution.

[11] Leithoff (2014), p. 26.

life insurance products). Moreover, huge investments were needed for development and launching (systems, admin, marketing, distribution) of unit-linked life products.[12]

In the 1980s, a professionalization of the German private equity scene could be clearly noted.[13] On the one hand, this is caused by the emerge of professional management teams in the insurance companies which are increasingly moving into the investment fund business by developing new insurance products. On the other hand, new business practices are also taking root to a greater extent, such as joint venture[14] i.e. the syndication which allowed holding companies to provide the funding resources or the selection of the IPO (Initial public offering)[15] as an exit channel. The private equity industry has begun to turn its attention to insurance industry and has put more efforts into this market segment.

The German reunification on 3 October 1990 led to a single increase in the insurance volume and showed a huge potential in private equity. The life insurance market at that time can be characterized as a complex, provincial, and quite difficult market to enter for foreign companies.[16] The insurance market at East Germany was quite underdeveloped. Risk management support was particularly important because many companies in Germany had lack of know-how to use a various type of sale channels. Only few insurance companies offered unit-linked insurance products (13 distributers) until 1994.[17]

The German insurance market went through a major change in the regulatory environment, specifically, the deregulation of the German insurance market in 1994 and the implementation of third generation Insurance Directive. The most important element of the Directive is the "EU passport system" (single licence) for insurers which makes cross-border business possible allowing companies based in the EU to set up operations in any other EU country from their home country.

Since the liberalization of the insurance market, independent multi-tied agent (*Mehrfachagent*) and foreign companies who have entered the German life insurance market, have offered more equity-exposed products via international framework agreements (IFAs). During that time, aspiration to offer unit-linked products increased and stock fund investments became more popular. Distributors started to search for equity oriented life products which provide fronted commissions because conventional products lost attractiveness. Moreover, increased efforts were made in attempts how to stabilize the German pension system which needed more private cover. German asset management companies (*Kapitalverwaltungsgesellschaften*)

---

[12] Bernhardt (2010), p. 29.

[13] Plagge (2006), p. 39.

[14] Joint ventures in Germany are subject to German and European Antitrust Law as well as the law of the home country of the parties if they fulfill certain requirements with regard to the turnover and market shares of the undertakings concerned.

[15] An IPO is the first sale of stock by a private company to the public.

[16] Hagelschuer (1983), p. 23.

[17] Unit-linked products were only sold as an add-on insurance (supplemental insurance) if client already had a conventional insurance product. Novikov and Wiesenewsky (2012).

identified unit-linked providers as sales channel and increased the fund offering. A variety of breakthrough technologies were set to stimulate a fundamental transformation of the insurance industry and enabling the creation of new insurance products like: index-linked policies, unit-linked annuity, mixture of conventional and unit-linked products.[18]

In 1996, private equity investments in Germany was only 0.04% of the GDP.[19] Even though a significant increase of private equity investment as a percentage of GDP can be noted since then, the acceptance of this investments is still limited in Germany.[20] The market for private equity in Europe only developed during the stock market boom in the 1980s and 1990s.[21]

The market developed its own dynamic during this time. However, these developments were greatly dampened after the stock market decline in 2001–2003 and unit-linked products lost some market share because customers lost confidence in equity investments. Thus, the share price losses on the national and international stock markets since 2001, have not been directly or indirectly affected by the long-term success of private equity investments. During that time, nearly all insurance companies have offered unit-linked insurance products. At same time, German insurance companies tried to diversify their portfolios by adding alternative investments such as private equity.[22]

However, the German market for private equity has still not recovered from the downturn when the Internet bubble burst begun. After the boom of the late 1990s, the equity market has undergone a 3-year consolidation. The adjustment in the portfolios of the financial investors did not come to a halt until the end of 2003. Since then, there has been a stagnation noticed in the new venture capital (VC) transactions, i.e. private equity investments into young innovative firms. When the High-Tech Start-up Fund and the ERP Start-up Fund were launched by public authorities, the situation became better and start-up financing eased again.[23]

Guaranteed interest rate declined down to 2.75% in 1/2004 and to 2.25% in 1/2007.[24] At the beginning of 2001, the German Tax Reduction Act of 23 October 2000 (*Steuersenkungsgesetz*) implemented sweeping tax changes and this reform not only reduced income tax rates, but also fundamentally changed the tax regime for German Corporations and the treatment of dividends received from corporations. Riester pension (*Riester Rente*) was introduced in 2002 and was supposed to compensate for a parallel reduction in the German Statutory Retirement Insurance

---

[18] Döring (2010), p. 50.

[19] C. Flowers became the first ever private equity backer of an insurance acquisition in Germany with its 'Württembergische & Badische Versicherungs-AG' investment at the end of 2004/beginning of 2005.

[20] Döring (2010), p. 52.

[21] Döring (2010), p. 50.

[22] The capital in private equity funds typically derive from institutional investors such as insurance companies, banks and pension funds; Kollmann (2008), p. 57.

[23] Reihlen and Werr (2012), p. 363.

[24] Gatzert and Schmeiser (2006), p. 4.

System ("*Gesetzliche Rente*").[25] The basic idea of this system is to use government subsidies as an incentive for people to secure their old age income with additional private old age provision. The Riester Pension Plan comes in five investing varieties: classical, unit-linked, bank savings plan, and two kinds of building loan contracts (Wohn-Riester).[26]

From 2001 to 2008, innovative life insurance products (unit-linked with guarantees, static hybrid products,[27] variable annuities (VAs),[28] dynamic hybrid products) have been offered in the German market with the intend to meet new consumer needs regarding stability and upside potential.

The Directive 2002/92/EC (Insurance Mediation Directive, abbreviated IMD) of 9 December 2002 on insurance mediation was adopted in January 2003. Originally, the Member States should have had transposed the IMD into national law by January 2005 but Germany failed to meet the deadline. Germany has implemented the IMD in December 2006 by adopting law named "*Gesetz zur Neuregelung des Versicherungsvermittlerrechts*" (the guideline of the IMD). Also, in 2008 German legislator decided to submit the German Insurance Contract Act (VVG) to an extensive reform. Consumer rights and the insurer's duties of disclosure and to provide information gained more relevance under this law. Innovations in the Insurance Supervision Act (*Versicherungsaufsichtsgesetz*—VAG (e.g. minimum level of appropriate profit sharing for policyholders) allowed development of investment-linked products.

The financial crisis of 2007–2008 deeply hit world's economy, but unlike almost all other countries, Germany emerged from the crisis quickly and stronger than before.[29] Guaranteed interest rate further declined down to 1.75% in 1/2012.[30] The business tax reform act of 2008 "*Unternehmensteuerreformgesetz* 2008" introduced a new tax system with a flat tax rate, which became effective for shareholders from the January 2009. The main aim of this reform was to increase Germany as attractive business location, to provide neutrality regarding the legal form and the financing structure of firms and to simplify tax planning for firms and the government. To

---

[25] For further details on Riester Pension System in Germany see Mierzejewski (2016), pp. 327 et. seq.

[26] Holzmann and Palmer (2006), p. 594.

[27] Static hybrid products were introduced in 1999 as the first hybrid products in Germany (hybrid products of the first generation); Kochanski and Karnarski (2011), pp. 173–198; Bohnert (2013), pp. 555–575.

[28] Variable annuities are unit-linked life insurance contracts with investment guarantees which, in exchange for single or regular premiums, allow the policyholder to benefit from the upside of the unit but be partially or totally protected when the unit loses value.

[29] Storm and Naastepad (2014), copy of the document available at URL: https://papers.ssrn.com/sol3/papers.cfm?abstract_id=2638053, accessed 11.05.2018.

[30] Gesamtverband der Deutschen Versicherungswirtschaft e.V., Absenkung des Höchstrechnungszinses hat kaum Einfluss auf die Ablaufleistung, copy of the document available at URL: http://www.gdv.de/2011/02/lebensversicherung-bleibt-attraktives-vorsorgeprodukt-absenkung-des-hoechstrechnungszinses-hat-kaum-einfluss-auf-die-ablaufleistung/, accessed 11.05.2018.

receive the tax-preferred life insurance status, an insurance policy must now meet the requirements such as life cover, wrapper policies,[31] and guaranteed annuity factors.[32]

The Directive Solvency II which entered into force in Germany on the 1 January 2016, contains a series of new requirements for insurance and reinsurance companies and its impact will extend, among other things, to unit-linked products.

1.3 The Implementation of the EU Regulations in Germany

The VVG 2008 entered into force on 1 January 2008 and the heart of the reform was to provide policyholders with a level of protection which is in line with modern EU concepts of consumer law. The new VVG imposes numerous duties on insurers to inform policyholders about their rights and obligations prior to, and at the time of, the conclusion of insurance contracts and also during the term of the contracts. In Germany,[33] the EU law has no direct effect on its citizens, but needs to transpose it, which means that the obligation must be laid down in national law.[34] The German record on transposing EU legislation is average and the legal system does not include any clear sanctions to ensure timely implementation.[35]

The Markets in Financial Instruments Directive (abbreviation—MiFID)[36] from 2004 was implemented into German law by the Act Implementing the Markets in Financial Instruments Directive *(Finanzmarktrichtlinie-Umsetzungsgesetz* abbreviation—FRUG)[37] in 2007. The German Federal Ministry of Finance published a

---

[31] A wrapper is a life assurance policy whose value is dictated by the value of a portfolio of investments selected by the life policy holder.

[32] Under a guaranteed annuity option, an insurer guarantees to convert a policyholder's accumulated funds to a life annuity at a fixed rate when the policy matures. Because of the way the guarantee was written, factors influenced the cost of these guarantees are stock market performance and mortality assumption.

[33] Germany was one of the founding members of the European Union (1952) and it became a member of the Schengen area when it was created in 1985 and has been a member of the Eurozone since its launching in 1999.

[34] The German legal system is strongly influenced by EU law and the law of European Communities exists as an independent legal system. EU Law is directly applicable, in most cases through so-called regulation (*Verordnungen*) which is binding in Germany after having been passed by means of one of the legislative procedures of the European Union. This basic process is the same for all EU Directives (*Richtlinien*) and directly applicable EU regulations. Specific national rules exit where important legal questions are not regulated by EU Law or where EU leaves room for additional national rules.

[35] OECD, Chapter 7 The interface between member states and the EU, Better Regulation in Europe Better Regulation in Europe: Finland 2010, p. 124.

[36] Directive 2004/39/EC of the European Parliament and of the Council of 21 April 2004 on markets in financial instruments.

[37] Gesetz zur Umsetzung der Richtlinie über Märkte für Finanzinstrumente und der Durchführungsrichtlinie der Kommission (Finanzmarktrichtlinie-Umsetzungsgesetz, FRUG),

draft bill for the Second Act Amending Financial Market Regulations (*Zweites Finanzmarktnovellierungsgesetz* abbreviation—2. FiMaNoG) on 29 September 2016 which implements most of the provisions of the Directive 2014/65/EU on Markets in Financial Instruments (abbreviation—MiFID2)[38] and accompanying Markets in Financial Instruments Regulation (MiFIR rules)[39] in Germany. Together with transposition of PRIIPs Regulation[40] in 2016, the 2. FiMaNoG aims the second pillar in reforming the existing regulation of the financial market in Germany. The 2. FiMaNoG was published in the Federal Law Gazette on 24 June 2017 and came into force on 3 January 2018.[41] Due to the 2nd FiMaNoG, amendments have been made, *inter alia*, to the German Securities Trading Act (*Wertpapierhandelsgesetz*), German Banking Act (*Kreditwesengesetz*) and German Stock Exchange Act (*Börsengesetz* abbreviation—BörsG).

Insurance Distribution Directive (abbreviation—IDD)[42] entered into force on 22 February 2016 and must be transposed into national law by 1 July 2018 and the application date of the IDD is 1 October 2018. Germany legislator approved Act implementing the Insurance Distribution Directive (IDD Implementation Act) on 7 July 2017 and it came into effect on 23 February 2018.[43] On 17 July 2018, the BaFin has published a new Circular no. 11/2018[44]—Guidelines on cooperation with insurance intermediaries, distribution-related activities and risk management in insurance product distribution in order to ensure the requirements of IDD Implementation. The Circular no. 11/2018 is also applicable to insurance undertakings from EU-/EEA-member states who conduct insurance business in Germany.

The implementation of the IDD mainly affects the German Trade, Commerce and Industry Regulation Act (*Gewerbeordnung* abbreviation—GewO), VAG and VVG.[45] EU Commission has defined standards for the format and content of the

BGBl. I 2007 S. 1330; 19.07.2007.

[38] Directive 2014/65/EU on Markets in Financial Instruments, of the European Parliament and of the Council of 15 May 2014 on markets in financial instruments, Official Journal of European Union, L 173/349.

[39] Regulation (EU) No 600/2014 of the European Parliament and of the Council of 15 May 2014 on markets in financial instruments, Official Journal of European Union, L 173/84.

[40] Regulation (EU) No 1286/2014 of the European Parliament and of the Council of 26 November 2014 on key information documents for packaged retail and insurance-based investment products.

[41] Zweites Gesetz zur Novellierung von Finanzmarktvorschriften auf Grund europäischer Rechtsakte (Zweites Finanzmarktnovellierungsgesetz—2. FiMaNoG), BGBl. I S. 1693.

[42] Directive (EU) 2016/97 of the European Parliament and of the Council of 20 January 2016 on insurance distribution, Official Journal of the European Union, L 26/19.

[43] Gesetz zur Umsetzung der Richtlinie (EU) 2016/97 des Europäischen Parlaments und des Rates vom 20. Januar 2016 über Versicherungsvertrieb und zur Änderung weiterer Gesetze, BGBl. I 2017 S. 2789.

[44] The Circular no. 11/2018.sets aside former Circular 10/2014. BaFin Journal, August 2017, p. 5. Copy of the document available at URL: https://www.bafin.de/SharedDocs/Downloads/DE/BaFinJournal/2017/bj_1708.pdf?__blob=publicationFile&v=5.

[45] For example, Sections 23, 48, 48b, 48c of the VAG; Section 34d of the GewO; Sections 1a, 6, 6a, 7, 7a, 7b, 7c, 7d, 59, 61, 66.

Insurance Product Information Document (IPID) and it is used from February 2018.[46] The IPID is a requirement under the IDD and it is implemented in Germany through the amendments in the Regulation on Information Obligations for Insurance Contracts (*Verordnung über Informationspflichten bei Versicherungsverträgen* abbreviation—VVG-InfoV). VVG-InfoV amendments have been made in order to align the provisions of the VVG-InfoV with PRIIPs Regulation and to ensure that only one information circular will be needed for insurance investment products.

On 23.10.2017, the Federal Ministry for Economic Affairs and Energy has submitted the draft bill for the new version of the Regulation on Insurance Mediation and Advice (*Versicherungsvermittlungsverordnung* abbreviation—VersVermV) which will further specify the new requirements for insurance sales. On 27.06.2018 the Cabinet of Germany (*Bundeskabinett*) adopted the draft bill of the new version of the VersVermV.

2 The Civil Liability of the Insurers and Insurance Intermediaries in Case of Distribution of Insurance-Based Investment Products

2.1 The Legal Framework for Liability in German Law: An Overview

The provisions relevant to establishing liability and damages, as well as provisions of law concerning obligations are contained in the second book of the BGB (*Recht der Schuldverhältnisse*). The second book of the BGB is not formally divided into two sections, but most authors use this classification for practical purpose. According to this, the second book of the BGB can be divided in two sections, a general part and special part.

The so-called "general part" of the second book of the BGB contains the provisions relating to the law of damages in Sec. 241-304 related to a contractual and non-contractual liability. General part of the second book of the BGB contains definition of fault and negligence in Sec. 276 and contributory negligence in Sec. 251. The provisions of the law of obligation are generally optional *(dispositive*) and the parties can develop atypical contracts and to modify rights and duties with existing type of contract. This legally approved factual flexibility of relationships includes the freedom to enter a contract and freedom to shape its conditions (i.e. to invent new types of contract) and it is constitutional guarantee of party autonomy.

Considering that the distribution of insurance-based investment products is carried out through various insurance companies and their agents, regarding the ques-

[46] Commission Implementing Regulation (EU) 2017/1469 of 11 August 2017 laying down a standardised presentation format for the insurance product information document, Official Journal of the European Union, L 209/19.

tion of liability, especially important is the issue of consumer protection and attribution of responsibility when several persons and participants are involved.

In the following section, we will review the evolution of the German legal doctrine and courts approach on the topic of liability of the insurers and insurance intermediaries.

2.2 *The Evolution of the German Legal Doctrine on the Topic of Liability of the Insurers and Insurance Intermediaries*

German insurance law was traditionally considered to be part of commercial law.[47] For that reason, insurance law was not included in the German civil code (*Bürgerliches Gesetzbuch*, abbreviated BGB) in 1896, arguing that it should either continue to be part of the older German HGB or be codified separately. In 1908, such a separate codification took place as a result of increasing economic significance of insurance and complex characteristics of insurance law. Insurance contract act (*Versicherungsvertragsgeset*, abbreviated VVG 1908), in force since 1910, was the first German codification of insurance contracts.[48] The VVG 1908 contained a number of provisions which favoured the interest of the insurer over the policyholder and many uncodified gaps especially for lines of business that have been introduced over the years.[49]

According to the VVG 1908, the policyholder had to disclose all material facts and circumstances to the insurer before making his contractual acceptance and there was no equivalent duty of disclosure for the insurer.[50] The insurer had no duty to advise and this duty could only follow from the BGB which requires that each party to take account of the rights, legal interests and other interests of the other party.[51] According to the art. 16 para 1 VVG 1908, there was no obligation on insurers to advise policyholders of the extent of their duty of disclosure which led to uncertainty of which information should be disclosed. The case law of the German courts over the years held in various decisions that there was no general duty for the insurer to give advice unless there was a reason to do so.[52]

---

[47] Neugebauer (1990), p. 47.

[48] Gesetz über den Versicherungsvertrag vom 30. Mai 1908, Deutsches RGBl. S. 263; The VVG 1908 was neither applicable to reinsurance nor to ocean marine insurance, the latter of which continued to be an integral part of the HGB until 2008.

[49] Koch (2010), pp. 163–171.

[50] Sec. 16 para. 1 VVG 1908.

[51] Sec. 241 para. 2 BGB.

[52] OLG Frankfurt, 21.11.2001 - 6 W 217/01; OLG Hamm, 23.08.2000 - 20 U 22/00; OLG Düsseldorf, 13.12.2005 - I-20 U 81/05.

German insurance law followed so-called “all-or-nothing principle” (*Alles-oder-Nichts-Prinzip*), but limit its scope be requiring gross negligence (*grob fahrlässig*) of the breach and a causal link between non-disclosure and the insured event.[53] Moreover, according to the provisions of VVG 1908, policyholders who violated their duties deliberately (*vorsätzlich*) or with gross negligence were not entitled to any claim under the insurance policy. Although, in cases of simple negligence (*einfache Fahrlässigkeit*), the insurer had to pay the full claim in case of an insured event. This regime led to legal uncertainty, which resulted to an excessively high number of court cases.[54]

So-called ‘all or nothing’ principle often led to unfair results for policyholders in third liability cases for injured parties. The courts often interpret the term gross negligence under the VVG 1908 more narrowly than under general contract law,[55] thereby setting aside the rule that the law be interpreted and applied uniformly (principle of uniformity of the legal order).[56]

German courts had to determine a distinction between simple or gross negligence which is difficult to make. The “all-or-nothing principle” expelled insurers of their liability in specific situations, e.g. in cases of causation of loss,[57] breach of duties, including breach of the duty of disclosure,[58] duties relating to an aggravation of risk,[59] etc. Another example of imbalance positions between insurer and policyholder comes from Sec. 12 para. 3 VVG 1908. According to this article, the policyholders had 6-month cut-off period for filing an action against the insurer after the insurer had denied the claim in writing.

The German legislator decided to submit the German Insurance Contract Act to an extensive reform that aimed at strengthening the position of the policyholder as well as the injured party. German Federal Ministry of Justice appointed in 2000 a Reform Commission to adapt the insurance contract law according to the factual and legal developments and also taking account of the way in which the law had developed in practice. The Reform Commission published its final report along with the draft bill of a new insurance contract law act in 2004. The new VVG 2008 entered into force on 1 January 2008 and the significance of this reform was to create more consumer protection.[60] Moreover, discussions about implementing institu-

---

[53] Art. 152 VVG 1908; Art. 67(2) VVG 1908; Art. 169, 170 VVG 1908 (life assurance); Art. 178 VVG 1908 (health insurance); Art. 181 VVG 1908 ((accident insurance).

[54] For further details see Endres (1991).

[55] Römer (2009), pp. 176, 182, copy of the document available at URL: http://www.humboldt-forum-recht.de/deutsch/13-2009/beitrag.html, accessed 31.05.2017.

[56] Julius von Staudinge, Rolf Sack, Neubearbeitung 2003, § 138 BGB Rn. 69.

[57] Art. § 61 VVG 1908.

[58] Art. 21 VVG 1908.

[59] Art. 25 VVG 1908.

[60] For more information and different views see Grote and Schneider (2007), pp. 2689, 2690; Werber (2001), p. 1313.

tional change to improve counselling and advice by insurance intermediaries in Germany is still ongoing.[61]

2.3 *The Evolution of the German Courts Approach on the Topic of Liability of the Insurers and Insurance Intermediaries*

Principles developed through court decisions and case law, carry considerable importance in the German legal system. Whether the judge made law (*Ricterrecht*) can be regarded as a source of law is constantly disputed. The strict doctrine of precedent (*Präjudizien*) does not exist in German doctrine and court decisions do not have any effect in future cases and only bind the parties to that case. The courts are bound to observe the requirements of statute law and justice[62] and prior decisions have some temporal effects. Decision of superior courts have a conclusive influence on all court decisions and newer decisions reached are taken into account by practitioners, academics and judges. The general requirement of legal certainty also demands consistency of court decisions and superior courts often formulate a type of headnote containing the *ratio decided* the case, which is printed at the head of published version of decision.

The consumers' complaints about unit linked insurance policies usually focus on the lack of transparency relating to the life insurance premium, costs charged and specific risks attached to the policy. The case law in Germany has provided some guidance on these issues.

The consumers are often being sold structured or complex investments that insufficiently meet their needs and requirements, for instance, due to failures to obtain sufficient information on the financial status or investment experience of the consumer. The Federal Court of Justice of Germany (*Bundesgerichtshof*—BGH) has started in the 1990s to consider lack of transparency as a ground of invalidity irrespective of any disparity of the parties' rights and obligations. The usual basis for a miss-selling claim of unit-linked life insurance policies in Germany is an alleged breach of an investment advisory contract.[63] The standards of transparency and the consequences of the change in transparency requirements on unit-linked insurance policies are not very clear in the German insurance market and emerge only in the course of development of case-law.

BGH passed a several verdicts[64] on 11.07.2012 in cases Clerical Medical Investment Group Limited (CMIG). CMIG has received a number of claims in the German courts, relating to Clerical Medical's life insurance policies. Clerical

---

[61] Hofmann (2011), pp. 287–307; Focht et al. (2013) pp. 329–350.

[62] Art. 20 para.3; art. 97 GG.

[63] BGH, 14.11.2012 - IV ZR 198/10.

[64] BGH, 11.07.2012 - IV ZR 164/11; IV ZR 122/11; IV ZR 151/11; IV ZR 268/10; IV ZR 271/10.

Medical's life insurance policies were sold by independent intermediaries in Germany (e.g. EMF AG Hamburg, LEX *Vermögensverwaltungs* AG), principally during the late 1990s and early 2000s.

The BGH ruled that the conditions of this policy wording and inclusion of policy terms in contracts were not transparent and clearly understandable to Clerical Medical's customers and it depends on the single individual case. The insurers denied liability on a number of grounds: that the VVG and previous case law clearly states that the insurer is not subject to any duties of information and advice where the product is mediated by an independent financial adviser selected by the customer; the policy schedule and the marketing material contained numerous general references to the standard terms and conditions, the standard terms and conditions contained a clause explaining that there was a risk of small capital gains and that the customers had been orally informed during the sales process that the regular payment of benefits would normally be lower than the interest owed on the financing loan.

In a series of so-called "leading decisions" (*Leitentscheidungen*), the BGH held that unit-linked life assurance policies as investment products and these decisions are unprecedented in German jurisprudence. In addition, the decisions did not attach any significance to the fact that unit-linked policies (without guaranteed benefits or participation rights) have been known and sold in Germany for years. The decisions were made in five test cases and dozens of similar cases are pending in different district courts and courts of appeals across the Germany.[65]

These judgments of the BGH that the CMIG is liable for its pre-contractual breach of duty are of great importance for the entire insurance sector in Germany. Unit-linked life insurance policies are for the first time qualified as investment products and are therefore retroactively subject to much firm case law rules developed by German courts over years.

The BGH has handed down another important decision on 14 October 2015[66] regarding extension of cancellation rights in a contract of unit-linked life insurance following failure to disclose the existence of this right to the policyholder. This court decision reinforced the rights of consumers to withdraw from life insurance policies and pension schemes. The BGH clearly decided a policyholder's right to withdraw from pension schemes and life insurance policies if they have not properly been informed about their option to withdraw.

According to the sec. 5a (2) sentence 2 of the VVG 1908, governing the conclusion of insurance contracts so-called "*Policenmodell*" (policy model), was that the insurance contract is considered concluded even if the policyholder has not yet received all the information required by the EU Life Directive. This was contrary to the principle laid down in the Second Life Assurance Directive (Council Directive 90/619/EEC) and Third Life Assurance Directive (Council Directive 92/96/EEC) stating that policyholders must be properly informed before they enter into a con-

[65] Clerical Medical Investment Group litigation in Germany involved more than 2000 individual claims brought by investors against a financial services provider.

[66] BGH, 14.10.2015 - IV ZR 284/12.

tractual obligation. Sec. 5a (2) sentence 4 of the VVG 1908 stipulates that the right of withdrawal expires no later than 1 year following payment of the first premium, and the ECJ[67] and BGH[68] have ruled that this provision is not in conformity with European Union law.

The new VVG 2008 abolished the "*Policenmodell*" and created an "application model" (*Antragsmodell)* in order to improve consumer protection. According to the Sec. 6 and 7 of the VVG 2008, the insurer has a duty to advise and to provide information before the policyholder releases his declaration of intent to conclude the insurance contract.[69]

While the BGH judgement initially applied to life insurance policies that were taken out in accordance with the so-called "*Policenmodell*" (policy model) between 1994 and 2007, the BGH extended this jurisprudence to policies concluded pursuant to "*Antragsmodell*" (application model). The requirement for withdrawal in such a case is that the consumer has not been fully informed about the contractual conditions or withdrawal periods (for example the client has received incomplete or inaccurate pre-contractual information about unit-linked insurance policy).

2.4 The Claim for Compensation Under Applicable National Rules

As already mentioned, the VVG 2008 was first introduced in 1908 and thoroughly reformed in 2007. The reform of the VVG 2008 apply on consumer and business insurance, although reinsurance, marine insurance and some large risks or open policies are explicitly excluded from the application of the VVG 2008.[70] Also, the German laws regulating insurance intermediation were significantly amended and these amendments were generated by the EU Directive 2002/92/EC which was implemented in Sec. 59 et seq. of the VVG 2008.[71] In Germany, the liability rule come from applicable EU directives and comprise failures resulting from neglect of information, counselling and documentation duties. Insurance contract law is linked to the BGB and some provisions in the BGB deal specifically with insurance contract law[72] and vice versa.[73] Moreover, the BGB is generally applicable wherever the VVG 2008 does not prescribe any special rules. In this chapter, the most important provisions of the applicable rules that affect questions of liability of the insurer and insurer intermediaries will be presented.

[67] Case number = C-209/12, Judgment of the Court (First Chamber), 19 December 2013, Walter Endress v Allianz Lebensversicherungs AG.

[68] BGH, 07.05.2014 - IV ZR 76/11.

[69] Schimikowski and Höra (2007), p. 136; Beenken (2010), p. 80.

[70] Sec. 209 and 210 of the VVG 2008.

[71] Directive 2002/92/EC o of 9 December 2002 on insurance mediation.

[72] Art.1045, 1046, 1127–1130 BGB.

[73] E.g. Sec. 4. para.1; Sec. 8. para. 4 VVG 2008 etc.

2.4.1 The Basis of the Claim for the Liability of the Insurer

Prior to adoption of a VVG 2008, the insurer's duty to inform the policyholder before conclusion of the contract was regulated by the VAG.[74] In the VVG 2008, the duty to provide pre-contractual information to the policyholder was set up as a central segment of his/her protection. The obligation to provide information and advice is valid for all types of insurance contracts (life insurance, general insurance, etc.). It comprises contents of the insurance contract and the general conditions of insurance that the insurer must inform the policyholder before conclusion of the insurance contract.[75]

The duty to inform exists for all policyholders, regardless of whether they are considered to be consumers or not. Moreover, the insurer must provide information as set out in the separate Regulation on information obligation for insurance contracts (*Verordnung über Informationspflichten bei Versicherungsverträgen* abbreviation—VVG-Info-Verordnung) which gives detail requirements regarding the order of the information provided and analyses the specifications regarding the content.[76] VVG-Info-Verordnung supplements the VVG 2008 and enables insurer regular fulfilment of pre-contractual and contractual duty to inform.[77] Insurer's failure to provide detailed advice and information to policyholders in a timely manner[78] may result in potential liability for damages.

As a general rule, under the VVG 2008 the insurer is required to give advice to policyholder before the conclusion of an insurance contract and it must be documented.[79] As opposed to Directive 2002/92, the VVG 2008 expands the duty to

---

[74] By transferring the provision duty to inform from the VAG to the VVG 2008 it is unequivocally confirmed its civil legal character.

[75] Sec. 7 of the VVG 2008 comprises all obligations of informing, including requirement to provide suitable advice to the customer and to document such advice. These obligations have its origins from EU directives.

[76] Based on Sec. 7, para. 2 VVG 2008.

[77] Considering that the duty to inform has been regulated by imperative and semi-imperative provisions, German Insurance Contract Act, cannot influence its contents i.e. possible changes. By submitting to the consumer, the documents which contain particularities of the contract in a brief, precise and understandable way, the assumptions are created that he/she will not make the hasty decision.

[78] German legislator only when regulating a time moment of informing the policyholder, uses the formulation of "in good time before the policyholder submits his contractual acceptance" or "before the contract is concluded". This should be interpreted in a way that the insurance contract is concluded on the basis of the insformations of the terms of contract, including the general terms and conditions of insurance, in the form of a document to a policyholder. The policyholder therefore should have all the information necessary for informed decision-making about conclusion of the contract not later than in the moment of initiation of offer for conclusion of insurance contract.

[79] Sect. 6 para. 1 VVG 2008. The insurer, unlike a broker (*Versicherungsmakler*) owe reasonable advice to the policyholder. In determining the reasonableness of the advice, it is generally accepted that all relevant information of the case including the demands and needs of the policyholder, the nature and complexity of the envisaged insurance contract and the amount of the premium to be paid.

advise to the insurer as well.[80] Provision from the Directive 2002/92 has as a consequence discrimination of the policyholders that conclude the contract directly with the insurer. By applying the provisions of the Directive 2002/92, policyholder who conclude the contract directly with the insurer has less protection than the policyholder who concludes the contract directly with the insurance intermediary.

The information that the insurer should provide to the policyholder must be provided in a clear and comprehensible manner (*klar verständlich zu übermitteln).*[81] The accent is placed on comprehensibility of information to an average consumer (*mündige Verbraucher*),[82] and information must be formulated that it leaves no dilemma with respect to the meaning (the insurer must avoid non-precise statements, complex formulations, too many technical terms etc.) Policyholder should be able to decide on the basis of the information given to him/her before making a contractual statement, whether he/she will conclude an insurance contract, i.e. whether he/she wants to keep the existing insurance cover.[83] Should there be a reason to do so, advice must be provided during the entire term of the insurance agreement.[84]

If the notified information is not in accordance with the request of clarity and comprehensibility, the transparency requirement is violated. The transparency requirement means that legal position of contractual partners must be regulated in a clear and transparent manner.[85]

---

[80] Finnern (2009), pp. 215–220.

[81] Sec. 6. para. 2 of the VVG 2008; In theory, it is pointed out that this provision has typically formal and substantive dimension. The language in insurance policy is ambiguous, contradictory or gives room to multiple interpretations and it is too difficult for insureds to understand it; Beckmann and Matusche-Beckmann (2009), p. 931.

[82] Many consumers for different reasons do not take into account the information that were told to them on the basis of the legal duty of the insurer. From the point of view of consumer protection, the important thing is that consumers are told all the information that the law considers to be the consuming ones (regardless of whether they will want/be able to use them in a legally prescribed manner). This is especialy relevent in the case of unit-linked life insurance policy. It is up to consumers to decide about conclusion of the contract. In that way, on one hand, consumers are supplied with the information necessary to overcome information assymetry, and on the other hand, they seem to be the only ones that are responsible for making the decision on the basis of analyzing and taking into account of all the information.

[83] Beckmann and Matusche-Beckmann (2009), p. 915.

[84] Sec. 6 para. 4 VVG 2008. For example, if the policyholder wishes to terminate a life insurance contract, the insurer must inform him about the option to continue the policy without premium payments. The documentation requirement is intended to facilitate the production of evidence for the policyholder (if he claims for damages for inappropriate advice). Policyholders may waive their right to receive advice and/or documentation by issuing a separate written declaration to this effect and such waiver is only valid if the insurer refers in the same document to the disadvantageous effects of the waiver. In this way, policyholders are protected from hasty waivers. More details: Rüffer et al. (2008), § 6 VVG note 31.

[85] Beckmann and Matusche-Beckmann (2009), p. 916; According to the German law, a standard term that lacks transparency will be subject to an unquestionable assumption of unreasonable discrimination (*unwiderlegbare Vermutung einer unangemessenen Benachteiligung*) against the contractual partner and discriminatory standard terms are null and void under Sec. 307. para. 1 BGB.

Under VVG 2008, a policyholder must disclose the circumstances in its sphere of risk which are relevant to the insurer's decision to conclude the contract. Where the policyholder deliberately (*vorsätzlich*) or with gross negligence (*gross fahrlässig*) has made incorrect statements, the insurer may withdraw (*zurücktreten*) from the contract.[86] If the policyholder acted without fault or was only guilty of simple negligence in violating these duties, the insurer may terminate (*kündigen*) the contract with 1 month's notice.[87]

In spite of withdrawal, the insurer may still be obliged to pay a claim if the non-disclosed circumstance is not responsible for the occurrence of the insured event that led to the claim or for the level of the insurer's liability.[88] The remedies available to the insurer in case of a breach of the insured's duty of disclosure. allows the insurer to terminate the contract and to avoid paying future claims by giving 1 month's notice (in cases of no more than slight negligence) or withdraw from the contract and consider the contract as void ab initio (to be treated as invalid from the outset in cases of at least gross negligence).[89]

In Germany, the doctrine of *Treu und Glauben* (literally fidelity and faith) is applicable in insurance contract law and it is generally recognized that the insurance relationship is governed to a special degree by such principle.[90] The principle of utmost good faith applies to all types of insurance contracts and particularly on insurance contracts with consumers. Both, the insurer and the insured are subject to the principle of utmost good faith (also an aggrieved party in some respect). The principle of utmost good faith is a constant duty to both insurer and insured throughout the contractual relationship and irrespective of whether or not an actual insurance contract is concluded.

The principle of good faith is provided in Sec. 242 BGB.[91] The insured's duty of disclosure which is contained in Sec. 19 of the VVG 2008 is the product of the principle of utmost good faith.[92] Sec. 19 VVG 2008 provides a detailed set of rules with regard to the insured's duty of disclosure[93] and the legal consequences following a violation of the disclosure.

---

[86] Sec. 19 para. 2, 3 VVG 2008.

[87] Sec. 19 para. 2 VVG 2008.

[88] Sec. 21.para 2. VVG 2008.

[89] Sec. 19.of the VVG 2008.

[90] Heiss (1989), p. 20ff; Fischer (1965), p. 197.

[91] § 242 BGB "*Der Schuldner ist verpflichtet, die Leistung so zu bewirken, wie Treu und Glauben mit Rücksicht auf die Verkehrssitte es erfordern.*" (An obligor has a duty to perform according to the requirements of good faith, taking customary practice into consideration).

[92] Honsell (1998), p. 2194.

[93] Sec. 19 para. 1 VVG 2008. Pursuant to this rule, the insured shall disclose to the insurer before making his contractual acceptance the risk factors known to him which are relevant to the insurer's decision to conclude the contract with the agreed content and which the insurer has requested in writing. If, after receiving the policyholder's contractual acceptance and before accepting the contract, the insurer asks questions about the risk factors, the policyholder shall also be under the duty of disclosure as regards these questions. Moreover, according to Sec. 20 of the VVG 2008 if the contract is concluded by a policyholder's representative, both the representative's knowledge and

The duty of utmost good faith applies at the pre-contractually and post-contractually stage. Sec. 19 VVG 2008 is primarily applicable but also the principle of utmost good faith applies during the pre-contractual stage.[94] Additionally, Sec. 23 of the VVG 2008 contain rules regarding the aggravation of risk which also constitute the written consequence of the principle of utmost good faith.[95] Sec. 6, 7 of the VVG 2008 prescribe the pre-contractual duty of utmost good faith for the insurer to inform and to advise. In addition, the principle of utmost good faith obliges the insurer to clarify any ambiguities.

Therefore, the key elements of duty to inform are the following: (1) it relates to all kinds of insurance contracts; (2) it comprises all the information prescribed by European insurance law[96]; (3) it contains an information significant for policyholder to make the decision whether or not to enter into the insurance agreement; (4) information are notified in writing (paper documents and electronic documents such as emails are allowed), floppy disk, CD ROM. However, the information that are contained in electronic data holder or on web page of the insurer are considered to be in written form only when they provides a record of the notification printed and given to the policyholder[97]; (5) for failure to fulfil this obligation, responsible can be

---

fraudulent conduct as well as the insured's knowledge and fraudulent conduct shall be taken into account.

[94] The principle of utmost good faith nevertheless still is applicable where positive rules do not exist.

[95] Pursuant to Sec. 23 of the VVG 2008 "after the policyholder has submitted his contractual acceptance, an aggravation of the risk insured occurs notwithstanding his intention, he must disclose the aggravation to the insurer without undue delay as soon as he has learned thereof".

[96] Directive 2009/138/EC (Solvency II) harmonizes certain aspects of insurance contract law in Title II (Art. 178 to 211 providing "Specific Provisions for Insurance and Reinsurance"), such as information duties of the insurer (Art. 183 to 185), the cancellation period in individual life insurance (Art. 186) and the free choice of a lawyer guaranteed and qualified in Art. 201 and 202; Directive 2002/92/EC (Insurance Mediation) provides provisions about contractual relationship between an insurer and its customer whenever an insurer is vicariously liable for a breach of duty committed by an agent, e.g. an inaccurate instruction on the contents of a particular product; Insurance Distribution Directive (IDD), Directive on Markets in Financial Instruments (MiFID II) and Regulation on Key Information Documents for Investment Products (PRIPs Regulation) provide special rules on insurance contracts which are investment instruments, such as funds-linked life insurance. Insurance contract law is also harmonized to a certain degree by directives on consumer contract law comprising consumer insurances, Directive 2002/65/EC (Distance Marketing of Financial Services) and Council Directive 93/13/EEC (Unfair Contract Terms), Council Directive 93/13/EEC (see Art. 8) and some of the provisions in Directive 2002/65/EC concerning information duties (Art. 4. para.2) provide EU minimum standards of consumer protection and allow Member States to adopt more protective measures.

[97] By arrangement of the duty to inform as a pre-contractual obligation, influenced is change of model of conclusion of insurance contract. Prior to adoption of the Insurance Contract Act, the contracts were concluded by submitting insurance policy (*Policenmodell*), and general and special conditions were submitted only after the conclusion of the contract. It was very unfair for policyholders who did not have an insight into significant data before final commitment. Considering that now the duty to inform has been regulated as a pre-contractual one, in practice is developed of conclusion of contract by giving an offer (*Antragsmodell*) or invitation to offer (*Invitationmodell*) and submission of the legally prescribed data circle before declaring contractual will. Beckmann and Matusche-Beckmann (2009), p. 918.

both the intermediary and insurance agent; (6) the information must be disclose to the policyholder in due time, before the conclusion of the contract.

The statutory manifestation of the pre-contractual duty relates to information and advice and insurer and insurance intermediaries (insurance agents and insurance brokers) have a duty to advise. But the insurer has exclusive statutory obligation to provide information. Even when the contract is concluded via insurance intermediary, the insurer must take care of execution of duty to inform.

If the insurer fails to comply with the obligation to provide a policyholder with information within legally stipulated deadline, the VVG 2008 gives the policyholder an unlimited right to revoke the policy and it can be exercised within a 2-week period or, in the case of life insurance, within 30 days. The time period does not start until the policyholder has received all policy conditions and information and has been properly informed about his revocation rights.

The German regulator (*Bundesanstalt für Finanzdienstleistungsaufsicht*—BaFin) in case of violation of the interests (constant breach by the insurer of its duty of utmost good faith in the form it has been adopted in statutory provisions) will demand from the insurer to remedy such inadequacy and has the authority to issue any order *vis-à-vis* the insurer (or/and insurer's management) which is necessary to remedy the situation. Violation of the duty to inform in pre-contractual stage presents a basis for submitting a claim against the insurer.

The question is posed how to settle collision of duties to inform and advise the policyholder when the insurance contract linked to investment funds is concluded by means of intermediaries or insurance agents. Who has the duty to advise? German law stipulates that the insurer has no duty to advise in the following cases: (1) when the insurance contract is concluded via insurance intermediary; (2) when insurance contract is concluded via internet and in general between the absent persons; (3) when large risks are insured; (4) when the policyholder waived the counselling. Although this obligation binds both, the insurer intermediary and the insurer, the duty to advise can be carried out only once.[98] The more complex is the requested insurance product (i.e. unit-linked policies), the more complex is duty to advise.

The insurer also can be exposed to the claim by the policyholder due to giving the wrong advice. Policyholders/insured persons can bring direct claims against an insurer but a third party is not allowed to bring it due to the fact that third parties do not have a direct legal relationship with the insurer.[99] If policyholder files a request for indemnity against the insurer due to violation of duty to advise, the policyholder should prove that assumptions for that have been fulfilled. The policyholder should prove the following: (1) that there is a duty to inform; (2) what is the reason for advice; (3) that the duty has not been fulfilled or that it has been fulfilled badly.

---

[98] van Bühren (2014), pp. 1629–1630.

[99] According to the Sec. 108 para. 2 of the VVG 2008, the policyholder can assign its indemnity claim against a liability insurer to the third party and that this assignment cannot be excluded in the general terms of insurance.

The VVG 2008 abolished so-called "all or nothing" principle and replaced it for a new principle of proportionality for questions of liability. Under the VVG 2008 payment of claims in cases of recklessness will not be excluded but will be reduced in proportion to the degree of fault depending on the policyholder's degree of responsibility. However, the insurer right to refuse payment and to terminate the contract is limited to cases in which the policyholder has acted with gross negligence.[100] In cases of ordinary negligence (failure to exercise the degree of care expected of a person of ordinary prudence), the entire amount of the insurance money will be payable. In contrast, the insurer can avoid the contract and he is free from liability in any event in cases of intentional or fraudulent behaviour by the policyholder.[101] The insurer is not obliged to return any premiums paid in case of withdrawal or avoidance.[102]

VVG 2008 gives the parties right to "contract-out" when major risks are concerned. In that case, general German statutory provisions on the freedom of contract apply, but conflicting terms always bear the risk of being ineffective, in particular when a clause disadvantages the policyholder inappropriately. The effectiveness of a disputed clause is subject to judicial review.

2.4.2 The Basis of the Claim for the Liability of the Insurance Agent and Insurance Broker

Provision 59 of the VVG 2008 describes insurance intermediation by distinguishing and defining two types of insurance intermediary "insurance agent" and "insurance broker" Pursuant to Sec. 59 para.2 of the VVG 2008, an "insurance agent' is anyone contracted by an insurer or another insurance agent to arrange or conclude insurance agreements on a commercial basis. Under Sec. 59. para.3. of the VVG 2008, an "insurance broker" is anyone who contracts to arrange or conclude insurance agreements for a client on a commercial basis without having being contracted to do so by an insurer or an insurance agent." Moreover, anyone who is giving impression that he is providing the services of an insurance broker to the person wishing to take out insurance, will be deemed as an insurance broker.[103]

The insurance intermediation is also subject of the provisions of the EU Insurance Mediation Directive (2002/92/EG), the German Trade, Commerce and Industry Regulation Act (*Gewerbeordnung*, abbreviated GewO), the Commercial Code

[100] Sec. 26. para 1. sentence 2, Sec. 28. para.2. sentance 2, Sec. 81. para.2, Sec. 82. para.3. sentence 2 and Sec. 86. para 2. sentence 3 of the VVG 2008; An insured's fraud under group insurance policies, does not prejudice the rights of the other insureds under the same contract and any (pre-contractual or later) fraud of the policyholder of the group insurance contract can have consequences for the insureds and endanger their cover.

[101] Sec. 26. para.1. sentence 1, Sec. 28. para.2. sentence 1, Sec. 81. para.1, Sec. 82 para.3. sentence 1 and Sec. 86. para.2, sentence 2 of the VVG 2008.

[102] Heiss (2013).

[103] For more information see Gebert et al. (2013), p. 173. Beckmann and Matusche-Beckmann (2009), p. 301.

(*Handelsgesetzbuch*, abbreviated HGB),[104] the Regulation on Insurance Mediation and Advice (*Versicherungsvermittlungsverordnung*, abbreviated VersVermV). These acts provide the requirements for the professional qualifications, the reliability, the duties to advice and documentation, and the financial circumstances for a job as an insurance broker and insurance agent. Moreover, VAG contains specific rules for insurance companies in their dealings with insurance intermediaries.[105]

All German insurance intermediaries, and thus also insurance brokers and insurance agents who acts on a professional basis, must be licensed by the relevant Chamber of Trade and Commerce (*Deutsche Industrie- und Handelskammertag*, abbreviated DIHK).[106] Pursuant to Sec. 34(d) para 2 GewO, the licence must not be granted, if: the applicant was convicted of a felony (*Verbrechen*) or certain property crimes within the last 5 years; insolvency proceedings have been initiated against the applicant; the applicant cannot provide proof of professional liability insurance; the applicant has not passed an exam offered by the DIHK proving she or he has the requisite expertise to operate as an intermediary.

In addition to these legal requirements insurance brokers and insurance agents have to prove a comprehensive knowledge because most insurance services and products are very complex (especially insurance based investment products), and therefore, an assessment of their features and the ability to choose among many diverse offers requires specialized knowledge. Because of high information asymmetries and high search costs and legal requirements, insurance intermediaries have to overcome it, by proving a comprehensive knowledge of the insurance business and the actuarial practice.

Insurance agents act as commercial agents in the name of a particular insurance company and in contrast to that, insurance brokers act as commercial brokers. This distinction also implies different legal duties and liability rules. Pursuant to Sec. 84 of the HGB, insurance agents act as commercial agents in the name of a particular insurance company. Insurance brokers are legally independent from insurance companies and they act as commercial brokers pursuant to the Sec. 93 of the HGB.[107] That means that an insurance agent is tied to a certain insurance company whose products he sells and can be compared to "front-line salesperson". Contrary to insurance agent, an insurance broker does not represent any insurance company, and he is free to choose from a variety of products available on the market of different companies.

[104] The HGB contains rules that affect insurance law (intermediaries and rules of liability), but these don't deal with contract law.

[105] Beckmann and Matusche-Beckmann (2009), pp. 298.et seq.

[106] Pursuant to section 34(d), para. 3 of the GewO, the authorities waive upon application the requirements of a license in the event that the applicant mediates insurance agreements as a supplement to the goods delivered or services rendered in the context of its primary activity. In such a case, the applicant would need to provide evidence that: he mediates insurance agreements as a contractor of an insurance intermediary holding a license or as a contractor of an insurance company; he is covered by a professional indemnity insurance; and he is reliable as well as appropriately qualified and does not live in disorderly financial conditions. Insurance mediation does not require any license in the context of ancillary activities if these are carried out in small scale.

[107] Beckmann and Matusche-Beckmann (2009), p. 310.

Insurance agent is independent from the insurer (usually self-employed if it is not a legal entity) and he is bound by an agency agreement with the insurer. An agency agreement binds the insurer and agent, and it is the source of some of the agent's express authority. The duties and responsibilities of an insurance agent are listed explicitly in the agency agreement, and it will generally include not only what the agent can do, but, also, what he cannot do, in representing the insurer. "Multiple agents" are selling insurance for a variety of companies and usually have contractual relationships with many insurance companies. They can be split into multiple agents representing several insurance companies in the same line of insurance or they can represent different insurers but only in different lines of insurance. Single agents represent one particular insurer. Anyone who is distributing insurance products on the basis of an employment agreement with an insurer would be acting on behalf of the insurer, and this includes insurer's duty to inform and to advise on behalf of the insurer, but not as an insurance agent according to the law.[108]

The duties imposed by the law on insurance brokers, with respect to the information that must disclose to customers before the conclusion of an insurance contract, are very strict. Moreover, insurance brokers represent the customers, and help them to find the right insurance company at the best price and the advice that insurance brokers give to their clients are sterner than for insurance agents.

According to the VVG 2008, intermediaries acting as brokers are only obliged to render advice in the pre-contractual phase,[109] in accordance with the provisions of the IMD. The main reason lies in the facts that consumers who are looking for some insurance are considered as the weaker party with weaker bargaining position and with lack of experience, in deciding what their rights and obligations shall be in insurance contracts. Insurance brokers have to prove a comprehensive knowledge because most insurance services and products are very complex (especially investment-linked insurance policies with life insurance and investment components), and therefore, an assessment of their features and the ability to choose among many diverse offers requires specialized knowledge.[110]

Also, insurance brokers are subject to stricter liability rules. Whereas insurance companies are liable for miscounselling by insurance agents, insurance brokers are liable themselves for a culpable breach of duty and for loss from misguided advise. Also, no liability insurance for financial losses is required from insurance brokers.[111]

Regional and higher regional courts (*Landgericht und Oberlandesgericht*) in Germany have been involved in lawsuits regarding counselling with misinformation

[108] These individuals are not subject to specific rules applicable to insurance mediation rather to certain rules of the HGB.

[109] Sec. 61 and 62 of the VVG 2008.

[110] Insurance Mediation Directive (IMD) ensures that insurance-based investment products sold by intermediaries meet the demands and needs of an individual consumer. The Insurance Distribution Directive (IDD) applies this requirement to all distributors and, in addition, introduces an assessment of the suitability and appropriateness of an insurance-based investment product.

[111] The liability rule arises from EU directives (IMD) and applies for failures resulting from neglect of information, advising and documentation duties.

in the last several years.[112] The liability rule is subject to German law pursuant to Sec. 63 of the VVG 2008 (*Schadensersatzpflicht*) and represents the basis for a claim. Section 6 of the VVG 2008 states: "The insurance intermediary shall be obligated to compensate for loss incurred by the person wishing to take out insurance on account of a breach of one of the duties under section 60 or section 61. This shall not apply if the insurance intermediary is not responsible for the breach of duty." For the insurance brokers, this liability rule is *lex specialis* compared to the general basis for liability in Sec. 280 para.1 BGB.[113]

According to the Sec. 63.par.1 of the VVG 2008, the insurance intermediary shall be obligated to compensate for loss incurred by the person wishing to take out insurance on account of a breach of one of the duties under Sec. 60 or Sec. 61. The VVG 2008 defines new personal liability with reference to all types of agents, either connect to only one insurance company, or in cooperation with multiple insurers.[114]

Joint liability means that insurance agent and the insurer are both liable to the same injured party for the same misconduct. Since the insurance broker represents interests of the customer, the insurer would generally not be liable for the broker's misconduct or fault, unless the broker acted on behalf of the insurer within the scope of a cooperation agreement. In this case, joint liability will depend on every single circumstance of misconduct.

The obligatory indemnification is basically triggered by a breach of one of following intermediaries duties.[115] Each intermediary is obliged to render advice prior to concluding a contract based on an analysis of a sufficient number of insurance contracts available on the market, Intermediary is in a position to make his recommendation, based on professional criteria (taking into account specific circumstances as well as the nature and complexity of the insurance contract), regarding which insurance contract is best suited to meet the needs of the person wishing to take out insurance. The main difference between insurance intermediaries is that a broker is obligated to base his advice on a sufficient number of insurance products and insurers available on the mark and an agent has to select a contract from his particular basis.

Likewise, a tied agent sell policies for only one insurance company which means that he has only one insurer to select from all market. When intermediary depends on a single insurer, the requirement becomes even more stricter. Considering that thorough risk assessment has become increasingly important to the success and longevity of any business, obligatory indemnification effects every intermediary. The policyholder must be given appropriate advice relating to his individual case in writing, including information about the reasons for that advice. If the intermediary

---

[112] For example: OLG Saarbrücken, 04.05.2011 – 5 U 502/10 – 76; OLG Hamm, 04.12.2009 - I-20 U 131/09; 33 O 136/10 LG Ingolstadt; 12/29/2010; 12 U 56/11 OLG Karlsruhe; 09/15/2011; 5 U 337/09 OLG Saarland; 01/27/2010; 14 U 129/10 OLG Schleswig; 09/16/2011.

[113] Sec. 280. para 1 BGB Damages for breach of duty.

[114] Dörner (2010), § 63 recital 1.

[115] Dörner (2010), § 63 recital 5,8.

fails to perform its duties (it effects every intermediary), he will be held accountable fora pre-contractual breach of his duty. Sec. 61. of the VVG 2008 provides that advice has to be documented in writing and each intermediary has to fulfil specific documentation requirements. Any breach of the advice duty that is due to fault (negligence or purpose) leads to a claim for compensation against the insurer or the insurance intermediary.[116]

The German legislation didn't formulate a special regulation concerning the plea of contributory negligence, regardless of implementation of concrete duties. The concept of contributory negligence (*Mitverschulde*) in German law is no defence for a breach of contract but a defence in contract law and leads to a reduction of the amount of damages to be paid.[117] In a case of contributory negligence, the provision of Sec. 254 BGB is applicable. Contributory negligence is defence for injurers which must be pleaded and proved by person invoking it. It results in partial compensation only whenever the consumer negligently violates a duty. The resulting compensation rate depends upon circumstances of the case and even though the primary standard is causation, the secondary standard is a review of the other circumstances (e.g. the question of negligence).

2.5 Liability Issues Regarding Insurance-Based Investment Products: Would the Liability of Insurance Intermediaries Remain Unregulated?

The insurance market has changed considerably in the present time and classical assertion of insurance law has recently been questioned due to all the technological advancements, new insurance products (e.g. investment products based on insurance) and level of protection in line with modern concepts of consumer law. Therefore, since it cannot keep pace with modern commercial practice, a classical approach of the issues regarding the liability of insurer and insurance intermediaries remain at the centre of attention and facing further calls for reform in order to cope with the developments in commercial transactions.

Based on the solutions inspired by the principle of good faith, new rules and institutions started to emerge, and MiFid and IDD principles are clear proof of that. The IDD introduced two general principles, providing that insurance distributors

[116] Sec. 6 para and Sec. 63 of the VVG 2008; From the consumers' point of view, missing documentation reduce the burden of proof.

[117] This is clearly express by the wording of section 254 BGB "(1) where fault on the part of the injured person contributes to the occurrence of the damage, liability in damages as well as the extent of compensation to be paid depend on the circumstances, in particular to what extent the damage is caused mainly by one or the other party. (2) This also applies if the fault of the injured person is limited to failing to draw the attention of the obligor to the danger of unusually extensive damage, where the obligor neither was nor ought to have been aware of the danger, or to failing to avert or reduce the damage. The provision of section 278 applies with the necessary modifications."

must "always act honestly, fairly and professionally in accordance with the best interests of customers" and that all information must be "fair, clear and not misleading". German courts determine what good faith requires in the circumstances of the specific case and the judge has to determine the requirements of good faith in such an objective way as possible. This raises a question, do the German courts rightly upholding high legal (ethical) standards for policyholders?

The "fairness" is the objective element. This objective element is combined with the notion of 'honesty', which is subjective and objective element. The test in determining whether the duty has been breached is an objective test based on subjective facts. In other words, would an objective person (a reasonable person), knowing what the insurer actually knows, act the same way? According to linguistic interpretations it means that distributors honesty, fairness, and professionalism are valued according to best interests of customers, and not according to the objective criteria. Consequently, it could be also interpreted that in any particular case, honesty, fairness and professionalism of distributors have to be valued according to the interest of policyholders.[118]

The revised VVG 2008 introduced a new rule of proportionality which replaced the former all-or-nothing principle for questions of liability. As already mentioned, the VVG 2008 provides that in cases of gross negligence on the part of the policyholder the insurer is required to pay a proportion of the claim depending on the degree of fault. This new flexibility can consequently create a legal uncertainty and courts may consider the policyholder's action as representing gross negligence in cases where under the former act they would have decided differently. German courts need to determine fault in accordance with the circumstances of a particular case and that require complex considerations of all facts and then reach a well-reasoned judgment which is mainly subjective element.

3 A Step Forward: The Possible Impact of the Implementation of IDD and PRIIPs on German Legal Doctrine and Courts Approach

As already mentioned, the BaFin has published a new Circular no. 11/2018 concerning a cooperation among insurance intermediaries and the guidance on insurance undertakings' risk management with regard to insurance distribution. This document explains in detail which obligations insurance undertakings have if they want to cooperate with tied agents (e.g. to check whether the tied agent is properly qualified), distinction between the cooperation with licensed insurance intermediaries and intermediaries who are exempt from the licensing requirement (especially ancillary insurance intermediaries).

[118] Tomic (2016), p. 206, available at: http://www.academia.edu/32903371/Strani_pravni_%C5%BEivot_4_2016; For further details see Gruber (2016), pp. 5–12; Di Nella (2015), pp. 767–774.

The Circular no. 11/2018 also deals with the cooperation with insurance advisers (*Versicherungsberater*) and "Tippgeber" (the person who doesn't moderate insurance contracts, but only make contact between potential policyholders and potential insurance undertakings). Moreover, the BaFin now expressly asks the insurance undertakings to take into consideration the provisions of the German Legal Services Act (*Rechtsdienstleistungsgesetz*)[119] if the activities, including complaints handling and policy administration, are outsourced to intermediaries. The German Legal Services Act prohibits legal services from being performed by brokers unless they are ancillary services to the original broking service.

In October 2017 EIOPA issued its Guidelines under the Insurance Distribution Directive on insurance based investment products that incorporate a structure which makes it difficult for the customer to understand the risks involved.[120] The EIOPA Guidelines have been developed pursuant to Sec. 30. para. 7 and 8 of IDD and it will help to evaluate the complex and non-complex insurance-based investment products to minimise the risks to consumers arising from mis-selling of these products in Europe. EIOPA guidelines are not legally binding but regulatory supervisors (including BaFin) are expected to incorporate it into its supervisory practice.

Directive IDD doesn't contain specific regulation regarding group insurance contract and neither expressly excludes nor includes the group policyholder in the definition of "insurance intermediary" or "insurance distributor".[121] The German legislator need to decide whether will implement specific national insurance distribution provisions regarding the group insurance policyholder or the final decision remain on the German courts.

German investment firms must provide retail clients with advisory minutes (*Anlageberatungsprotokoll*) when providing investment advice at the present time. In the case that retail client trades before the receipt of the advisory minutes and these are wrong, the client can revoke the trade within 1 week. The German advisory minutes will be replaced according to the Sec. 25 para 2 MiFID II to suitability minute but content will remain relatively the same.

The PRIIPs Regulation provides a period for the investment funds until 31 December 2019 which means that funds can still produce and use UCITS KIIDs or AIF-KIIDs (alternative investment fund) in German market if such a fund is "wrapped" into a life insurance product. The amended rules of the German Securities Trading Act (*Wertpapierhandelsgesetz*—WpHG) just refers to the PRIIPs Regulation with regard to financial instruments which are within the scope of the PRIIPs Regulation. For other financial instruments (e.g. investment funds,) an investment adviser must provide a retail client with a short form information paper even if no PRIIPs KID is available.

---

[119] Legal Services Act of 12 December 2007, Federal Law Gazette I p. 2840, as last amended by Article 6 of the Act of 12 May 2017, Federal Law Gazette I p. 1121.

[120] See https://eiopa.europa.eu/Publications/Guidelines/EIOPA-17-651-IDD_guidelines_execution_only_EN.pdf.

[121] Recital (49) of the IDD.

Conventional life insurance contracts with profit sharing (e.g. endowment life and annuity insurance policies, basic pension (*Basis-Rente*), Riester pension (*Riester-Rente*) do not have the typical characteristics of PRIPs such as: no package i.e. no contractual link to a concrete reference value (a share in a fund, an index or other securities) and no investment risk. A policyholder who has concluded a conventional life insurance contracts is protected by the insurer against the risk of loss upon the termination of the insurance contract or upon certain contractually agreed insured events and contractual commitments to provide benefits are covered by solvency capital.[122]

According to the Recital (7) of PRIIPs: "Individual and occupational pension products, recognised under national law as having the primary purpose of providing the investor with an income in retirement, should be excluded from the scope of this Regulation". Recital (37) of the PRIIPs further provides that the Commission should assess whether to maintain the exclusion of pension products 4 years after the entry into force of the PRIIPs.

In Germany, dynamic hybrid products are generally pension contracts which are often criticized for the lack of standardized information that lead to a lack of transparency and difficult for the average consumer to understand it.[123] Therefore, information requirements for these products were introduced in 2001 with the Act on Certification of Old-Age Provision and "Basic Pension" Contracts (*Gesetz über die Zertifizierung von Altersvorsorge- und Basisrentenverträgen*—AltZertG). For the purposes of consumer protection, exclusion of pension products from the scope of the PRIIPs, any uniform brief information covering these different product groups would be a qualitative setback and it would lead to unnecessary duplication of information requirements.

4 Conclusion

The German insurance contract act was completely revised in 2008 and applies to all contracts commenced on or after 1 January 2008 and contracts commenced before that day are governed by the VVG 1908. The new VVG 2008 act generalizes the Directive 2002/92/EC provisions, laying down a comprehensive regime on the duty to advise and protection of policyholders. It imposes numerous duties on insurers to inform and advise policyholders of their rights and obligations in a timely manner, and the advice must be documented and given to the policyholders. Those duties are supposed to solve the problems that occur from asymmetrically distributed information and inadequate counselling regarding insurance products. The failure to comply with this obligation may result in potential liability for damages.

[122] This is a difference compared to UCITS (Undertakings for the Collective Investment of Transferable Securities).

[123] Menzel (2008), pp. 9–12. For further details on the dynamic hybrid products in Germany see Bohnert (2013), pp. 555–577; Radstaaki (2017), p. 46.

VVG-Info-Verordnung contains in detail the information that must be given to a policyholder before the submission of his contractual statement, as well as separate product information sheet with key details of the insurance policy, information about the provision of the policy and general terms and conditions of insurance coverage should be given to policyholders. In Germany, supervisory authorities require for unit linked life policies an explicit pre-contractual information for insurers and insurers intermediaries because it cannot be expected that a consumer has expert knowledge and discovers failures, gaps or inconsistencies in their insurance coverage.

The so-called "policy model" ((*Policenmodell*) has been abolished and replaced with an "application model" (*Antragsmodell*) under the insurer must fulfil his clarification, consultation and information duties before the insured releases his declaration of intent to conclude the insurance contract. Should the insurer violate his information duties, the period for the right of appeal of the insured will not be initiated. In case of failure to comply with the obligation to provide a policyholder with information, the German law gives the policyholder an unlimited right to revoke the policy (after he received all policy conditions and information and has been properly informed about his revocation rights) and it can be exercised within a 2-week period or, in the case of life insurance, within 30 days.

The VVG 2008 abolished the "All-or-Nothing Principle" and replaced it with rule of proportionality for questions of liability. Discharge of liability of an insurer is limited and depends on the policyholder's degree of fault. Moreover, under the VVG 2008, the policyholder is obliged to respond to written enquiries from the insurer about the risk and the insurer's right to withdraw from the policy is excluded in cases of negligence of the policyholder's disclosure obligation.

The new IDD introduced two general principles, providing that insurance distributors must "always act honestly, fairly and professionally in accordance with the best interests of customers"; and that all information must be "fair, clear and not misleading". Accepting a general principle "to always act honestly, fairly and professionally" does not necessarily mean that parties to insurance contracts will be subject to new or more extensive "good faith" duties in Germany. The general organizing principle will not impose a pre-fabricated set of specific legal duties that need to be observed by the parties. Rather, it requires the parties in general terms to perform their contractual duties honestly, fairly and professionally in accordance with the best interests of customers. As the IDD is a minimum harmonisation Directive, German lawmaker may elect to implement additional measures at national level, if the lawmaker deems this necessary for the purposes of consumer protection. However, this may lead to unnecessary administrative burden and would have a negative effect on the Single Market. The implementation of the IDD might not change the regulatory landscape in insurance distribution in Germany because a number of the regulatory requirements that are now being introduced by the IDD are already in place. Bearing in mind the above-mentioned, this leaves some space for a doubt how the implementation of the IDD will improve consumer protection and transparency in the market and what level of harmonisation the IDD will achieve in practice.

References

Beckmann RM, Matusche-Beckmann A (2009) Versicherungsrechts-Handbuch Gebundene Ausgabe. C.H. Beck, München

Beenken M (2010) Der Markt der Versicherungsvermittlung unter veränderten rechtlichen Rahmenbedingungen: unter besonderer Berücksichtigung von Sourcingstrategien des Versicherungsvermittlerbetriebs, VVW Karlsruhe

Bernhardt J (2010) Private Equity als Anlageklasse für Fondsgebundene Lebensversicherungen. Gabler Verlag

Bohnert A (2013) The market of dynamic hybrid products in Germany: concept, risk-return profiles, and market overview. Ger J Risk Insur 102(5):555–575

Di Nella L (2015) Der Schutz der Kunden nach der MiFID 2 und MIFIR – Eine Skizze des Regelwerks und systemorientierte Schlussfolgerungen, Privatrecht, Wirtschaftsrecht, Verfassungsrecht Privatinitiative und Gemeinwohlhorizonte in der europäischen Integration, Cordula Stumpf, Friedemann Kainer, Christian Baldus (Hrsg)

Döring N (2010) Teilung von fondsgebundenen Versicherungen im Rahmen des neuen Versorgungsausgleichs, Reihe "Versicherungswirtschaft", Band 62, Eul Verlag

Dörner H (2010) §§ 59–73. In: Prölss ER, Martin A (eds) Versicherungsvertragsgesetz, vol 14. Beck'sche Kurz-Kommentare, C.H. Beck, München

Eichengreen B, Ritschl A (2008) Understanding West German economic growth in the 1950s. In: Working Papers No. 113, Barry Eichengreen, Berkeley, & Albrecht Ritschl, LSE

Endres A (1991) Okonomische Grundlagen des Haftungsrechts. Physica-Verl, Heidelberg

Finnern C (2009) Der Vertragsabschluss im Versicherungsrecht: Die Besonderheiten des geltenden Rechtes, die Vorgaben des europäischen Gesetzgebers und die Reform des deutschen Versicherungsvertragsrechtes. Saarbrücker Verlag für Rechtswissenschaften, Saarbrücken

Fischer R (1965) Treu und Glauben im Versicherungsrecht, Versicherungsrecht – VersR Zeitschrift für Versicherungsrecht, Haftung und Schadensrecht

Focht U, Richter A, Schiller J (2013) Intermediation and (mis-)matching in insurance markets: who should pay the insurance broker? J Risk Insur 80(2):329–350

Gaida M (2002) Venture Capital in Deutschland und den USA. Finanzierung von Start-ups im Gefüge von Staat, Banken und Börsen, Deutscher Universitäts-Verlag

Gatzert N, Schmeiser H (2006) Implicit options in life insurance: valuation and risk management, Working papers on risk management and insurance No. 26. Institute for Insurance Economics, University of St. Gallen

Gebert Y, Erdmann KU, Beenken M (Hrsg) (2013) Praxishandbuch Vermittlerrecht, Verlag Versicherungswirtschaft GmbH, Karlsruhe

Gesamtverband der Deutschen Versicherungswirtschaft e.V, Statistisches Taschenbuch der Versicherungswirtschaft 2016. http://www.gdv.de/wpcontent/uploads/2016/09/Statistisches_Taschenbuch_2016_Versicherungswirtschaft_GDV.pdf

Gesamtverband der Deutschen Versicherungswirtschaft e.V., Absenkung des Höchstrechnungszinses hat kaum Einfluss auf die Ablaufleistung. http://www.gdv.de/2011/02/lebensversicherung-bleibt-attraktives-vorsorgeprodukt-absenkung-des-hoechstrechnungszinses-hat-kaum-einfluss-auf-die-ablaufleistung/

Grote J, Schneider C (2007) VVG 2008: Das neu Versicherungsvertragsrecht Auswirkungen für gewerbliche Versicherungen, Betriebs-Berater, Heft 50

Gruber M (2016) Die Versicherungsvertriebsrichtlinie, Zeitschrift für Finanzmarktrech, Heft 5

Günter L, Frommann, H (1998) Eigenkapital für den Mittelstand, Venture-Capital im In- und Ausland. C. H. C. H. Beck'sche Verlagsbuchhandlung

Hagelschuer PB (1983) Lebensversicherung. Gabler

Heiss H (1989) Treu und Glauben im Versicherungsvertragsrecht: Eine rechtsvergleichende Untersuchung deutscher und österreichischer höchstrichterlicher Judikatur, Orac (Wien)

Heiss H (2013) Proportionality in the New German Insurance Contract Act 2008. Erasmus Law Rev 5(2):105–114

Hofmann N (2011) Information cost, broker compensation, and collusion in insurance markets. Schmalenbach Bus Rev 63:287–307

Holzmann R, Palmer EE (2006) Pension reform: issues and prospects for non-financial defined contribution (NDC) schemes. In: Proceedings of the NDC Conference in Sandhamn, Sweden, September 28–30, 2003, The World Bank, Washington, DC

Honsell H (1998) Berliner Kommentar zum Versicherungsvertragsgesetz: Kommentar zum deutschen zum deutschen und österreichischen VVG. Springer

Koch R (2010) German reform of insurance contract law. Eur J Commer Contract Law 2(3):163–171

Kochanski M, Karnarski B (2011) Solvency capital requirement for hybrid products. Eur Actuarial J 1(2):173–198

Kollmann R (2008) Private Equity als Kapitalanlage deutsche Lebensversicherungen: eine empirische Analyse, Karlsruhe: Verl. Versicherungswirtschaft

Leithoff T (2014) Die fondsgebundene Versicherung: Rechtliche und fachliche Grundlagen zur Konzeption und Vermittlung von Fondspolicen, Versicherung Journal Verlag, Auflage: 2

Menzel P (2008) Optionen in Dynamischen Hybridprodukten, Der Aktuar 14(1):9–12

Mierzejewski AC (2016) A history of the German public pension system: continuity amid change. Lexington Books

Neugebauer R (1990) Versicherungsrecht vor dem Versicherungsvertragsgesetz Zur Entwicklung des modernen Binnenversicherungsrechts im 19. Jahrhundert, Verlag: Frankfurt am Main: Klostermann

Novikov V, Wiesenewsky U (2012) Unit linked business in Europe Development of the unit linked market in Germany, Towers Watson

OECD (2010) Chapter 7 The interface between member states and the EU, Better Regulation in Europe Better Regulation in Europe: Finland

Plagge A (2006) Public policy for venture capital: a comparison of the United States and Germany. Deutscher Universitätsverlag

Pyka A, Hanusch H (eds) (2006) Applied evolutionary economics and the knowledge-based economy. Edward Elgar

Radstaaki S (2017) Kapitalanlagemanagement bei Lebensversicherungsunternehmen für Hybridprodukte unter Solvency II und im aktuellen Niedrigzinsumfeld, Verlag Versicherungswirtsch

Reihlen M, Werr A (eds) (2012) Handbook of research on entrepreneurship in professional services. Edward Elgar

Römer W (2009) Die Reform des Versicherungsvertragsrechts, Humboldt Forum Recht, No.13. http://www.humboldt-forum-recht.de/deutsch/13-2009/beitrag.html

Rüffer W, Halbach D, Schimikowski P (2008) *Versicherungsvertragsgesetz: VVG-Handkommentar*, 2 Auflage

Schimikowski P, Höra K (2007) Das neue Versicherungsvertragsrecht. Bundesanzeiger Verlag

Storm S, Naastepad CWM (2014) Crisis and Recovery in the German Economy: The Real Lessons, Institute for New Economic Thinking Working Paper Series No. 10. https://papers.ssrn.com/sol3/papers.cfm?abstract_id=2638053

Tomic K (2016) The principle of good faith in European and National insurance law foreign legal life. Inst Comp Law, 4. http://www.academia.edu/32903371/Strani_pravni_%C5%BEivot_4_2016

van Bühren HW (2014) Handbuch Versicherungsrecht, 6 Auflage, Deutscher Anwaltverlag & Institut der Anwaltschaft GmbH

von Staudinge J, Sack R (2003) Staudinger-Kommentar zum BGB, Neubearbeitung

Werber M (2001) Der Versicherungsmakler im Vergaberecht, Versicherungsrecht (VersR), VVW

Italy

Diana Cerini and Santa Nitti

Contents

Sections 1–2 are attributed to Diana Cerini. Sections 3–8 are attributed to Santa Nitti. Last updated June, 2017.

D. Cerini (✉)
Dipartimento di Giurisprudenza-School of Law, University of Milano Bicocca, Milano, Italy
e-mail: diana.cerini@unimib.it

S. Nitti
Department of Private Law and Legal history, University of Milan "La Statale", Milano, Italy
e-mail: Santa.Nitti@unimi.it

P. Marano, I. Rokas (eds.), *Distribution of Insurance-Based Investment Products*, https://doi.org/10.1007/978-3-030-11668-2_7

1 Introduction: Insurance Intermediation in the Italian Legal System

Insurance intermediaries are a vital link in the sale of insurance products and in the offer of connected services. They also play an important role in protecting the interests of insurance clients, primarily by offering them advice and assistance and by analysing their specific needs. In simple words, intermediaries are a major element in the functioning of the Single European Market for insurance. This is confirmed by the fact that the distribution and sale of insurance products through intermediaries has always prevailed over direct sales by insurance companies, both in Italy and in other markets.[1]

This general trend is now changing slightly due to a more mature approach to the market by insurance companies, which is more consistent with consumer protection policies. On the one hand, insurers aim to improve their image and enhance clients' confidence in financial services; in addition, the evolution of distance selling techniques allows insurance companies to acquire more visible areas in the distribution chain without having to open market points in the territory.[2] This does not mean that insurance intermediaries will disappear, especially in the light of a more complex market, because of the coexistence of diversified products and of local and foreign companies operating in accordance with freedom of services and establishment. The role of insurance intermediaries is nonetheless called to evolve into a more sophisticated and attentive activity of assistance to clients, in order for insurance to be a 'service' rather than a mere 'product' to be sold.

Before dealing with the specific topic of this paper, it is essential to recall some major characteristics of Italian regulations and rules on insurance intermediation. In this direction, it is quite surprising that despite the importance of the role of insurance intermediaries as the essential link between insurance companies and their clients since centuries, their activity remained essentially unregulated in Italy for a very long time. This period of this substantial lack of regulation stretched from medieval times, when a prototype of the 'mediation man' first made its appearance (called a *sensale* at the time), up to the last decades of the twentieth century, when Law no. 49/1979 on insurance agents and, some years later, Law no. 792/1984 on insurance brokers were finally approved in order to implement the first Directive on insurance mediation (Directive EC/77/92 of 13 December 1976). In particular these laws gave rise to "*albi*" (registers) for agents and brokers.

The legislative situation completely changed after the implementation of Directive 2002/92/EC on insurance mediation, which occurred by approving the

---

[1] Donati and Volpe Putzolu (2014), p. 249.

[2] It should be pointed out that the model of 'intermediate selling' developed over the years involved a clear distinction and lack of communication between insurance companies, on the one side, and their clients, on the other; the possibility for insurance companies to acquire a true understanding of their clients' needs was thus inevitably restricted, weakening consumer confidence.

*Codice delle Assicurazioni Private (*in brief referred to as "CAP"), Title IX, from Articles 106–121. The pillars of the reform can be summarized as follows:

(a) the adoption of a broad definition of insurance intermediaries in line with Article 2 of the second Directive. In fact, Article 106 CAP provides that the activity of an insurance intermediary consists of presenting and proposing insurance and reinsurance products, as well as providing assistance and advice in the preparation of such contracts or assisting in the administration and performance of such contracts;
(b) the creation of a single register for all intermediaries (Article 109 CAP). In particular, Article 109 CAP provides that the register is divided into five sections ("*Sezioni*", specifically dedicated to each single category of intermediaries and organized as follows: section (a) insurance agents; section (b) insurance and reinsurance brokers; section (c) free producers; section (d) banks, investment companies and Poste Italiane–divisione bancoposta (bank departments of post offices); section (e) any other subject who cooperates with the abovementioned intermediaries.
(c) the acceptance of the principle of the single European passport for all insurance intermediaries (Article 116 CAP);
(d) the requirements of professional skills and good repute for all insurance intermediaries (Articles 110 to 112 CAP); the specific standard of professional skills will have to be determined by IVASS with further regulations (in particular regulations no.5/2006 and no.35/2010, as later amended);
(e) the establishment of the duties and responsibilities of insurance companies and intermediaries for damages deriving from intermediaries' services (Article 119) as well as information requirements (Article 120). More specifically, art. 106 CAP provides the definition of intermediation along with an indication of the activities that fall within that notion. Article 107 identifies the subjects to whom the reference system applies and in particular, the set of rules that govern the conditions of admission to intermediation, entry in the public register (so-called "R.U.I.") and the corresponding control over these activities, in addition to operating rules.

The subjects who, when carrying out any activity falling within the definition set out in article 106, are thus regulated by Italian laws on intermediation are identified, above all, according to the location of their activity: in fact, Italian operating rules, as established by C.A.P., apply to all natural and legal persons that reside or have their registered offices in the Republic of Italy and in relation to the activities they carry out both in Italy and in other member states under the freedom of establishment or the freedom to provide services, and for insurance and reinsurance intermediation services connected with risks and commitments situated outside the European Union. The provision thus transposes the *Home Country Control* principle, i.e. the application of the operating rules of the country of origin and the corresponding control by the supervisory body of the country of origin.

In addition, para. 1 also adds what follows: Italian subjects have the obligations set out in Chapter IX whenever they carry out intermediation activities, as defined in article 106, provided the activity is carried out for a fee. In other words, intermediation rules apply when the subject carries out one of the activities stated in article 106, provided such activity is somehow remunerated.[3]

The "onerousness" requisite referred to by the legislator should be clarified. First of all, such onerousness is to be intended as referring to any type of payment, including any form of profit-sharing pertaining to the broker, or cost savings or the attribution of other benefits by the insurance company though also by other intermediaries with whom the subject collaborates. In actual fact, this reference to onerousness is used to confirm the professional performance of the intermediation activity: it is obvious that, wherever there is some sort of remuneration, it is likely that the activity will not be carried out occasionally; rather, it will be part of a collaboration with a company or with another intermediary or also on appointment from clients. Besides, it would be rather difficult to argue that an activity, let's imagine not paid, carried out by a subject who professionally and therefore habitually, provides intermediation services—let's assume an agent—is not subject to the rules protecting users only because, in that specific case, there is no payment of a fee or any other benefit. It must therefore be concluded that the onerousness requisite imposed by legislation refers to the habitual execution of insurance brokerage services, thus remunerated or in any case not carried out for free, with the identification of a "*status*" (that of a broker) which is connected, in turn, to enrolment in the RUI.

Para. 2 of the said art. 107 identifies the activities which, albeit functionally traceable to the notion of intermediation described in art. 106 above, do not imply the application of the rules of intermediation to the subjects that perform such activities.

The first case (art. 107, para. 2, lett. a) appears obvious as it concerns the activities carried out directly by insurance companies and their employees. In said case, the exclusion is justified as there is no intermediated activity, since the subject that offers the product is the same as the company that creates and offers such product: there is not third party *medium*.

Secondly, art. 107, para. 2, lett. b) excludes pure information activities, provided as an ancillary part of another professional activity, from the scope of application of the regulations on intermediation, provided such information is not designed to assist the insured party in stipulating or executing an insurance contract. This is the case, for example, of the legal advisor who gives an opinion on a given product; likewise, any subject who gives mere insurance advice is not required to fulfil the obligations related to insurance brokerage: the role of the insurance consultant, who simply provides advisory services without collaborating in the offer of insurance products, will therefore not only be legitimate, but will also not be subject to the obligations of registering with the RUI and to insurance supervision.

The third case (art. 107, para. 2, lett. c) is more complex and brings together a large number of situations in which a number of requisites must be met, regarding both the product offered and the conditions of the offer, thus justifying a "reduction" of users' protection. In particular, the obligation of enrolment and of compliance

[3] See Volpe Putzolu, quoted, 315.

with the entire chapter of rules on intermediation is excluded where the product requires only knowledge of the coverage provided (1), is not a life insurance or third party liability insurance contract (2), the offer is made by a subject who does not carry out the activity on a professional basis (3) and the amount of the annual premium does not exceed five hundred euros and the contract, including any renewals, does not last more than 5 years (4). If we exclude the reference, somehow tautologic, made by *sub* 1, which concerns a product that requires solely knowledge of the guarantee offered, we can see—also by reading the provision together with IVASS regulation no. 5/2006—that the legislator has excluded all the situations where, albeit in the presence of an activity that can be placed in the context of intermediation, the product is provided as an accessory to another product or service, since in these cases it would have been too burdensome to require the subject offering the insurance product to meet the obligations of registration, training and control set out in Chapter IX of C.A.P.

Para. 3 mentions something that seems obvious, i.e. the subjects that are entered in section d) of the RUI, i.e. banks and financial intermediaries, are subject to controls by insurance supervisory authorities, with regard to observance of the provisions on the rules of conduct set out in Chapter III, informing and collaborating with the other authorities involved. This specification, albeit obvious, is necessary as it confirms a separation of the supervision by segment of activity and intends to reaffirm, in particular, the existence of the supervisory, regulatory and inspection powers that Chapter II of C.A.P. and articles 5 and 6 of C.A.P. attribute to IVASS, the insurance control authority, even where applied to bodies that are already subject to other forms of supervision for their industry.

Article 6, in particular, states that IVASS exercises its own functions in relation to insurance and reinsurance companies (a), financial groups and conglomerates (b), but also subjects, bodies and organizations that carry out functions that are partly included in the operational cycle of insurance or reinsurance companies, limited to insurance and reinsurance profiles (c), and insurance and reinsurance brokers, insurance appraisers and any other operator in the insurance market. In any case, the key standard for supervision remains that set out in art. 3, now integrated by art. 3-*bis* transposing Solvency II, according to which "*Supervision is designed for the good and prudent management of insurance and reinsurance companies and the transparency and fairness of the conduct of all companies, intermediaries and other operators in the insurance sector, having regard to the stability, efficiency, competitiveness and good operation of the insurance system, the protection of the insured and other subjects entitled to insurance services, as well as consumer information and protection*".[4]

[4] Volpe Putzolu, quoted, 20.

2 The Near Future: Possible Scenarios for the Transposition of the "IDD": Insurance Distribution Directive

The regulatory framework dedicated to insurance intermediation is about to incorporate new amendments to implement Directive 2016/97 dated 20.1.2016 on insurance distribution (so-called "IDD Directive"). As the term of entry into force of the new rules provided by the IDD has been postponed to October 2018 by the EU Commission, a further delay in the internal implementation has to be denounced, being actually in course the discussion of a project of law.[5] Nevertheless, the IDD and the project of implementation do not seem to affect the notion of insurance intermediation (adding, on the contrary, a new definition of distribution), which will remain untouched, probably with the same wording contained in art. 106 C.A.P.

The main amendments, in fact, will concern essentially some of the information and assistance obligations established by the Insurance Code and the implementation regulations enacted by the supervisory authority (IVASS) which will be later mentioned.[6] In any case, it should first be said that Directive 2016/97/CE introduces common rules for insurance *distribution* which includes, as can be seen from the term used, not only intermediated offers but also direct sales by insurance companies. Therefore, the IDD wrong-foots those who expected a "second edition" of the Intermediation Directive (IMD of 2002): the change is not just a linguistic one, as the intention of the European legislator is to confer *unitariness* to the insurance product-service offer phase, an activity that can be carried out by intermediaries and directly by companies. The difference compared to the previous legislation that had separately regulated the subjects concerned (intermediaries), is all too clear. Directive 2016/97/EC thus adopts a functional approach as clearly indicated in the 7th Recital, where it states that "*Insurance undertakings which sell insurance products directly should be brought within the scope of this Directive on a similar basis to insurance agents and brokers*". At least on paper, the Directive thus aims to place companies and intermediaries on the same level, in order to guarantee a minimum set of protection for users receiving insurance services. This functional approach can be better understood by looking at the definition given for "insurance distribution": it includes "*the activities of advising on, proposing, or carrying out other work preparatory to the conclusion of contracts of insurance, of concluding such contracts, or of assisting in the administration and performance of such contracts, in particular in the event of a claim, including the provision of information concerning one or more insurance contracts in accordance with criteria selected by customers through a website or other media and the compilation of an insurance product ranking list, including price and product comparison, or a discount on the price of*

[5] *See* Schema di decreto legislativo for implementation of EU Directive 2016/97 on insurance distribution approved by Consiglio dei ministri 8 February, and delivered to Chamber of Deputies (Camera dei Deputati) on the 21 February 2018.

[6] *See* here after, § 3-8.

an insurance contract, when the customer is able to directly or indirectly conclude an insurance contract using a website or other media".

A careful observer will notice that the identification of precise information obligations both in the case of direct distribution, i.e. carried out by the insurance companies, and in the case of intermediation, can already be found in the systematic reading of the Insurance Code of Private Insurances which, on the one hand, identifies the rules for intermediation in Chapter IX, specifically focusing on articles 119-120 that deal with intermediaries' duties and their responsibilities; and on the other hand (articles 185 et seq. dedicated to the contract) refers indifferently to the information obligations that companies and intermediaries should fulfil when offering products to their clients, *in primis* in relation to the need to offer suitable products.

We also need to evaluate the interaction between the obligations set out by the insurance class and the ones established for the case when the product is also a financial product. The sections below are dedicated to this issue.

3 The Notion of Insurance-Based Investment Products

In the current Italian legal system, insurance products with an "investment content"—defined by art. 2, para. 1 of Leg. Decree No. 209, dated 7 September 2005 (Private Insurance Code)—are the so-called linked policies, split into the two subtypes of unit-linked and index-linked (class of insurance III) and capital redemption operations (class of insurance V).[7] As known, linked insurance is characterised by the fact that, in its contractual structure, it offers, alongside the typical life insurance contract, an investment element. More specifically, unlike a traditional insurance contract—where the insurer undertakes to pay, when an event concerning human life occurs, either capital or annuity—preestablished at the time when the contract is stipulated—, these products are characterized by the fact that the benefits are exposed, wholly or in part, to the value of the units of investment funds (namely Undertakings for Collective Investment in Transferable Securities) or internal funds, or to indexes or other reference values.

Before the enactment of Law no. 262 dated 28 December 2005 on the protection of savings and the governance of financial markets (so-called Savings Law), insurance products with a financial content were not subject to a specific set of regulations that took into account their particular characteristics.

In such a legal framework, these products (and in particular unit-linked policies) have been the subject of long discussions by scholars and Courts regarding the applicable rules. In particular, it was wondered (though the debate is still somehow

[7]The classification by "class of insurance" was introduced by the First Directive 79/267/EEC, concerning admission to the direct life assurance activity. Alpa (2006), p. 77 ff. It analyses the financial structure of linked policies. E. Piras, *Polizze "index linked" collegate ad obbligazioni Lehman Brothers*, in Banca borsa tit. cred., 2012, II, 76 ff.; D. Cerini (2012), Insurance law in Italy, *International Encyclopoedia of Laws, Kluwer.*

ongoing) whether, given the significant financial nature of these products, these policies were subject to protection models created for financial instruments, pursuant to the Consolidated Finance Act (TUF). In resolving the dispute on the applicability (or non-applicability) of the new regulation to contracts concluded prior to the Savings Law, the national Courts clarified a series of interpretive principles and criteria to define the exact nature of the policies in question and thereby establish the applicable regulations. This gap, as stated above, was filled by the Savings Law (and later Legislative Decree 29 December 2006, n. 303—so-called Pinza Decree), that reformed, among other things, the rules on the sale and distribution of insurance products with an investment content.[8] In particular, with the said legislative intervention, article 25-bis "Financial products issued by banks and insurance companies" was introduced in the TUF, which provides for the application to the linked policies and to the capital redemption operations of similar rules to the one applicable to strictly financial products.

More specifically, art. 25-bis provides that the subscription and placement of financial products issued by insurance companies are to be regulated by articles 21 (rules of conduct for the supply of investment services and activities) and 23 (Contracts) of the TUF; in addition, Consob can exercise its own regulatory, inspection and information supervision power in relation to these products and to the companies, including insurance companies, which distribute them. What is most interesting in this respect is that the legislator, with reference to the distribution activity, equalised insurance-financial products issued by insurance companies to more purely investment products, placing the distribution of these policies within the scope of application of the above mentioned articles 21 and 23 of the TUF, which was previously limited to the provision of investment services (and additional services).

As a result of this choice, Consob has the power to issue detailed regulations on the matter. On this point, articles 83 et seq. of the Consob Intermediary Regulations[9] consequently establish specific obligations for intermediaries engaged in the distribution of insurance financial products (defined as "subjects authorised to engage in insurance intermediation") including, among other things, obligations of information to clients, contracts, evaluation of suitability and appropriateness, client order management, bonuses, reports, offers outside of the office and distance selling, and internal organization. Similar regulations are in place for insurance companies that directly distribute insurance financial products.

It must be pointed out that, unlike products from life classes of business III and V, policies under class I—although with an investment component—and so-called

[8] Art. 1, para. 1, lett. w-bis, of the TUF defines "financial products issued by insurance companies", these meaning "policies and operations referred to in the life sectors III and V set out in Article 2, subsection 1, of the Legislative Decree no. 209 dated 7th September 2005, with the exclusion of individual pension scheme according to article 13, subsection 1, letter b), of Legislative Decree no. 252 of 5th September 2005".

[9] Consob Regulation no. 16190 of 29 October 2007.

"multi-class" policies[10]—which consist in the combination of traditional segregated assets (class I) with a unit-linked investment fund (class III),[11] have been excluded from the definition of "financial products issued by insurance companies" set out in the TUF and are only governed by insurance regulations.[12]

---

[10] On this matter, it is interesting that, in December 2007, a consultation was commenced by IVASS and Consob for a joint communication aimed at governing the distribution of these policies; the document draft submitted for market evaluation also included obligations regarding pre-contractual information and information during the contract, reporting and advertising, and specific rules regarding client knowledge and the evaluation of product suitability. However, such consultation did not lead to the issue of the final text of the communication by the Authorities.

[11] On this matter, it is interesting that, in December 2007, a consultation was commenced by IVASS and Consob for a joint communication aimed at governing the distribution of said policies; the document draft submitted for market evaluation also included obligations regarding pre-contractual information and information during the contract, reporting and advertising, and specific rules regarding client knowledge and the evaluation of product suitability. However, such consultation did not lead to the issue of the final text of the communication by the Authorities.

[12] As for the reconstruction of the legislative measure, it should be recalled that in the course of the overall review of the financial market regulations—which then ended up in MiFID II—the EU legislator felt the need to regulate the cases regarding "Investments that involve contracts of insurance that are often made available to customers as potential alternatives or substitutes to financial instruments" (see recital 87 of MiFID II) on the basis of the consideration that said investments were more and more popular among retail clients, who thus needed greater protection from potential distortions linked to the absence of any harmonisation of the treatment of insurance and financial products. On this matter, art. 91 of MiFID II—while awaiting the future union legislation on insurance intermediary and insurance company activities (which arrived in January 2016 with the IDD)—introduced chapter III-bis in Directive 2002/92/EC on insurance mediation (so-called "IMD"), which was specifically dedicated to insurance investment products. The reform of the MiFID II centred around two essential elements: firstly, the introduction of the innovative (for the EU legislation) category of "insurance-based investment product" defined as "an insurance product which offers a maturity or surrender value and where that maturity or surrender value is wholly or partially exposed, directly or indirectly, to market fluctuations" [The definition was then later included into Regulation (EU) no. 1286/2014 (so-called "PRIIPs") on key information documents for packaged retail and insurance-based investment products]. It is clear that the EU definition of insurance-based investment products is inevitably wider and general, with particular reference to the exposure of the maturity or surrender value "wholly or partially, directly or indirectly, to market fluctuations" and therefore subject to interpretation; on this matter, it will be interesting to understand which products on the market must actually come under this category, since the MiFID II does not provide for inclusions, but only exclusions for certain non-life insurance products, life insurance contracts with services due only in the event of death or accident and pension schemes. The new category of insurance-based investment products thus appears to significantly expand the definition currently given by article 83 of the Intermediaries' Regulations of "insurance-based financial product" (which, as mentioned, includes the policies and operations of life sectors III and V): class I policies with separate management and "multi-sector" policies, so far excluded according to Italian law, can fall within the regulations established for insurance-based investment products. A de facto distinction between life policies and damage policies might therefore arise in a more distinct way, which would undermine in the future, from a classification point of view, the separation of policies into "sectors". However, since the aforesaid MiFID II provisions have been repealed as a result of the enactment of IDD—which includes a more detailed regulation of the topic, starting from the new definition (and exemptions) of insurance-based investment products already given by MiFID II (and the PRIIPS regulations)—it is appropriate to recall the important aspects introduced by this Directive with specific emphasis on insurance-based products.

In classification terms, the regulation of financial products issued by insurance companies is too poor to identify exactly their boundaries, and therefore the task of evaluating which regulations are applicable lies with the interpreter.

Generally speaking, life insurance is defined by the regulations contained in the Civil Code and by article 1, para. 1, lett. *b*) CAP, as "insurance policies and operations stated in article 2, paragraph 1", i.e. insurance activity falling within the six different "classes of life business". Traditionally, life insurance contracts were conceived in the past to provide fixed capital or annuity upon human life, in which the investment element, albeit present, was represented simply by the fact that the premium and capital insured were calculated on the assumed capitalisation of the premium at a pre-set interest rate (the so-called "technical rate"), which kept the relationship between the contracting parties unchanged for the entire duration of the contract, with the consequence that the investment risk was placed entirely on the insurer. The structure of the life insurance contract was characterised precisely by the certainty of insurance benefit due, both for the *an* and the *quantum*, based on the assumption that the insurer took upon itself both the so-called demographic risk, i.e. the risk regarding the duration of human life (death or survival of the insured party), and the investment risks embedded in the contract.

The evolution of the insurance market has brought about the connection between life insurances and financial instruments. Pursuant to article 2 (Classification by class of business) of the CAP, policies in life class III are insurance policies on the duration of human life, marriage and birth insurance contracts, whose main services are directly connected to the value of shares of external collective investment fund or internal funds (i.e. unit linked policies) or to indexes or other reference values (i.e. index linked policies).

These particular life policies, given their significant financial component, have been included in the TUF by Legislative Decree No. 303 of 29 December 2006 which, amending art. 1, para. 1, TUF, has included letter *w-bis*, which defines the policies and operations set out in life classes III and V (Article 2, paragraph 2, CAP) as "financial products issued by insurance companies", excluding the individual pension schemes according to article 13, para. 1, letter *b)*, CAP. Therefore, these products are identified with direct reference to life classes III and V, with insurance "class" meaning: "the classification, according to a homogeneous group of risks or operations, which describes the activity that the company can exercise when it is issued the corresponding licence" (art. 1, CAP).

This legislative provision is useful to distinguish these products from other financial products, from which they differ because they are issued by insurance companies and concern insurance policies; yet there are no legislative indications that are precisely aimed at outlining their distinctive traits compared to "traditional" life insurance policies. In fact, the provision contained in the TUF reveals that all class III life contracts are insurance-based financial products, though the permanence of an insurance function in insurance-based financial products cannot be easily affirmed without analysing each single contract.

Quite certainly, the distinguishing feature of life class III contracts is the presence of a investment component; yet, the distinction between life class I products and financial products issued by insurance companies in class III cannot be identified either in the subject that issues the product (an insurance company in both cases) or in the presence of a general investment risk for the insured party, intended in a broad sense. As a confirmation of this point, it can be seen that while it is true that, in "normal" with-profit life insurances (which fall under class I), the investment risk lies with the company and the policyholder has the right to receive a minimum assured sum (possibly revalued at a guaranteed rate), it is also true that the profit of the policyholder depends on the performance of a segregate fund of assets.

Therefore, the distinction compared to class I life insurance contracts must be found elsewhere, and it can probably be found in the fact that class III products (although endorsing the traditional logic of life insurance products regarding the determination of events that cause the supply of the service) determine that the amount to be paid to the policyholder (or beneficiary, as the case may be) is not predetermined, rather it is connected to financial market performance. The consequence is that, in the absence of a minimum capital and/or yield guarantee by companies, most of the financial risk (and not only the risk of not receiving a remuneration higher than the technical rate or minimum guaranteed rate) lies with the policyholder rather than with the company.

Compared to capital redemption operations under class V, index and unit-linked policies can be distinguished because they are contracts in which the determination of the services to be provided is strictly linked to the "duration of human life", maintaining, just like traditional life policies, a demographic risk for the company. Capital redemption operations, instead, are characterised by the fact that the sums owed by the insurer do not depend on the occurrence of events related to the insured party's life, and there is no insurance risk intended in the traditional sense, whereas there is, instead, a purely financial risk. To conclude, in spite of the legislative gap and in the presence of a classification by classes that replicates insurance practice, rather than outlining specific notions, we can rightfully argue that class III policies have two distinguishing features: the first is the assumption of a significant investment risk by the policyholder, which is the distinctive trait compared to class I life policies; the second is the presence of an insurance function—mostly represented by the so-called demographic component, which is indicative of a risk that remains with the insurance company—that distinguishes them from capital redemption operations.

4 The Liability of Insurance Intermediaries: Key Principles

The topic of intermediaries' liability in the distribution (to use the words of the new directive on insurance distribution, the so-called IDD) or, in more general terms, in the placement of insurance products, is closely connected to the issue of consumer protection. To speak about insurance consumer protection means to start with an essential premise, namely the idea that insurance consumer protection hinges on two different areas that can be referred to two different phases of the insurance contract cycle.

On the one hand, the placement of the contract, which essentially coincides with the entire pre-contractual phase; on the other hand, the contract management phase, which concerns not only its content but also the execution of the contract itself.

As a third and final level, we should not underestimate the issue of consumer protection at any critical time of the relationship and thus also in the event of a dispute. Having indicated the levels of the discussion, it should be firstly recalled that the pre-contractual phase is extremely delicate, and the concept of transparency and information asymmetry, and the consequent need to remedy the consumer's situation of inferiority, are all closely connected to this issue. The area of protection of the pre-contractual phase is highly regulated, both by primary and secondary or regulatory rules. In addition, when dealing with insurance contracts, there arises the rather sensitive problem of the sources of insurance regulations, i.e. the intersection between Civil Code, Insurance Code and Consumer Code; in particular the insurance contract falls within the general regulations of the civil code, even if important provisions are laid down both in the Insurance Code and in the Consumer Code. In particular, the Consumer Code extensively regulates the pre-contractual phase. We could even say in absolute terms that the consumer legislator has specifically focused on the rules aimed at protecting the product offer; in fact it is no coincidence that one of the pillars of the consumer code is precisely chapter II, called "Information for consumers".

In the case of insurance contracts, the rules on the offer or generally on the pre-contractual phase are strongly identified with the rules on insurance intermediation.

In fact, the insurance market is substantially an intermediated market, i.e. the distribution of products is entrusted to insurance intermediaries who now, due to EU laws, have their own well-defined legal status.

On this point, it should be remembered that the so-called "direct sale" of products by companies is still very limited. Direct sales by online companies are much discussed, yet they still represent a limited case, mostly connected to the car sector.

The pre-contractual phase is extensively regulated by a very incisive set of rules that apply to intermediaries and, quite obviously, to companies in the case of direct sales. Specifically, reference should be made to chapter XIII of the CAP, entitled "Transparency of operations and protection of the insured party".

This chapter lays down a set of general rules of absolute importance, from the characteristics that advertising should have, to the rules of conduct for intermediaries and the obligations of information represented by the delivery of the so-called information notes that come with insurance contracts. Insurance intermediaries must meet conditions of professionalism and good reputation, and primary legislation introduces a set of incisive rules of conduct that range from the obligation to act with diligence, fairness and transparency toward insured parties, the obligation to propose and place contracts that are suited to the "insurance or pension" needs of the contracting party, and rules regarding conflicts of interest and the corresponding obligations of disclosure "about possible negative effects".

Therefore the conduct of those offering said products is specifically regulated.

These principles are now implemented in detail in the regulations issued by IVASS including, first of all, Regulation no. 5 of 2006 on insurance intermediation, Regulation no. 35 of 2010 on insurance product information and advertising obligations,[13] Regulation no. 40 of 2012 on the minimum content of insurance contracts.

Therefore, the entire pre-contractual phase is highly regulated, at both a primary and secondary level in our system, and in all European systems, and has now been assimilated by operators. In actual fact, the latter often complain strongly about the costs of implementing the rules on insurance offers, which are often claimed to be unsustainable by intermediaries, especially small ones. In fact, this system implies strict compliance, also through the organisation of corresponding controls, to try and avoid or at least limit the severe pecuniary sanctions and reputational risks, which are in any case a deterrent to violating these regulations.

Therefore, in relation to his professional liability, the intermediary, just like other professionals, regardless of the existence of special legislation or regulations, is exposed to complaints if he fails to perform his services with due care, fairness and transparency towards the contracting parties.

On this point, for the purpose of correctly assessing the intermediary's liability in the distribution of an insurance product, we should refer to the principles of conduct and to the evaluation criteria established by civil law, i.e. the professional standards of diligence that the legislator, together with the scholars and the Courts, have always requested for specialised operators.

Indeed, the conduct of an intermediary, just like other professionals, must meet the principle of diligence set out in art. 1176, para. 2, civil code, which establishes that, when carrying out a professional activity, diligence must be evaluated with regard to the nature of the activity performed.[14]

---

[13] Regulation 35 at present stage when the present paper has been delivered to the Editor, is under review by IVASS see Consultation Document 3/2017 which will implement the new set of pre-contractual documents information for non life insurance product.

[14] The Court of Cassation has endorsed this approach, holding in particular that the primary duties of insurers and brokers "arise from articles 1175, 1337 and 1375 civil code; and that violation thereof amounts to negligence, pursuant to art. 1176, para. 2, civil code." Civil Court of Cassation 24 April 2015, n. 8412. In this case, the Court of Cassation discussed how the general duties of conduct according to good faith and fairness, set out in articles 1175, 1337 and 1375 Civil Code, had an impact on the conduct of professionals in an insurance contract. Following an interesting reasoning, the Court held that the primary duties of the insurer and his brokers or promoters included those of providing "thorough, clear and complete information and of offering the contracting party insurance policies that are actually useful for the insured party's needs", i.e. "consistent with the profile of risk or pension needs" manifested thereby. These duties, continued the Court, "are general in nature" and "prevail over regulatory standards, such as the supervisory authority's rules and, a fortiori, over the indications given in documents with no regulatory power, such as memorandum from the supervisory authority".

5 The Distribution of Insurance-Based Investment Products: The Current Legal Framework in the Civil Code, Insurance Code and MiFID

Therefore, with regard to distribution channels and in light of the regulations examined above, the following scenario can be envisaged: subjects authorized to carry out insurance intermediation, traditional insurance intermediaries (i.e. Agents as per section A RUI and brokers section B RUI), EU investment companies, banks, financial intermediaries under art. 107 Consolidated Bank Act (TUB) corresponding to section D of the RUI; insurance companies. It is clear that the MIFID regulations can be considered applicable to:

- The insurance company when it distributes its insurance/financial products directly.
- The "qualified entities", as listed in art. 1, par. 1 *r*) of the TUF, when the insurance company distributes its insurance/financial products through an authorized intermediary. However, it has to be underlined that among the "qualified entities" as listed by the abovementioned art. 1 there are banks and asset management companies (SIM) but not insurance intermediaries.

The distribution channel of banks and financial intermediaries (registered under section D of RUI), when they distribute insurance/financial products, are subject to the rule set by TUF and consequently to obligations aligned with MiFID requirements, just like insurance companies, when they distribute these products directly. The other channels (traditional insurance intermediaries) are subject instead, even when they distribute insurance/financial products, to the Insurance Directive and therefore to the rules transposed into the Insurance Code and the regulations issued by the Insurance Supervisory Authority (IVASS): these are two very similar sets of regulations, though the latter is considered to be less sophisticated. In other words insurance agents and insurance brokers are subject to the Insurance Code and to the supervision of the competent Authority (IVASS), even when they distribute insurance/financial products as the unit linked policies. Therefore, the scenario is marked by different applicable regulations to different intermediaries. This is clearly due to the typical structure of the Italian model, which has maintained a dual supervision (CONSOB for the market and financial operators, and IVASS for the market and insurance operators) which, in terms of regulations, applies according to subjects rather than products. This diversity has repercussions on the types of liability though, above all, on the consequences of the infringement of the various obligations. We thus need to analyse each obligation to understand the actual extent of this complex system that has developed over time.

5.1 *Disclosure Obligations and Codes of Conduct for Insurance Intermediaries*

5.1.1 The Notion of Insurance Suitability and the Parallel Notion in the Financial Sector

Article 183 of the Insurance Code, called Rules of conduct and protection of the insured, essentially replicates article 21 of the Consolidated Finance Act[15] (TUF) and contains the directives that the undertakings and intermediaries must abide by when providing their services. It is designed to guide the general activity of insurance companies and intermediaries in all its manifestations, regardless of the contractual activity in the strict sense; in fact, the provision expressly deals with the duties that insurance companies and intermediaries must follow when offering and executing the contract; therefore, these are duties that must be fulfilled continuously in the daily pursuit of an entrepreneurial or intermediation business.

Although the provision is formulated broadly and sets general principles, it is immediately cogent. In terms of regulatory technique, it can be seen that the legislator, acknowledging the complexity of the issue, which cannot be framed in specific, unchangeable rules, and the need to create a system that is "up to date" with the evolution of the markets, simply sets general principles, delegating the issue of specific provisions to the Supervisory Authority. The legislator thus grants to such Authority a legal implementation power, replicating a scheme and a technique already adopted in previous texts, especially for life insurance, although the regulatory power attributed nowadays to IVASS is broader than in the previous insurance system (as for the regulatory powers of IVASS, see article 191 of the insurance code).

It must be noted that the general obligation to make sure that the contracting party is always suitably informed is laid down together with the obligation to acquire therefrom the information needed to evaluate his/her insurance needs. If the former obligation is a specification of fairness and transparency, the latter, instead, should be related to the criterion of diligence, so that letters *a)* and *b)* of the article should be interpreted together, for they are intended to achieve the same result.[16]

---

[15]The section is called General Criteria in the financial markets regulations. On this matter see Alpa and Gaggero (1996), p. 65. In relation to the intersection between insurance regulation and finacial regulation see P. Marano, *The 'Mifidization': The Sunset of Life Insurance in the EU Regulation on Insurance?* (August 31, 2016). Liber Amicorum for Professor Ioannis Rokas, 2016. Available at SSRN: https://ssrn.com/abstract=2832952.

[16]Art. 183 Insurance Code:

1. Before the conclusion and during the term of the contract undertakings and intermediaries

   shall:

   (a) behave with diligence, fairness and transparency towards policyholders and insured persons;
   (b) acquire from policyholders the information necessary to evaluate their insurance or pension

   needs and act in such a manner that they are always appropriately informed (Omissis).

The subjects that are required to fulfil these obligations are both the company and the intermediary; since this is a several obligation, the fulfilment by one party does not release the other from the same obligation and, in fact, the principle of suitability is recalled, in relation to intermediaries, by article 120, para. 3.

The general obligation to acquire information about the insured party finds its "model" in the rules on financial intermediation and, specifically, in the general principle that is known as "*know your customer*" [see. art. 21 para. 1 letter *b)* of the TUF art. 48, para. 2, CONSOB resolution no. 16190 dated 29 October 2007]. The said principle aims at enabling the undertaking and intermediary to carry out their services in the best way possible, suggesting insurance products that are suited to the type of policyholder and his insurance needs. Indeed, the collection of information is the prerequisite for application of the further standard of *suitability* i.e. the evaluation, by the intermediary, of the suitability of the insurance product according to the profile of the policyholder.

Therefore, the suitability of information is a different concept from the suitability of the operation with regard to the client's specific needs.

The law does not specify what information should be acquired and what information should be provided, and simply refers generally to necessary and suitable information. On the basis of this general provision and detailed rules, the information to be acquired is essentially the client's profile, i.e. personal details, information regarding the client's financial means, insurance needs, the subjects to be protected; such information is necessary to achieve the goal laid down in the said rules, namely the offer of suitable insurance products. Quite obviously, the content of the obligation changes according to the insurance product requested or sought, depending on whether it is non life or life insurance.

As for the fulfilment of the duty in question, we believe that the obligation to acquire information and to provide adequate information takes on a different content for the insurer and the intermediary. For the insurer, the identification of necessary information presumably depends on an evaluation process carried out "upstream" thereby, in relation to the insurance products offered on the market; the obligation to collect information has therefore an objective quality since the collection of information have primarily the function to assess the risk, which the undertaking is going to accept. The intermediary, on the other hand, is directly in touch with the client, so that the need for information should be related to the individual's subjective profile, especially because the collection of information is the prerequisite for evaluating the suitability of the insurance product offered with respect to the client's needs.[17] Art. 120 paragraph 3, in fact, confirms the obligation of the intermediaries to acquire information on the client and to suitably inform the latter, emphasising the further duty to propose suitable products to the client. The provision, in fact, states that the intermediary must "*recommend a suitable product*"

[17] This differentiation could be reduced in the light of IDD implementation and product governance discipline. Chapter V of IDD entitled "Information requirements and conduct of business rules" includes art. 25 that specifically applies to the product and oversight arrangements. For an overview of the impact of POG discipline see Velliscig (2018).

"based on the information provided by the contracting party", "previously illustrating the essential characteristics of the contract".

Therefore, if the collection of information is functional for the intermediaries to meet his obligation to propose contracts to clients that are suited to their needs, it can be argued, also on the basis of experience in the parallel financial sector, that this goal can be pursued by the intermediary only by "personalising" his relationship with the client. In this respect, it cannot be ignored that, in line with the general standardisation trend in insurance (not only in relation to contracts), questionnaires have become widely used and are often drawn up by the company and used by intermediaries too. This leads us to assess the value that a questionnaire holds in the contractual economy, especially in evidential terms. The Courts have wavered on the value of questionnaires as a diriment or merely evidential element; in fact, they initially recognised their value only for evidential purposes, as stated by the Supreme Court in ruling no. 4682/99, whereby a questionnaire does not have the function of "typifying" the possible causes of cancellation of contracts, and "the drawing up of a questionnaire by the insurer shows the latter's intention to attach particular importance to certain requisites, inducing the contracting party to pay attention to give full, truthful answers", so that the Courts should consider the existence of a questionnaire when examining the decisive nature of consent to inaccuracies or reticences, and are obliged to provide suitable reasons if they believe such relevance should be ruled out.[18] In the last decade of the last century, probably with the intent to reasonably circumscribe the extent of the insurer's duty to collaborate in the precontractual phase, the Courts identified, based on the general principle of good faith set out in article 1337 Civil Code, the duty for the insurer to "provide a reference framework of the circumstances that he intends to gather information on such as to reasonably reduce the room for indeterminacy about facts which he is interested in learning about, with the consequence that, failing this, any doubts about the relevance of any circumstances not declared or inaccurately declared, remain the responsibility of the insurer that caused them".[19] There is no doubt that the Supreme Court thus tried to rebalance the contractual parties in an insurance operation, though I would personally be less optimistic in viewing this approach, which is based on the more general principle of good faith of the insurer, as the touchstone of the problem of information asymmetries in the insurance contract.[20]

Turning to the obligation to provide suitable information to the policyholder, this should be seen as an application of the general duty to act in good faith, a principle that finds several applications in the regulations in question and in specific provisions adopted by the Supervisory body over the years (i.e. the Regulation regarding

[18] See in this respect Civil Cassation, 12 October 1998, no. 10086.

[19] The first ruling where this trend can be found is Civil Cassation, 20 November 1990, no. 11206; likewise Civil Cassation, 4 April 1991, no. 3501; Civil Cassation, 17 May 2004, no. 9342, Civil Cassation, 24 November 2003, no. 17840; Civil Cassation, 19 January 2001, no. 784.

[20] See Bugiolacchi (2009), p. 1598; Nitti (2010), pp. 527–603.

pre-contractual information and information during the contract that must be provided by the company to a party to a life insurance contract).

In particular, during the pre-contractual phase, the subjects involved in the negotiations are required to fulfil the information obligations set out by law. The minimum content of the insurer's and intermediary's information obligations is regulated on two levels: for the intermediary, by article 120, called *Pre-contractual information and rules of conduct,* ruling that intermediaries must provide information to the contracting parties before stipulating the contract, and which gives IVASS the task of detailing such information (art. 120 para. 3); for the insurance undertaking, by article 185, called *Information notes,* which gives the supervisory authority the task of enacting a regulation with specific details on the content of these information notes, listing minimum information requirements and setting the principles that the IVASS regulations must abide by (paragraphs 3 and 4).

The intermediary is required to provide two types of information; information on his relations with the insurer and information on the "*essential characteristics of the contract and the services that the insurance company is required to provide*". The insurer's information obligations are broader. The latter must provide an information note containing necessary information "*so that the contracting party and the insured party can form their own grounded opinion on their contractual rights and obligations and, where suitable, on the company's financial situation*" (art.185 para. 2).

We should now examine whether the obligation to provide suitable information, set out in article 183, para. 1, letter b), is met by merely fulfilling the above duties or whether it also includes the duty to provide any other information and relevant circumstance for the purpose of stipulating the contract.

On the basis of what is suggested by a comparison with experiences in other sectors, it seems plausible to argue that this obligation for the insurer is basically translated into the preparation of Information Document suited to the characteristics of the product offered, in accordance with the provisions set out by the Supervisory Body, especially bearing in mind the meticulousness of the provisions issued to date by the Body on the content of such information notes, whilst not ruling out, *a priori*, the residual applicability of art. 183 para. 1 lett. *b*). Namely the provision on the preparation of the Offer Prospectus.

For the intermediary, instead, this obligation is broader. These information obligations to be fulfilled by this intermediary cannot be deemed met by merely delivering a standard document, for the latter must guarantee his own assistance and advice to the contracting party. In other words, the intermediary should modulate his conduct and the content of information according to the particular nature of the relationship with the contracting party, and provide the same with possibly additional information to that included in the standard document drawn up by the insurer. In other words, the intermediary, if necessary, must "leave" the realm of objective information, with the information obligation taking on an individual content.

Also with respect to the execution phase of the contract, art. 183 para. 2 sets specific obligations for the company and intermediary: in particular, reference can be made to the obligations indicated by the supervisory body regarding information provided during the contract, once again relating to the transparency of operations, just like the obligation to quickly communicate any changes that affect the contract and any loss of value in case of financial contracts.

5.1.2 Diligence, Transparency and Fairness

Pursuant to letter *a)* of art. 183 of the code, when offering and executing contracts, insurers and intermediaries must behave diligently, fairly and transparently in the interest of the contracting-insured parties. Diligence, fairness and transparency are standards of conduct that are functional to the protection of the interests of each contracting-insured party, although they do not complete their effects within the scope of single relationships. In fact, since an insurance relationship is based on the condition of mutuality that characterises insurance activities, the duties of conduct become important primarily in relation to the protection of each insured party and, indirectly, they protect the interests of all the insured clients.

In this perspective of a contextual protection of interests, the legislator recalls the general clauses of diligence and fairness contained in the Civil Code, in the same manner as the rules on financial intermediation (see art. 21 of the TUF). It is not clear why this special law reiterates general clauses that would have nonetheless been deemed applicable to insurance services, though this may have been done to make their violation autonomously prosecutable by IVASS or by Consob. This interpretation appears to be confirmed by the legal implementation power granted to the supervisory body, and particularly by the fact that said power is connected to the attribution thereto of precautionary and prohibiting powers under art. 184 CAP.

As for fairness, the concept recalls the criterion set out in article 1175 Civil Code, a criterion that should inspire the reciprocal conduct of the parties involved in a relationship that lays down obligations therefor. Its relevance is expressed in the obligation to protect the counterparty's interests and applies also to extra-contractual economic relations.

According to most scholars,[21] the reference to the general duty of fairness is designed to supplement the contractual obligation as a further source of the agreement. Therefore, in the performance of insurance services, fairness is a general clause that integrates the relationship between the insurer and the intermediary, on the one hand, and the contracting-insured party on the other. This is a source of an autonomous legal obligation intended to protect the insured party. In this light, the principle of fairness implies that insurer and intermediary should, in all circumstances, favour the contracting-insured party's interests, both when establishing the insurance relationship and during pre-contractual negotiations as well as when drawing up the contract, up to the time when the contract is executed. It should be added that, unlike other rules, fairness does not require a given conduct with a pre-set content, rather different conducts depending on the tangible circumstances

---

[21] See S. Rodotà, *Diligenza (diritto civile)*, in EdD, 1962; L. Rovelli, *Correttezza*, in Dir. Civ., 1989; A. Di Majo, entry *obbligazione (teoria generale)*, in EGI, 1990.

of the contract. The principle is also intertwined with the rules of conduct set out in the subsequent points of the article, such as those regarding conflicts of interest and information obligations.

The relevant provisions also recall the principle of diligence, reiterating a criteria that was previously established by the *ius commune*. To understand the value of this criterion, we should recall that, according to most scholars, diligence is a fundamental criterion to determine the service and also to assess liability. As a criterion of liability, diligence indicates the steps that the debtor should take to avoid any breach or inaccuracy in contract fulfilment; as a criterion for the determination of a service, instead, diligence indicates the model of accuracy and technical ability which the performance should meet.[22]

The "model" and criterion for the assessment of the debtor's conduct differs according to the debtor's experience and sphere of activity. In relation to insurance services, since insurers and intermediaries perform a professional activity, the evaluation of diligence cannot be the one that applies to the average man. Diligence must be evaluated more strictly, taking account of the specific expertise that is usually expected of an insurer or intermediary, or according to professionalism, based on article 1176, paragraph 2. This means that the insurer's and intermediary's liability should be assessed according to the nature of the services performed thereby and to the complexity of the insurance product offered; in the event of breach, these should be held liable if their conduct differs from the conduct that an insurer or intermediary would have had in similar circumstances.

It should also be recalled that art. 178 CAP says that, in disputes on compensation for damages claimed by the contracting-insured party, it is the company's responsibility to prove that it acted with the specific diligence required. This provision is aimed at imposing on the professional the burden of proving his due diligence and is thus beneficial to the contracting-insured party. Since we are dealing with specific diligence, we can confirm that the general criterion of diligence set out in article 183 refers to article 1176 paragraph 2 civil code.

Turning to the general criterion of transparency, also based on what is suggested by the rules on investment services and by financial regulations,[23] it is plausible to argue that this expression refers to objective transparency, which the operator should abide by when conducting his business. The obligation applies to insurers and intermediaries.

As we said earlier on, there is no "legal" definition of transparency, neither does the obligation of transparency appear in the Civil Code. The expression is commonly understood as standing for fairness and diligence, and in recent years the transparency criterion has taken the shape of a detailed series of information obliga-

[22] On this point M. Bianca, in *Diritto civile*, book IV, *L'obbligazion*e, 1990, p. 90; P. Perlingieri, *Recenti prospettive nel diritto delle obbligazioni*, in Vita not., 1976.

[23] As for the transparency of investment services and for a short discussion of banking transparency, please refer to C. Rabitti Bedogni, *Commentary to art. 21*, in *Il testo unico della intermediazione finanziaria*, Commentary to Leg. Decree 24 February 1998, n. 58, 1998, p. 175; L. Gaffuri, *I Servizi e le attività di investimento,* Milan, 2010.

tions to be met by the insurer, becoming a tool to remedy the imbalance of information in relationships "characterised" by information asymmetry.

We believe that the reference to transparency contained in letter *a)* of the article in question should be intended broadly, also to distinguish it from the provision contained in letter *b)* of the same article, which establishes the insurer's and intermediary's obligation to operate in such a way that the contracting-insured party is always adequately informed, and from the obligation of transparency that involves the preparation and delivery of the information note referred to in article 185 and, with respect to the intermediary only, from the information obligations imposed thereon by art. 120 of the code. By interpreting the legislation in this way, transparency refers to the objective supply of insurance services, regardless of the establishment of a contractual relationship, of a specific request by the contracting party or of any information due, according to specific provisions. In terms of content, transparency consists in the provision of complete and objective information regarding the service offered, the contract and the insurance product.

This general criterion has been further detailed in regulations issued by IVASS, pursuant to the second paragraph of the article 183 in question.

5.2 *Conflict of Interest*

Speaking of the protection of contracting party's rights, letter *c)* of the first paragraph of art. 183 and paragraph 1-*bis* of art. 21 of TUF address the problem of conflicts of interests,[24] one of the most delicate and important issues for the protection of the contracting/insured party-investor. This aspect set by IVASS with Regulation n. 35/2010[25] has a clearly financial matrix, which can be inferred from a comparison with art 21, para. 1, lett. *c)* of TUF.

Although conflicts of interest[26] are associated, in practice and in the public opinion, with the idea of bias, it is not easy to establish when the insurer and the intermediary can find themselves in a "legally relevant" situation of conflict of interests with the insured party, also and above all because the legislator sets this general principle of conduct without giving the operator and the interpreter a parameter of evaluation; this uncertainty is worsened by the fact that situations of conflict do not always clearly give rise to a bias to the detriment of the insured party. While carrying out insurance services, there are many cases in which conflicts of interest can arise—and sometimes they are unavoidable—both when looking at the relationship between the client, on the one hand, and the insurer or intermediary on the other,

[24] In relation to critical aspects of conflict of interest as means of disclosure see Kochenburger et al. (2010), p. 21.

[25] It is to point out that in the insurance sector conflict of interest was first addressed by IVASS in its Circular 551/2005, than abrogate by Regulation n. 35/2010. The regulation of conflict of interest will be revised in light of the implementation of IDD.

[26] Kochenburger et al. (2010), p. 21.

and when looking at the relationship between the single insured and other clients. A broad rule thus runs the risk of producing a globalising effect which would paralyse the activity.

Neither does case-law offer support in this respect, since there are no rulings on contracts stipulated by insurance companies in a conflict of interest. The problem has arisen, instead, in the financial services sector, where the prevalent approach is that a conflict of interests exists whenever the financial intermediary has an economic interest in placing a financial product offered to the client.[27]

However, according to a recent decision, a conflict of interest does not exist where the bank purchases securities from another bank within the same group, at a better price than that charged by other subjects, not causing damage to the client.

The preferential ground for the provision is represented by life insurance, especially life insurance where the policyholder usually bears the investment risk (the mentioned unit-linked and index-linked insurance policies). In fact, in this case the enhancement of the investment component gives rise to the need to involve multifunctional subjects in the management and production process, who are holders of "different" economic interests than those of the insured party. The diffusion of these products on the market and their similarity with financial products prompted the supervisory body in the past to anticipate the legislator in this respect. In fact, article 29 of ISVAP Circular no. 551 nowadays abrogated, contemplated a regulation of conflicts of interests. Without providing a definition of conflict, the memorandum described a rather general case that encompassed economic conflicts of interests though also covered *group relations, company's business relations or business relations of group companies.*

Returning to article 183 of the Insurance Code, we can see that the provision intervenes on two levels: firstly, by trying to prevent conflict of interest situations; secondly, by establishing that, if a conflict of interest situation does arise, the intermediary and the insurer must protect and safeguard the insured parties' interests. For the first issue, it establishes that insurers and intermediaries should organise themselves in such a way as to identify and avoid conflicts of interest; for the second issue, the provision says that the professional should act with the utmost transparency, pointing any detrimental effects to the insured party, and in any case is required to manage the conflict in such a way as to avoid it causing damage thereto. Therefore, the provision does not place a prohibition on insurers and intermediaries to carry out operations in a conflict of interests. Such a decision can be endorsed: it comes from an acknowledgement that the presence of conflicts of interests is sometimes inevitable in the insurance field; therefore, a regulation imposing prohibitions would not produce any result, so that a regulation that ensures transparency and adequate information to clients is more effective. Yet, in recent measures IVASS has imposed specific bans, regarding given operations considered to be in a conflict of interests

[27] Court of Milan, 25 July 2005; Court of Rome 13 June 2005; more recently Court of Appeal of Milan, 25 January 2008, in BBTC, 2010, 2, II, p. 150 with note by Houben; Court of Milan, 19 April 2011, in BBTC, 2011, 6, II, p. 748 with note by Girino; Court of Milan, sect. VI, 12 November 2013.

(reference is hereby clearly made to Provision no. 2946 that introduced paragraph 1 *bis* in art. 48 of regulation no. 5/2006 which, in relation to policies linked to mortgages or loans, requires banks and financial intermediaries not to act as beneficiaries and intermediaries at the same time, in relation to the proposed insurance contract). This was a widely criticized choice; indeed, whilst acknowledging the intention to protect clients in a sector like that of linked policies, where there has been a certain level of abuse by operators, prohibitions do not appear to be the most suitable tool, since conflicts in the financial sector have always been regulated through information and disclosure,[28] both because this is the trend that can be found in other systems, like in England, and because it is the same method followed by the European Union with the Insurance Distribution Directive (IDD).

6 Information Obligations for Insurance-Based Investment Contracts in the Consolidated Financial Act

6.1 Pre-contractual Information

The rules governing the pre-contractual phase is similar in the two sets of regulations. For intermediaries (so called authorised subject under section D of the Register) and undertakings, reference is made both to pre-contractual information under MiFID for investments services and to specific additional regulations replicating, at least for some aspects, the former. IVASS regulation no. 5/2006 on insurance intermediation must also be taken into consideration. Efforts have surely been made by CONSOB to join the two sets of regulations.

In particular, information is mandatory for shareholdings exceeding 10% in/from insurance companies; it should be specified whether the intermediary gives "impartial advice". In practice, the intermediary must specify whether he sells the product on the basis of a mandate given by a company or whether he is independent of the company whose product is sold (though, in this case, the facts should prove that the distributor is in the required conditions, i.e. he can have access to a wide range of products).

Lastly, the reasons why a certain product is recommended should be "illustrated" (ex post verification of the soundness of the advice given): this is a new concept for the MiFID.

[28] A principle recently confirmed also by the Courts, cfr. Court of Milan, VI, 12 November 2013, where the court held: *Authorized intermediaries cannot carry out operations with or on behalf of their own clients if they have, directly or indirectly, a conflicting interest, also deriving from group relations, unless they previously inform the investor about the nature and extent of their interest in the operation and the investor consents in writing to the operation.*

6.2 Classification of Clients

Authorised subjects, as previously defined, and insurance companies must classify their clients and notify them of their classification, which is important for the assumption of them having sufficient experience and adequate financial resources, for the purpose of the suitability test, whereas no classification is required to insurance intermediaries. With respect to the preexisting regime—in which the qualified operator was distinguished from the mass of the investors, for which the order allowed the non application of certain normative provisions (essentially of an informative nature)—the current system provides for three different categories of customers: (1) Retail customers: are the category to which the order reserves the utmost information protection. This type of clientele, in fact, is considered to be deprived of the knowledge required to make a conscious choice; (2) Professional customers for whom the legal system assumes the existence of high experience, knowledge and competence. Skills that allow to make informed choices with an intermediate level of information; (3) Qualified counterparties or the same subjects considered as professional clients by law, who, in the performance of certain investment services, do not require many of the safeguards provided. This specific rule differs from the rules of the insurance mediation, where, as known, the policyholder, with the exception of the sector of "large risks", is always considered as a consumer with recognition of the relevant protections.

6.3 Suitability

The "suitability assessment" is required to authorised subjects and companies and only if advice is given, in accordance with MiFID, i.e. when a product is presented as "suitable" to the client's personal characteristics. This "appears to be the normal case". The "suitability test" may be replaced by a simple "appropriateness test" if the product is sold without being presented, i.e. by means of execution only transaction. In the event that the "suitability test" is negative, i.e. if the client does not have the right characteristics, then the financial intermediary must be kept from placing the contract. Whereas in insurance sector, intermediaries has simply the duty to advice the client that the product is not adequate.

In this respect, we should also consider the different notion of advice in the two sectors (insurance and financial). For insurance intermediaries, advice is always considered to be provided though with the prohibition to "propose or recommend" unsuitable products; however, in this case such advice is not "impartial", for it depends significantly on the relationship between the intermediary and the insurance company (mandate limits for agents, greater autonomy for brokers etc.). For insurance intermediaries, the suitability test should refer to the client's "insurance and pension needs". There is no obligation to illustrate the client's requests and needs or the reasons for any advice given in the absence of accurate information. If the test is negative, the client must be given a written notice, giving reasons therefor, with which the contracting party acknowledges such unsuitability, declares he has been informed and, in spite of this, wishes to stipulate the contract. This difference in approach has necessarily also implications for the intermediary's liability regime and above all on remedies granted to the contractor in the event of breach of intermediary's duty to advise an appropriate product.

6.4 Best Execution

The best execution concept set by the MIFID implies that the firm must execute the customer's orders in a manner consistent with the best possible results for the same. This specific rule does not apply to authorized subjects and insurance companies. A similar concept applies instead to insurance intermediaries: contracts should be proposed "at the best possible conditions", considering the time, size and nature of the operation. There is an obligation to obtain the "best possible result in relation to the relevant goals". In practice it appears more like a specification of the general obligation to act with diligence, transparency and fairness towards the contracting party.

6.5 Incentive System

This does not apply to insurance intermediaries or "single mandate" agents (who are part of the company and not real "third parties"). Multiple mandate agents should justify the incentive received from the company by providing advice and offering access to a vast range of products (which is also required to provide "impartial" advice).

6.6 The Rules on Conflicts of Interest

Authorized subjects and insurance companies are required to identify and manage—taking all reasonable measures—any conflicts of interest that can cause serious damage to clients. Disclosure is necessary in the event of inefficient management. Insurance intermediaries are required to avoid conflicts of interest. If the conflict is unavoidable, they should operate in such a way as to avoid causing damage to the contracting party. There is also an obligation to identify and manage conflicts in a way suited to the size and complexity of the activity.

7 The State of the Art of the Italian Case-Law

It should first be pointed out that, in relation to insurance-based investment contracts, Italian Courts have focused in recent times almost exclusively on the legal nature of these contracts. In this respect, the Courts have translated the scholars' debate discussed above into rulings. Indeed, a given theory expounded by scholars has already been repeatedly endorsed by the Courts, reclassifying insurance contracts as financial contracts. The reclassification of insurance contracts as financial contracts, implemented by the ruling in question, implies a serious consequence: policy placement amounts to the performance of an investment service, regulated by the TUF. This reclassification has two main effects: firstly, the operators who sell these products must make sure that the contract is in writing; secondly, the rules of conduct laid down for financial intermediaries must be complied with.[29]

In particular, these rulings have confirmed the cancellation of the contract, with the ensuing return obligations on the insurer, where the master agreement is not in writing. Besides, in the operations of financial intermediation, the master agreement must be kept separate from the operations implementing the same: the master agreement only contains general and abstract regulations of the intermediation relationship between the parties, which is followed by one or more investments. This distinction cannot be applied *tout court* to the different, standard insurance relationship which involves no financial investments. In fact, where linked policies are classified as financial products, TUF is applied. One of the most important provisions to be applied is article 23 of the TUF on the written condition of the contract; the absence of a written form can thus be claimed, causing the nullity of the contract. An important part of disputes between investors and financial intermediaries can be easily settled precisely for the lack of the written form of intermediation contracts. The nullity of the contract for this reason prevails, in fact, over any other issue, for example over the potential breach of the rules of conduct for intermediaries.[30]

---

[29] A further consequence of the reclassification of the contract is the non-applicability of article 1923 Civil Code on the prohibition of executive or precautionary actions. Several rulings have confirmed the non-applicability of art. 1923 civil code to linked policies. See, for example, Court of Cagliari, 2 November 2010, in Riv. giur. sarda, 2011, I, 387 ff. with note by Landini, who stated that contracts stipulated by insurance companies, where not entailing the demographic risk, cannot be classified as pure insurance contracts, so that they can be encompassed in the bankrupt's estate. See also Court of Parma, 10 August 2010, in Assicurazioni, 2010, 781 ff. with note by de Francesco; in Giur. it., 2011, 1560 s., with note by Gobio Casali; in Nuova giur. civ. comm., 2011, I, 189 s., with note by Palmentola; in Società, 2011, 55 ff. with note by Guffanti; according to whom the ban on executive and precautionary actions provided for in art. 1923 Civil Code does not apply to index linked and unit linked life policies if it is ascertained that they do not have a pension function, which is typical of life insurance, but are instead true financial investments.

[30] On the matter of nullity of a contract by reason of a defect of form, the applicable provision is article art. 1418 para. 2 Civil Code, whereby non-fulfilment of one of the conditions set out in article 1325 Civil Code produces the nullity of the contract. One of the conditions required by this provision is the written form "when it is required by law or else the contract is null". In the case of financial intermediation contracts, the written form is required by law otherwise the contract is null: article 23 paragraph 1 of the TUF, in fact, provides that contracts for the provision of invest-

As regards the written condition relating to financial intermediation contracts and insurance contracts, the solution adopted by the legislator is different: in the first case, the written form is required or else the contract is invalid,[31] in the second case it is required for purely evidential reasons. Insurance contracts need not be in writing for validity purposes. Art. 1888 para. 1 Civil Code only states that insurance contract must be proven in writing.[32] As is known, the main effect of the written form condition *ad probationem* is stated in article 2725 para. 1 Civil Code: when a contract must be proven in writing, witness evidence is admitted only where the contracting party has lost the document that gave such evidence, through no fault of his own. Since this case (the loss of the document without fault) is a rare occurrence, in actual fact—in the absence of a written contract—it is very difficult to give evidence of the content thereof. The Courts have confirmed, as already explicitly indicated by the law, that the written condition for insurance contracts applies only for evidential purposes.[33] However, this interpretation or, rather, this reclassification, has been applied by some Italian Courts indifferently to all insurance-financial contracts, without making any distinction as to the time when the contract was stipulated. Reference is hereby made to the circumstance that, in some cases, the Courts have not distinguished the contracts entered into before Law 28.12.2005 no. 262 (the famous "Savings Law") and leg. decree 29.12.2006 no. 303 (enacted by exercising the delegation contained in art. 43 of the same law no. 2005/262), from the contracts entered into after that date.[34] The Supreme Court itself[35] has established that in case of a life insurance contract stipulated before the entry into force of law 28 December 2005 no. 262 and leg. decree 29 December 2006 no. 303, where it is established that the premiums paid by the insured party are paid into the insurer's

---

ment services are drawn up in writing and that these contracts are null if they are not in the required form.

[31] Baratella, *La forma scritta e i c.d. contratti di intermediazione finanziaria nella ricostruzione giurisprudenziale,* in Resp. civ., 2010, 688 ff..; Barenghi, *Disciplina dell'intermediazione finanziaria e nullità degli ordini di acquisto (in mancanza del contratto-quadro): una ratio decidendi e troppi obiter dicta*, in Giur. mer., 2007, 59 ff.; D'Auria, *Forma "ad substantiam" e uso selettivo della nullità nei contratti di investimento*, in Corr. mer., 2011, 703 ff.; Della Vecchia, *Forma dei contratti e obblighi informativi nella prestazione dei servizi di investimento*, in Società, 2011, 682 ff.; Della Vedova, *Sulla forma degli ordini di borsa,* in Riv. dir. civ., 2010, II, 161 ff.; Maragno, *La nullità del contratto di intermediazione di valori mobiliari per difetto di sottoscrizione dell'intermediario*, in Nuova giur. civ. comm., 2010, I, 932 ff.; Nocco, *Ordine di negoziazione di titoli "Parmalat" ed inosservanza della forma scritta*, in Danno resp., 2011, 865 ff.; Sangiovanni, *Mancata sottoscrizione e forma del contratto di intermediazione finanziaria*, in Corr. mer., 2011, 140 ff.

[32] On the written condition for insurance contracts, see the recent Bracciodieta, *Commento all'art. 1888*, in Il contratto di assicurazione. Disposizioni generali, Milan, 2012, 81 ff.

[33] In this sense, for example, Cass. 11 January 2005, no. 367; Cass., 3 April 2000, no. 4005; Cass., 18 February 2000, no. 1875.

[34] Justice of the Peace, Palermo, 25 January 2012; Court of Turin, 17 March 2016; Court of Naples, 17 April 2013, n. 5060 see in *Banca Borsa Titoli di Credito*, 2014, 4, II, 445 with note by Camedda.

[35] Civil Cassation sect. III 18 April 2012, no. 6061 in Dir. economia assicur. (From 2012 Fiscalità assicur.), 2013, 1,I with note by Gagliardi.

internal or external investment funds, on expiry of the contract or on occurrence of the corresponding event the insurer is required to pay the insured party a sum equal to the value of the investment fund shares at that time (unit linked-policies); the trial judge, in order to establish whether the issuing company, the intermediary and the promoter have violated the rules of fair conduct laid down by specific legislation and by article 1337 Civil Code, must interpret the contract—and this interpretation cannot be disputed by the Court of Cassation if it is consistently and logically grounded—in order to establish whether the contract, apart of its *nomen iuris*, should be identified as a life insurance policy (where the risk concerning an event in the insured party's life is taken by the insurer) or as an investment in a financial instrument (where the performance risk is entirely assumed by the insured party). On this point, however, no firm stance has been taken by the Courts, since opposite sentences have equally been passed. In fact, we should mention a decision by the Court of Bologna[36] according to which no regard should be had to the argument which, giving priority to the financial nature of insurance products called Unit-Linked or Index-Linked Life Insurance Policies or Insurances and attributing a merely interpretive nature to the legislative amendments set out in law no. 262/2005, introducing art. 25-*bis* in leg. decree no. 58/1998, claims that the TUF and its implementation regulations should apply also to policies and contracts stipulated prior to 1.7.2007.

Pension savings find a consistent and rational development in specific regulations applicable in the field, which is characterised by basic pensions (marked by the certainty of the amounts due) and supplementary pensions, intended to increase income also with financial investments that are characterised by the absence of a guaranteed result. There ensues a graduation of the pension function, a function that is undoubtedly weakened in index linked policies where, alongside the pension component, there is definitely an investment purpose. As regards specifically the duties of intermediaries in the distribution phase, and partially confirming what has already been said above in general terms, the Supreme Court[37] has ruled on the applicability of the general principles of good faith and fairness, holding the applicability of the duties set out in articles 1175, 1337, and 1375 of the Civil Code, to provide clear and truthful information, whose violation gives rise, pursuant to art. 1176 of the Civil Code, to the intermediary's negligence. The ruling is relevant since, also in this instance, the case concerned a unit-linked policy stipulated in 2000 and thus not only prior to the TUF reform mentioned above, but also in a legislative context in which insurance intermediaries' and insurance companies' duties were totally different from the current and stricter legislative-regulatory framework.

[36] Court of Bologna, sect. III, 06 July 2015, no. 2146 see in DeJure.

[37] Civil Cassation, sect. III, 24 April 2015, no. 8412, in Diritto & Giustizia 2015, and Responsabilità civile e Previdenza 2015, 3, 970.

8 Insurance-Based Investment Products: Perspectives Under IDD

The Insurance Distribution Directive (IDD) establishes specific obligations to the distribution of insurance investment products in addition to those applicable to all products. It should be immediately stated that, as in the Italian system, insurance financial products are currently subject to Leg. Decree 58/1998 (TUF), which lays down more detailed rules than those introduced by the IDD Directive, the IDD Directive is not expected to have a significant impact on this category of products.

However, by analysing its specific provisions, we can see that, as for its scope of application, the following are not considered insurance investment products: (1) non-life insurance products as listed in Annex I to Directive 2009/138/EC (Solvency II); (2) life insurance contracts where the benefits under the contract are payable only on death or in respect of incapacity due to injury, sickness or disability; (3) pension products which, under national law, are recognised as having the primary purpose of providing the investor with an income in retirement and which entitled the investor to certain benefits; (4) occupational pension schemes; (5) individual pension products for which a financial contribution from the employer is required and where the employer or the employee has no choice as to the pension product or provider.

A condition for the applicability of the additional conditions set out in Chapter VI of the IDD Directive is that the insurance investment products must be distributed by: (a) an insurance company or (b) an insurance intermediary.

The section on insurance investment products lays down obligations on conflicts of interest, information on products and associated costs and charges, as well as the assessment product suitability where advice is given.

As regards conflicts of interests, insurance companies and insurance intermediaries are required to maintain and operate effective identification and management arrangements with a view to taking all reasonable steps designed to prevent conflicts of interest with their clients. If these procedures are not sufficient to prevent the conflict, insurance companies or intermediaries must inform the client of this circumstance prior to stipulating the contract.

With regard to information obligations, insurance companies and insurance intermediaries must provide the client with appropriate information about: (1) when advice is provided, the periodic assessment of the suitability of products; (2) appropriate guidance on, and warnings of, the risks associated with the insurance-based investment products or in respect of particular investment strategies proposed; (3) all costs and related charges to be disclosed, including the cost of advice, where relevant, the cost of the insurance-based investment product and how the customer may pay for it.

Art. 29 of the IDD Directive also establishes that insurance intermediaries or insurance undertakings are regarded as fulfilling their obligations under the Directive where they are paid any fee or commission, or any non-monetary benefit from any party except the client, only where the payment or benefit does not have a detrimental impact on the quality of the relevant service and does not impair compliance with the insurance intermediary's or insurance undertaking's duty to act in accordance with the best interests of its client. In any event, Member States may prohibit or further restrict the acceptance of fees, commissions or non-monetary benefits from third parties in relation to the provision of insurance advice. In addition, Member States may require that, where an insurance intermediary informs the client that advice is given independently, the intermediary must assess a sufficiently large number of insurance products available on the market which are sufficiently diversified with regard to their type and product providers.

Art. 30 of the IDD Directive also deals with the obligations to assess the suitability and appropriateness of insurance investment products when providing, or not providing, advice, which is defined in art. 1 as "*the provision of a personal recommendation to customers, either upon their request or at the initiative of the insurance distributor, in respect of one or more insurance contracts*".

Without prejudice to the general information obligations set out in article 20, insurance intermediaries and investment companies offering advice must: (1) obtain the necessary information regarding the customer's knowledge and experience in the investment field relevant to the specific type of product or service, that person's financial situation including that person's investment objectives (2) recommend to the customer the insurance-based investment products that are in accordance with that person's risk tolerance and ability to bear losses. When no advice is provided, the intermediaries and companies can limit their requests for information solely to the client's knowledge and experience.

Similarly to what was established in the previous directive, if the insurance intermediary or insurance undertaking considers, on the basis of the information collected, that the product is not suitable or appropriate for the customer, the insurance intermediary or insurance undertaking must warn the customer to that effect. Where clients do not provide the information required, the insurance intermediary or insurance undertaking must warn them that they are not in a position to determine whether the product envisaged is suitable or appropriate for them. That warning may be provided in a standardised format.

The IDD Directive also allows Member States to introduce a simplified distribution system for intermediaries or companies, where no advice is given, according to a system that is reminiscent of the execution-only service of financial intermediation. In particular, insurance intermediaries or insurance undertakings can be exempted from the obligation to obtain information on the client's knowledge and experience where the following conditions are met: contracts which only provide investment exposure to financial instruments deemed non-complex; the insurance distribution activity is carried out at the initiative of the client; the client has been informed that the insurance intermediary or the insurance undertaking is not required to assess the appropriateness of the product or insurance and thus does not benefit from the corresponding protection; the insurance intermediary or insurance undertaking complies with its obligations on the management of conflicts of interest.

The other obligations imposed on intermediaries and companies include, in particular, the obligation: (1) to establish a record that includes documents that set out the rights and obligations of the parties and the other terms of performance of the services; (2) to provide adequate reports on a durable medium, including those on costs; (3) when providing advice, to provide the client with a suitability statement specifying how that advice meets the client's needs.

On the basis of a preliminary assessment of the specific rules established by the IDD on insurance-financial products, it appears that these will not have a significant impact on operators (increasing or changing the required conduct), since many of them appear to mirror the current content of the financial regulations examined above. Rather, an issue that might be interesting to consider, though we need to wait for the legislator's implementation thereof, is the possibility that, given the specific enactment of detailed regulations on financial insurance products, the debate on the legal status of these products (which are mixed by definition) might be settled once and for all, and also that the divergence of applicable rules between "traditional" distributors and distributors in the financial sector, such as bankassurance, might be eliminated.

From a systematic point of view, it is clear that the IDD will be implemented by amending chapter IX of the Insurance Code; therefore, we hope the rules will be realigned and, above all, that the legislative and regulatory framework will be made consistent.

References

Alpa G (2006) I prodotti assicurativi finanziari. In: Amorosino S, Desiderio L (eds) Il nuovo codice delle assicurazioni. Giuffre, Milan, p 77 ff

Alpa G, Gaggero P (1996) I servizi di investimento in valori mobiliari nel decreto eurosim. Giuffre, Milan, p 65

Bugiolacchi L (2009) Disclosure dell'assicurato e cooperazione dell'assicuratore nella determinazione dell'informazione rilevante. RCP 7–8:1598

Cerini D (2012) Insurance law. Kluwer Law International

Donati A, Volpe Putzolu G (2014) Manuale delle assicurazioni private. Giuffrè, Milan, p 249

Kochenburger P, Zhiyan Li R, Marano P (2010) Conflict of interest of insurance brokers-recent developments in US and China and prospects for the regulation in the European Union. Insur Law Rev 1:21

Nitti S (2010) Duty of disclosure e contratto di assicurazione comparazione tra modello italiano e inglese. Dir.Economia asscur (From 2012 Fiscalità assicur.), pp 527–603

Velliscig L (2018) Season 3: Product governance. Rethinking retail customer protection in the EU insurance market. Global Jurist 18(1):20170016

Poland

Dariusz Fuchs

Contents

D. Fuchs (✉)
Department of Civil Law and International Private Law, Faculty of Law and Administration of the Cardinal Stefan Wyszyński University, Warszawa, Poland

Law Firm, Katowice, Poland
e-mail: d.fuchs@dariuszfuchs.pl

P. Marano, I. Rokas (eds.), *Distribution of Insurance-Based Investment Products*, https://doi.org/10.1007/978-3-030-11668-2_8

Abbreviations

CC	Polish Civil Code
IDD	Directive on Insurance Distribution
IRA	Insurance and Reinsurance Act
MA	Insurance Mediation Act

1 Introduction

To discuss comprehensively the issue of legal rules of distribution of investment-based insurance products, also in the context of insurer's liability for agent's activities in connection with the so-called additional activities performed by the agent in the light of Polish law, it is necessary to analyse the applicable legal circumstances, above all the CC,[1] and the regulations of the so-called insurance act package, with particular focus on the Insurance and Reinsurance Act of 11 September 2015 (IRA)[2] and the Insurance Mediation Act of 22 May 2012 (MA).[3] In this context, we cannot ignore the acquis communautaire of the European Union, and in particular the EU law in the area of business insurance.[4] Therefore, reference is made to the already prepared works under the Principles of European Insurance Contract Law (PEICL) prepared by the so-called Insurance Restatement Group.[5] As in practice the issue of performing additional activities by a mediator (including an agent) occurs in particular in the area of personal insurance, the text focuses on the considerations based on the example from this area, i.e. a unit-linked life insurance contract, which constitutes a representative example of regulations of investment-based insurance instruments distribution under Polish law. At the same time, the text emphasises the status of an agent, who (as a consequence of the MA regulations) may act in the insurance mediation service market as an exclusive agent or as a so-called multiagent. By its nature, the status of a broker has been ignored in this approach, as the role of a broker in the distribution of investment-based insurance products does not demonstrate the specific legal features relevant to the considerations. In the opinion of the author, for the proper assessment of the relations between an insurer and an agent in the context of distribution of these types of insurance products, it is necessary to present, first of all, the essence and the nature of the insurance contract in Polish law.

[1] Journal of Laws of 1964 No. 16 item 93 as amended.

[2] I.e. Insurance and Reinsurance Act of 11 September 2015, Journal of Laws of 2015, item 1844 as amended.

[3] I.e. Insurance Mediation Act of 22 May 2003, i.e. Journal of Laws of 2016, item 2077.

[4] Cf. Fuchs (2006), p. 526 et al.; Fuchs (2004), p. 443 et al.

[5] D. Fuchs, Insurance Restatement jako przykład jednolitego prawa wspólnotowego o umowie ubezpieczenia, Studia Ubezpieczeniowe No. 127 of 2009, p. 307 et al. and idem: Fuchs (2009), p. 125 et al.

2 Specific Nature of Insurance Contract Regulations in the Context of the Scope of Legal Operations of an Insurance Company (Insurer) and an Insurance Mediator in Relation to the Distribution of Investment-Based Insurance Products

2.1 Explanation

It should be emphasised that entry into force on 1 January 2004 of the amendment to the CC (pursuant to Art. 233 of the previously applicable Insurance Act[6]) failed to introduce a change *verba legis* in the definition of an insurance contract in Art. 805 § 1 of the CC, and the content of the Insurance Act (taking into account its subsequent amendments) allows for drawing conclusions in relation to the characteristics of the benefits of the insurance company (insurer).[7] The subsequent amendment to the Civil Code, which has been applicable in relation to Art. 805 of the CC since 10 August 2007, also failed to introduce *expressis verbis* any "revolutionary changes" to the definition of an insurance contract included therein, apart from the (advocated for years) change in the name of the party to the contract from the insurance company to the insurer, while emphasising the fact that it enters into an obligation as part of the insurer's business. Thus, consequently the insurer provides its service in connection with the professionally conducted business (so-called qualified activity), which, *nota bene*, allows for referring to the insurance contract as a unilaterally qualified contract. Without going here into detailed considerations in this subject, we may assume that, nevertheless, the amendment resulted in the broader context than previously in the need to analyse in practice the essence of the insurance contract in the framework of the Insurance Act applicable then and now. In fact, the legislator has bound by this means to use the legal consequences resulting from the Public Law Act regulations (that the Insurance Act constitutes in principle, governing the public-law status of an insurer) during the analysis of both the features of the insurance contract and the characteristics of the benefits of the parties to the contract.

[6] Cf. the inapplicable Insurance Activities Act of 22 May 2003, Journal of Laws of 2003 No. 124 item 1154 as amended.

[7] Details: D. Fuchs, Ochrona ubezpieczeniowa jako świadczenie główne ubezpieczyciela, Prawo Asekuracyjne No. 2 of 2006, p. 40 et al.

2.2 *The Essence of the Statutory Definition of Insurance Activity According to Polish Law*

Art. 4(1) of the IRA includes a definition, according to which "Insurance operations shall be understood as performance of insurance activities related to offering and providing coverage in case of risk of the occurrence of fortuitous events."

There is no doubt that the above definition outlines (similarly to its equivalent in Art. 3(1) of the inapplicable Insurance Act of 2003) the permitted framework of operations for the insurance company (insurer), *ergo*: when concluding, e.g. under Art. 805 of the CC, an insurance contract (which is one of insurance activities), the insurer shall provide protection under such contract (*scil*: insurance coverage). It is irrespective of whether the funds derived from the premium are invested or not, including of whether such investment relates to the entire funds or only their parts.

An example may be the aspect of the operations of a mediator acting as an agent and using in this respect persons cooperating as entities performing agency activities in order to conclude an insurance contract related to the unit-linked insurance. The very statutory definition of insurance related to the unit-linked insurance was included by the legislator, which is characteristic albeit raising dogmatic concerns, not in the CC but in the IRA. It is a fund present in the insurance referred to in section I in group 3 of the Appendix to the Insurance Act,[8] *separated fund of assets constituting a provision created from insurance premiums, invested in the manner stipulated in the insurance contract (Art. 3(50) of the IRA).*

An agent acting for the benefit of the insurer brings about the conclusion of insurance contracts, including unit-linked life insurance contracts, i.e. based on open investment funds. Contracts concluded by such a mediator in this case are classified according to Section I of Annex to the IRA, where in sec. 3 (patterned on the EU law) the domestic legislator allowed for life insurance if it is related to the unit-linked insurance, as a type of insurance different from the life insurance *sensu stricto*. The concept was taken from the content of the First Directive of the Council of 24 July 1973 (73/239/EEC) on the coordination of laws, regulations and administrative provisions relating to the taking-up and pursuit of the business of direct insurance other than life assurance.[9]

Such ascertainment is consolidated by the fact that in the definition of the insurance operations, the Polish legislator refers to a fortuitous event as defined in the IRA as a future and uncertain event, independent of the will of the policy holder or the insurer, the occurrence of which causes damage to personal interests or material interests or an increase in material need of the policy holder or any other person covered by insurance (Art. 3(57) of the IRA).

[8] "Life insurance, if it is related to the unit-linked insurance, and life insurance where the service of the insurance company is determined based on specific indexes or other reference values".

[9] Official Journal of 1973, L 228 p. 3, Cf. Malinowska (2005), pp. 34–35; Maśniak (2004), p. 324; Fuchs (1998), p. 287 et al.; Fuchs (2006), p. 532.

The aforementioned definition may suggest that the intent of the legislator was to define a fortuitous event relevant for business insurance in the manner that at the same time characterises the basic features "traditionally" attributed to an indemnifiable accident, i.e. as a future and uncertain event, independent of the will of the policy holder.

3 The Essence of Insurance Mediation and Liability in Relation to the Distribution of Investment-Based Insurance Products

Consequently, pursuant to the definition of mediation included in the MA, an insurance mediator is also obliged to perform only the (actual or legal) activities related to the conclusion or execution of the insurance contract, which excludes, under the applicable law, its participation e.g. in the procedure of concluding contract for granting an insurance guarantee. The fact remains that in the IRA the legislator allows the insurance companies to commission the activities in the area of activities related to granting and performing guarantees to the authorised insurance mediators.

Such approach allows for the *a priori* formulation of one more reflection. Namely, that it should be taken into account that apart from the mediator himself/herself, the entity most interested in the classification of performed activities, also due to the practical system of remuneration for mediators, will be the insurer or any other entity in the insurance relation, for which the mediator operates in a given case. Any possible mistakes will consequently burden not only the mediator but also the entities for the benefit of which specific activities are performed by a given mediator. It appears that such analysis is useful precisely in the interest of insurers. Therefore, in the present applicable environment there is a paradox consisting in the fact that although an insurance company may commission the performance of insurance activities in the area of the guarantee relation to insurance mediators, in the light of the mediation definition, the mediator acting to the order of the insurance company (the exclusive agent or the multiagent), cannot perform such activities without violating the applicable law, since, as it was demonstrated hereinabove, performing activities related to concluding and performing an insurance contract shall not mean allowing for performing analogous activities in relation to the insurance guarantee relationship.

On this occasion, it is rightly emphasised that acting for and on behalf of one of the parties to the insurance contract does not exclude acting also in one's own economic interest, as the mediator, as an entrepreneur, must take into account this aspect of his/her operations.[10] Such activity (pursuant to Art. 2(2) of the MA) is assigned only to insurance agents and brokers, except for distinctiveness in the form

[10] Cf. Wieczorek (2010), p. 1101.

of reassurance brokers. The above means that other entities, e.g. entrepreneurs benefiting from the principle of freedom of business activity, guaranteed in principle by the rules of the public law, are not allowed to enter this zone with impunity, as they are exposed to various sanctions, including criminal sanctions (Art. 47 of the MA).

At the same time, this means that if a given entity acts as a mediator (irrespective whether as a broker or e.g. an exclusive agent), it may operate only in the area related to the conclusion, or, possibly, execution of the insurance contract. Its activity should be, as a consequence of the essence of the insurance contract as derived hereinabove, targeted at the provision and execution of the insurance protection. The insurance mediator is remunerated for such activities, which, *nota bene*, he/she is entitled to under the statutory regulation (Art. 2(1) of the MA). Therefore, the legislator requires the insurance mediator to mandatorily provide the information specified in detail in Art. 12(2), Art. 13(1)(4 and 4a) or Art. 26(1)(1, 2 and 4) and Art. 26(2) of the MA to every person seeking insurance protection or to a current customer in the following form:

(1) on paper or on any other durable medium available and accessible to the person seeking insurance protection or for the customer;
(2) in a clear, accurate and comprehensible manner;
(3) in an official language of the EU Member State, where the insurance contract is concluded or in any other language agreed by the parties.

At the same time, which is a certain specific nature of Polish law, detailed duties related to the investment-based insurance, are included by the legislator not in the Mediation Act but in the Insurance Act. First of all, they apply to group insurance, as part of which investment-based insurance instruments are used in Poland. Accordingly, in case of insurance for a third party, in particular in group insurance, the insurer shall not receive the remuneration or other benefits in connection with offering the possibility of benefiting from the insurance protection or the activities related to the execution of the insurance contract. It does not exclude the possibility of the insured's commitment with respect to the insurer to finance the cost of the insurance premium. The aforementioned prohibition applies also to the persons acting for or on behalf of the policy holder.

Pursuant to Art. 21 of the IRA, prior to the conclusion of an insurance contract within the scope of unit-linked insurance instruments, as referred to in section I in group 3 of the Appendix to the Insurance Act, an insurance company shall receive from the policy holder, in the form of a survey, the information on the policy holder's needs, knowledge and experience in the field of life insurance and the policy holder's financial situation, so that the insurance company could assess which insurance contract is suitable for the needs of the policy holder. In case of an insurance contract concluded for a third party, in particular group insurance, as referred to in section I in group 3 of the Appendix to the IRA, the insurance company shall receive, in the form of a survey, the information concerning the insured, before the insured agrees to be covered with insurance protection as part of the insurance contract concluded by the policy holder, so that the insurance company could assess if the insurance contract is suitable for the needs of the insured. Based on the analysis of the information referred to hereinabove, the insurance company shall present the policy holder with the proposals of insurance corresponding to the policy holder's needs together with the justification, which shall include in particular the identification of the policy holder's needs and the explanation how these needs are met by the presented proposals. In case when according to the information analysis, the needs of the policy holder are inadequate to the policy holder's experience, knowledge of life insurance field or financial situation or there is no insurance corresponding to the policy holder's needs, the insurance company shall communicate that to the policy holder with a warning the analysis result or the offer of the insurance company prevents offering relevant insurance. The policy holder shall confirm the receipt of this information in writing and shall submit a written statement that the policy holder has become acquainted with the warning. In such case an insurance contract may be concluded only based on a written request of the policy holder. And according to Art. 22 of the IRA, prior to the conclusion of a life insurance contract, if it is unit-linked, as referred to in section I in group 3 of the Appendix to IRA (*scil*: investment-based insurance products), the insurance company shall provide the person interested in the conclusion of such a contract with the basic information concerning this contract on paper or (providing that the policy holder agrees to that) on any other durable medium.

The information referred to hereinabove shall include in particular:

(1) the purpose and the nature of the contract;
(2) a list of benefits granted under the contract and a list of offered insurance funds;
(3) titles and amounts of fees collected by the insurance company;
(4) specification of risk profile of the unit-linked insurance plans;
(5) the recommended minimum contract duration together with the justification of the recommendations, including the investment horizon of the unit-linked insurance plan;
(6) the information on the investment risk of the policy holder or the insured, if any.

The information for the eligible person shall specify the venue and the manner of obtaining additional information on unit-linked insurance plans, and they shall be formulated in a comprehensive and not misleading manner and communicated unambiguously.

5. In case of an insurance contract, if it is unit-linked, as referred to in section I in group 3 of the Appendix to the IRA, concluded for a third party, in particular group insurance, the policy holder shall provide the person interested in entering into such a contract with the aforementioned information on paper or (providing that the policy holder agrees to that) on any other durable medium. In addition, in a life insurance contract, if it is unit-linked, as referred to in section I in group 3 of the Appendix to IRA, the insurance company shall specify:

(1) a list of unit-linked insurance plans offered under the insurance contract;
(2) the principles of determining the value of benefits under the insurance contract for the death of the insured and in case when the insured is still living on the

insurance coverage maturity date, as well as the principles of determining the value of the total and partial insurance buy-out;
(3) the rules for investing funds of the unit-linked insurance plan;
(4) the principles and the terms of the evaluation of participation units of the unit-linked insurance plan;
(5) titles and amounts of the fees collected from insurance premiums, from the assets of unit-linked insurance plans or by the surrender of the participation units of the unit-linked insurance plans;
(6) the principles of the allocation of funds derived from insurance premiums in participation units of the unit-linked insurance plan, the dates of changing insurance premiums into participation units and the principles of surrendering the participation units of the unit-linked insurance plan and changing them into cash.

And the rules for investing funds of the unit-linked insurance plan shall specify the following:

(1) the investment purpose of the unit-linked insurance;
(2) types and kinds of securities and other proprietary rights that are the subject of deposits of the unit-linked insurance;
(3) characteristics of the assets composing the unit-linked insurance, criteria for the selection of assets and the principles of their diversification and other investment limitations;
(4) the information on the investment risk of the policy holder or the insured.

In the life insurance contract, if it is unit-linked, the insurance company shall specify the latest dates when the following will occur:

(1) allocation in participation units of the unit-linked insurance after the insurance premium payment;
(2) surrender of the participation units of the unit-linked insurance after the submission of the application for payment of the benefit under the insurance contract and the benefit disbursement, as well as the application for the payment of the total or partial buy-out of the insurance and the disbursement of the value of the total or partial insurance buy-out.

Within the scope of the life insurance contract, if it is unit-linked, the insurance company shall additionally:

(1) evaluate the participation units of the unit-linked insurance plan, not less frequently than once a month;
(2) publish, not less frequently than once a year, on the insurance company's website, the value of the participation unit of the unit-linked insurance plan, as determined in the month preceding the month when it is published;
(3) prepare and publish annual and semi-annual reports of the insurance fund

The following principles shall refer directly to the status of the mediator within the scope of the distribution of the discussed insurance products, also specified by the legislator's will in the Insurance Act.

In the life insurance contract, if it is unit-linked, concluded for the period not longer than 5 years, with respect to the remuneration of the insurance mediator, an insurance company shall be guided by the principle of the equal distribution over time of expenses for the commission of the insurance mediator in the insurance period set forth in the insurance contract. At the same time, in such circumstances, with respect to the remuneration of the insurance mediator, an insurance company shall be guided by the principle of the equal distribution over time of expenses for the commission of the insurance mediator in the period not shorter than 5 years. However, it should be emphasised that the above 2 rules shall not be applied to the insurance contract where the guaranteed amount of the benefit for the death of the insured due to any reason is higher than ten times the annual premium due under that contract in each of the first 5 years of the insurance.

In a separate case of the life insurance contract, where the benefit amount is determined based on the determined indices or other base values (Art. 24 of the IRA), as referred to in section I in group 3 of the Appendix to IRA, the insurance company shall notify of:

(1) the assets in which the insurance premium is or will be invested and the proportion in which parts of the premium are or will be invested in individual assets;
(2) indices or other base values, based on which the benefits amount is determined, in the manner allowing for their identification;
(3) the principles of determining the value of benefits under the insurance contract for the death of the insured and in case when the insured is still living on the insurance coverage maturity date, as well as the principles of determining the value of the total and partial insurance buy-out;
(4) the guaranteed amount of benefits under the insurance contract, if the terms of the insurance contract provide for the guaranteed amount of benefits;
(5) time limits when the values of indices or other base values are determined and used for the establishment of the value of benefits under the insurance contract;
(6) sources of information on the values of indices or other base values used for the establishment of the value of benefits under the insurance contract;
(7) titles and amounts of fees collected by the insurance company;
(8) the method of the settlement of the parties to the insurance contract in case when:

    (a) determination of the benefit value is not possible due to the fact that it is impossible to determine the value of the index or other base value during the term of the insurance contract, or
    (b) in the opinion of the insurance company, during the term of the insurance contract, the method for the determination of the value of the index or any other base value was significantly changed;

(9) the time limits and methods for the provision of information on the value of indices or other base values, based on which the benefits amount is determined.

In case of a life insurance contract, where the amount of the benefit is determined based on specific indices or other base values, concluded for a third party, in particular group insurance, the policy holder shall provide the person interested before entering into such a contract with the aforementioned information on paper or (providing that the policy holder agrees to that) on any other durable medium.

In relation to a mediator, in a life insurance contract, where the benefit amount is determined based on specific indices or other base values, concluded for the period not longer than 5 years, with respect to the remuneration of the insurance mediator, an insurance company shall be guided by the principle of the equal distribution over time of expenses for the commission of the insurance mediator in the insurance period set forth in the insurance contract.

As a consequence, in such a contract concluded for the period longer than 5 years or for an indefinite period of time, with respect to the remuneration of the insurance mediator, an insurance company shall be guided by the principle of the equal distribution over time of expenses for the commission of the insurance mediator in the period not shorter than 5 years.

It should be also emphasised in principle that the legislator clearly separated the scope of rights and obligations of an agent and a broker, establishing that the former (irrespective whether as an exclusive agent or a multiagent), when performing agency activities, acts for and on behalf of the insurance company, and a broker performs analogous activities for and on behalf of the person seeking protection (Art. 4(1 and 2) of the MA).

Thereby, the legislator specifies also the principal objective of insurance activities performed by the insurance company, and, consequently, also by the insurance mediator (an agent in particular), which is to be executed by the provision of insurance coverage.

In this context is necessary to underline that it have appeared some interesting court decisions recently that resolved problems raised on *acien regime* (not actually binding law). For instance, during District Court in Częstochowa, the institution of the "redemption value" in a way that allowed the defendant to retain more than 80% of the funds paid by the plaintiff as a redemption of shares was contrary to good morals and grossly infringed the interests of the plaintiff. Clearly, it requires that the meaning of redemption is reduced to the payment of the funds deposited in the insured's account should be forbidden. "The discount mechanism used in the present case, which is used in the present case, is, in fact, a sanction for resigning from the continuation of the contract without reference to the actual costs incurred by the defendant".[11] In the other court decision's example, we should referred to the Polish Supreme Court ruling. According to the Supreme Court, the seller of the insurance life insurance contract, if it is unit-linked, the must deliver to the prospective client

[11] Court decision form 12 08 2016 (signature.: VI Ca 88/16), vide: www.rf.gov.pl.

the General Terms of Insurance (GTC) before the contract is concluded. The Supreme Court held that it was not enough to familiarize the insured with the general terms and conditions of insurance, or even his signature, that this was the case, so as to say that the client was sufficiently informed about such insurance, which he bought.[12]

The one of most stressed Polish court decisions we can find in the case District Court decision form Warsaw, according to the such policies (raised on *ancient regime* Insurance Activity Act form 2004) should be forbidden totally. Court says: "In the case of ordinary investment policies, customers are at risk of losing money only if they retire from their investments (when liquidation charges are deducted from their payments), structured policies make the most of the loss of value of this special investment fund. This discount is based on a mechanism not disclosed in the contract, a mechanism dependent solely on the insurer."[13]

4 A Catalogue of Insurance Activities

Therefore, the obligation of the insurer, providing that the insurer does not use an additional (supplementary—cf. Art. 4(9) of the IRA) basis for its operations, which is Art. 4(7 and 8) of the IRA, may only mean the obligation to provide the benefit which at the same time results from the catalogue of insurance activities which, apart from the insurance contract, include:

(1) concluding insurance contracts, insurance guarantee contracts or commissioning the conclusion thereof to authorised insurance mediators, within the meaning of the Insurance Mediation Act, as well as performing these contracts;
(2) concluding reinsurance contracts or commissioning the conclusion thereof to reinsurance brokers, within the meaning of the Insurance Mediation Act, as well as performing these contracts, in the scope of assigning the risk from the insurance contracts or insurance guarantee contracts (passive reassurance);
(3) making declarations of will regarding claims for damages or other benefits due under the contracts referred to in paragraphs 1 and 2;
(4) calculation of premiums and commissions due under the contracts referred to in sec. 1 and 2;
(5) establishing, by way of civil law activities, proprietary or personal collaterals if it is directly connected with the conclusion of the contracts referred to in sec. 1 and 2;
(6) risk assessment within personal and property insurance and in insurance guarantee contracts;

[12]Vide: "Rzeczpospolita"(Nr z 18.12.20115 r.).

[13]Court decision on 23 03 2015, (signature: III C 1453/13), vide: finanse.uokik.gov.pl/ufk/; this court decision was non-final one.

(7) payment of damages and other benefits due under the contracts referred to in sec. 1 and 2;
(8) taking over and selling objects or rights acquired by an insurance company in connection with the execution of the insurance contract or the insurance guarantee contract;
(9) conducting the control of compliance, by the policy holders or the insured, with obligations and safety rules indicated in the contract or general terms and conditions of insurance with regard to the objects covered by the insurance;
(10) conducting recourse proceedings and receivables collection proceedings with regard to the performing of:

  (a) insurance contracts and insurance guarantee contracts,
  (b) reinsurance contracts in the scope of assigning the risk under insurance contracts and insurance guarantee contracts;

(11) investing assets of the insurance company;
(12) performing other activities provided for the insurance company as specified in separate acts.

5 The Concept of Insurance Protection (Coverage) as the Effect of the Investment-Based Insurance Product

Despite the diversity of the above catalogue, each of those activities, in accordance with the intent of the legislator, is related to offering and providing protection. Thus, it may be reasonably assumed that the basic type of service that the insurer undertakes to perform within the scope of operations of its undertaking is precisely the provision of insurance coverage in case of the possible occurrence of events generating damage to the protected goods.

For the insurance contract, as an insurance activity that the insurer is entitled to conclude (due to the eligible nature of the insurance contract), a special role is played also by Art. 15(1) of the IRA, which stipulates, *explicite*, the obligation of providing the insurance coverage by the insurer, where it is stated that "...shall provide insurance protection on the basis of insurance contract concluded with the policy holder." Thus, neither the insurer nor the policy holder, nor even the insured (*scil*: the person eligible under the insurance contract—entitled to request the provision of benefits under the insurance contract from the insurance company; the eligible person under the insurance contract shall be deemed to be also an injured party in case of third-party liability insurance, Art. 3(1)(52) of the IRA) has impact on such a result of the concluded contract that is the source of the insurance protection, which the insurer is obliged to provide.[14]

[14] Interesting reconsideration of this opinion is included in the study by M. Orlicki: Roszczenie o zapłacenie składki za czas, w którym nie była świadczona ochrona ubezpieczeniowa, Prawo Asekuracyjne No. 1 of 2006 p. 42.

In the event of the occurrence of an indemnifiable accident (*scil.*; a fortuitous event), the aforementioned protection will oblige the insurer to provide additional benefits, usually of a monetary nature, which are within the scope of the insurance coverage (constitute its supplementation) and constitute the fulfilment of the compensation function of business insurance.

Such a position is also present in the judicial decisions of the Polish Supreme Court, as may be illustrated above all by the judgement of 28 May 1997, where it was stated that "The insurance contract shall serve protective function; therefore, the point of view of the one who is protected shall be meaningful for the interpretation of its provisions."[15]

And the relation between the premium and the insurance coverage was taken into account by the Supreme Court in 2001 by deciding that "the premium is the benefit incurred by the policy holder for the insurer in consideration of the insurance coverage."[16] Therefore, the judicial decisions also notice the premium correlate in the insurance coverage, which also allows for arguing the thesis on the provision of insurance protection as the so-called main service of the insurer.[17] As a consequence, the operations of the mediator also have to be generally aimed at the achievement of this result; and this is due to the content of the aforementioned definition of insurance mediation, specified in Art. 2 in connection with Art. 4(1) of the MA, where the legislator linked the activities performed for and on behalf of the insurance company or a person seeking protection with the insurance contract, which, by its nature, needs to provide protection as specified hereinabove. (Art. 4(1) of the MA activities for and on behalf of the insurance company, hereinafter referred to as "agency activities", consisting in winning customers, performing preparatory activities aimed at concluding insurance contracts, concluding insurance contracts and participating in insurance contract administration and execution, as well as in compensation cases, and in organising and supervising agency activities).

The assumption that the principal service of the insurance company in the insurance contract is the provision of the insurance coverage by taking over the risk incumbent primarily only on the person whose protected goods may be damaged as a result of the occurrence of a fortuitous event, constitutes also an argument by reciprocity, as at such moment, the objections are overruled that concern the absence of equivalence of the premium paid by the policy holder to the insurance company, which in turn (according to the theory of the random nature of the insurance contract), provides its service only in case of the occurrence of an indemnifiable accident.[18] If the Insurance Act characterises in the aforementioned manner the definition

[15] III CKN 76/97, LEX No. 50796.

[16] V CKN 199/00, LEX No. 52419.

[17] Details: Fuchs (2003), p. 43 et al.

[18] Cf. the still valid considerations of Wąsiewicz (2002), pp. 46–47. In the domestic literature, W. Czachórski is definitely in favour of the random nature of the insurance contract: Czachórski (2003), pp. 513–514; B. Rozmus, G. Kuczyński, Kilka mitów z zakresu teorii umów, Gdańskie Studia Prawnicze, Volume VII, pp. 316–317 emphasise the absence of equivalence of benefits of the parties to the insurance contract.

of the insurance operations with the use of *iuris cogentis* rules, it shall be considered that in the same manner it also decides on the permitted scope of operations of the insurance company. Therefore, it is difficult to defend the position according to which, despite such wording of the statutory definition of the insurance operations, in consideration of the premium that the policy holder is obliged to pay, the insurance company is, in turn, only obliged to perform services in case of an accident; as in this manner it would lead to the violation by the insurance company of the mandatory legal regulations, which, after all, are both the limitation of the contractual freedom (Art. 353[1] of the CC) and the condition for validity of a legal activity under Art. 56 of the CC.

Thus, the consent of the parties to the contract to include in the insurance contract the benefits of the insurance company only in the context of cash benefit, the obligation to comply with which depends on an accident, could lead to invalidity of the insurance contract. In this manner, it can be assumed that the legislator has definitively prejudged that the insurance company has a synallagmatic nature, through the acceptance that the benefit of the insurance company is the provision of protection in the insurance contract in consideration of the insurance premium.[19]

Similarly, if we were to search for comparisons with the EU law, we would need to decide that it also assumes (in the Insurance Restatement project, officially: Principles of European Insurance Contract, PEICL) linking the insurance contract with the provision of the insurance protection by the insurer. This is clearly provided for in Art. 1:201(1) of PEICL, where the insurance contract is defined as a contract under which one of the parties (the insurer), in consideration of the premium, provides the protection to the insured in connection with specific risks.[20]

6 The Essence of Duties of the Agent as a Mediator

The obligation to provide the insurance protection by the insurer to the other party to the contract, as stressed several times hereinabove, is also the effect of the unquestioned another feature of business insurance, which is the classification of this contract as a contract of the highest trust. This means that in each insurance contract, irrespective of whether it is of property or personal nature, the parties shall use their best endeavours in the performance of their obligations, while respecting the legitimate interests of the other party. The natural consequence of that is finding that, similarly, *contractus uberrimae fidei* is the insurance contract where the insurance mediator is present, e.g. a multiagent or an exclusive agent. Undoubtedly, this statement is supported by the fact that in Art. 760 of the CC both parties to the agency

[19] Details: Fuchs (2005), pp. 920–925.

[20] More: D. Fuchs, Nowelizacja kodeksu cywilnego w zakresie wybranych przepisów ogólnych o umowie ubezpieczenia w świetle prac Project Group on a Restatement of European Insurance Contract Law, Wiadomości Ubezpieczeniowe, No. 7/8 z 2007, p. 32 et seq.

contract are obliged to mutual loyalty with respect to each other.[21] At the same time, it is stated in the Mediation Act itself that agency activities shall be performed with diligence set forth in Art. 355 § 2 of the CC (Due diligence of a debtor within the scope of the business operated by the debtor shall be stipulated while taking into account the professional nature of such operations and good practice (Art. 8 of the MA).

After all, pursuant to the Mediation Act, his/her activities are also to be aimed at acquiring customers for the insurance company, and then at efficient administration of a given insurance on behalf of the insurer. Just as the insurer, he/she should endeavour to provide to the fullest possible extent, within the insurance existing between the parties, the protection of the interests of the policy holder. It would be against logic if his/her actions could be assessed differently or if it would be possible to question his/her professionalism (competence) due to the fact that he/she made efforts (permitted by law) intended to provide the standard of service higher than the one commonly met in the insurance market. Thus, performing activities, e.g. by a multiagent, that may make the insurer's offer more attractive, bind (in a legal manner) the policy holder for the future with a given insurance company, are as close as possible to the essence of agency operations. Certainly, if such activities were performed only in the interest of the entity entitled to benefits, it would be the domain of the broker. Similarly, such possibility of operation shall not be refused to the exclusive agent, whose relation with a specific insurer by its nature is even closer.

Nevertheless, while assuming that it has been previously approved by the insurance company represented by the exclusive agent, the presented standard provides them with customers and, certainly, is also an activity performed in the business interest of the agent. Thus, in accordance with the law, the insurance company promotes the activities aimed at promotion of the insurance protection. In such case, there are no grounds to assign liability to the insurer in case when, e.g. the exclusive agent performs such additional activities. Certainly, it is a different matter if the agent commits a tort during the performance of such additional activities. In such case, the insurer's liability will occur, with the exclusion of the possibility to refer by the insurer to the content of Art. 429 of the CC, which in practice will mean, above all, lack of possibility of discharging from liability for the damage inflicted by the exclusive agent due to the fact that this agent has the status of an entrepreneur (Art. 5 of the Mediation Act).

In relation to the multiagent, such, even hypothetical attempt to assign liability to the insurance company would end up in a failure, due to content of Art. 11(2) of the MA.

[21] Cf. Ogiegło (2001), pp. 413–414.

7 The Case of a Life Insurance Contract Related to the Unit-Linked Insurance

This "product" allowed in the so-called II Section of the Appendix to the IRA is composed by its nature of two separate insurance scopes (insurance activities): of classical life insurance and of the financial service, consisting in the assistance in investing funds in investment funds according to the instructions of the policy holder.

If, however, the domestic insurer (in accordance with applicable law) allowed for the conclusion of these types of insurance contracts, the consequence of this fact was at first the concern of the insured about the financial fate of the frequently significant part of the insurance premium invested in the fund, which on the part of the insurer should generate (due to the insurance protection concept considered hereinabove and the feature of the highest loyalty with respect to the contracting party) the necessity to provide the policy holder with sufficient instruments to make, frequently in a very dynamic manner, financial decisions related to the allocation of funds invested in funds.

Due to this reason, the practice of performing additional activities by the agent in the form e.g. of providing information to the insured about currency exchange rates or listing shares of individual listed companies should be, in principle, considered to be acceptable in the light of the applicable law, as it will constitute an additional service, supporting at the stage of the execution of the insurance contract and functioning in the interest of the insurer represented in a given case by the agent.

Certainly, such a methodological assumption causes that a possible contract which is the basis for the access to the data related to the situation on the stock exchange market should, first of all, satisfy the regulations of personal data protection, as well as guarantee free will of a given policy holder to accept such a possibility, by the adaptation of the model content of such a contract, maintained, e.g. on the website, pursuant to Art. 384 § 4 of the CC. Here, additional attention should be paid to Article 384^1 of the CC.

Art. 384^1 of the CC may serve as a particular example which is *explicite* omitted by the legislator in Art. 805 § 4 of the CC (as it refers only to Art. 385^1-385^3), and whose application to the insurance contract was noticed in practice and in literature in the previously applicable legal environment, and that with respect to the no longer binding content of Art. 384 § 5 of the CC. According to Art. 384^1 of the CC "a standard contract delivered during a continuous contractual relationship is binding on the other party if the requirements set forth in Article 384 are met, and the party concerned has not terminated the contract with notice on the earliest possible termination date."

First of all, the principal issue shall be determined whether this is a standard assigned only to the consumer market, i.e. the one that is applicable when a party to the contract is a consumer within the meaning of Art. 22^1 of the CC. ("A natural person who carries out a juridical act which is not directly related to his economic or professional activity shall be considered a consumer"). A positive answer would prove that it could be applied e.g. to the insurance contract or to the contract between an entrepreneur and a natural person at most, only in case when the policy holder is a consumer. However, both the linguistic interpretation and the systemic argument incline us to the opposite conclusion, as in its content Art. 384[1] of the CC fails to make reference to the term of a consumer and consumer market, and, after all, Title III Book III of the CC does not provide for the consumer market but for general regulations concerning contractual obligations. According to Art. 384[1] of the CC, a standard contract delivered during a continuous contractual relationship is binding on the other party if the requirements concerning the contract template delivery (as set forth in Art. 384 of the CC) are met, and the party concerned has not terminated the contract with notice on the earliest possible termination date.

If the above statement is correct, another question is raised—whether with the use of linguistic interpretation and the systemic argument we arrive in a legitimate manner at another conclusion that Art. 384[1] of the CC applies to all contractual relationships of a continuous nature, where the standard applies in the manner described in the hypothesis.

In this regard, in the domestic literature it has been rightly noticed that Art 384[1] of the CC may not be applied to all continuous contracts, which depends, above all, on whether the length of the period is closely related to the nature of the benefit (as in the example of the insurance contract), or if it is neutral to the nature of the obligation.[22] If there is such an immanent relation, the modification according to this procedure is impossible as it makes the protection of the contracting party-proponent illusory; although, as it is noticed, the literal wording of the provision could induce to opposite conclusions; however, in this context, in principle, no attention is paid to the specific continuous contractual obligations.[23] The aforementioned position was supported in the judicial decisions concerning legal relationships similar to the insurance contract, such as for instance: a bank account contract.[24]

If such a position is justified, and, thus, it is possible *prima facie* to represent the opinion that in accordance with the purpose-bound interpretation, it should not be allowed *ex definitione* to apply Art. 384[1] of the CC in all contractual relations of a continuous nature. If we decide that in the insurance contract the insurer's benefit is the provision of insurance coverage, which by its nature is spread in time and, in principle, depends on the performance of a one-time benefit, which is the premium payment by the policy holder, due to the aforementioned reasons, the application of Art. 384[1] of the CC to the insurance contract should be refused. Additionally, it should be noted that adoption of a different position would be contrary to the very nature of the insurance contract expressed more and more commonly also in the domestic literature by considering it to be the contract of the highest trust (*contractus uberrimae fidei*). Unfortunately, with respect to the legislator's will expressed *explicite* in Art. 830 §4 of the CC, which allows for the application of the regulation from Art. 384 [1] of the CC to the life insurance contract, one can at most talk about

[22] Żuławska (1999), p. 125.

[23] Popiołek (2002), p. 797 and the literature quoted therein.

[24] Cf. the catalogue of decisions: Patulski (2000), pp. 306–307.

the inconsistency of the prevailing conditions with the views of the doctrine, which, however, should be an inspiration for changes in the regulation in the future as soon as possible.

In the discussed case of the life insurance contract with the unit-linked insurance, it is an argument on the possibility of applying negative consequences to such a contract, resulting from Art. 384[1] of the CC, which, also due to the fundamental adaptability of this standard to the market, may also apply to the fate of the contract between the insured and the entrepreneur running the information service, whose data the insured has access to, pursuant to the content of the contract separate to the insurance contract.

The contract under which relevant information would be provided for the insured should also satisfy the Act on Prevention of Unfair Market Practices[25] and the regulation applicable with respect to the consumer rights[26] in the part referring to the protection of legitimate interests of consumers. After all, it should be assumed that *gros* of policy holders, wishing to benefit from such an additional service, will do so as natural persons—consumers in the light of Art. 22[1] of the CC, and in such case, particular attention should be paid to the consumer law in this respect.

Referring to the relation agent *versus* entrepreneur, who is for instance the owner of the information service whose final user will be the insured, it should be emphasised that improving the quality of the insurance service consists in the mentioned case in making available the possibility of using the appropriate "information service". The very acceptance of such possibility on the part of the policy holder does not result in performing activities by the agent that go beyond acting as a mediator in the conclusion and performance of the contract due to (as it was stressed hereinabove) the close relation of such project with the interests of the insurer. Thus, such practice does not give rise to the formulation of objections addressed to the insurance company, or to raising claims for indemnity pursuant to Art. 11(1) of the MA. Therefore, the contractual obligation created in this manner between the policy holder (*vel*: the insured) and the owner of the information and financial service is a legal relationship independent of the insurance contract, concluded and performed by the insurer with the policy holder with the participation of an agent, which certainly does not eliminate the functional relations between such contracts, as it was discussed hereinabove.

The situation is different if the entrepreneur, who is neither the exclusive agent nor the multiagent, performs such auxiliary activities or those "supporting" the insurer's position in the market by himself/herself. In such case the collision with Art. 2 and the sanction mentioned in Art. 47 of the MA are possible. On the other hand, such situation would also fail to entail liability of the insurance company as in the aforementioned factual circumstances such entrepreneur, who is not an agent,

[25] Act on Prevention of Unfair Market Practices of 23 August 2007, Journal of Laws of 2007 No. 171 item 1206 as amended.

[26] Consumer Rights Act of 30 May 2014, as amended Journal of Laws 2014 item 827, and other residual provisions of the Act of 2 March 2000 on the protection of consumer rights and liability for damage caused by dangerous products, Journal of Laws of 2000 No. 22 item 271 as amended.

may not be considered to be the exclusive agent; hence, Art. 11(1) of the MA will not apply in this case and the entrepreneur will be personally liable for any possible damage inflicted to third parties. Thus (apart from the case when such entity acts with the knowledge and agreement of the insurer, without the relevant legal status of a mediator), the practical dimension of the liability of the insurance company is highly limited.

8 What Will Change in Poland After 1 October 2018?

8.1 Objective and Subjective Scope of the New Legislation

In order to properly understand legal conditions of the distribution of insurance products in 2018 in Polish law it is necessary to refer not only to the IRA regulations, but also to the legislative solutions that ultimately implement the IDD. A basic example is here the Insurance Distribution Act, IDA, which is due to come into force as of 1 October 2018.[27] The objective scope of the IDA specifies the rules for carrying out activities in the distribution of personal and property insurance and reinsurance distribution. The act also includes legal definitions of basic terms and legal institutions characteristic for insurance distribution, although the constructions of such definitions are often different.

For example, a broker is defined more precisely than an insurance agent[28] because he is defined as a natural or legal person who holds an authorization from a regulatory authority for pursuing brokerage activities related to *insurance*, and is entered in the register of brokers. Both of these basic categories are recognized under the IDA as entities carrying out insurance intermediation—pursuit of *insurance distribution* or reinsurance *distribution* by insurance intermediaries. On the other hand, the category of an insurance intermediary itself may include: insurance agent, ancillary *insurance* agent, insurance broker and reinsurance broker who carry out *insurance distribution* or reinsurance *distribution* for remuneration.

The key definitions (as quoted above), as per the IDD, are included in the glossary for the act (Art. 3 of the IDA). A reinsurance distributor is, *verba legis*, a reinsurance undertaking, *insurance* undertaking or reinsurance broker, whereas an insurance distributor is an insurance undertaking, insurance agent, ancillary insurance agent or insurance broker. Another similarly fundamental definition is the statutory definition of a customer defined, for *insurance* contracts, as a person seeking insurance protection, insuring party or insured party, and for insurance guarantee

[27] Insurance Distribution Act from 1512 2017, Journal of Laws. Z 2017 item. 2486 as amended.

[28] *Scil*: insurance agent—an entrepreneur other than an agent offering supplementary insurance (compare Art. 3(1)(2) of the IDD, definition is analogical to IDD) who carries out agency activities under an agency agreement made with an insurance company and entered in the register of agents (Art. 3(1)(1) of the IDA); cf. J. Nowak in: P. Czublun, Ustawa o dystrybucji ubezpieczeń. Komentarz, Warszawa 2018, s. 20 I nn.

contracts, as an insurance guarantee applicant. The term "customer" is made more precise by the status of a person seeking insurance protection, namely a person who expressed towards the *insurance* distributor his/her intention to take actions in order to make an *insurance* contract.

8.2 Casus of the General (Public) Good

Due to the UE character of the regulation (because of the statutory implementation of the IDD), the Polish legislator had to refer to the notion of the general (public) good which has been subjected to insurance regulation in the Polish legislation in that manner (by means of general clauses, as a matter of fact). According to Art. 3(1)(23) of the IDA the rules of the common good mean basic legal norms relating to the practice of *insurance distribution* or reinsurance *distribution* in the territory of a given member state of the European Union, and intended for entities that have their registered offices or domicile in another member state of the European Union, who are interested in carrying on *insurance distribution* or reinsurance *distribution* via a branch or in a manner other than via a branch, as part of the free provision of services, in the territory of that member state of the European Union.[29]

8.3 Distribution in the Light of the IDA

According to the IDA insurance distribution means in principle (Art. 4(1)) the activities performed exclusively by a *insurance* distributor and consisting in:

(1) advising on, proposing, or carrying out other work preparatory to the conclusion of *insurance* contracts or insurance guarantee contracts;
(2) concluding *insurance* contracts or insurance guarantee contracts on behalf of an *insurance* undertaking, on behalf and for the benefit of a customer or directly by an insurance undertaking; provision of assistance by an insurance intermediary in administering *insurance* contracts or insurance guarantee contracts and the performance thereof, as well as in claims for compensation or benefit.

As part of their agency activities an insurance agent and an ancillary *insurance* agent perform actions related to *insurance distribution* on behalf and for the benefit of an insurance undertaking (the so-called *agency activities*). Whereas, an insurance broker performs actions related to *insurance distribution* on behalf and for the benefit of a customer, known in the Act as insurance brokerage activities.

According to the IDA an insurance undertaking is authorized to carry out direct activities related to *insurance distribution* via an employee authorized by such

[29] Details on the public good under the rule of secondary law on business insurance: Fuchs (1998), s. 299-301 a przede wszystkim: Fuchs (2002).

insurance undertaking (distribution activities of an *insurance* undertaking). Insurance distribution also includes organizing and supervising agency activities at an insurance agent's or ancillary insurance agent's and insurance brokerage activities at an insurance broker's.

On the other hand, reinsurance *distribution* means the activities performed exclusively by a reinsurance distributor and consisting in:

(1) advising on, proposing, or carrying out other work preparatory to the conclusion of reinsurance contracts,
(2) concluding reinsurance contracts on behalf of an *insurance* undertaking or reinsurance undertaking or directly by an *insurance* undertaking or reinsurance undertaking;
(3) assisting in the administration and performance of reinsurance contracts.

As part of its brokerage activities a reinsurance broker carries out reinsurance distribution activities on behalf of or for the benefit of an *insurance* undertaking or reinsurance undertaking, known in the IDA as reinsurance brokerage activities. An insurance undertaking or reinsurance undertaking may directly perform reinsurance *distribution* activities via an employee authorized by such insurance undertaking or reinsurance undertaking (*scil*: distribution activities of a reinsurance undertaking). Reinsurance *distribution* also involves organizing and supervising brokerage activities related to reinsurance at a reinsurance broker's.

8.4 Duties of the Insurance Distributor and His Responsibility

While pursuing *insurance distribution* activities an insurance distributor acts in a fair, reliable and professional manner, to the best interests of his customers. The manner of remunerating the *insurance* distributor and the persons with the help of whom agency or brokerage activities related to *insurance* are carried out, and the persons via whom distribution activities of an insurance undertaking are performed, cannot be contrary to the duty to act in the best interests of customers. In particular, an *insurance* distributor cannot make any arrangements related to remuneration, sales targets and other arrangements that may be an incentive for proposing a specific *insurance* contract or insurance guarantee contract to a customer in a situation where the *insurance* distributor could propose other contract that would better fit the customer's needs. Before concluding an *insurance* contract or an insurance guarantee contract the *insurance* distributor specifies, based on the information received from the customer, the customer's demands and needs and provides him/her with objective information in a comprehensible form about the insurance product to allow him/her to make an informed decision. Any proposed *insurance* contract or insurance guarantee contract should be consistent with the customer's demands and needs related to insurance protection or guarantee protection.

Persons performing agency activities, persons performing *insurance* brokerage activities, persons performing reinsurance brokerage activities, persons performing distribution activities of an *insurance* undertaking and persons performing distribution activities of a reinsurance undertaking must improve their professional skills and are required to complete at least 15 h of professional training every year on selected topics specified in an annex to the IDA.

According to an annex to the Act on Insurance and Reassurance Activity an insurance broker, insurance agent and ancillary *insurance* agent who perform agency activities for more than one *insurance* undertaking within the same category of insurance, must reply to a complaint from a customer who is a legal person or an unincorporated entity within 30 days from the date of receipt thereof, in the scope not related to the insurance protection provided. To comply with the time limit it is sufficient to send a reply before the expiry thereof, which may be extended, in a justified case, up to 60 days from the date when the intermediary received the complaint.

Agency activities should be pursued with all diligence as specified in Art. 355 § 2 of the CC[30] and in line with best practices. According to Art. 20 of the IDA an *insurance* undertaking for the benefit of which an agent acts, is responsible for damage caused by such insurance agent or ancillary *insurance* agent in connection with the performance of agency activities. Art. 429 of the CC[31] is not applicable. An insurance agent and ancillary *insurance* agent performing agency activities for more than one *insurance* undertaking within the same category of *insurance* are responsible, according to the annex to the Act on Insurance and Reinsurance Activity, for damage arisen as a result of such activities caused to a customer or a person entitled under the *insurance* contract or insurance guarantee contract. As regards the responsibility for damage arisen as a result of agency activities an insurance agent who performs agency activities for more than one *insurance* undertaking within the same category of *insurance*, (also according to the annex to the Act on Insurance and Reinsurance Activity) is subject to a compulsory civil liability *insurance*. A civil liability *insurance* contract and an insurance guarantee contract cover damage caused by an insurance agent or an ancillary *insurance* agent in connection with activities performed in the territory of the Republic of Poland and other member states of the European Union.

According to Art. 28(1) of the IDA an insurance broker and a reinsurance broker are subject to a compulsory civil liability *insurance* on account of their brokerage activities in the area of *insurance* and reinsurance. Such compulsory civil liability insurance covers damage caused to a customer, a person entitled under an *insurance* contract or insurance guarantee contract, *insurance* undertaking or reinsurance undertaking, respectively, and also includes damage caused by natural persons with the help of whom an insurance broker or reinsurance broker performs brokerage

[30] Art. 355. §2: The due care of a debtor in his business activity is specified with consideration taken of the professional nature of this business.

[31] Art. 429. Anyone who entrusts an act to another person is liable for any damage caused by the perpetrator when performing the act unless he was not at fault when choosing that person or he entrusted the act to a person, enterprise or establishment which performs such acts within the scope of its professional activity.

activities in the area of *insurance* and reinsurance. A civil liability insurance contract covers damage caused by an insurance broker or reinsurance broker in connection with activities performed in the territory of the Republic of Poland and other member states of the European Union.

The issue of the EU freedom of establishment related to insurance distribution intermediation and problems related to the provision of cross-border services in business insurance distribution are regulated in detail in Chapter 4 of the IDA.

9 Conclusion

The additional scope of duties of the insurer and the mediator in relation to investment-based insurance products according to Polish law, in particular on the occasion of executing unit-linked life insurance contracts is, in principle, an acceptable example in the light of the applicable internal law and it also fails to face any obstacles in the EU law. A separate issue is respecting, within the freedom of contracting, various specific rights relating to the protection of personal data and, particularly, to the protection of the consumer; which is further reinforced by the European law. At the same time, it should be concluded that making it possible for the policy holders to make better thought-out financial decisions, related to investing some of paid premiums to appropriate investment funds, increases the protection level and contributes to the fact that these specific insurance becomes a service more similar to classical business insurance, which is the responsibility of the insurance company, and, thus, may be also performed by its mediator, who is an exclusive agent or a multiagent.

Certainly, the detailed structure of the model of legal relations between the agent and the entrepreneur who is, e.g. the owner of the information service, or who provides stock market data, values of prices of raw materials, real property etc., and the policy holders who benefit from such data, cannot also lead to the violation of standards relating for instance to the prohibition of surreptitious advertising or misleading advertising. The content of this information should be left for the free assessment of the interested party—the policy holder. For the interests of the insurer, performing such additional activities by agents, which, on one hand, are to support the insurance protection, and, on the other hand, are to make the insurance product more attractive, should be evaluated positively and, in the author's opinion, do not give rise to the definite risk for insurer's liability. In the opinion of the author, this comment is also significant in the context of the prepared regulation of the Mediation Act, in the light of the new directive on mediation prepared at the EU level. Certainly, detailed relationships should be always analysed *ad casum*.

It is also worth emphasising that at present, due to the initiative of The Association of Polish Brokers, a draft act was prepared concerning in its content the implementation of the IDD to Polish law. It was provided to the Minister of Finance in December 2016. The draft provides for the maintenance of the division of the insurance mediation profession into agents and brokers, as well as the presence, in accordance with the law, of other entities distributing insurance services. It should be noted that some informative obligations required under the IDD, as specified hereinabove, are exercised in the content of the Insurance Activity Act. Implementation of the IDD to Polish law according to the prepared draft will make it possible to meet the required standards of the EU law.[32]

At the same time it should be emphasised that in the realities of the Polish practice, the distribution of the investment-based insurance instruments is also performed by the conclusion of group insurance contracts for third parties.[33] Therefore, on 28 November 2014, a draft amendment to the CC was prepared, aimed at adding Section IV to the Polish regulation on the insurance contract, included in the Civil Code: "Group insurance for third parties". It was prepared by the Problem-Focused Insurance Contract Team of the Civil Code Codification Committee.[34] Upon the completion of the works of the Committee, under a decision of the Minister of Justice, the draft has not been accepted by the legislator. Currently, there are works in progress on the amendment in this respect as part the Academic Draft of the Civil Code.[35]

References

1. Sources of Law

Act on Prevention of Unfair Market Practices of 23 August 2007, Journal of Laws of 2007 No. 171 item 1206 as amended

Act of 2 March 2000 on the protection of consumer rights and liability for damage caused by dangerous products, Journal of Laws of 2000 No. 22 item 271 as amended

Consumer Rights Act of 30 May 2014, as amended Journal of Laws 2014 item 827

Civil Code, Journal of Laws of 1964 No. 16 item 93 as amended

First Directive of the Council of 24 July 1973 (73/239/EEC) on the coordination of laws, regulations and administrative provisions relating to the taking-up and pursuit of the business direct insurance other than life assurance, Official Journal of 1973, L 228 p. 3

Insurance and Reinsurance Act of 11 September 2015, Journal of Laws of 2015, item 1844 as amended

Insurance Mediation Act of 22 May 2003, i.e. Journal of Laws of 2016, item 2077

Insurance Distribution Act from 1512 2017, Journal of Laws of 2017 item 2486 as amended

www.projektkc.uj.edu.pl

[32] Comparison of the IDD and the Polish law de lege lata: Szaraniec (2017), p. 141 et al.

[33] Cf.: Fras (2015).

[34] Composed of: M. Romanowski and D. Fuchs, draft text: www.ms/kkpc.

[35] The author hereof is a member of the Academic Draft of the Civil Code: www.projektkc.uj.edu.pl.

2. Literature

Act on Prevention of Unfair Market Practices of 23 August 2007, Journal of Laws of 2007 No. 171 item 1206 as amended
Czachórski W (2003) Zobowiązania zarys wykładu, Warsaw
Fras M (2015) Umowa ubezpieczenia grupowego. Aspekty prawne. Wolters Kluwer, Warszawa
Fuchs D (2004) Reforma wspólnotowej regulacji ubezpieczeń na życie a stan rozwoju europejskiego prawa kontraktów. In: Mik C (ed) Unia Europejska w dobie reform, Toruń
Fuchs D, Insurance Restatement jako przykład jednolitego prawa wspólnotowego o umowie ubezpieczenia, Studia Ubezpieczeniowe No. 127 of 2009
Fuchs D (2009) Restatement of European Insurance Contract Law a koncepcja polskiego kodeksu ubezpieczeń. In: Kowalewski E (ed) O potrzebie polskiego kodeksu ubezpieczeń, Toruń
Fuchs D, Ochrona ubezpieczeniowa jako świadczenie główne ubezpieczyciela, Prawo Asekuracyjne No. 2 of 2006
Fuchs D (1998) Dyrektywy III generacji prawa ubezpieczeniowego oraz ich implementacja w wybranych prawodawstwach państw członkowskich Unii Europejskiej. In: Mik C (ed) Implementacja prawa integracji europejskiej w krajowych porządkach prawnych, Toruń
Fuchs D (2006) In: Kowalewski E, Fuchs D, Mogilski WW, Serwach M (eds) Prawo ubezpieczeń gospodarczych, Bydgoszcz - Toruń
Fuchs D (2003) Konsekwencje nowelizacji art. 805 § 1 kodeksu cywilnego dla umowy ubezpieczenia. In: Koch A (ed) Umowa ubezpieczenia. Aktualne problemy prawne, Bydgoszcz – Poznań
Fuchs D (2005) Wpływ wejścia w życie przepisów tzw. pakietu ustaw ubezpieczeniowych na charakterystykę cech umowy ubezpieczenia, Księga Pamiątkowa Profesora Maksymiliana Pazdana, Zakamycze
Fuchs D, Nowelizacja kodeksu cywilnego w zakresie wybranych przepisów ogólnych o umowie ubezpieczenia w świetle prac Project Group on a Restatement of European Insurance Contract Law, Wiadomości Ubezpieczeniowe, No. 7/8 z 2007
Fuchs D (2002) Dobro powszechne (ogólne) jako wyznacznik ewolucji wspólnotowego prawa ubezpieczeń gospodarczych, [w:] C. Mik, Prawo gospodarcze Wspólnoty Europejskiej na progu XXI wieku, Toruń
Malinowska K (2005) In: Brodecki Z, Serwach M (ed) Prawo ubezpieczeń gospodarczych, Komentarz, Zakamycze
Nowak J (2018) In: Czublun P (ed) Ustawa o dystrybucji ubezpieczeń. Komentarz, Warszawa
Maśniak D (2004) Prawo ubezpieczeń. In: Brodecki Z i inni, Finanse, Warszawa
Ogiegło L (2001) Umowa agencji. In: Rajski J (ed) System Prawa Cywilnego, vol 7, Prawo zobowiązań – część szczegółowa, Warszawa
Orlicki M: Roszczenie o zapłacenie składki za czas, w którym nie była świadczona ochrona ubezpieczeniowa, Prawo Asekuracyjne No. 1 of 2006
Patulski W (2000) Kodeks cywilny w praktyce gospodarczej z orzecznictwem, Gdańsk
Popiołek W (2002) In: Pietrzykowski K (ed) Kodeks cywilny, vol 1, Warsaw
Romanowski M, Fuchs D, draft text: www.ms/kkpc
Rozmus B, Kuczyński G, Kilka mitów z zakresu teorii umów, Gdańskie Studia Prawnicze, Volume VII
Szaraniec M (2017) Działalność gospodarcza pośredników ubezpieczeniowych. Studium publicznoprawne. Difin, Warszawa
Wieczorek E (2010) In: Brodecki Z, Serwach M, Glicz M (eds) Prawo ubezpieczeń gospodarczych, vol I, Issue 2, Warszawa
Wąsiewicz A (compiled by M. Wąsiewicz) (2002) Umowa ubezpieczenia. In: Sangowski T (ed) Ubezpieczenia w gospodarce rynkowej, vol. 4, Bydgoszcz – Poznań
Żuławska Cz (1999) In: Komentarz do Kodeksu cywilnego. Zobowiązania, vol 1, Warszawa

The United Kingdom

Matthew Channon

Contents

Abbreviations

CIDRA	Consumer Insurance (Disclosure and Representations Act) 2012
ECA	European Communities Act 1972
EU	European Union

Thanks go to Dr Timon Hughes-Davies for advice on parts of this chapter.

M. Channon (✉)
University of Exeter, Devon, South West England, UK
e-mail: M.Channon2@exeter.ac.uk

P. Marano, I. Rokas (eds.), *Distribution of Insurance-Based Investment Products*, https://doi.org/10.1007/978-3-030-11668-2_9

FCA	Financial Conduct Authority
FSMA	Financial Services and Markets Act 2000
IBIPS	Insurance Based Investment Products
KFI	Key Features Illustrations
KID	Key Information Document
SYSC	Senior Management Arrangements, Systems and Controls sourcebook
UK	United Kingdom

1 Introduction

The UK has significant complexity regarding the regulation of Insurance Based Investment Products (IBIPS), partially due to the fact that there are several statutory and extra-statutory areas which affect their regulation and enforcement, from both the UK and the EU.[1] It is evident that, this is growing even more complex due to the UK's departure from the EU in March 2019. With the EU regulating much of this area, UK law on IBIPs is certainly going to be examined again and will be the significant subject of debate regarding the retention of harmonised laws. However, as liability is very much a national issue, left to national law (which will be discussed later), there is moreover uncertainty with regards to this.

This Chapter will examine the key regulation of IBIPs in the UK and their effect along with the UK's liability regime relating to them. It will begin by examining the key sources of law such as the Insurance Act, and will then go onto examine IBIPs in detail, finishing with the complexities surrounding Brexit.

2 Insurance Regulation in the UK

2.1 EU Law

EU Law has longed reigned Supreme in the UK since the introduction of the ***European Communities Act 1972***. UK Courts have further long since held the supremacy of EU law, particularly since the well-known ***Factortame*** litigation.[2] As PRIIPs is an EU regulation, and is therefore directly applicable,[3] it does not require transposition into UK law, it automatically becomes part of UK law. However, this still requires that the UK does not have regulation which contradicts this, with potential ***Francovich***[4] damages resulting from serious breach. The Financial

[1] See for example the Insurance Act 2015, the Consumer Insurance (Disclosure and Representations Act) 2012 (CIDRA).

[2] (No 2) Case C213/89 (1990) ECR 2433; (1990)3 CMLR 867.

[3] See Article 288 Consolidated Version Of The Treaty On The Functioning Of The European Union, Journal of the European Union C 326/47.

[4] Francovich v Italy (C-6/90) [1993] 2 C.M.L.R. 66.

Conduct Authority (which will be discussed later in this chapter) have significantly consulted upon and have altered their rules to ensure that there is consistency and no overlaps.

Alternatively the Insurance Distribution Directive (IDD),[5] aimed at the harmonisation of both insurance and reinsurance distribution,[6] will require the UK implementation as it is not directly applicable.

It is important to note, however, as mentioned above in the introductory paragraph, that the EU's supremacy over UK law is likely to come to an end due to '*Brexit*', with significant potential to disrupt the UK's insurance market. The potential impact of Brexit on this area will be discussed later. However, before examining the law directly related to IBIPS it is important to examine the potential impact of UK general insurance law.

2.2 The Insurance Act 2015

The ***Insurance Act 2015*** came into force on the 12th August 2016 after significant consultation from the UK Law Commission,[7] regulation by the ***Insurance Act 2015*** of IBIPs is rarely discussed. Moreover due to the fact that the Act is still relatively new, there is limited interpretation of the Acts' provisions, it is rather interpreted by academics. Consequently, until the Act is interpreted through the courts, and provisions are clarified, significant uncertainty will continue to exist.

The ***Insurance Act 2015*** does not specify the types of insurance contracts (such as consumer or business) that it regulates, apart from provisions within the Act which expressly state whether that provision is addressed to either business insurance contracts, or consumer insurance contracts. However, the Act may regulate certain IBIPs, so far as a contract of insurance has been made. The ***Insurance Act 2015*** is the most significant change in the UK on insurance law since the ***Marine Insurance Act 1906***. It regulates significant aspects of the formation of an insurance contract. This part will only deal with them briefly but the significant parts are as follows:

- The Duty of Fair Presentation (***Section 3***)- The insured must make a fair presentation of risk (***Section 3 (1)***). Remedies for Breach of this are found in Schedule 1 of the Insurance Act
- Warranties in non-consumer contracts (***Section 10***). Breach of a warranty will not discharge the insurers' liability if the breach of warranty has been remedied before the loss. Basis of the contract clauses are also prohibited.

[5] Directive (Eu) 2016/97 Of The European Parliament And Of The Council.

[6] Ibid, [2].

[7] See the UK Law Commission Insurance Contract Law webpage containing all of the consultation documents https://www.lawcom.gov.uk/project/insurance-contract-law/ [Accessed 09/10/2017].

- Reduces use of exclusions which are not relevant to the loss (***Section 11***). There are limitations of this provision as it does not apply to 'terms defining risk as a whole' and that non-compliance would have increased the risk of loss.
- Alteration to the law of Fraudulent Claims (the insurer is not liable for a fraudulent claim and can terminate but cannot use the doctrine of utmost good faith to avoid a contract for fraud) (***Section 12 (1)***)

Some of these will therefore not apply to consumers who are effected by IBIPS, instead, they may be able to use CIDRA which will be discussed below. The Insurance Act is a significant departure from the law previously, particularly in terms of exclusions and warranties which have been limited, as well as remedies.

2.3 Consumer Insurance (Disclosure and Representations) Act 2012

The ***Consumer Insurance (Disclosure and Representations) Act 2012*** (CIDRA) is more likely to affect PRIIPS than the ***Insurance Act*** since it is aimed specifically at consumers. The Act has a number of provisions:

- The insured has the duty to take reasonable care not to make a misrepresentation to the insurer (***Section 2 (2)***)
- Remedies for Misrepresentation: This are distinguished between deliberate or reckless and careless (***Schedule 2***)
- The circumstances in which 'reasonable care' is found (***Section 3 (2)***[8])
- Representations cannot be turned into warranties ('basis of the contract clauses') (***Section 6***). These were used to turn pre-contractual statements on the proposal form into warranties, therefore unjustly denying the insured a remedy if they made a small error on the proposal form.

Similar to the Insurance Act 2015, as ***CIDRA*** is relatively new, it requires a substantial amount of interpretation by the Courts. Consequently, the law in relation to insurance contracts is uncertain and their application is open to significant interpretation.

[8] Including:

(a) the type of consumer insurance contract in question, and its target market, (b) any relevant explanatory material or publicity produced or authorised by the insurer, (c) how clear, and how specific, the insurer's questions were, (d) in the case of a failure to respond to the insurer's questions in connection with the renewal or variation of a consumer insurance contract, how clearly the insurer communicated the importance of answering those questions (or the possible consequences of failing to do so), (e) whether or not an agent was acting for the consumer.

2.4 The FCA Handbook

2.4.1 General Information

The main area of rules which effect IBIPs in the UK, and which will be addressed more significantly in this paper, is through the Financial Conduct Authority (FCA) Handbook.[9] The FCA (alongside the Prudential Regulation authority), replaced the Financial Services Authority in 2013 and introduced a new 'Twin Peaks' system, which is designed to be a more "judgement based"[10] approach to financial regulation, and which is more interventionist.[11]

The FCA's role is in embracing the conduct of business of all financial firms, and the micro-prudential supervision of smaller firms.[12] The Handbook is an instrument which covers many areas of financial regulation, including IBIPS. The Handbook is available online[13] making it more accessible. The FCA is given its power under the ***Financial Services and Markets Act 2000*** and has the power to fine, withdraw a firm's authorisation to carry out activities, or through injunctions.

2.5 Preparing for Introduction of PRIIPS and IDD

In relation to PRIIPS, the FCA introduced a consultation paper in July 2016 to set out how it was going to deal with the introduction of the PRIIPS regulation through alterations to its handbook. The paper stressed that:

> As a regulation, the PRIIPs Regulation is directly applicable without any additional domestic legislation being passed. Therefore, from that date firms in the EU will need to comply with the PRIIPs Regulation[14]

Much of the Consultation was in relation to altering the FCA Handbook so that there were no clashes once the PRIIPS regulation was enforced. In particular, previous to the PRIIPs regulation, Key Features Illustrations (KFI's) (COBS 13.1.1R (2) and 14.2.1R (1)) and Key Features Documents (KFD's) (COBS 13.1.1R (1) and 14.2.1R (1)), were required, which would clash with the PRIIPS regulation in relation to the need for Key information documents (see Article 5 (1) PRIPPS regulation).

---

[9] The Handbook can be found online here https://www.handbook.fca.org.uk/handbook [Accessed 02/06/2018].

[10] Hill and Ligere (2013), p. 156.

[11] Ibid.

[12] See Mcmeel and Virgo (2014).

[13] www.handbook.fca.org.uk [Accessed 01/09/2017].

[14] Financial Conduct Authority Consultation Paper "Changes to disclosure rules in the FCA Handbook to reflect the direct application of PRIIPs Regulation"(CP16/18, July 2016).

Interestingly there is some confusion as to whether the PRIIPS regulation would apply to non-EEA persons dealing with EEA clients, the FCA stated that, *'Subject to further clarification from the EU Commission and/or ESAs, our view is that the PRIIPs Regulation does have application to persons outside the EEA dealing with EEA retail clients'.*[15] Meaning, that all non-EEA persons dealing with EEA clients will have to give KID's to their EEA clients.

The FCA later published its final disclosure rules, setting out how it would change its handbook on the 2nd May 2017.[16] The FCA found that respondents that the FCA would need to amend or delete its disclosure requirements which would duplicate or conflict with the requirement to provide a KID.[17] Moreover, that firms may need to provide additional disclosures to supplement the KID.[18]

The FCA have released a number of Consultation papers in relation to the IDD.[19] Unlike with the PRIIPs regulation, the IDD is not directly applicable[20] and therefore requires implementation into UK law. In its' Consultation number two, the FCA stated:

> We propose to introduce the minimum standards of the IDD into our Handbook through intelligent copy-out. However, in some cases we are proposing changes that go beyond the IDD minimum requirements[21]

An example of the IDD implementation with reference to IBIPs can be found on Page 14 which states:

> We propose to introduce new rules in COBS 7.3 (for non-advised sales), COBS 9A (for advised sale of IBIPs) and COBS 9 (for advised sale of other life policies) to cover the enhanced IDD requirements on demands and needs for both advised and non-advised sales[22]

Moreover, a number of IBIP disclosure requirements were suggested as a result of the IDD which will apply in relation to all customers purchasing or receiving advice in relation to IBIPs. These proposals are a rather significant alteration to the FCA Handbook.

The FCA received a number of responses to its consultation paper. Concerns were displayed by some regarding the training and knowledge of insurance distributors, particularly with regards to Continuous Professional Development of 15 h

---

[15] Ibid, [341].

[16] Financial Conduct Authority, " FCA's disclosure rules following application of PRIIPs Regulation Feedback to CP16/18 and final rules" (Policy Statement PS17/6**, May 2017).

[17] Ibid, 6.

[18] Ibid.

[19] Financial Conduct Authority "Insurance Distribution Directive Implementation – Consultation Paper I" (CP17/7, March 2017), Financial Conduct Authority, "Insurance Distribution Directive Implementation – Consultation Paper 2" (CP17/23***, July 2017), Financial Conduct Authority, "Insurance Distribution Directive Implementation – Consultation Paper 3" (CP17/33, September 2017).

[20] See Article 288 TFEU (n 4).

[21] FCA (n 20), [3.1].

[22] Ibid, 14.

proposed with some arguing that this was too much[23] whilst others were not sure whether this was required.[24] The majority of other proposals from the FCA were accepted, although there were some issues regarding the media in which information should be provided to customers (on paper and free of charge[25]), it was argued that making paper a 'default' was a backwards step due to reasons including the environment,[26] the FCA refuted that this was the default and that the customer should be given choice.[27] It is notable that there is potential for the FCA to go back to previous regulation post Brexit or address some concerns shown.

On January 19th 2018 the FCA released its final policy statement (number 3)[28] on the IDD which contained the 'near final rules'. In its Statement, the FCA noted that it had included a transition period for firms in its' near final rules to clarify that firms may adopt the IDD early.[29] In May 2018, the FCA introduced a Handbook notice confirming final rules,[30] the Notice laid out the changes that would be made to the Handbook as a result of IDD implementation.[31]

3 Distribution of IBIPS

Having examined the general UK insurance law regime within the previous chapter and the UK's preparation for PRIIPS and the IDD, we now turn to examine the definitions and actors involved in the distribution of IBIPS.

3.1 Defining IBIPs in the UK

The FCA has provided its definition of an IBIP which is identical to the definition provided by the EU. It states that an IBIP is an "*insurance product that offers a maturity or surrender value that is exposed to market fluctuation*".[32] The FCA very

[23] Ibid, [3.10].

[24] Ibid.

[25] Ibid, [5.26].

[26] Ibid, [5-28].

[27] Ibid [5.31], 19.

[28] Financial Conduct Authority "Insurance Distribution Directive implementation – Feedback and near-final rules for CP17/23, CP17/32, CP17/33, CP17/39 and near-final rules for CP17/07", January 2018, Policy Statement PS18/1.

[29] Ibid, [1.12].

[30] FCA 'Handbook Notice no 55', May 2018, available here https://www.fca.org.uk/publication/handbook/handbook-notice-55.pdf [Accessed 02/06/2018].

[31] Ibid, 5.

[32] Financial Conduct Authority, 'Priips Disclosure: Key Information Documents' https://www.fca.org.uk/firms/priips-disclosure-key-information-documents [Accessed 1/09/2017].

much follows the EU in terms of what is encompassed within an IBIP, although as stated in its PRIIPS disclosure documents,[33] it includes Holloway Sickness Policies, with profits policies, and other unit linked policies.

3.2 *Those Involved in the Insurance Distribution Process*

3.2.1 Insurer

Under the **FSMA,** those who carry out a regulated activity within the UK must be authorised (***Section 19***).[34] Without authorisation, those who carry out a regulated activity are liable for prosecution. As noted within the ***Financial Services and Markets Act 2000 (Regulated Activities) Order***, effecting and carrying out an insurance contract is a regulated activity.[35] The register of authorised persons who can undertake business practise can be found here https://register.fca.org.uk/.

3.2.2 Intermediary

As stated by Section 39 ***FSMA***:

> (1) If a person (other than an authorised person)– (a) is a party to a contract with an authorised person ("his principal") which–
>
> (i) permits or requires him to carry on business of a prescribed description, and
>
> (ii) complies with such requirements as may be prescribed, and
>
> (b) is someone for whose activities in carrying on the whole or part of that business his principal has accepted responsibility in writing,
>
> he is exempt from the general prohibition in relation to any regulated activity comprised in the carrying on of that business for which his principal has accepted responsibility

The ***Financial Services and Markets Act (Regulated Activities) (Amendment No.2) Order 2003*** is concerned with the authorisation of intermediaries. This amended the ***Financial Services and Markets Act 2000 (Regulated Activities) Order 2001.***

---

[33] Ibid.

[34] An exemption is an insurer which is authorised and established in any other EEA Member State for requirements in relation to this see Merkin (2016), D-0962.

[35] Ibid [14-018].

4 Liability in the Context of Distribution

4.1 *FCA Handbook*

In UK law, liability arises both through breach of the FCA's handbook. This opens up either a statutory claim (through the FSMA) or through standard avenues of tort. In relation to the statutory claim, ***Section 138D (2)*** of the ***FSMA 2000*** states:

> A contravention by an authorised person of a rule made by the FCA [the Financial Conduct Authority] is actionable at the suit of a private person who suffers loss because of the contravention, subject to the defences and other incidents applying to actions for breach of statutory duty'

This consequently gives a person who has been damaged due to the breach of the FCA Handbook the opportunity to gain compensation for any losses that may have resulted. As stated by Stanton:

> Section 138D(2) itself creates no single tort. What it does is make actionable breach of a large number of detailed regulatory rules enacted in the FCA's Handbook. Indirectly, the section creates a host of different tortious obligations[36]

Stanton further notes that the provision creates '*strict liability statutory tort*'[37] which gives recovery for pure economic loss, meaning that negligence is not a requirement in awarding damages for breach of this tort.[38] This is an interesting point by Stanton particularly with regards to the idea of strict liability which essentially increases the risk of falling foul of these provisions, meaning that those operating within the FCA Handbook should take greater care not to breach relevant provisions.[39]

4.2 *Private Person*

It is important to note that use of the remedy under Section 138D FSMA 2000 is only available to a '*private person*'. As will be discussed later in this chapter, failing to meet this criterion will not necessary mean an absence of compensation, as there would continue be a possibility to claim in negligence.

Nevertheless, the interpretation of '*private person*' has caused the courts significant issues, as it opens up the debate as to whom the Handbook should seek to protect. Should business be treated the same as individuals if they are a '*victim*' of Handbook breach? The definition of private person is therefore difficult, as by providing a very wide interpretation, it could open up the liability to those for whom it

---

36 Stanton (2017), p. 154.

37 Ibid.

38 Ibid.

39 Ibid.

is not meant, if too narrow then there is potential to unfairly restrict those who have been a '*victim*' of any breach.

The definition of '*private person*' is found in ***Regulation 3(1) of the Financial Services and Markets Act 2000 (Rights of Action) Regulations 2001*** which states:

> In these Regulations, "private person" means--
>
> (a) any individual, unless he suffers the loss in question in the course of carrying on-
>
> (i) any regulated activity; or
>
> (ii) any activity which would be a regulated activity apart from any exclusion made by article 72 of the Regulated Activities Order (overseas persons); and
>
> (b) any person who is not an individual, unless he suffers the loss in question in the course of carrying on business of any kind.

This clearly restricts businesses from being incorporated within this definition. It is submitted that this definition, however, is unsatisfactorily vague, although the courts have been required to interpret this. In ***Titan Steel Wheels Limited v The Royal Bank of Scotland Plc***,[40] the Judge held that that 'business of any kind' should be read widely. In ***Sivagnanam v Barclays Bank Plc***,[41] an action brought by a sole director and shareholder loss, as a "private person", from the alleged mis-selling of interest rate hedging products to his companies. It was clear that there had been no claim for breach of a duty owed specifically to the director personally. The Judge held that it is

> clear beyond argument that the rules were designed to protect the customers who constituted private persons within the meaning of Section 138D. It was not intended that the Act should apply to a different group of people who fell outside that category to whom no duty was owed and in respect of whom no breach of duty has even been pleaded. In short, the claimant is not a person whom the legislation was designed to protect[42]

This therefore highlights the narrowness of the meaning of '*private person*' and rules out substantial bodies or businesses from being able to use this to gain compensation. This is arguably a satisfactory conclusion, as the intended beneficiaries of the Section are those much weaker parties, i.e. the individual. The ***Titan*** case, however, is particularly difficult, due to the advising banks' superiority in terms of knowledge and technical expertise, and therefore ***Titan*** were not in a position to assess the risk of the products. Gray noted, however, that:

> the contractual documentation also made it crystal clear that Titan would obtain independent advice if needed and was not placing any reliance on the Bank but was making its own independent decisions. English Courts never have set aside clearly agreed express contractual terms between commercial contracting parties and historically certainty and sanctity of

[40] [2010] EWHC 211 (Comm).

[41] [2015] EWHC 3985.

[42] Ibid [10].

> contract has been one of the most fundamental building blocks of English commercial life through the centuries.[43]

This therefore meant that not only could the investor not count as a private person, but that the contractual terms further negated any other potential claims. This, it is submitted, is a difficult position to be in. As further noted by Gray it is "*interesting, yet unsurprising*"[44] for this to continue in "*contemporary post-financial crisis litigation involving highly complex financial transactions between corporate and financial customers of the financial services behemoths*".[45] This, is a fair point to make, the case therefore gives '*private person*' greater importance. The difficulty here, is whether to treat businesses equally as falling outside of '*private person*' or whether those smaller and more vulnerable businesses should also be included in the remedy available. It is submitted that, if the scales are unbalanced significantly in terms of business size then it is difficult to see the difference between that relationship and a relationship concerning an individual.

As will be discussed later, this does not mean that there is no remedy open to non-private persons but this would fall rather under the law of negligence. Moreover, there is potential for contract law to be used in order to provide some protection by the insertion of contractual terms.

4.3 Restricting Use of Section 138D (2) in Section 138D (3)

It is important to note, as stated in ***Section 138D (3)*** of the ***FSMA***, the FCA can restrict the use of ***Section 138D*** in certain provisions of the Handbook if stated within the handbook. As can be seen in the "*Insurance Distribution Directive Implementation – Consultation Paper*"[46] the FCA has utilised this exception particularly in the Senior Management Arrangements, Systems and Controls sourcebook (SYSC) within SYSC 11 to SYSC 21, SYSC 22.8.1R or, SYSC 22.9.1R or SYSC 23. The proposed SYSC 23 within the consultation paper is important because it contains:

> rules and guidance relating to the minimum knowledge and competence requirements in relation to insurance distribution activities undertaken by a firm[47]

Meaning that any breach of this would not fall within **Section 138D of the FSMA 2000**, although again there is a potential for claims outside of this provision.

---

[43] Gray (2010), p. 300.

[44] Ibid.

[45] Ibid.

[46] See Financial Conduct Authority, "Insurance Distribution Directive Consultation Paper 1" CP 17/7 https://www.fca.org.uk/publication/consultation/cp17-07.pdf [Accessed 12/07/2017].

[47] Ibid.

4.4 Section 138D

4.4.1 Causation

Section 138D requires that the breach of ***Section 138D*** causes the loss, causation is also required to be proven below in relation to breach of tortious duty and therefore will be discussed in this part also. The burden of proof for causation is on the claimant to show on the balance of probabilities.[48]

In ***Rubenstein***[49] the claimant wanted to invest the proceeds of the sale of a property pending the purchase of a subsequent property. The claimant was led to believe that he was investing in a product which gave him security equivalent to a cash deposit. However, the product was exposed to market risk and later depreciated. The Court utilised the 'but for' test in causation, that had Mr Rubenstein not been given the assurances that he had been given, he would not have made the investment.

In ***Zaki v Credit Suisse (UK) Ltd***,[50] even though it was found that a breach of the FCA's COB Sourcebook had been proven, on the balance of probabilities the damage would have been caused anyway, as the investor was taking a rather careless approach to investment. As noted by Stanton,[51] this follows the traditional '*but for*' test in causation.

4.4.2 Remoteness

Stanton notes an important question which is *"to what extent does a professional obligation to a client raise a duty to protect that client from market movements?"*.[52] This is clearly an important issue and remoteness has the potential to trip up a liability claim. This has been dealt with by the ***Rubenstein***[53] (as noted above) case, where it was noted that money lost at the time of the 2008 Financial Crash, was recoverable, as this was the type of movement that the defendant should have protected the claimant from.[54] Milner[55] argues that this is '*clearly helpful to the claimants bringing or contemplating proceedings arising out of the mis-selling of investments*'.[56] However, he further argues that this '*should not be overestimated...* (as the) *facts*

[48] Matthew Bradley "Three years post Rubenstein: causation and loss revisited" http://www.hendersonchambers.co.uk/wp-content/uploads/2015/11/02-Matthew-Bradley-on-causation-in-financial-mis-selling-post-Reubenstein.pdf [Accessed 07/06/2018].

[49] [2012] EWCA Civ.

[50] [2013] EWCA Civ 14.

[51] Stanton (2017), p. 168.

[52] Ibid.

[53] [2013] PNLR 9.

[54] Stanton (2017), p. 168.

[55] Milner (2013).

[56] Ibid, 61.

were particularly stark'[57] and the '*bank clearly failed to make any serious attempt to comply with its obligation*'.[58] Consequently, investors will have to take this case cautiously and '*will face more difficulty than Rubenstein in establishing negligence or breach of statutory duty'*[59] in relation to remoteness. This case therefore provides an interesting example the remoteness example particularly in light of the financial crisis. Consequently, it provides an additional risk on advisors that they cannot take financial collapse as automatically too remote.

4.5 Tortious Liability

As noted above, a claim under the tort of negligence is potentially useful for those whom are barred from claiming under ***Section 138D*** because they are not a '*private person*'. As stated by Stanton, "*the majority of cases in this area assume, without discussion, that the existence of and restrictions applicable to the statutory tort do not impact on a claim brought in negligence*".[60] Stanton further notes that, "*this is exactly the kind of proximate, akin to contractual, professional relationship which would lead to the tort of negligence imposing a duty of care in relation to pure economic loss under the Hedley Byrne principle*".[61]

Gorham[62] re-enforces this and further highlights that the lack of remedy from the FCA does not rule out a claim in negligence. As stated by Pill L.J:

> In my judgment, the stress placed upon the statutory code as a decisive ground for refusing a remedy is misplaced … I do not … discern a parliamentary intention to eliminate the power of courts to decide whether a duty of care arises in a situation and, if so, what its extent is. Had Parliament not intervened, remedies for the abuses which existed in this field would almost certainly have been developed by the courts.[63]

It is now therefore important to examine the requirements of finding liability in negligence. The often most difficult criteria is the duty of care, although in a financial setting this may be less difficult.

[57] Ibid.

[58] Ibid.

[59] Ibid.

[60] Stanton (2017), p. 169.

[61] Stanton (2017), p. 144.

[62] [2000] 1 W.L.R. 2129.

[63] Ibid, 2141.

4.6 Duty of Care

For liability in negligence to be determined, a duty of care between the claimant and the defendant needs to be found. In Hedley Byrne & Co Ltd v Heller & Partners Ltd [1964] A.C. 465, 529. The House of Lords held that the Court would examine whether there is an 'assumption of responsibility'.

In Caparo v Dickman,[64] three requirements were examined in determining a duty of care. Reasonable foreseeability, a proximate relationship, and it must be fair, just and reasonable to impose a duty.[65] However, in the Supreme Court case of *Robinson v Chief Constable of West Yorkshire Police [2018] UKSC 4*, Lord Reed stated that (at [21]) 'The proposition that there is a Caparo test which applies to all claims in the modern law of negligence, and that in consequence the court will only impose a duty of care where it considers it fair, just and reasonable to do so on the particular facts, is mistaken'. Instead the law should develop 'incrementally'. Further, his lordship noted, (at [27]) 'It is normally only in a novel type of case, where established principles do not provide an answer, that the courts need to go beyond those principles in order to decide whether a duty of care should be recognised'. In NRAM Ltd (formerly NRAM plc) v Steel and another ([2018] UKSC 13), the Supreme Court utilised the assumption of responsibility test from Hedley Byrne in terms of negligent misrepresentation and noted that, 'It has therefore become clear that, although it may require cautious incremental development in order to fit cases to which it does not readily apply, this concept remains the foundation of the liability'.[66]

In their book 'Financial Services Law' George Walker, Robert Purves and Michael Blair QC note a list of factors (See Chapter 15 for the list of factors) in determining whether a bank owes a duty of care to an investor, including 'the investors financial sophistication'. [para 15–85].[67] Further as well as a duty of care, it must be proven that the duty of care was breached and further that the breach caused damage. The standard of care in negligence for skilled persons is found in Bolam v Friern Hospital Management Committee [1957] 1 W.L.R. 582 whereby Macnair J held (at 587) that 'he is not guilty of negligence if he has acted in accordance with a practice accepted as proper by a responsible body... skilled in that particular art'. Whilst this case involves a medical context, this would also extend to other professions including the financial profession (see for example Mr Les O'Hare & Mrs Janet O'Hare v Coutts & Co.[2016] EWHC 2224 (QB)). In relation to the provision of financial advice the most likely test would be the materiality test as found in Montgomery v Lanarkshire Health Board [2015] A.C. 1430 [87]. This was seemingly applied in O'Hare v Coutts. However, as noted by Vincent Ooi: 'While it is true that in O'Hare v Coutts Kerr J did expressly reject the Bolam test, the test he

[64] [1990] 2 A.C. 605.

[65] Caparo, (n 67), 617.

[66] ibid, [27].

[67] Walker et al. (2018), para 15–85.

eventually did apply was not the Montgomery test. Kerr J appears to have applied the COBS rules instead, which, although they make reference to certain duties to inform the client, crucially do not include a test of materiality'.[68]

There are clear similarities between the claim under the Tort of negligence and the claim under Statute. There are also number of differences between the tort and statute, for example, the '*private person*' test in the statute which is not required negligence.

Stanton notes as to the relationship between tort and statute, "*The provisions contained in the FCA Handbook determine what amounts to taking reasonable care of a client's interests*".[69] This follows the approach of Rix LJ who stated:

> It would seem therefore that, at any rate in the context where the COB rules apply to investment advice provided to a private person, the applicable principles in contract and/or tort will be guided by the focus and purpose of the statutory provisions[70]

5 Brexit

5.1 Impact of Brexit on UK Law: The Current Situation

As much of the law relating to IBIPs comes from the European Union, it is important to discuss any potential effect of the now inevitable scenario of the UK leaving the Union. This is very much open, as little is known about the UK's future arrangements due to a lengthy negotiating phase with the EU Commission. The most certain thing to note, is that although the UK has triggered Article 50 of the TFEU, it continues to remain a Member of the EU until March 2019 at the earliest. This means that the UK will continue to be subject to the supremacy of EU law and must continue to comply with the Insurance regulation coming from the EU. After March 2019, unless all Member States are agreed in extending the time that Article 50 takes, the UK will leave the supremacy of the EU, and is free to repeal and or replace any laws that it wishes. An additional note, however, is that there is likely to be a transition period whereby the UK will continue to pay into the EU budget and comply with EU laws, much of the transition period has been agreed and will last until December 31st 2020.[71]

Post Brexit the UK could seek to retain membership of the Single Market or the European Economic Area. Retaining membership of the Single Marker or the EEA would mean disruption to the financial sector in the UK will be '*minimised*'[72] and the '*UK financial institutions will continue to benefit from the passport regime by*

[68] Ooi (2018), p. 182.

[69] Stanton (2017), p. 171.

[70] This was quoted in Ibid Rubenstein v HSBC Bank plc [2013] PNLR 9, [46].

[71] "*The UK and EU agree terms for Brexit transition period*" https://www.bbc.co.uk/news/uk-politics-43456502 [Accessed 10/06/2018].

[72] Peihani (2017), p. 364.

operating through branches or providing direct cross-border services'.[73] Prebble notes that the continuance of passporting rights for insurers will likely require the participation in the Single Market, either as a member of the EU or the EEA. Due to the absence of public appetite for these,[74] Prebble submits that:

> Firms should assume that the most likely outcome is that there will be in due course some form of bi-lateral agreement between the EEA and the UK but not necessarily with rights akin to existing passporting rights[75]

It is recognised, however, that this still would be a far less attractive that an EEA type passport.[76] An alternative to this exists whereby the UK would seek to create a trade deal with the EU which is completely bespoke,[77] allowing access to passporting style arrangements, meaning minimum disruption to insurers. However, there is always possibility for the UK to walk-away from EU negotiations, the UK insurance industry has already warned against this outcome as this would provide maximum disruption to the UK insurance market.[78]

It is, however, clearly in the UK's best interest to continue to replicate EU laws as much as possible and to try and retain its position within the EUs passporting regime. As stated by the Association of British Insurers:

> Our judgement is that the British Government will have difficulty trying to replicate the passporting regime. All that we can say for sure is that insurers will face a period of uncertainty as to the future regulatory regime. Regulatory uncertainty is bad news.[79]

This is undoubtedly a concern for the insurance industry, and therefore there is likely to be continued lobbying by the industry of the Government in order to protect their passporting ability.

It is further important to note that the potential detriment for the UK is not just for the insurers who are doing business, but also for consumers. Any reduction in the Insurance Distribution requirements or liability within EU laws, it is submitted, have the potential to significantly affect consumers.

---

[73] Ibid.

[74] Ashley Prebble, "Brexit: Passporting and equivalence implications for the UK insurance sector" https://www.cliffordchance.com/briefings/2016/08/brexit_passportingandequivalenceimplication.html [Accessed 06/09/2017].

[75] Ibid.

[76] Ibid.

[77] There is some support for this, see "Britain will secure a bespoke trade deal after Brexit, French President Emmanuel Macron suggests", (The Telegraph, 20th January 2018) https://www.telegraph.co.uk/news/2018/01/20/britain-will-secure-bespoke-trade-deal-brexit-french-president/ [Accessed 26/06/2018].

[78] Oliver Ralph, 'No Brexit deal 'unacceptable', UK insurers warn' https://www.ft.com/content/69c9ee7d-5fb3-3ca2-9e8a-76625989b1f5 [Accessed 02/06/2018].

[79] Ibid.

6 Conclusion

To conclude, the regulation of IBIPS in the UK is complex and difficult. There are a number of different regulatory sources of IBIPs with the core regulation coming within the FCA Handbook. The UK has followed the EU law in relation to much of the regulation of IBIPs. In relation to liability it is clear that there are two potential avenues, through statute or through tort. Both are overlapping in terms of requirements, although it is clear that the tortious route will be followed more by those who are not deemed 'private persons'.

Finally, this chapter has examined the impact of Brexit on the UK. This is very uncertain as there is little clue as to the future potential direction of the UK at the present time. However, it is submitted that it is unlikely that the UK will make it difficult for itself or its insurers in carrying out activities across the EU.

References

Gray J (2010) Titan Steel Wheels Ltd v. Royal Bank of Scotland Plc (High Court: Queen's Bench Division: Commercial Court: Mr Justice David Steel. JFRC 18(3):293–300

Hill J, Ligere E (2013) The UK's new financial services regulatory structure - the shape of things to come. JIBLR 28(4):156–159

Mcmeel G, Virgo J (2014) Financial advice and financial products, 3rd edn. Oxford University Press, Oxford

Milner A (2013) Liability for negligent investment advice following extraordinary market turmoil: case comment'. J Prof Negligence 29(1)

Ooi V (2018) "Decisional" and "operational" negligence. J Professional Negligence 34(4):171–189

Peihani M (2017) Brexit and financial services: a tentative analysis of possible exit scenarios'. JBL 5:357–375

Prebble A, "Brexit: Passporting and equivalence implications for the UK insurance sector" https://www.cliffordchance.com/briefings/2016/08/brexit_passportingandequivalenceimplication.html [Accessed 06 Sept 2017]

Stanton K (2012) Legislating for economic loss. In: Steele J, Arvind TT (eds) Common law, statute and the dynamics of legal change, 1st edn. Hart Publishing, Oxford. Chapter 13

Stanton K (2017) Investment advice: the statutory remedy. PN 33(2):153–174

Stace V (2016) Mis-selling financial products: when can the customer claim in negligence?. JBL 6:517–535

Walker G, Purves R, Michael Blair QC (2018) Financial services law, 4th edn. Oxford University Press, Oxford

Books

Merkin R (2016) Colinvaux and Merkin's law of insurance (Sweet and Maxwell, 11th edn, [14-018]

News

"The UK and EU agree terms for Brexit transition period" https://www.bbc.co.uk/news/uk-politics-43456502 [Accessed 10 June 2018]

Oliver Ralph 'No Brexit deal 'unacceptable', UK insurers warn' https://www.ft.com/content/69c9ee7d-5fb3-3ca2-9e8a-76625989b1f5 [Accessed 02 June 2018]

Consultations

See Financial Conduct Authority, "Insurance Distribution Directive Consultation Paper 1" CP 17/7 https://www.fca.org.uk/publication/consultation/cp17-07.pdf [Accessed 12/07/2017]

Financial Conduct Authority Consultation Paper "Changes to disclosure rules in the FCA Handbook to reflect the direct application of PRIIPs Regulation" (CP16/18, July 2016)

UK Law Commission Insurance Contract Law webpage containing all of the consultation documents https://www.lawcom.gov.uk/project/insurance-contract-law/ [Accessed 09/10/2017]

Financial Conduct Authority "Insurance Distribution Directive implementation – Feedback and near-final rules for CP17/23, CP17/32, CP17/33, CP17/39 and near-final rules for CP17/07", January 2018, Policy Statement PS18/1

FCA 'Handbook Notice no 55', May 2018, available here https://www.fca.org.uk/publication/handbook/handbook-notice-55.pdf [Accessed 02 June 2018]

Financial Conduct Authority, 'Priips Disclosure: Key Information Documents' https://www.fca.org.uk/firms/priips-disclosure-key-information-documents [Accessed 1 Sept 2017]

Financial Conduct Authority "Insurance Distribution Directive Implementation – Consultation Paper I" (CP17/7, March 2017)

Financial Conduct Authority, "Insurance Distribution Directive Implementation – Consultation Paper 2" (CP17/23, July 2017)

Financial Conduct Authority, "Insurance Distribution Directive Implementation – Consultation Paper 3" (CP17/33, September 2017)

MIX
Papier aus verantwortungsvollen Quellen
Paper from responsible sources
FSC® C105338

If you have any concerns about our products,
you can contact us on
ProductSafety@springernature.com

In case Publisher is established outside the EU,
the EU authorized representative is:
Springer Nature Customer Service Center GmbH
Europaplatz 3, 69115 Heidelberg, Germany

Printed by Libri Plureos GmbH
in Hamburg, Germany